PRACTICAL
BIBLE
Illustrations

PRACTICAL
BIBLE
Illustrations

FROM
YESTERDAY AND TODAY

Compiled by
Richard A. Steele, Jr. and Evelyn Stoner

AMG
PUBLISHERS
Chattanooga, TN 37422

PRACTICAL BIBLE ILLUSTRATIONS
FROM YESTERDAY AND TODAY

ISBN 0-89957-231-6

Library of Congress Catalog Card Number: 96–86820

Printed in Canada

07 06 05 04 03 02 –T– 8 7 6 5 4 3

Contents

Actions

1   *The Most Dangerous Kind of Actions*

There are three sorts of actions: those that are good, those that are bad, and those that are doubtful; and we ought to be most cautious of those that are doubtful, for we are in most danger of these doubtful actions, because they do not alarm us. And yet they insensibly lead to greater transgressions, just as the shades of twilight gradually reconcile us to darkness.

2   *Your Duty*

"What I must do," says Emerson, "is all that concerns me, and not what people think. This rule, equally arduous in actual and in intellectual life, may serve for the whole distinction between greatness and meanness. It is the harder because you will always find those who think they know what is your duty better than you know it. It is easy in the world to live after the world's opinion; it is easy in solitude to look after your own; but the great man is he who in the midst of the crowd keeps with perfect sweetness the independence of solitude."

3   *Good Deeds Performed Unconsciously*

A farmer goes to market to purchase grain. He puts the bags containing it into his wagon, and drives slowly home. As the wagon jolts over the stony road, one of the bags becomes untied, and the grain is scattered along the way. The birds catch some of the grain and fly off with it, and drop it in distant places. Some is blown in different directions by the winds. Thus the farmer goes on for miles, without knowing what he is doing; but the next summer finds the scattered seed. It starts and grows, and when he sees his own grain he does not know it. He did not even know that he lost it. And so it is with good deeds. Men often perform them unconsciously, and they bear fruit, and when they see that fruit they do not know that it is the result of anything they have done.

—Beecher

4   *Daily Actions*

"It is the bubbling stream that flows gently," observes Barnes, "the little rivulet which runs along day and night by the farm-house, that is useful, rather than the swollen flood or warring cataract. Niagara excites our wonder; and we stand amazed at the powerful greatness of God there, as He pours it from the hollow of His hand. But one Niagara is enough for the continent of the world, while the same world requires thousands and tens of

1

thousands of silver fountains and gently flowing rivulets, that water every farm and meadow, and every garden, and shall flow on every day and night with their gentle, quiet beauty. So with the acts of our lives. It is not by great deeds, like those of the martyrs, good is to be done, but by the daily and quiet virtues of life."

5   *Our Actions Should Have an Aim*

Bishop Hall points out that the lives of most are misspent for lack of a certain end to their actions: ". . . wherein they do as unwise archers, shoot away their arrows they know not at what mark. They live only out of the present, not directing themselves and their proceedings to one universal scope; whence they alter upon every change of occasions, and never reach any perfection; neither can do other but continue in uncertainty and end in discomfort. Others aim at one certain, but a wrong one. Some, though fewer, level at a right end, but amiss. To live without one main and common end is idleness and folly. To live at a false end is deceit and loss. True Christian wisdom both shows the end and finds the way; and as cunning politics have many plots to compass one and the same design by a determined succession, so the wise Christian, failing in the means, yet still fetcheth about to his steady end with constant change of endeavors; such one only lives to purpose, and at last repents not that he has lived."

Admonition

6 The Criticism That Heals

The admonition of a good man of character resembles the compound "fuller's earth." It not only removes spots from his character, but it will rub off when it is dry.

"I have met with some unexpected 'rubs,'" explained one preacher, "but not one more than was necessary to humble my proud heart."

John Foster said once: "Considering how many difficulties a friend has to surmount before he can bring himself to reprove me, I ought to be very much obliged to him."

To reprehend well is the most necessary and the hardest part of friendship. Who is there that does not sometimes merit an admonition. Yet how few will endure one.

If you cannot bear to be handled, it is proof you have ugly sores on your conscience, which would not be worse for wear to be skinned over!

7 An Infidel Reproved

When Rev. Newton heard an infidel say in jest, "I always spend the Sunday in settling my accounts," that venerable minister turned around and said, in an accent of deep solemnity, "You may find, sir, that the day of judgment is to be spent in exactly the same manner."

8 A Christian Duty

A man who had been led to see his sinfulness and his fearful doom, being surprised that he was allowed to go on quietly in his obstinate lifestyle, exclaimed, "No one ever spoke to me of my salvation." There were in the place many Christians who professed to long for the conversion of souls. If he had been sick, someone would have sent for a physician. If he had been starving, someone would have given him bread. If he had been naked, someone would have clothed him. But his soul was wretched, and miserable, and poor, and blind, and naked, yet no one pitied him. He was banned, he was shunned, but he was not treated as a fellow-creature whose soul was exposed to eternal wrath ought to be treated.

Is there any one living near you that can say, "No one ever spoke to me of my salvation"? You talk about the weather and the crops, and births, accidents, and deaths: do you ever speak to anyone about Jesus? Do you ever affectionately tell any to flee from the wrath to come? If not, is it kind? Is it faithful? Is it honest to your Christian profession? Does it accord with your prayers? Can you consistently pray for a revival of religion? Can you have any compassion for souls or any love for Christ? Never let anyone die in your neighborhood, or even live there long, and be able to say, "No one ever spoke to me of my salvation." A tear, a sigh, a kind word, a pressure of the hand of Christian sympathy, a verse of the Bible, a page of religious reading, with the blessing of the Holy Spirit, may save a soul from death, and hide a multitude of sins.

"It is the fact of responsibility that makes existence so solemn a thing."

9 Looking at the Clock

While the Rev. R. Watson was preaching one Sabbath morning at Wakefield, in Yorkshire, he observed a man rise from his seat to look at the clock in front of the gallery, as though he wished to give the preacher a hint to bring his sermon to a conclusion. Mr. Watson observed, in a very significant manner: "A remarkable change has taken place among the people of this country, in regard to the public services of religion. Our forefathers put their clocks on the outside of their places of worship, that they might not be too late in their attendance. We have transferred them to the inside of the house of God, lest we should stay too long in

His service. A sad and ominous change!"

10 Trade or Man?

It is remembered as one of the liberal axioms of George III, that "no British subject is by necessity excluded from the Peerage." Consistently with this sentiment, he once checked a man of high rank, who lamented that a very good speaker in the Court of Aldermen was of a lowly trade, by saying with his characteristic quickness, "What signifies a man's trade? A man of any honest trade may make himself respectable if he will."

11 Undesigned Admonition

Lady Huntingdon once spoke to a workman who was repairing a garden wall, and pressed him to thoughtfulness on the state of his soul. Some years afterwards, she was speaking to another man of the same subject, and said, "Thomas, I fear you never pray, nor look to God for salvation." "Your ladyship is mistaken," answered the man; "I heard what passed between you and James at such a time, and the word you designed for him took effect on me." "How did you hear it?" "I heard it on the other side of the garden through a hole in the wall, and shall never forget the impression I received."

Adversity

12 Carefulness in Details

General Hill, writing of Stonewall Jackson, says: "Invidious critics have attributed many of Jackson's successes to lucky blunders, or at best to happy inspirations at the moment of striking. Never was there a greater mistake. He studied carefully (shall I add prayerfully?) all his own and his adversaries' movements. He knew the situation perfectly, the geography and topography of the country, the character of the officers opposed to him, the number and material of his troops. He never joined battle without a thorough personal reconnaissance of the field. That duty he never trusted to any engineer officer."

13 Trials

Whitefield says that: "All trials are sent for two ends—that we may be better acquainted with the Lord Jesus, and with our own wicked hearts."

14 Miscellaneous Illustrations on Adversity

The Latin poet Horace lays down the axiom that "adversity has the effect of eliciting talents which in prosperous circumstances would have lain dormant."

Sir Walter Scott compares adversity to the period of the former and of the latter rain—cold, comfortless, unfriendly to man and to animal; yet from that season have their birth the flower and the fruit, the date, the rose, and the pomegranate.

15 God's Dealings with Men

It was said by Robert Hall that, "God, in His moral government of the world, has various methods and complicated machinery by which He excites the heart, the constitution of which none can know so well as He. Some He terrifies by His frowns, some he wins by his smiles; to some He throws in rich profusion all the bounties of His providence, to excite their gratitude; some He bereaves of their all, and tracks their footsteps with misfortune and desolation, in order that they may know the vanity and real worthlessness of all earthly possessions and enjoyments, and feel the full consolation of that refuge of which they may always avail themselves, in order that they may seek, like some battered bark, broken and tempestworn, some haven, secure from the storms which sweep over the open ocean."

16 Bearing Adversity

In a fair wind every fool may sail, but wise behavior in a storm commends the wisdom of the pilot. To endure adversity with a positive attitude is both the sign and glory of a brave spirit. As there is no worldly gain without some loss, so there is not worldly loss without some gain. If you have lost your wealth, you have also lost the trouble that often comes with wealth. If you are degraded of your honor, you are also freed from the stroke of envy. If sickness has blurred your beauty, it has also delivered you from pride. Set your gains against your losses, and you will find no great loss. He loses little or nothing who keeps the favor of his God and the peace and freedom of his conscience.

17   Uses of Adversity

It is good for man to suffer the adversity of this earthly life, for it brings him back to the sacred retirement of the heart, where only he finds he is an exile from his native home, and ought not to place his trust in any worldly enjoyment. It is good for him also to meet with contradiction and reproach, and to be evil thought of, and evil spoken of, even when his intentions are upright and his actions blameless, for this keeps him humble, and is a powerful antidote to the poison of vain-glory: and then chiefly it is that we have recourse to the witness within us, which is God, when we are outwardly despised, and held in no degree of esteem and favor among men. Our dependence upon Him ought to be so entire and absolute that we should never think it necessary, in any kind of distress, to have recourse to human consolation.

Advice

18 Miscellaneous Anecdotes on Advice

Advise not what is most pleasant, but what is most useful.

He who is wise enough in youth to take the advice of his seniors, unites the vivacity and enterprise of early with the wisdom and gravity of later life.

19 How to Tender Advice

"Our advice," says Seed, "must not fall like a violent storm, bearing down and making those to droop whom it is meant to cherish and refresh. It must descend as the dew upon the tender herb, or like melting flakes of snow; the softer it falls, the longer it dwells upon and the deeper it sinks into the mind. If there are few who have the humility to receive advice as they ought, it is often because there are few who have the discretion to convey it in a proper vehicle, and to qualify the harshness and bitterness of reproof against which corrupt nature is apt to revolt, by an artful mixture of sweetening and agreeable ingredients. To probe the wound to the bottom with all the boldness and resolution of a good spiritual surgeon, and yet with all the delicacy and tenderness of a friend, requires a very dexterous and masterly hand. An affable deportment and a complacency of behavior will disarm the most obstinate; whereas if, instead of calmly pointing out their mistake, we break out into unseemly sallies of passion, we cease to have any influence."

7

Affliction

20   Fruitful Affliction

Dr. Thomas Goodwin, who was President of Magdalen College, lost half of his library, some five hundred pounds worth of his best books, in the terrible fire of London in 1666. His son remembers how his father lamented this, and said of it, that in taking away these precious possessions God had struck him in a very tender place. Later he said, "I loved my books too well, and God corrected this by affliction." But of this sore trial came the volume, *Patience and its Perfect Work,* a work that has enabled thousands to say "God's will be done." Goodwin's loss has been the Church's gain and enriching through the centuries.

21   Affliction Compensated For

That blind people have extra keenness of their other senses, especially that of hearing, has been universally observed: but it is now asserted and with much show of authority, that they actually have a sort of sixth sense. The echoes made in walking are to the blind equivalent to light and shadow; the compression of air that occurs as you approach a wall or closed door, tells them of danger. All these delicate and subtle hints, unnoticed by us, trained to perfection by long years of practice, enable them to be aware of obstacles, and to recognize landmarks in finding their way.

22   Affliction Overruled

Noticing that window-glass exposed near the seashore soon loses its polish by the sand constantly blown against it, an American has invented a new way of grinding and etching glass. Instead of the usual acid, he uses fine quartz sand, and this is driven with great force by a blast of air against the glass, and in fifteen or twenty seconds an embossed design can be produced. The parts meant to be deadened are exposed, while those intended to remain polished are covered. The storm of wind and sand work the lovely design. So God often makes afflictions work soul-beauties in us that else would never be seen.

23   Affliction Symbolized by the Sea

As the sea, if it were not tossed with the winds, would stink; even so the godly man, if he were not tested with troubles and afflictions, would be the worse.

8

24 Affliction Blessed

As incense, when it is put into the fire, gives greater aroma; or as spice, when it is pounded and beaten, smells sweeter; as the earth, when it is torn up with the plow, becomes more fertile; the seed in the ground, after frost and snow and winter storms, blossoms into new life, the closer the vine is pruned to the stalk, the greater grapes it yields; the grape, when it is most pressed and beaten, makes the sweetest wine; and linen, when it is washed and wrung and beaten, is made so fairer and whiter: even so the children of God receive great benefit by persecution; for by it God washes and scours and educates and nurtures them, so that through many tribulations they may enter into their rest.

25 Disguised Blessing

A young man who had long been confined with a diseased limb, and was near dissolution, said to a friend, "What a precious treasure this affliction has been to me! It saved me from the folly and vanity of youth; it made me cleave to God as my only portion, and to eternal glory as my only hope; and I think it has now brought me very near my Father's house."

26 Fortunate Affliction

When Gilpin was on his way to London, to be tried because of his religion, he broke his leg by a fall, which much delayed his journey. The person in whose custody he was, took occasion from this circumstance to remind him of an observation he used frequently to make, "that nothing happens to the people of God but what is intended for their good;" asking him "whether he thought his broken leg was so." He answered meekly, "I make no question, but it is." And so it proved; for before he was able to travel, Queen Mary died. Being thus providentially preserved from probable death, he returned to Houghton through crowds of people, who expressed the utmost joy, and blessedness for his deliverance.

27 Patient Suffering

There was a little boy who was so crippled that he could not open his Bible, which he had always had before him. A gentleman asked him why he was so fond of reading it. "I like to read the Bible," said the boy, "because it tells me of Jesus Christ." The gentleman asked, "Do you think you have believed on Jesus Christ?" "Yes I do," said the boy. The gentleman then asked, "What makes you think so?" And the boy responded, "Because He enables me to suffer my afflictions patiently."

28 School of Trial

A minister was recovering from a dangerous illness, when one of his friends addressed him thus: "Sir, though God seems to be bringing you up from the gates of death, yet it will be a long time before you will sufficiently retrieve your strength, and regain vigor enough of mind to preach as usual." The good man answered: "You are mistaken, my friend; for this six weeks' illness all my past studies and all my ten has taught me more divinity than years' ministry put together."

Age

29 Happy Old Age

To the intelligent and virtuous, old age presents a scene of tranquil enjoyments, of obedient appetite, of well-regulated affections, of maturity in knowledge, and of calm preparation for immortality. In this serene and dignified state, placed as it were on the confines of two worlds, the mind of a good man reviews what is past with the complacency of an approving conscience in the mercy of God, and with devout aspirations towards His eternal and ever-increasing favor.

30 Youth in Age

Beecher said, "Be you young until you die, so far as energy, persistence, ambition, and augmentation of resources are concerned. There are some things that curl over easily in the autumn. Their leaves become sere and yellow, and fall to the ground before there are any signs of frost in the air. I do not like such vegetables; I do not have them in my garden. Others carry their green leaves clean down into freezing before they give up. These I like. And I like to see men that can look at God's frosts and not be blighted, but remain green and succulent and growing, even into the edges of winter."

31 Sweet, Old Age

"It is a noble thing when a man grows old, retaining something of youthful freshness and fervor all the time. It is a fine thing to *ripen without shriveling:* to reach the calmness of age, yet keep the warm heart and ready sympathy of youth."

32 Renewing Our Youth

Queen Victoria remarked to a guest at a garden party at Buckingham Palace, about the time of the great Jubilee exercises, "This jubilee means one thing: it means I am a very old woman." Even the Queen of England can not help being the prisoner of old age; and yet in another sense she may, in common with the humblest washer-woman, find freedom and renew her youth as the "prisoner of Jesus Christ." Paul, as such a prisoner, could say in the face of approaching age, "We know that if our earthly house of this tabernacle were dissolved, we have a building of God, a house not made with hands, eternal in the heavens (2 Cor. 5:1).

33 Growing Sweeter with Age

Old violins in general produce their tones with much less effort on the part of the player than is necessary for new ones. New violins are associated with a certain stiffness and a lack of ready response which wear away slowly with time and use. Long-sustained tones from a new violin may sound quite as well as from an old one, but when rapid runs and chords are played the superiority of the mature instrument is very evident to the listener. The tones of all violins become more mellow with age and use. When new, they have a certain thickness or woodiness of tone, which, in most of them, degenerates into an actual harshness, but which in the best ones, is so slight as to be detected only by those who are accustomed to hearing high-class old instruments. Where this woodiness is very marked the violin seems to the player to have a very powerful tone, but to the listener stationed at a little distance the tone may sound very weak. Stiff-toned, heavily wooded instruments are usually the most harsh and raw in tone when new, and it takes these a longer time than more thinly wooded ones to acquire mellowness of tone. The human heart is like a violin. When taken up with the things of the world it has a worldly tone that may sound very strong and splendid to the player (that is, the man himself), but people who look on feel discord. Our hearts ought to be like violins in that they grow more mellow and sweeter in tone with age. An old man or woman whose heart becomes mellow with heavenly notes as the end of the journey draws near, is the most splendid testimony to Christianity, for the devil has no happy elderly people.

Alcoholism

34   The Folly of Strong Drink

An amusing but pathetic incident happened in New York, many years ago, when a man with a wooden leg became so drunk that when he got home at night he lay down on the floor and dropped into a heavy drunken slumber. He turned over in his troubled stupor, and rested his wooden leg against the stove, and it finally caught on fire. When the policeman broke into the house, after first calling the fire department, he found the poor wretch snoring away while his wooden leg was burning brightly. What stupid fools drink makes of men! A wise man of old said of the drunkard: "Thou shalt be as he that lieth down in the midst of the sea, or as he that lieth upon the top of a mast. They have stricken me, shalt thou say, and I was not sick; they have beaten me, and I felt it not: When shall I awake? I will seek it yet again." If Christians have any duty, surely it must be to interpose in behalf of intelligent manhood, and save it from such waste and folly.

35   Murder and Suicide in the Drink

How monotonously the tragic results of the drink-curse repeat themselves, over and over, in every day's news stories. A young man of only twenty-one years of age attempted suicide by jumping off a bridge into the Tennessee River. Paramedics arrived at the scene promptly, and pulled him out of the river, but by the time he entered the emergency room, he was in a comatose state and virtually brain-dead. He died only a week and a half later. What makes a young person with so much potential, want to take his own life? It turns out, his father had a long bout with alcoholism and substance abuse. He had been sober for nearly a decade, but his disease left deep emotional and psychological scars on his family, particularly his children. Almost all of his children have or have had alcohol problems. This particular son was no exception. He, too, had received help from a clinic, and had been sober for four years, but the pressure of his recovery process evidently was so demanding, he had lost all desire to live. This sad story could have been avoided, had the father and sons heeded the warnings of God's Word: "Wine is a mocker, strong drink is raging: and whosoever is deceived thereby is not wise" (Prov. 20:1).

13

36 *The Worst Foe of All*

The chief mission of the church is to save souls. Anything that harms men or women or children is the deadly foe of the church. This makes the liquor industry the worst foe on earth to the modern church. Its wrecks are everywhere. In Mount Vernon, New York, a man who had once been a brilliant lawyer, had a brilliant home, a lovely wife and daughter, and more than $100,000 worth of property, walked into a barroom and ordered a drink of whiskey. He swallowed the liquor with a smack of his lips; he called for another, and then another, and then said to the bartender: I have been in a treatment center trying to cure my desire for liquor, but it's no use. You see, I have gone back to my old habits; tonight you will find my dead body on the nearby railroad tracks. I am going to end it all!" He took another drink, and walked straight to the railroad platform, and, flinging himself in front of an express train, was crushed to death. If the church of Jesus Christ will not fight such a foe, then surely nothing could arouse her to action.

Ambition

37 *True Greatness*

I had a good friend who preserved the axle of the cart in which he wheeled home his goods when he first came to London. It was placed over his front door, and he never blushed to tell how he came up from the country, worked hard, and made his way in the world. I like this a deal better than the affected gentleness which forgets the lone half-wit which worked in solitude with nothing in their pockets when they entered this city.

They are indignant if you remind them of their poor old father in the country, for they have discovered that the family is very ancient and honorable; in fact, one of their ancestors came over with the Conqueror. I have never felt any wish to be related to that set of vagabonds; but tastes differ, and there are some who think that they must be superior beings because they are descended from aristocrats.

Nobodies suddenly swell as if they were everybody. Observe that Jacob does not say, "Years ago I was at home with my father Isaac, a man of large estate." Nor does he talk of his grandfather Abraham as a nobleman of an ancient family in Ur of the Chaldees, who was entertained by kings. No, he was not so silly as to boast of aristocracy and wealth, but he frankly owns his early poverty:—"With my staff, a poor, lonely, friendless man, I crossed this Jordan, and now I am become two bands." It humbles him to think of what he was, but at the same time it strengthens him in prayer; for in effect he pleads "Lord, hast thou made two bands of me that Esau may have the more to destroy? Hast thou given me these children that they may fall by the sword?" So again I say, that which humbled also encouraged him: he found his strength in prayer in those very things which furnished motives for lowliness.

—C. H. Spurgeon

38 *Holy Ambition*

The famous Battle of Marathon had been fought, in which Miltiades led his little army of ten thousand men against a force of 300,000 Persians. After his glorious victory, Miltiades became for the hour a nation's idol. Themistocles, then a youth, was observed to be remarkably pensive and sad, refusing to join in his accustomed amusements, and often spending whole nights in thought and wakefulness. When asked the cause of this change in his deportment, he answered, "The trophies of Miltiades will not suffer me to sleep." His whole soul was possessed with the desire to become similarly distinguished among his countrymen. To this end he bent every purpose of his soul. Scorning fatigue and ease, he planned, and labored, and studied, until he had placed his name high on the scroll of fame. He created a navy, which enabled Greece to cope with Persia on the sea, and to win a glorious and decisive victory over the great leader Xerxes.

Yet what were the perishing honors of Miltiades compared with the glorious crown set before the faithful young soldier of the cross? If a perishing garland of laurel or bay could so fire the heart, what should be the enthusiasm of one who has immortal glory before him? What care, what pains and watchings, are too great to expend for such a prize? If Themistocles could thus give up the follies and pleasures of youth to make himself a strong and valiant soldier, can you not forego whatever would disqualify you from becoming a good soldier of Jesus Christ? There are powerful foes to be met both without and within, and the soldier must be ever at his post.

39   Miscellaneous Anecdotes on Ambition

Ambition is often established in men upon performing the most degrading tasks; so climbing is performed in the same posture with creeping.

A slave has but one master; the ambitious man has as many masters as there are persons whose aid may contribute to the advancement of his future.

40   Ambition a Snare

Ambition, arising either from a discontented mind or from a false estimate of our powers, leading us to seek a high position, will be sure to prove a snare. The pathway of pride leads upwards, but the summit of the hill is so enwrapped with mist, that those who climb lose themselves in the darkness, and at last topple over a precipice, at the bottom of which they groan, with no friends near to pity, until destruction becomes their lot.

41   Ambition to be Avoided

"I see that candle," says Warwick, "makes small show in the day which at night yields a glorious lustre, not because the candle has then more light, but because the air hath the more darkness. How prejudicial then is that ambition which makes me seem less than I am, by presuming to make me greater than I should be! They whose glory shines as the sparks amongst stubble, lose their light if compared to the Sun of glory. I will not seat myself higher than my place, lest I should be disgraced to a humility; but if I place myself lower than my seat, I may be advanced to the honor of 'Friend, sit up higher.' I had rather be exalted by my humility, than be brought low by my exaltation."

Angels

42 *The Chariots of God*

Angels are called the chariots of God. "The chariots of God are thousands of angels" (Ps. 68:17). That is, they are the chariots of His will, they bear His will about to every part of the universe. This is their delight. They bless God, who rewards them with service. But when they have fulfilled God's message, then they return back to Him by whom they were sent forth. They return back to Him, and stand before Him, drinking in fresh streams of life, and strength, and purity, and joy from His presence.

43 *Angelic Ministration*

Listen to what Beecher has to say about angels: "I did not see, early in the morning, the flight of those birds that filled all the bushes and all the orchard trees, but they were there, though I did not see their coming and heard their songs afterward. It does not matter whether they have ministered to you, or how you perceive angelic existence. The fact that we want to bear in mind is, that we are environed by them, that we move in their midst. How, where, what the philosophy is, whether it be spiritual philosophy, no man can tell, and they least that think most about it. The fact which we prize and lay hold of is this, that

angelic ministration is a part, not of the heavenly state, but of the universal condition of men, and that, as soon as we become Christ's, we come not to the home of the living God, but to the 'innumerable company of angels (Heb. 12:22).' "

44 *Angels–both Good and Bad*

A wicked angel came to Eve, in order that through her man might be separated from God. A good angel came to Mary, that through her God might be united to man.

45 *What Are Angels?*

"The very names assigned to angels," says Dwight, "by their Creator, convey to us ideas preeminently pleasing, fitted to captivate the heart and exalt the imagination; ideas which dispel gloom, banish despondency, enliven hope, and awaken sincere and unmingled joy. They are living ones; beings in whom life is inherent and instinctive; who sprang up under the quickening influence of the Sun of Righteousness, beneath the morning of everlasting day; who rose expanded, and blossomed in the uncreated beam, on the banks of the river of life, and were nourished by the waters of immortality. They are spirits, winged with activity, and

17

formed with power, which no labor wearies and no duration impairs; their faculties always fresh and young, their exertions unceasing and wonderful, and their destination noble and delightful, without example, and without end. They are burning ones, glowing with a pure and serene, with an intense and immortal flame of divine love; returning, without ceasing, the light and warmth which they have received from the great central Sun of the universe, reflecting with supreme beauty the image of that divine luminary; and universally glorious, although differing from each other in glory."

46   *Angels and Men*

The angels glorify, men scrutinize; angels raise their voices in praise, men in disputation; they conceal their faces with their wings, but man, with a presumptuous gaze would look into God's unspeakable glory.

Anger

47 Art of Self-Defense

"Do you think it would be wrong for me to learn the noble art of self-defense?" a religiously-inclined young man asked of his pastor.

"Certainly not," answered the minister; "I learned it in youth myself, and I have found it of great value during my life."

"Indeed, sir! Did you learn karate, kung fu, or some other system?"

"I learned Solomon's system."

"Solomon's system?"

"Yes, you will find it laid down in the first verse of the fifteenth chapter of Proverbs: 'A soft answer turneth away wrath.' It is the best system of self-defense of which I know."

48 Calm in the Heat of Debate

It is said that in the earlier part of Robert Hall's ministry, he was impetuous and sometimes overbearing in argument; but if he lost his temper he was deeply humbled, and would often acknowledge himself to blame. On one of these occasions, when a discussion had become tense, and he had displayed unusual agitation, he suddenly closed the debate, left his seat, and retiring to a remote part of the room, was overheard by a lady who was just entering, to ejaculate with deep feeling: "Lamb of God, Lamb of God, calm my perturbed spirit!"

49 Gentle Words

Anthony Blanc, one of Felix Neff's earlier converts, was very earnest in winning souls to Christ. The enemies of the gospel were very angry at his success, and used threatening words against him. One night, as he was returning home from a religious meeting, he was followed by a man in a rage, who struck him with a violent blow on the head. "May God forgive and bless you!" was Anthony's quiet and Christian response. "Ah!" replied his assailant furiously, "if God does not kill you, I'll do it myself!" Some days afterwards, Anthony met the same person in a narrow road, where two persons could hardly pass. "Now I shall be struck by him again," he said to himself. But he was surprised, on approaching, to see this man, once so bitter towards him, reach out his hand, and say to him, in a tremulous voice, "Mr. Blanc, will you forgive me, and let all be over?" Consequently, this disciple of Christ, by gentle and peaceful words, had made a friend out of an enemy.

50 Anger in a Marriage

"I have heard of a married couple," says Matthew Henry, "who were both passionate naturally, but who lived very happily together, by simply observing this rule: never to be both angry at the same time."

It is said of Julius Caesar, that, when provoked, he used to repeat the whole Roman alphabet before he suffered himself to speak.

51 Don't Fuel the Fire

"It is an easy matter," says Plutarch, "to stop the fire that is kindled only in hair, wool, candle-wick, or a little chaff; but, if it once has taken hold of matter that hath solidity and thickness, it soon inflames and consumes. Just so, he that observes anger while it is in the beginning, and sees it by degrees smoking and taking fire from some speech, or chaff-like scurrility, he need take no great pains to extinguish it, but oftentimes puts an end to it only by silence or neglect. For, as he that adds no fuel to fire has already as good as put it out, so he that doth not feed anger at the first, nor blow the fire in himself, hath prevented and destroyed it."

52 Anger and Sunset

John, patriarch of Alexandria, had a controversy with Nicetas, a chief man of that city, which was to be decided in a court of justice. John defended the cause of the poor, and Nicetas refused to part with his money. A private meeting was held, to see if the affair could be adjusted, but in vain; angry words prevailed, and both parties were so obstinate that they separated more offended with each other

than before. When Nicetas was gone, John began to reflect on his own pertinacity, and although his cause was good, "Yet," said he, "can I think that God will be pleased with this anger and stubbornness? The night draweth on, and shall I suffer the sun to go down upon my wrath? This is impious, and opposed to the Apostle's advice." He therefore sent some respectable friends to Nicetas, and charged them to deliver this message to him, and no more: "O sir, the sun is going down!" Nicetas was much affected, his eyes were filled with tears; he hastened to the patriarch, and saluting him in the most gentle manner, exclaimed, "Father, I will be ruled by you in this or any other matter." They embraced each other affectionately, and settled the dispute instantly.

53 Two Brothers

Euclid, a disciple of Socrates, having offended his brother, the latter cried out in a rage, "Let me die, if I am not revenged on you one time or other!" To which Euclid replied, "And let me die, if I do not soften you by my kindnesses, and make you love me as well as ever!"

54 Righteous Anger

High and gusty passions that sweep through the soul are sometimes like fierce summer storms that cleanse the air and give the earth refreshment by strong winds and down-pelting rains. Men are better for knowing how to be angry, provided the sun does not go down on their wrath, and provided it is justified by the occasions of it.

55 The Slave to Anger

"What a chain of evils," exclaims St. Ephraim, "does that man prepare for himself who is a slave to anger! He is the murderer of his own soul; yea to the letter he is so, for he lives in a continual torment. He is devoured by an inward fire, and his body partakes of his sufferings. Terror reigns around him; every one dreads lest the most innocent, the most trifling occurrence, may give him a pretext for quarrel, or rouse him into fury. A passionate man is odious alike to God and man, and is insupportable even to himself."

56 The Power of Evil Passions

A man should always be on his guard, otherwise his evil passions will run away with him. A small sickly boy on the back of a great cart-horse pulls with all his might to stop the powerful beast, but in vain, for the cart-horse takes him just where he pleases. It is just the same when evil passions get the better of a man, for they carry him away like the cart-horse, without his having the power to control them, and he seldom if ever will get out of a passion without finding that he has lost something he should have kept.

57 Anger Controlled

"We must not forget," says Hickman, "to make our prayers to God, that He who giveth wisdom liberally and upbraideth not would teach us the wisdom of governing our passions, and by the aid of His Holy Spirit give us the victory over them; that he would create in us a clean heart, and renew a right spirit within us, and sanctify us throughout. When an unruly passion is subdued and a bad temper corrected, we have as it were obtained a new nature; and this is to be born anew, or of God. For these depend upon God by daily prayer. And all our vigilance and pains with ourselves, and our earnest entreaties at the throne of grace, we must particularly apply against 'the sin which doth so easily beset us'" (Heb. 12:1).

58 Anger Harbored

Speech ends anger, silence nourishes it. Much malice and grudge would be avoided, and the very poison of it drawn out, did we but give it a vent at first, by reasoning with the party that wronged us, and expostulating the injury, which most times is but a mere mistake. Now many, on the contrary, harbor this viper in their bosoms till it has eaten to their hearts; they not only let "the sun go down," but go its whole round, "upon their wrath" (Eph. 4:26), and cannot find time from one end of the year to the other to utter their minds and compound their discords. Not only Abraham, but Aristippus shall rise up in judgment against such pseudo-Christians, and condemn them. For when Æschines and he had been at long debate, and there was "I stout," and "Thou stout," and neither could find in their hearts to go to the other, Aristippus went at length to Æschines and said unto him, "Shall we not agree to be friends before we make ourselves a common scorn to the whole country?" Whereunto, when Æschines answered that "he was content to be friends with all his heart," Aristippus replied, "Remember, then, that although I was the elder and the better, yet I first sought you." "In very deed," said Æschines, "you are a far better man than I; for I began the quarrel, and you have been first in making up the breach:" and these two became friends forever.

59   Coolness in Debate

An artisan who used to attend the public debates held at the Academy, was once asked if he understood Latin. "No," replied the man, "but I know who is wrong in the argument." "How?" asked his friend. "Why, by seeing who is angry first."

60   Death in Anger

A person of property and eminence, who lived in habits of impiety and profaneness, was seized by an illness which compelled him to seek a physician; but, being disappointed for a time by his absence from home, he fell into a violent agitation, which was vented in horrid imprecations. As soon as the physician arrived, he was saluted with a volley of oaths. The violence of the man's agitation broke a blood vessel; so that oaths and blood continued to flow from his mouth till he could speak no longer, and in this situation he died.

Aspiration

61 Christian Enterprise

It does not matter whether you have the Gospel in a penny testament, printed on thin paper with black ink, and done up in cloth, or in an illuminated book glowing in gold and color, painted with loving care on fair parchment, and bound in jeweled ivory. And so it matters little about the material or the scale on which we express our devotion and our aspirations; all depends on what we copy, not on the size of the canvas on which, or on the material in which, we copy it.

62 Christian Ambition

In all regions of life a wise classification of men arranges them to their aims, rather than their achievements. The visionary who attempts something high and accomplishes scarcely anything of it, is often a far nobler man, and his poor, broken, foiled, restless life, far more perfect than his who aims at marks on the low levels and hits them full. Such lives as these, full of yearning and aspiration, though it be for the most part vain, are:

Like the young moon with a
　　ragged edge
E'en in its imperfection beautiful.

63 Treasures in Heaven

God's treasures, where He keeps His children's gifts, will be like many a mother's secret store of relics of her children, full of things of no value, what the world calls "trash," but precious in His eyes, for the love's sake that was in them.

64 Good Deeds

The deeds that stand highest on the records of heaven are not those which we vulgarly call great. Many "a cup of cold water only" will be found to have been rated higher there than jeweled chalices brimming with rare wines

65 Noble Aspiration

Spurgeon often used an illustration taken from a person who taught the art of growing taller. Spurgeon, himself, did not believe in such an art but compared his teaching techniques with those of a Christian growing in faith:

". . . But part of this professor's exercise is, that in the morning, when you get up, you are to reach as high as ever you can, and aim a little higher every morning, though it be only the hundredth part of an inch. By that means you are to grow. This is so with faith. Do all you can, and then do a little more:

and when you can do that, then do a little more than you can. Always have something in hand that is greater than your present capacity. Grow up to it, and when you have grown up to it, grow more. By many little additions a great house is built. Brick by brick up rose the pyramid. Believe and yet believe. Trust and have further trust. Hope shall become faith, and faith shall ripen to full assurance and perfect confidence in God Most High."

Assurance

66 Assurance Is Job

Assurance is Job sitting in the dust, covered with sores, and saying, "I know that my redeemer liveth" (Job 19:25), "Though He slay me, yet I will trust in Him" (Job 13:15).

67 The Fruit of Faith

Assurance is rather the fruit of faith than faith itself; it is in faith, as the flower is in the root. Faith in time, after much communion with God, acquaintance with the Lord, and experience of His dealings with the soul, may flourish into assurance; but as the root truly lives before the flower appears, and continues when the flower has shed its beautiful leaves and is gone again, so does true justifying faith live before assurance comes and after it disappears. Assurance is, as it were, the cream of faith. Now there is milk before cream; this cream does not appear until after the milk has stood for some time; and there remains milk after the cream is skimmed off. How many of the precious saints of God might one shut out from being believers if their faith did not reach to that which amounts to assurance!

68 Illustration of the Lack of Assurance

To illustrate the lack of Christian assurance, the Rev. J. C. Ryle takes two English emigrants and supposes them set down side by side in the colony of New Zealand or Australia. He says:

"Give each of them a piece of land to clear and cultivate. Let the portions allotted to them be the same both in quantity and quality. Secure that land to them by every needful legal instrument; let it be conveyed as freehold to them and theirs forever; let the conveyance be publicly registered, and the property made sure to them by every deed and security that man's ingenuity can devise.

"Suppose then that one of them shall set to work to bring his land into cultivation, and labor at it day after day without intermission or cessation. Suppose in the meantime that the other be continually leaving his work, and going repeatedly to the public registry, to ask whether the land is really his own, whether there is not some mistake—whether, after all, there is not some flaw in the legal instrument which conveyed it to him. The one shall never doubt his title, but just work diligently on. The other shall hardly ever feel sure of his title, and spend half his time in going to Sydney or Auckland with needless inquiries about it. Which now of these men will have made most progress in a year's time? Who will have done the most for his land, got the greatest breadth of soil under tillage, have the best crops to show, be altogether the most prosperous?"

69 *A God That Can Shake the World*

During an earthquake that occurred many years ago, the inhabitants of a small village were generally very much alarmed, and at the same time surprised, at the calmness and apparent joy of an old lady, whom they all knew. At length one of them, addressing the old lady, said, "Mother, aren't you afraid?"

"No," she replied, "I rejoice to know that I have a God that can shake the world."

70 *Where Is Your Hope?*

When David Livingstone appeared at the University of Glasgow to receive the honorary doctor of law degree, he was received with silent respect. He was gaunt and weary from 16 years of exposure to Africa's hardships. One arm hung useless at his side because of an attack by a lion.

Livingstone asked, "Shall I tell you what supported me through all those years of exile among a people whose language I could not understand and whose attitude toward me was always uncertain and often hostile? It was this: 'Lo, I am with you alway, even unto the end of the world'" (Matt. 28:20).

Atheism

71 Witnesses

As the Lord Verulam observes, God never produced a miracle to convince an atheist, because His ordinary works may convince him; and unless men will be willfully and stubbornly blind, they must needs subscribe to that of St. Paul: "God hath not left Himself without witness in that He doth good, and gives us rain from heaven, and fruitful seasons, filling our hearts with good and gladness;" (Acts 14:17) and "The invisible things of God are clearly seen from the creation of the world, being understood by the things that are made, even His eternal power and Godhead: so that they are without excuse" (Rom. 1:20). When we see footsteps evidently imprinted on the earth, shall we not easily deduce that certainly someone hath passed that way? When we see a stately fabric built according to all the rules of art, and adorned with all the riches and beauty that magnificence can expend about it, must we not presently conclude that certainly there was some skilful architect that built it?

It can be said that every creature is a footprint of God; we may observe His footsteps in each footprint, and see how His attributes, His wisdom, His goodness, and His power have passed along that way. And the whole world is a stately fabric, a house that God hath erected for Himself: the magnificence and splendor of it are suitable to the state of the Great King: it is His palace, built for the house of His kingdom and the honors of His majesty; and we may easily conclude that so excellent a structure must needs have an excellent architect, and that the builder and maker of it is God.

72 The Difference

Many years ago, a well-known minister delivered a series of sermons against atheism in an American town in which some of the citizens were known to be skeptical. A few days afterwards he took passage in a steamer ascending the Mississippi, and found on board several of the citizens of that town, among whom was a noted atheist. So as soon as he discovered the minister, he began his blasphemies; and when he perceived him reading at one of the tables, he proposed to his companions to go with him to the opposite side of the table and listen to some stories that he had to tell upon religion and religious men, which he said would annoy the old preacher. Quite a number, prompted by curiosity, gathered around him to listen to his vulgar stories and anecdotes, all of which were pointed against the Bible and its ministers. The preacher did not raise his eyes from the book which he was reading, nor appear to be in the least disconcerted by the presence of the rabble. Finally, the blasphemer walked up to him, and rudely slapping him on the shoulder, said, "Old fellow, what do you think of these things?" The minister calmly pointed towards the land, and said, "Do you see that beautiful landscape spread out in such quiet loveliness before you?" "Yes," the atheist answered. The minister then replied, "It has a variety of flowers, plants, and shrubs that are calculated to fill the beholder with delight." "Yes," the atheist answered once again. "Well," the minister responded, "if you were to send out a dove, he would pass over that scene and see in it all that was beautiful and lovely, and delight himself in gazing at and admiring it; but if you were to send out a buzzard over precisely the same scene, he would see in it nothing to fix his attention, unless he could find some rotten carcass that would be loathsome to all other animals. He would pounce and gloat upon that with exquisite pleasure." "Do you mean to compare me to a buzzard, sir?" said the atheist, his face turning deeply red from embarrassment. "I made no allusion to you, sir," said the minister, very quietly. The atheist walked off in confusion, and went by the name of "The Buzzard" during the remainder of the trip.

Atonement

73 *The Atonement Must Be Proclaimed*

Spurgeon states on this subject: "The other day, when I was inquiring about the welfare of a certain congregation, my informant told me that there had been few additions to the church, although the minister was a man of ability and industry. Furthermore, he let me see the reason of the failure, for he added, 'I have attended there for several years, and during all that time I do not remember hearing a sermon upon the sacrifice of Christ. The atonement is not denied, but it is left out.' If this be so, what is to become of our churches? If the light of the atonement is put under a bushel, the darkness will be dense. In omitting the cross you have cut the Achilles tendon of the church: it cannot move, nor even stand, when this is gone. Holy work falls to the ground: it faints and dies when the blood of Jesus is taken away. The cross must be put in the front more than ever by the faithful, because so many are unfaithful."

74 *Christ Suffering in Our Stead*

Spurgeon also told a story first made famous by D. L. Moody, of a man in the wars between England and France who was drafted as a soldier, but did not have to go to battle because a friend had stepped in, and was accepted as his substitute. The substitute served in the war till he was killed in battle. The man for whom he substituted was drafted a second time, but he refused to serve. He was forced to appear before a judge, and he pleaded that he had been drafted once, had served in the war by means of his substitute, and should now be considered as being dead, because his substitute had been killed. He claimed that his substitute's service was practically his service, and it is said that the law allowed his plea. Spurgeon comments: "assuredly it is according to divine equity, even if it be not according to human law. No criminal can be hanged a second time; one death is all the law requires: believers died in Christ unto sin once, and now they pennaly die no more. Our condemnation has spent itself upon our gracious representative. The full vials of divine wrath against sin have been poured upon the head of the great Shepherd, that this sheep might go free; and therein is our joy, our comfort, our security. 'There is therefore now no condemnation to them which are in Christ Jesus'" (Rom. 8:1).

75 Atonement and the Transformed Character

Bronson Alcot, a schoolmaster in America, resolved to substitute his own voluntary chastisement in place of the punishing of a pupil who had disobeyed school rules, and watch its effect on his students. "One day," he says, "I called up a boy who had broken an important rule. The scholars looked on with deepest interest. I put the ruler into the transgressor's hand, and told him to strike. That instant I saw a great struggle going on in the lad. A new light sprang up in his countenance. A new set of shuttles seemed to be weaving a new nature within him. I kept my hand extended, and the school was in tears. The boy at last struck once, and then himself burst into tears. He seemed transformed by the thought that I had taken chastisement in place of his punishment. He went back to his seat, and was ever afterwards one of the most docile of all the pupils in the school, although at first he had been one of the roughest."

76 The Christian's Ruby Ring

One of our kings once gave a ring to his favorite, and said to him, "I know that at the council tomorrow a charge of heresy will be brought against you; but, when you come in, answer them if you will, but you need be in no fear; if you find yourself brought to desperation, simply show them the ring, and they will go no further."

It is even so with us; the Lord has given us the precious blood of Christ to be like a ruby ring upon our finger, and now we know how far conscience may go, and how far accusations from Satan may go; we have only to produce that token and bar all further proceedings. "He that believeth on him is not condemned" (John 3:18), neither can he be.

—C. H. Spurgeon

Avarice

77 *Injustice from Avarice*

"Sir William Smyth, of Bedfordshire, who was my kinsman," relates King, "when he was near seventy was wholly deprived of his sight. He was persuaded to be operated on by Taylor, the oculist, who, by agreement, was to have sixty guineas if he restored his patient to any degree of sight. Taylor succeeded in his operation, and Sir William was able to read and write without the use of spectacles during the rest of his life; but as soon as the operation was performed, and Sir William perceived the good effects of it, instead of being overjoyed, as any other person would have been, he began to lament the loss (as he called it) of his sixty guineas. His contrivance therefore now was how to cheat the oculist. He pretended he had only a glimmering, and could see nothing perfectly; for that reason the bandage on his eyes was continued a month longer than the usual time. By this means he obliged Taylor to compromise the bargain, and accept twenty guineas for payment; for a covetous man thinks no method dishonest which he may legally practice to save his money. Sir William was an old bachelor, and at the time Taylor performed his eye surgery, had a fair estate in land, a large sum of money in the stocks, and not less than five thousand or six thousand pounds in his house."

78 *Deathbed Avarice*

"I once attended" says the Rev. Leifchild "at the miserable deathbed of an individual who resided at a little distance from my own neighborhood. He had amassed considerable property, which he tenaciously retained, and seldom broke in upon by liberality. Though he made a profession of godliness, he lived principally to himself, and was not rich towards God. Age stole upon him apace; and he was then naturally compelled to think of relinquishing all he possessed, and of leaving it amongst his surviving relatives, who displayed great eagerness to lay their hands upon it.

"After the service on Sabbath morning, one of his married daughters, who belonged to my congregation, entreated me to accompany her to her father's sick chamber, and in the interval between the services of the day, to soothe him and prepare him for his last hour. Little suspecting the other object which she concealed under this general one, and which she hoped to find me instrumental in accomplishing, I consented. On our arrival we found the dying man, propped up in his bed, wearing a perplexed and anxious countenance, though somewhat relieved by my presence, and by the recollection of my character and office. His other married daughter had already arrived, and, when I entered the room, was occupied in warmly entreating him, ere he departed this world, to cancel a bond for a considerable amount which he had lent to her husband. Upon hearing this, my guide, his other daughter, as earnestly besought him not to comply with her sister's petition, and thus to deprive her family of what they thought themselves entitled to expect. Hesitating and trembling, he looked first to one daughter, then to the other, and finally to me, and entreated me to persuade his daughters to leave him in quiet, and afterwards to administer to him some religious instruction and comfort. One of them, on the contrary, now appeared to have brought me as an advocate on her behalf, and wished me to use my influence on her side. It was in vain, therefore, that I sought and awaited an opportunity to question and instruct the sufferer. I more than once attempted to ascertain from him the state of his mind, but was interrupted by the renewed entreaties of his daughters addressed to their father, and their altercations with one another. As his strength declined, theirs seemed to increase; their eagerness respecting the bond growing as their father's interest in the topic declined. He desired to turn to more important matters; they to fix him to this. It was not his approaching death that troubled them so much as the approaching decision by death in the affair of the lent money. Scarcely any scene could be more powerfully illustrative of the accursed passion of avarice. Here were four persons present in the chamber of death; the dying man in vain, and very feebly, more by looks than words, supplicating repose; two daughters urging their respective claims in the very face of death; and a minister of the Gospel deeply distressed at the whole, yet unable to effect an alteration, and prevented from exercising the duties of his office by those who ought to have been the first to wish them performed.

"As the time for evening service was now drawing on, I explained the necessity for my departure, and turned towards the door. When I looked back, ere leaving, I saw the wretched man casting at me an imploring look, which exceedingly distressed me, and haunted me as I went to my residence. What followed I cannot recount; for I took no trouble to inquire concerning the parties, having been so pained by that short interview that I was unwilling to recur to the event or revive the circumstances. 'Surely,' I said within myself, 'every man walketh in a vain show; surely he is disquieted in vain; he heapeth up riches, and cannot tell who shall gather them'" (Ps. 39:6).

Backsliding

79 *Spiritual Decline*

"The symptoms of spiritual decline," says Dr. Payson, "are like those which attend the decay of bodily health. It generally commences with loss of appetite and a disrelish for wholesome food, prayer, reading the Scriptures and devotional books. Whenever you perceive these symptoms, be alarmed, for your spiritual health is in danger: apply immediately to the great Physician for a cure."

80 *Backsliders of Scripture*

Leifchild says: "No instance of backsliding can be more aggravated than that of the apostle Peter, and yet no recovery was more signal. While that stands upon record, no traitor to his Lord and Master is justified in saying, 'The door of hope is closed against my return.' The Scriptures contain several instances in which the lamentable and disgraceful lapses of God's people are shown to be followed by their recovery and restoration. Frequently such characters, after they have been corrected and chastened of the Lord, have risen to stations of great eminence in His Church. David in the Old Testament, and Peter in the New, while both illustrating the shame and sorrow of a backsliding state, stand forth as monuments of that sovereign grace which can forgive the penitent wanderer, and once more infuse into his heart the 'peace that passeth all understanding'" (Phil. 4:7).

81 *St. John and the Robber Captain*

When the Apostle John, it is stated, was once on a tour, visiting the Christian Churches of that day, observing a youth of a remarkably interesting countenance, he warmly recommended him to the care of a particular pastor. The young man was baptized, and, for a time, lived as a Christian; but, being gradually corrupted by bad company, he was rendered idle and intemperate, and at length so dishonest as to become the captain of a band of robbers. Some time afterwards, the Apostle had occasion to inquire of the pastor concerning the young man, who told him that he was now dead to God, and that he inhabited a mountain over against his church. John, in the vehemence of his charity, went to the place, and exposed himself to be taken by the robbers. "Bring me to your captain," said the Apostle. The young robber beheld him coming; and, as soon as he knew the aged and venerable Apostle, he was struck with shame, and fled. John followed him, and cried, "My son, why fliest thou from thy Father, unarmed and old? Fear not; as yet there remaineth hope of salvation. Believe me, Christ has sent me." Hearing this, the young man stood still, trembled, and wept bitterly. John prayed, exhorted, and brought him back to the society of Christians; nor did he leave him, till he felt assured that he was fully restored by Divine grace.

Benevolence

82 Miscellaneous Quotes on Benevolence

"The disposition," remarks Howels, "to give a cup of cold water to a disciple is a far nobler property than the finest intellect. Satan has a fine intellect, but not the image of God."

Seneca, the great Roman orator, said: "As benevolence is the most sociable of all virtues, so it is of the largest extent; for there is not any man, either so great or so little, but he is yet capable of giving and of receiving benefits."

83 Active Benevolence

A woman visited New York City, and saw on the sidewalk a ragged cold, and hungry little girl, gazing wistfully at some of the cakes in a shop window. She stopped, and, taking the little one by the hand, led her into the store. Though she was aware that bread might be better for the cold child than cake, yet, desiring to gratify the shivering and abandoned one, she bought and gave her a cake she wanted. She then took her to another place, where she purchased for the girl a shawl and other items of comfort. The grateful little girl looked at the woman right in the eyes, and with precious simplicity said, "Are you God's wife?"

84 A Grateful Family

Reuben Rouzy, of Virginia, it is said, owed General George Washington about a thousand pounds. While President of the United States, one of his agents took legal action in an effort to obtain the money. Judgment was executed against the defendant, who was taken to jail. He had a considerably large estate, but this kind of property could not be sold in Virginia for debts, unless at the discretion of the person. He had a large family, and for the sake of his children preferred lying in jail to selling his land. A friend hinted to him that probably President Washington did not know anything of the proceeding, and that it might be well to send him a petition, with a statement of the circumstance. He did so, and the very next post from Philadelphia after the arrival of his petition in that city brought him an order for his immediate release, together with a full dismissal of the debt and a severe reprimand to the agent for having acted in such a manner. Poor Rouzy was restored to his family, who never laid down their heads at night without praying to Heaven for their "beloved Washington." Providence smiled upon the labors of the grateful family, and in a few years Rouzy enjoyed the exquisite pleasure of being able to lay the thousand pounds with interest, at the feet of this truly great man. Washington reminded him that the debt was dismissed. Rouzy replied that the debt of his family to the father of their country and preserver of himself could never be dismissed; and the President to avoid the pressing importunity of the grateful Virginian, who would not be denied, accepted the money, only, however, to divide it among Rouzy's children, which he immediately did.

85   Freely Given

A poor widow contributed to the Dorpation Branch of the Russian Bible Society a ruble; and, to the question of whether that sum was not too much for one in her circumstances, she answered, "Love is not afraid of giving too much."

86   Guyot and His Aqueduct

A man by the name of Guyot lived and died in the town of Marseilles, in France. He amassed a large fortune by laborious industry and severe habits of abstinence and privation. His neighbors considered him a miser, and thought that he was hoarding up money from mean and avaricious motives. The populace pursued him, whenever he appeared, with hootings and denouncements, and the boys sometimes threw stones at him. Later, he died, and in his will were found the following words:

"Having observed from my infancy that the poor of Marseilles are ill supplied with water, which can only be purchased at a great price, I have cheerfully labored the whole of my life to procure for them this great blessing; and I direct that the whole of my property shall be laid out in building an aqueduct for their use."

87   Luther's Unselfishness

Disinterest was a leading feature in the character of Luther; superior to all selfish considerations, he left the honors and awards of this world to those who delighted in them. The poverty of this great man did not arise from wanting the means of acquiring riches, for few men have had it in their power more easily to obtain them. The Elector of Saxony offered him the produce of a mine at Sneberg; but he nobly refused it, "lest," said he, "I should tempt the devil, who is lord of these subterraneous treasures, to tempt me." The enemies of Luther were no strangers to his contempt for gold. When one of the Popes asked a certain Cardinal why they did not stop that man's mouth with silver and gold, his Eminence replied, "That German beast regards not money!" It may easily be supposed that the liberality of such a man would often exceed his means. Once, after hearing a poor student tell him of his poverty, Luther asked his wife to give him a sum of money; and when she informed him that they had none left, he immediately seized a cup of some value, which accidentally stood within his reach, and giving it to the poor man, told him to go and sell it, and keep the money to supply his needs. In one of his letters, Luther says:

"I have received one hundred guilders from Taubereim; and Schartts has given me fifty; so that I begin to fear lest God should reward me in this life. But I will not be satisfied with it. What have I to do with so much money? I gave half of it to P. Priorus, and made the man glad."

88 "Making a Man Glad"

One of Bishop Burnet's parishioners, being in great distress, applied to him for assistance. The Prelate requested to know what would serve him, and reinstate him in his trade. The man named the sum, and Burnet told the servant to give it to him. "Sir," said the servant, "it is all that we have in the house." "Well, give it to this poor man; you do not know the pleasure there is in making a man glad."

89 Trying to Do Good

Lady Holland was ever lamenting that she had nothing to do; that she did not know what to be at, or how to employ her time. "I recommended her," said the poet Rogers, "something new—to try to do a little good." Once fairly engaged in that business, one will never have to complain of nothing to do. It is a good cure-all for laziness or listlessness.

90 Well-Spent Life

Dr. Cotton Mather, who was born in Boston in the seventeenth century, commenced a life of the most active beneficence when very young, and at the age of sixteen adopted as a maxim that a power and opportunity to do good not only gives the right of doing it, but makes it a positive duty. On this maxim he determined to act, and continued to do so during the remainder of his days. Accordingly he began in his father's family, by doing all the good in his power to his brothers and sisters, and to the servants. After he had attained to man's estate, he imposed on himself a rule "never to enter any company where it was proper for him to speak without endeavoring to be useful in it; dropping, as opportunities might offer, some instructive hint or admonition." By way of improving every moment of his time, he avoided paying or receiving unnecessary visits; and, to prevent intrusion, he produced a sign, written in large characters, over the door of his study, containing these admonitory words, "Be short." Not a day passed without some contrivance on his part "to do good," nor without his being able to say, at the close of it, that some part of his income had been distributed for noble purposes.

Bible

91 The Charm of the Bible

Says Spurgeon: "There is such a charm about the Bible, that he who reads it little may never perhaps feel the whole of it. It is something like the Maelstrom you heard of, only in a different and more excellent sense. The Maelstrom is a great whirlpool on the coast of Norway. A ship at a long distance from it will feel a little of its attracting influence, a very little, yet enough to make it veer from its course; but the nearer it floats to the center the stronger becomes the current, and the more forcibly is the vessel carried along by it, until at last, if the ship should be so unhappy as to near it, it would whirl round at a tremendous rate until it was thoroughly engulfed in its depths. In a higher and better sense the like is true of the Bible. The nearer you go to it, and the more closely you study it, the more rapidly do you revolve in its circles, the more voraciously do you devour its contents, until at last you are swallowed up in its glory, and long for nothing else than to prove the heights and depths of this bliss unfathomable—the love of God revealed to us in Christ, in His sacred Word. Truly, of this book, we may say, ". . . Thou hast the dew of thy youth" (Ps. 110:3).

92 The Neglected Bible

Spurgeon tells a story of how a woman once came to speak to him in private; he spoke to her about her soul, and she told him how deeply she felt, how she had a desire to serve God, "but she found another law in her members." Mr. Spurgeon then led her to a passage in Romans, and read to her, "The good that I would I do not; and the evil which I would not that I do!" (Rom. 7:19). She said, "Is that in the Bible? I did not know it." Spurgeon could not blame her, because he knew that she had no interest in the Bible till then; but came to this conclusion about society in general: "Ah, you know more about your ledgers than your Bible; you know more about your day-books than what God has written; many of you will read a novel from beginning to end, and what have you got? A mouthful of froth when you have done. But you cannot read the Bible; that solid, lasting, substantial, and satisfying food goes uneaten, locked up in the cupboard of neglect; while anything that man writes, a catch of the day, is greedily devoured."

93 The Eternal Word of God

The Librarian of Edinburgh University once inquired of Professor

Simpson: "How many books shall I reserve in the library for your students?" and he replied: "You may set aside every book that is not more than ten years old." The majority of men's writings are out of date in a few years; but the Word of God is perennially new, and abides forever. It has the dew of its youth through the Word of the Ancient of Days.

94 The Indestructible Word

Antiochus Epiphanes, perhaps the cruelest tyrant the world has ever known, was furious in his hatred of the Scriptures. He had a search conducted for all the Hebrew manuscripts and had them all burned to ashes. He then issued a proclamation throughout Judea that every Jew who had a copy of the Old Testament should deliver it up to be destroyed or else be executed. But many of the devout preserved their manuscripts at the risk of their lives. Today, Bible publishers print and circulate millions of Bibles in all languages of the earth. It is the Word of God, and lives and abides forever!

95 God's Word Preserved

Wondrously has the Spirit of God watched over and preserved the Scriptures. The original copy of the *Magna Charta*, on which hung all the greatest liberties of the British people, was once nearly destroyed. Sir Richard Cotton was in a tailor's shop and the great scissors were opened to cut it in pieces. The man into whose hands it had fallen knew

nothing either of its nature or value. But it was rescued and remains today in the nation's keeping as the priceless charter of its freedom. The Bible is the charter of the soul's freedom, and many and many a time its enemies have sought to exterminate it, but God has watched over it, preserved it by numerous miracles, and today it is still declaring liberty to countless spiritual captives all over the world.

96 The Bible, the Great Classic

Mr. Leslie Stephen says: "A writer is entitled to be called a classic when his books have been read for a century after his death. It takes a very powerful voice and a very clear utterance to make a man audible to the fourth generation." If this is true, what a testimony to the Word of God, and the words of Jesus therein. The Bible is sold and read by millions, and while our Lord continues to declare "My words shall not pass away" (Matt. 24:35), even His enemies confess, "Never man spake like this man" (John 7:46).

97 What Does It Mean?

Once a theological student went to his pastor with the complaint that there were some passages in the Bible that he did not understand. The pastor, however, knew how to answer the complaint. "Young man," he said, "allow me to give you one word of advice: You must expect to let God know a few things that you do not understand."

98 Eating God's Word

Spurgeon says: "I have many an old book in my library in which there have been bookworms, and I have sometimes amused myself with tracing a worm. I do not know how he gets to the volume originally, but being there he eats his way into it. He bores a hole in a direct line, and sometimes I find that he dies before he gets half-way through the tome. Now and then a worm has eaten his way right through from one wooden cover to another; yes, and through the cover also. This was a most succesful bookworm. Few of us can eat our way quite so far. I am one of the bookworms that have not gotten half-way into my Bible yet; but I am eating my way as fast as I can. This one thing I have proved to myself beyond all question: I shall never, never exhaust this precious Book; much less shall I exhaust the wondrous person of my divinely-blessed Lord. He is that bread which came down from heaven. He is utterly inexhaustible."

99 God's Treasure

Many of the river sands of Ceylon consist of fragments of rubies, sapphires and garnets intermixed with others of quartz and mica. The bed of the Manickganga in particular is so full of ruby, as to remind one of the story of Sinbad. Such is the Book of God in spiritual enriching and beauty. No wonder that as those that find great spoil, devout hearts can say "Thy word is better unto me than thousands of gold and silver" (Ps. 119:72).

100 Bible, a Delight

One day when walking through Wales, Mr. Hone, an author, stopped at a cottage door and found a little girl reading a Bible. He asked for a glass of water, but she replied, "Oh, yes; mother will, no doubt, give you some milk." He went in, and after a little conversation with the girl, asked her if she liked learning her task out of the Bible. "Oh, it is not a task to read it. I love it." Seeing his surprise, she added, "I thought everybody loved the Bible." The arrow went home. Hone pondered over it, and was led to read for himself, and from that time was a great reader and ceased being an opponent to the Bible.

101 Bible by Heart

On the subject of Scripture memory in the Sunday-school class, the following quote by Dr. Talmage, given years ago, is still so fitting for our churches today: "They should learn the first chapter of Genesis, that they may know how the world was made; the third chapter, that they may know how it fell; the first chapter of John, that they may know how it is to be redeemed; and the twenty-first chapter of Revelation, that they may know how it is to be re-constructed."

102 Bible Committed to Memory

An Irish boy, under threats, was commanded to burn his Bible, when he said, "I thank God that you cannot take away the twenty chapters that I know by heart."

103 Bible Facts Worth Knowing

Though bound in one cover, contains sixty-six books.

Takes in a period of over 1,600 years.

Written at different times by more than forty men.

Its writers were men of different ranks—law-givers, kings, princes, physicians, peasants, and fishermen.

It is read in every pulpit in the land.

It finds a place in the palace of the President, and the cottage of the peasant.

It has a message for everyone— the aged man, the little child, the weary, the glad, and the sad.

The New Testament tells us Christ *did* come, as the Old Testament said He *would* come.

104 A Long Lake

The following illustration is by Robert M. Metcalf:

"When we come to the Bible, we may think of ourselves as looking at a long lake. It is one body of water, not bucketfuls lifted out here and there.

"I have learned to look on God's Word as that long lake, a body of water slowly moving along as it is fed from water upstream, a river flowing into it. That river is made up of truths flowing from the Almighty Giver of the Word.

"At a certain point, the lake suddenly widens into an even larger body of water. That is where the New Testament begins, where God himself comes personally on the scene as the Son, Jesus Christ. That wider lake is so dominant as a part of the whole that it causes me to view the beginning part (the Old Testament) in the light of the wider lake.

"Then I learned to think of that 'Scripture lake' in one other way: I would not only view it from above in seeking the truths **it as a whole** conveyed, I would also imagine myself being **immersed** in it—saturating my very being in it, to make the 'Bible lake' more and more a part of my very life.

"And I think of my Bible in this way as having one other feature: The water flows out in many rivulets. They go out over a wide area. These streams are the **truths** which God gives us through His Word, and they are truths that cover **all** of life and living on this earth. They not only apply to one's personal life and to the church in how it is to be organized and carried on in its broad-scale work; there are such truths coming out of that 'lake of Scripture' that apply to **everything** humankind does on this earth: the way it organizes and runs its families, its schooling, its civil governments, its economy, its working life, its arts expressions, and so on and on. God's Scriptures have specific or clearly derived principles for all manner of life on this planet."

105 Bible Study

Many an erudite scholar that has studied the Bible all his life, has missed the purpose for which it was given; and many a poor old woman in her shack has found it.

106 Obedience to Commandments

"If ye love me keep my commandments" (John 14:15). That draws all the agitations and fluctuations of the soul after it, as the rounded fullness of the moon does the heaped waters in the tidal wave that girdles the world.

107 The Grand Secret of Scripture Study

A man may find much amusement in the Bible, variety of prudential instruction, abundance of sublimity and poetry; but if he stops there, he stops short of its great end; for "the testimony of Jesus is the spirit of prophecy" (Rev. 19:10). The grand secret in the study of the Scriptures is to discover Jesus Christ therein, "the Way, the Truth, and the Life" (John 14:6).

108 God Revealed in His Word

In the fabulous records of pagan antiquity we read of a mirror endowed with properties so rare that, by looking into it, its possessor could discover any object which he wished to see, however remote, and discover with equal ease persons and things above, below, behind, and before him.

Such a mirror, but infinitely more valuable than this fictitious glass, do we possess in the Bible. By employing it in a proper manner, we may discern objects and events past, present, and to come. Here we may contemplate the all-encompassing circle of the eternal Mind, and behold a perfect portrait of Him whom no mortal eye hath seen, drawn by His own unerring hand.

109 Blind Guides

A learned Oriental, upon visiting the library of a French convent, writes thus to his friend in Persia, concerning what had passed:

"Father," said I to the librarian, "what are these huge volumes which fill the whole side of the library?" "These," said he "are the interpreters of the Scriptures." "There is a prodigious number of them," replied I; "the Scriptures must have been very dark formerly, and be very clear at present. Do there remain still any doubts? Are there now any points contested?" "Are there!" answered he with surprise. "Are there! There are almost as many as there are lines." "You astonish me," said I; "what then have all these authors been doing?" "These authors," said the librarian, "never searched the Scriptures for what ought to be believed, but for what they did believe themselves. They did not consider them as a book wherein were contained the doctrines which they ought to receive, but as a work which might be made to authorize their own ideas."

110 Casting Bread Upon the Waters

During the time of the Russian war, several regiments of French soldiers were quartered at Toulon, waiting for orders to embark for the Crimea. A noble person in the neighborhood, thinking that among the men he might find some opportunities of usefulness, visited the camp, taking with him a number of French Testaments; these he distributed to the men, many of whom seemed pleased with the gift. He had given away all the Testaments, with the exception of one copy; this he offered to a man standing near him. The man took it, opened it, and turning to a companion, said, sneeringly, "Oh! This will do to light my pipe with" (a discouraging enough reception); but the book having been once given was beyond recovery. About a year and a half after this occurrence, the distributor of the Testaments was on a short journey through the South of France, and stopped on his way at a roadside inn for refreshment and a night's lodging. On entering the house, he soon perceived that something of a melancholy nature had transpired. On inquiring of the landlady what it was, she informed him that her eldest son had been buried that very week. She went on very naturally to boast of his many excellences, and spoke of his happy deathbed. "And, sir," said she, "all his happiness was got from a little book that was given him some time ago." The gentleman inquired further concerning the little book. "You shall see it," said the mother: "it is upstairs." She gave him a small book. Upon opening it, he found it to be a French Testament, and further identified it as the very one he had himself given, so many months before, to that seemingly unpromising soldier at Toulon. He discovered that five or six pages had been torn out, thus proving that the man had actually commenced the fulfillment of his threat of using the book to light his pipe with. This was not all; on the fly-leaf was written these words: "Given to me at Toulon, on—day; first despised, then read, and finally blessed to the saving of my soul."

111 Delights of Bible Study

In a conversation with a friend, a short time before his death, Dr. Buchanan was describing the minute pains he had been taking with the proofs and revisions of the Syriac Testament, every page of which passed under his eye *five* times before it was finally sent to press. He said he had expected beforehand that this process would have proved irksome to him but that every fresh perusal of the sacred page seemed to unveil new beauties. Here he stopped, and said to his friend, as soon as he recovered himself, "I could not suppress the emotion I felt, as I recollected the delight it pleased God to afford me in the reading of His Word."

112 Peasant's New Testament

An Irish peasant, understanding that a gentleman had a copy of the Scriptures in the Irish language, begged to see it. He asked whether he might borrow the New Testament in his own tongue, that he might take a copy from it. The gentleman said that he could not obtain another copy, and that he was afraid to lend it to the peasant for the purpose of copying the Testament in writing. "Where will you get the paper?" asked the gentleman. "I will buy them." "Where will you find a place?" The peasant replied, "If your honor will allow me your hall, I will come after I have done my work in the day, and take a copy by portions of time in the evening." The gentleman was so struck with his zeal that he gave him the use of the hall and a light in order to copy the Testament by writing. The man was firm to his purpose, finished the work, and produced a copy of the New Testament in writing by his own hand. A printed copy was given to him in exchange, and the written one was placed in the hands of the President of the British and Foreign Bible Society, as a monument of the desire of the Irish to know the Scriptures.

113 Priest and Bible

A woman at Montreal, of the Roman Catholic belief, having obtained a Bible, was visited by her priest, who earnestly endeavored to persuade her to give it up. Finding he could not persuade her to relinquish her treasure, he attempted to induce her to sell it; offering first five, then ten, fifteen, and at last twenty dollars. The good woman, after refusing these offers, finally consented to sell it for twenty-five dollars. The priest agreed, the money was paid, the obnoxious volume was given up, and he departed in triumph. But the woman set off immediately to Montreal, and, with the priest's twenty-five dollars, purchased twenty-five new Bibles for herself and neighbors.

114 Progress of Conviction

"The process of enlightenment in many unconverted minds," says a Christian worker, "is shadowed forth by the experience of one whom I saw but recently. He sat down to read the Bible an hour each evening with his wife. In a few evenings he stopped in the midst of his reading, and said, 'Wife, if this book is true, we are lost.' Riveted to the book, and deeply anxious, he still read, and in a week more joyfully exclaimed, 'Wife, if this book is true, we may be saved!' A few weeks' more reading, and, taught by the spirit of God, through the exhortations and instructions of a city missionary, they both placed their faith in Christ, and are now rejoicing in hope."

115 Stray Verses

In a London missionary's narrative of his experiences we read: "On board a vessel at Horselydown, I found only an old shipkeeper. I asked him if he could read; he replied that he could. On asking him what books he read, his reply was, 'The Bible.' I then gave him two tracts, and remarked that I had sometimes seen parts of the Bible in cheesemonger's shops, which I thought very wrong. He said he differed from me. On asking his reason, he stated that he was formerly a great smoker, and on going to purchase some tobacco it was put up in part of a Bible. One verse struck him very forcibly; and he was induced to purchase a Bible, and has read it daily to the present time; and, said he, 'Blessed be God, I would not part with it, and the hopes I have of salvation, for ten thousand worlds.' "

116 Torn Leaves

A young shopkeeper once took up a leaf of the Bible, and was about to tear it in pieces, and use it for packing some small parcel in the shop, when a devout friend said, "Do not tear that: it contains the word of eternal life." The young man, though he did not relish the reproof, folded up the leaf, and put it in his pocket. Shortly after this, he said within himself, "Now I will see what kind of life it is of which this leaf speaks." On unfolding the leaf, the first words that caught his eye were the last in the book of Daniel: "But go thou thy way till the end be: for thou shalt rest, and stand in thy lot at the end of the days" (12:13). He began immediately to inquire what his lot would be at the end of the days, and the train of thought thus awakened led to the formation of a religious character.

117 Translators Converted

A German clergyman at St. Petersburg once asked two Mongul Tartar chiefs to assist him in preparing a translation of the Gospels into the language of their country, and they spent some time every day in study. After a length of time, the work was completed, the last correction was made, and the book was closed on the table before them. Still they sat, serious and silent. The minister inquired the cause, and was equally surprised and delighted to hear them both avow themselves converts to the truths of the blessed volume. "At home," they said, "we studied the sacred writings of the Chinese, and the more we read the more obscure they seemed; the longer we have read the Gospel, the more simple and intelligible it becomes, until at last it seems as if Jesus was talking with us."

Bible Principles

118 A Swarm of Bees

Be Converted.	Acts 3:19
Be Renewed.	Eph.4:23
Be Obedient.	Eph.4:23
Be Content.	Heb. 13:5
Be Sober.	1 Pet. 1:14
Be Thankful.	Col. 3:15
Be Gentle.	2 Tim. 2:24
Be Wise.	1 Cor. 3:8
Be Faithful.	Rev. 2:10
Be Vigilant.	1 Pet. 5:8
Be Ready.	1 Pet. 3:15
Be Glad.	1 Pet. 4:13
Be Good.	2 Cor. 5:10
Be Holy.	1 Pet. 1:16
Be Perfect.	1 Cor. 13:11
Be Christ's.	Gal. 3:29

119 Waiting for the Shadow

Job 7:2: "As a servant earnestly desireth the shadow . . ." The people of the East measure time by the length of their shadows. Hence if you ask a man what time it is, he immediately goes into the sun, stands erect, looks where his shadow terminates, then he measures the length with his feet, and tells you nearly the time. Thus they earnestly desire the shadow which indicates the time for leaving their work. A person wishing to leave his toil says, "How long my shadow is in coming." If he is asked, "Why did you not come sooner?" he replies, "Because I waited for my shadow."

120 A Sheep in Court

A man in India was arraigned for stealing a lamb. He was brought before the judge, and the supposed owner of the lamb was also present. Both of these men claimed the lamb, and had witnesses to prove their claim, so that it was difficult for the judge to decide to which the lamb belonged. Knowing, however, the custom of shepherds, and the habits of the animal, he resorted to the following expedient. He had the lamb brought into court, and sent one of the men into an adjoining room, while he told the other to call the lamb, and see if it would come to him; but the poor animal, not knowing the "voice of a stranger," would not go to him. In the meantime the other claimant, who was in an adjoining room, growing impatient, and probably suspecting the nature of the experiment which was going on, gave a kind of "cluck," upon which the lamb bounded away towards him without a moment's delay. This "cluck" was the way in which he had been used to calling his sheep, and it was at once decided that he was the real owner. Thus we have presented to us incidentally a beautiful illustration of John 10:4, 5: "And the sheep follow him, for they know his voice. And a stranger will they not follow, but they will flee from him; for they know not a voice of a stranger."

121 He Goes Before Them, and the Sheep Follow Him

In Judea and other eastern countries, where flocks and herds constituted the riches, and the feeding of them the chief employment of the principal inhabitants, practices prevailed very different from what we have been accustomed to see. Instead of a keeper following the sheep, and employing dogs on all occasions to drive them (for the use of dogs in Judea was to defend the flocks from the wild beasts of the forest and the field, and to give notice of their approach), the shepherd himself walked before the sheep, whether he led them to pasture, water, or the fold. The shepherd's going before the sheep and leading them to pure waters and verdant pastures, is a very striking and beautiful representation of God's preventing grace and continual help.

122 "Inasmuch As Ye Did It unto the Least of These, Ye Did It unto Me"

Certain little incidents that find casual record, reveal his relation to the children in the happiest way; such as this, while they sat one evening at supper. For when one of the boys had said the pious grace, "Come, Lord Jesus, be our guest, and bless what Thou hast provided," a little fellow looked up, and said, "Do tell me why the Lord Jesus never comes? We ask Him every day to sit with us, but He never comes." "Dear child, only believe, and you may be sure He will come; for He does not despise our invitation." "I shall set Him a seat," said the little fellow; and just then there was a knock at the door. A poor frozen apprentice entered, begging a night's lodging. He was made welcome; the chair stood empty for him; every child wanted him to have his plate; and one was lamenting that his bed was too small for the stranger, who was quite touched by such uncommon attentions. The little one had been thinking hard all the time, "Jesus could not come, and so He sent this poor man in His place; is that it?" "Yes, dear child, that is just it. Every piece of bread and drink of water that we give to the poor, or the sick, or the prisoners, for Jesus' sake, we give to Him. 'Inasmuch as ye have done it unto one of the least of these My brethren, ye have done it unto Me'" (Matt. 25:40). The children sang a hymn of the love of God to their guest before they parted for the night, and neither he nor they were likely to forget this simple Bible comment.

Blessings

123 Undiscovered Mercies

"If one should give me a dish of sand," says Holmes, "and tell me there were particles of iron in it, I might look for them with my eyes, and search for them with my clumsy fingers, and be unable to detect them; but let me take a magnet, and sweep through it, and how would it draw to itself the most invisible particles by the mere power of attraction! The unthankful heart, like my finger in the sand, discovers no mercies: but let the thankful heart sweep through the day, and, as the magnet finds the iron, so it will find in every hour some heavenly blessings; only the iron in God's sand is gold."

124 Right Use of Blessings

"Even the best things," remarks Bishop Hall, "ill used, become evils, and contrarily, the worst things, used well, prove good. A good tongue used to deceit, a good wit used to defend error, a strong arm to murder, authority to oppress, a good profession to dissemble, are all evil. Even God's own Word is the sword of the Spirit, which, if it kill not our vices, kills our souls. Contrariwise (as poisons are used to wholesome medicine), afflictions and sins, by a good use, prove so gainful as nothing more. Words are as they are taken, and things are as they are used. There are even cursed blessings."

125 A Poison or a Blessing?

The following is from the *Tract Journal:*

"Father," said Clara, "I never could understand how the same wind can take ships in such different directions. There goes one in toward the port, and there is another standing out to sea." "It depends upon the position of the sails," her father answered. "It is much the same with men in the world as with ships at sea. One sails heavenward by the same breeze which sweeps another on to destruction. I was thinking of poor Fred Merril, who has come home from the same college where our Edmund graduated with such honor, and from which he returned to be our pride and comfort. Fred has fallen into bad habits, and is a source of untold anxiety and distress to his parents. So differently did college life affect the two. And it is the same with all the influences which surround us: they are a blessing to one, and poison to another. Gaining wealth makes one man generous and another miserly; domestic trouble hardens one and softens another."

Care

126 Cowper on Care

"Quick is the succession of human events; the cares of today are seldom the cares of tomorrow; and when we lay down at night, we may safely say to most of our troubles, 'Ye have done your worst, and we shall meet no more.'"

127 Treasuring Up Cares

"Last week I met a brother," says Beecher, "who, describing a friend of his, said he was like a man who had dropped a bottle, and broken it, and put all the pieces in his bosom, where they were cutting him perpetually. I have seen persons with troubles and cares that seemed like one that had fragments of glass in his bosom, that cut him, and that cut him the more the tighter he pressed them to his heart."

128 Emblem of Care

One winter day, some boys had made a snowball, and rolled it along until it had grown too large and heavy for them to move. "Here," said Gotthold, "we have an agreeable emblem of human cares. These are often little and insignificant; but we magnify them, by impatience and unbelief, till they become greater than we can bear. Many a one keeps night and day revolving his trouble in his mind to no better purpose than these boys. All they accomplish by their pains is to set up for those who pass a sign that children have been at play; and he gains nothing by this but a head more confused and a heart more sorrowful than before."

129 God's Children Free from Care

"The children of God have the only sweet life," points out Archbishop Leighton. "The world thinks not so—rather looks on them as poor, discontented, lowering creatures; but it sees not what an uncaring, truly secure life they are called to. While others are turmoiling and wrestling, each with his projects and burdens for himself, and are at length crushed and sinking under them . . . the child of God goes free from the pressure of all that concerns him, it being laid over on his God. If he use his advantage, he is not racked with musings, 'Oh, what will become of this and that?' but goes on in the strength of his God as he may, offers up poor but sincere endeavors to God, and is sure of one thing, that all shall be well. He lays his affairs and himself on God, and so hath no pressing care; no care but the care of love, how to please, how to honor his Lord. And in this, too, he depends on Him both for skill and strength; and, touching the success of things, he leaves that as none of his to be burdened with, casts it on God, and since He careth for it they need not both care, His care alone is sufficient. Hence springs peace, inconceivable peace. 'Be careful for nothing, but in everything by prayer and supplication, with thanksgiving, let your requests be made known unto God. And the peace of God, which passeth all understanding, shall keep your hearts and minds through Christ Jesus'" (Phil. 4:7)

Character

130 Character Defined

The original and simple meaning of the word "character" is an engraving—something carved or inscribed in a man's nature; it is the potential fact about the man—the inmost truth of him written upon his personality, which on the whole his fellow men can read and perceive accurately, and from which God at last will judge him. When the books are opened in the Day of Judgment, it is not some scroll or parchment, accurately chronicling his deeds and posted up to date in Heaven that will be produced. It is the man's own character, the writing engraved within upon himself which shall be read, and which shall determine his doom or bliss.

131 Independence of Character

Chief Justice Chase once stopped at a little railway station in Virginia, and was informed that it was the birthplace of Patrick Henry. He immediately went out upon the platform, and admiring the magnificent scene which met his gaze, exclaimed, "What an atmosphere, and what a view! What glorious mountains! No wonder that Patrick Henry grew here!" "Oh! yes, sir," replied a native standing near, "that is very true. Yet, so far as I have heard, that mountain and landscape have always been here; but we haven't seen any more Patrick Henrys." Man is not the product of his surroundings, as so many social libertarians tell us today. Though a Judas was among the twelve, Jesus grew up a spotless and perfect soul, amid the moral hatefulness of Nazareth.

132 Attracting Beauty

A scientific observer of wide experience and observation declares that all nectar-gathering insects, such as the common honeybee, manifest a strong preference for the finest flowers. The more perfect in form, color, and fragrance, the more they are attracted to it, as they seem to know by instinct that there they will find the richest supply of honey. It is from the characters and lives of those who are most like Him who is the Altogether Lovely that the souls of others can gather the most sweetness of God's love and grace. To be Christlike, is to be winsome; to grow in grace, to grow in Divine attractiveness.

133 Estimate of Real Genius

The girl to whom Mozart was first engaged to be married became discontented with her choice when she saw more of the world, and gave up the composer. She thought him too diminutive. "I knew nothing of the greatness of his genius," she afterwards explained; "I saw him only a little man." How many of us act in the same way. We look on the outward person only, and forget that a very homely, even shabby exterior, may contain much goodness and greatness.

134 The Evolution of Christian Character

H. W. Beecher gave the following quotation on character: "No man ever suddenly cleared up forty acres of land. A man may begin such a work suddenly. No man ever began to do a thing without making up his mind to do it. No man ever began to be a Christian without a volition; and no volition was ever anything but a flash—an instantaneous thing. But the volition is the beginning. The evolution of Christian character is gradual."

135 Coming into the Harbor

Human life is often compared to a voyage. It is perhaps as apt a figure as could be used. Strong character can only be built up through battling with the waves. It is a glorious thing to make the harbor of a successful life in the teeth of the gale.

A splendid sight was witnessed from the Golden Gate, off San Francisco, one evening. There had been a great storm outside, and beginning seven miles off shore the whitecaps could be seen rushing shoreward, and by the time they reached the Seal Rocks they had grown into overwhelming billows

that rose fully thirty feet above the largest rocks and dashed their spray to the second balcony of the Cliff House. Enormous breakers would wash over the highest Seal Rock, and submerge the herd of seals that had climbed to the topmost point for protection against the heavy waves. Even the birds were driven inland, finding no foothold on the rocks, and being unable to rest upon the water even inside the little channel between the shore and the home of the seals. But despite the war of the elements, the white sails of ships and trailing smoke of steamers came out of the misty distance, and steadily battled toward the entrance to the harbor. At first it was difficult to distinguish between white-capped wave and glistening sail, but as the vessels came in with all canvas set, they presented such pictures as are never seen on painters' walls, for the lights and shades, the colors and tones, the tints and multichromes, were such as no human mind could invent, and no mortal hand could arrange.

136 The Tattooed Character

A magazine once published a striking and interesting article on the strange fashion in some circles, even among very well-to-do persons, of tattooing the body. Instances are given of famous paintings being tattooed on the backs of persons. Some people pay large sums of money to have strange and unique pictures tattooed on them, until every inch of their bodies is covered with this evidence of silly and absurd barbarism. But silly as that is, it is innocent when compared to the horrible tattooing of the moral nature which some men and women acquire at such a fearful cost. Some who take the greatest care of their bodies would blush with shame if their tattooed characters were exhibited to the public gaze. It is worse yet when they have become so hardened in iniquity that they are not ashamed, but flaunt the marks of their degradation before the eyes of their fellows.

137 How to Build Strong Character

We are told that, years ago, an Arab sultan's champion wrestler Ismail Yousarf, came to the United States to see whether any man in America could put him on his back. The Turk never lost a fall, it is said, and those who saw him in exercise claimed that his equal never lived. His boast of strength brought up the old and always interesting question whether any one race or nationality can produce the strongest men in the world. That involves as important differences in climate, food, and habits as in size and physical appearance. However it may be of physical strength, we know that spiritual strength is equally within the reach of all nationalities. Whoever gives Christ the right of way in his heart is nerved with the same divine power that made him spotless and pure and victorious amid all the world's sin and defilement. We can do all things if we have his strength (Phil. 4:13).

138 The Saving Power of a Good Character

In a terrible storm, on the San Antonio and Aransas Pass road, a large number of Mexican laborers who were camped on the embankment were washed into the bay. When morning dawned after the cyclone, scores of them were missing, and, it was thought, drowned. As a matter of fact not a single Mexican lost his life. For days afterward they could be seen coming across the sand-marsh, each man wheeling his wooden wheelbarrow. When the men realized that they were doomed to risk a watery grave, every one of them grabbed his wheelbarrow and floated away in it. The wheelbarrows all grounded as the storm subsided, and the workmen made their escape. A good character is such a refuge when the storm comes and sweeps away every other source of safety. Many a man has tided over the recent hard times and come up safe in the more promising days because his good character floated him on the waves.

139 Character Developed by Little Deeds

It takes a great quantity of fresh-cut flowers to supply a great city like London. Many years ago, there was a florist in the Covent Garden Market which sometimes sold as much as $150,000 worth of cut flowers a week. One of the interesting features of the supply of flowers for this great city was that they came largely from abroad, and from small growers. Baskets of flowers left from southern France in the evening, and were ready for all the early morning markets of England two days later. These flowers were grown largely by industrious French cottagers, each sending a few baskets from their little well-worked garden plots. Human life is like that in many ways. It is the little things that make up the beauty and fragrance of a character. Christian manhood and womanhood grow by little restraints, little self-denials, deeds that seem insignificant, taken alone; but the aggregation is a character and a life fragrant with the whole variety of Christian graces.

140 The Christian as an Enduring Monument

There was a great deal of curiosity aroused at one time in society circles in Naples, Italy, concerning a beautiful shaft of Carrara marble which had been set up in the cemetery there, and on which the leading sculptors were constantly at work, beautifying it with delicate designs in subtle carvings. Its splendid art and magnificence aroused the admiration of critics, and, as there was no name on it, its unknown destiny kindled widespread curiosity and interest. But later all curiosity was satisfied when a sculptor's chisel carved the name "Crispi" near the base. They knew then it was to mark the resting-place of the great Italian statesman when his life work was ended. This suggests a significant truth. Every one of us is building up steadily and surely a character, either good and beautiful or ugly and repulsive, that is to be a more enduring monument than ever was carved from a block of Carrara marble. On what ideal are we forming our character?

141 The Building of Character

To the geologist the east coast of Florida is one of the most interesting portions of the earth's surface. In the eyes of science it was but yesterday when the surf beat on what is now the western shore of the St. Johns River. East of this line, the corals built a long bar; gradually this caught the earth washed from the shore, and on this plants grew and then trees. This made of the St. Johns a long saltwater lagoon. As the coast widened, and the coral worked, the lagoon filled in and drainage from both sides made it fresh. So character is built up. For good or bad, our thoughts and meditations are constantly leaving their sediment in our heart, and as we meditate and muse in certain lines, a reef is thrown out that catches the wash of our thinking and doing, until after a while it becomes the bedrock principle on which we think and act. To make sure of a good character one must be certain to keep guard over his or her thoughts.

142 Scratches Won't Come Off

The story is told of a little boy who was scratching on a window-pane. "Don't scratch on that windowpane," his sister said. "Why not?" asked the little boy. "The scratches will not come off," his sister replied.

Scratches on the human brain and on character will not come off either. Men are never better because they have sinned. Sam Jones was a great preacher in spite of the fact that he had been a drunkard. But having been a drunkard did not make him a great preacher. It is better to be saved when we are young before sin has wrecked us than it is to be saved after we have been wrecked.

Where sin abounds grace does much more abound (Rom.5:20). This means that the grace of God is sufficient to save any sinner; but even after men are saved, they carry the marks of early dissipation.

Young people, remember, it is better to be saved before you become a drunkard, a libertine or a degenerate, than it is to be saved after sin has wrecked you physically, mentally and morally.

—Dr. Bob Jones, Sr.

143 Two Exams Every Time

George Sweeting wrote about the desperate need for honesty in our culture. He referred to Dr. Madison Sarratt, who taught mathematics at Vanderbilt University for many years. Before giving a test, the professor would admonish his class like this:

"Today I am giving two examinations, one in trigonometry and the other in honesty. I hope you will pass them both. If you must fail one, fail trigonometry. There are many good people in the world who can't pass trig, but there are no good people in the world who cannot pass the examination of honesty."

144 Are You Discouraged?

Remember this: When Abraham Lincoln was a young man, he ran for the legislature in Illinois and was badly defeated. He next entered business, failed, and spent seventeen years of his life paying off the debts of a worthless partner. He was in love with a beautiful young woman to whom he became engaged—but then she died. Reentering politics, he ran for Congress and again was badly defeated. He then tried to get an appointment to the United States Land Office, but failed. He became a candidate for the U.S. Senate and was badly defeated. In 1856 he became a candidate for the Vice-presidency and was again defeated. In 1858 he was defeated by Douglas. One failure after another—bad failures, great setbacks. In the face of all this, he eventually became one of the country's greatest men, if not the greatest.

When you think of a series of setbacks like this, doesn't it make you feel kind of small to become discouraged just because you think you are having a hard time in life?

145 Luther's Resolute Character

There were many Christian men in Wittemberg who said to Martin Luther, "You don't mean that you are going to hang those up on the church door?" Said Luther "They are true; they assail damning error; my Fatherland is bowing down to

Antichrist." "Pause," said the men who would stand well with everybody. "Is not this zeal without knowledge? Think how you will scandalize the University; how you will drive off men who would follow you in more discreet course." "Away!" said the Reformer. "The people are perishing in ignorance. The crowds of the common people who come into the city to market will read these words. Yours is not discretion, but cowardice." He did the deed; and, as the result of that act, Wittemberg received the *Ninety-Five Theses,* Europe received the Protestant Reformation, and the night of the Middle Ages was ended.

146 Associations

If a wafer be laid on a surface of polished metal, which is then breathed upon, and if, when the moisture of the breath has evaporated, the wafer be shaken off, we shall find that the whole polished surface is not as it was before, although our senses can detect no difference; for if we breathe again upon it, the surface will be moist everywhere except on the spot previously sheltered by the wafer, which will now appear as a spectral image on the surface. Again and again we breathe, and the moisture evaporates, but still the spectral wafer reappears. This experiment succeeds after the lapse of many months, if the metal be carefully put aside where its surface cannot be disturbed.

If a sheet of paper, on which a key has been laid, be exposed for some minutes to the sunshine, and then instantaneously viewed in the dark, the key being removed, a fading spectre of the key will be visible. Let this paper be put aside for many months where nothing can disturb it, and then in darkness be laid on a plate of hot metal, the spectre of the key will again appear. In the case of bodies more highly phosphorescent than paper, the spectres of many different objects which may have been laid on in succession will, on warming, emerge in their proper order.

This is equally true of our bodies and our minds. We are involved in the universal metamorphosis. Nothing leaves us wholly as it found us. Every man we meet, every book we read, every picture or landscape we see, every word or tone we hear, mingles with our being and modifies it.

147 How Character Is Made

As you begin the day's work, what is your aim and purpose? You may say, "I intend to do as much business and get through as much work as I can." But what else, what beyond? You may answer, "I mean to support my family, to keep even with the world, and if possible, to lay aside something against bad times or old age."

This is good as far as it goes— very good; but you will remember that the beaver builds his hut, and the bee constructs her cell, and the ant fills her storehouse upon the same principle. They toil to supply present wants, and they make a provision for the future, and they look forward to a season of rest and plenty as the reward of the labor and forethought of today. In a beaver, or a bee, or an ant, this is sound policy, and I would that all who profess and call themselves men came up to this standard: such habits would soon sweep away nine-tenths of the poverty found in the land. Still, even this purpose is altogether too low for a man. Reason ought to go beyond instinct, and religion beyond reason; and, therefore, that which is praiseworthy in these little creatures would be utterly unworthy of a man and a Christian.

Do not forget that, amid the cares of business, as a man thinks in his heart, so is he (Prov. 23:7). If in his daily work the thought of a man's heart reaches only to his own comfort and credit and competence, then is his life sheer organized selfishness. Himself and his family are everything; Christ and His kingdom are nothing; and every such man is literally "without God in the world" (Eph. 2:12). It is for you to say whether your daily labor shall be a sin or a sacrifice. It is true everywhere and at all times, that the thought of the heart determines character, and character gives quality to conduct. This holds good, not only on the Sabbath and in religious duties, but also and equally on the weekday and in secular work. Whatever he may be doing, as a man thinketh in his heart, so is he; if his aims are low and his plans earthly, so is he; and if his motives are pure and his purpose high and heavenly, so is he; and as he is, so is his work.

Christians

148 Christ Is All in All

Christ is all in all to His people. He is all their strength, wisdom, and righteousness. They are but the clouds irradiated by the sun, and bathed in its brightness. He is the light which flames in their gray mist and turns it to a glory. They are but the belt and cranks and wheels; He is the power. They are but the channel, muddy and dry; He is the flashing life which fills it and makes it a joy. They are the body; He is the Soul dwelling in every part to save it from corruption and give movement and warmth.

Thou art the organ, whose full
    breath is thunder;
I am the keys, beneath Thy
    fingers pressed.

149 Jesus, the True Hero

From the beginning, the true "Hero" of the Bible is God; its theme is His self-revelation culminating forevermore in the Man, Jesus. All other men interest the writers only as they are subsidiary or antagonistic to that revelation. As long as that breath blows them they are music; else they are but common reeds.

150 "Brand Plucked Out of the Fire"

An American missionary one day overtook one of his converts in the woods, and after some conversation asked him, "Tell me what your heart says of Jesus." The Native American stood still, paused awhile, and then replied, "Stop, and I will show you." Stooping down, he gathered some dry leaves into a circle, in the middle of which he left an open space, and dropped a worm into it: he then set fire to the leaves. The flames quickly ran round them, and the poor insect, beginning to feel the heat, writhed and wriggled about in all directions, seeking in vain some way of escape from the torment. At last, exhausted with its fruitless efforts, it sank motionless. The native stretched out his hand, lifted up the worm, and laid it on the cool ground, beyond the reach of its place of torture. "This Jesus did for me," said the native; "and this is what my heart tells me I owe to him."

151 Call of Christ

In the second century, Celsus, a celebrated adversary of Christianity, distorting our Lord's expression, complained: "Jesus Christ came into the world to make the most horrible and dreadful society; for He calls sinners, and not the righteous, so that the body He came to assemble is a body of profligates, separated from good people, among whom they before were mixed. He has rejected all the good, and collected all the bad."

Origen says in reply: ". . . our Jesus came to call sinners—but to repentance. He assembled the wicked—but to convert them into new men, or rather to change them into angels. We come to Him covetous, He makes us liberal; lascivious, He makes us chaste; violent, He makes us meek; impious, He makes us religious."

152 Last Comfort

"I have taken much pains," says the learned Selden, "to know everything that was esteemed worth knowing among men; but, with all my disquisitions and reading, nothing now remains with me to comfort me at the close of life but this passage of St. Paul: 'It is a faithful saying, and worthy of all acceptation, That Christ Jesus came into the world to save sinners:' [1 Tim. 1:15] to this I cleave, and herein I find rest."

153 Looking Unto Christ

A traveler, once fording the Susquehanna River on horseback, became so dizzy as to be near losing his seat. Suddenly he received a blow on his chin from a hunter who was his companion, with the words, "Look up!" He did so, and recovered his balance. It was look-

ing on the turbulent water that endangered his life, and looking up saved it.

154 One Mediator

A gentleman full of deistical principles said to Mr. Greenfield, "Can you give me the reason why Jesus Christ is called the Word? What is meant by the Word? It is a curious term." Mr. Greenfield, unconscious of the motive or the sceptical principles of the inquirer, replied, "I suppose, as words are the medium of communication between us, the term is used in the sacred Scriptures to demonstrate that He is the only medium between God and man; I know no other reason."

155 Peace in Christ

"A person whom I once knew," says Mr. Hervey, "was roused from a habit of indolence and supineness to a serious concern for his eternal welfare. Convinced of his depraved nature and aggravated guilt, he had recourse to the Scriptures and to frequent prayer, he attended the ordinances of Christianity, and sought earnestly for an interest in Christ, but found no steadfast faith, and tasted very little comfort. At length he applied to an eminent divine, and laid open the state of his heart. Short but weighty was the answer: 'I perceive, sir, the cause of all your distress: you will not come to Christ *as a sinner.* This mistake lies between you and the joy of religion; this detains you in the gall of bitterness, and take heed, oh take heed, lest it consign you to the bond of iniquity.' This admonition never departed from the gentleman's mind, and it became the means of removing the obstacles of his peace."

156 Vine and Branches

Taking this subject in a Sunday-school class, a teacher was trying to show the dependence of the branches upon the vine—for if the vine dies, the branch dies too—and the teacher said earnestly, "Jesus is the vine, we are the branches of the vine, and derive all our comfort and happiness from Him." "Yes," said a bright little fellow of eight years, "Jesus is the vine, the grown-up people are the branches, and we (the children) are the little buds;" showing that he clearly understood the parable, and giving to the great truth a simplicity which the minds of the smaller children could hardly fail to comprehend. Imitate Christ.

Let us imitate Him who sought the mountain-tops as His refreshment after toil; but never let duties undone or sufferers unrelieved in pain. Let us imitate Him who turned from the joys of contemplation to the joys of service without a murmur when His disciples broke in on His solitude with "All men seek Thee"; but never suffered the outward work to blunt His desire for, nor to encroach on, the hour of still communion with His Father. Lord, teach us to work; Lord, teach us to pray.

—Alexander Maclaren

157 The Great Physician

"I wish you would go with me to see my physician," a lady said to a friend who seemed to be in declining health. "I am certain that he could cure you if you would go at once."

"Wait till I feel better, and I will go with you," returned the invalid, looking up with a pale smile.

"But I said a physician," the friend explained, somewhat impatiently. "It is because you are sick that I wanted you to go to him."

The invalid only shook her head. "I believe all you say about him," she said, "but I want to get my system toned up a little before I go to him. I don't think he can do anything for me till I am stronger."

It is not difficult for us to see the folly of such an answer. The same thing is not always so plain to us when sick souls are to be brought to the great Physician.

158 If You Had Known

John 4:10.

In his intercourse with men, Jesus more than once virtually said that if they had really known who He was, their course of action would have been widely different.

It was so of the whole Jewish nation. They had long waited and sighed for the coming of their Messiah, but when He came they knew him not. A young man was taken prisoner and was to be executed at sunrise. As he lay upon the ground that night between his sleeping guards, his heart was full of bitter thoughts. Oh, for a single sight of the dear ones at home! What would he not give to be free once more? Suddenly he saw a solitary figure steal out from behind a clump of bushes. The man saw that he was awake and began to make signs as though trying to communicate with him. He crept nearer and nearer. The soldier thought he could see a grin of derision on the man's face. Evidently one of his enemies had heard of his plight and had come here to taunt him. He was mad with rage. It was enough to have to die like a dog, but this cruel mocking was more than he could endure. With a shriek of anger he sprang up. In a moment his guards had awakened and the entire camp was in an uproar. In the midst of the excitement the stranger had fled, and the condemned man never knew that the one he repulsed was a friend who had come to deliver him from the hands of his enemies.

There are many men who will find out when it is too late that they allowed themselves to be blinded to their day of opportunity. If they had known that the trial they rebelled at was but a message of mercy! If they had known that the invitation they treated lightly was the last chance for escape! "If thou knewest the gift of God, and who it is that saith unto thee, Give me to drink; thou wouldest have asked of him, and he would have given thee living water" (John 4:10).

159 Seeing Christ

In a work of fiction from many years ago, an account is given of a burglar, who, while ransacking a room, became so uneasy at the sight of a face of Christ in a picture that, unable to finish his work while its eyes were upon him, he deliberately turned it around to the wall. Many a soul would have been saved from yielding to evil if only it could have remembered that Jesus was there. The "real presence" of the real Christ destroys the power of temptation. It was this that preserved Joseph, who in Genesis 39:9 recoiled from sin with "How then can I do this great wickedness, and sin against God?"

160 What Think Ye of Christ?

Rabbi Duncan says in his *Colloquia Peripatetica:* "Christ either deceived mankind by conscious fraud, or He was Himself self-deceived and deluded, or He was Divine. There is no getting out of this dilemma. It is inexorable." This is a true saying, and all attempted explanations of Christ can be categorized under one of these three. Either an imposter, or a mad fanatic; or the Son of God with power, the Savior of the world. To each one of us comes His own question with majestic authority, demanding our answer, and so deciding our attitude towards Him, "What think ye of Christ?" (Matt. 22:42).

161 Author and Finisher

We often go back to our ancient history and think about the original Olympic games in Greece. In the ancient Olympic games the stadium was an ellipse or circle, and the starting point was also the goal; instead of running from one end of the racecourse to the other in a straight line, the athlete ran around the curve at its far end and returned to the point where he started. The Christian life has Jesus as Author and Finisher because we begin with Him on earth as Savior, we finish with Him as Lord and Rewarder in heaven.

162　The Great Advocate

President Lincoln was one day assured by a friend that he was prayed for as no man before had ever been remembered, and he replied: "I have been told so, and have been greatly helped by just that thought." Then he slowly and solemnly added: "I should be the most presumptuous blockhead if I for a moment thought that I could discharge the duties which come upon me in this place without the help of One Who is stronger and wiser than all others." If prayer was help for him, so is it for the lowliest Christian. Thank God, the "I have prayed for thee" of Jesus is always ours. He ever lives to make intercession for us.

163　B.C. or A.D.

"I once asked a man," says an eminent preacher, "what he thought of Christ and he replied frankly that he never thought of Him at all. Then I inquired when he was born. He gave the date. 'B.C. or A.D.?' I kept on. He smiled, but I repeated soberly, 'Before Christ or after Christ?' He was silent, and I continued, 'Have you been putting dates

on your letters for twenty years without even recognizing that you were daily commemorating the nativity of Christ? Have you actually formed no opinion concerning that personage whose advent among men changed the reckoning of time, whose birthday shook the race into a new era, as His crucifixion shook the planet with a new earthquake?'"

164　Christ in the Old and New Testament

A weaver, who made an elaborate piece of tapestry, hung it, stretched upon a line, in his yard. That night it was stolen. A piece of tapestry was found by the police officers, which seemed to answer the description, but as the pattern was not unlike that of other fabrics, there must be definite proof. It was brought to the weaver's yard, and there the perforations in the fabric were found to correspond precisely to the hooks upon which it was hung on the line. This was demonstration. In like manner, if we place the life of Christ over against all the prophecies of Messiah in Scripture a perfect correspondence will be found.

165　Christ as a Copy

When Agesilaus was invited to hear a man who mimicked the nightingale with wondrous art, he replied, "Why should I, when I have heard the nightingale herself?" So a man who has Christ and His life before him, is without excuse if he persists in copying the questionable life of others.

166 A Genuine Thirst

A naturalist, writing of the habits of certain animals, says that though there is abundant evidence that many animals can exist without water for long periods of time, this abstinence is not voluntary, and when unduly protracted causes suffering and loss of health. Many suppose that cats do not care for water and never provide them with waterpans. This is a mistake; the cats, like the tigers and jaguars, thirst for water, and the numerous cases of cats upsetting and breaking the flower-vases on tables are usually due not to mischief but to the cat's effort to drink the water in which the flowers are set. Jesus puts the hungry and the thirsty among those specially marked for blessing in the Beatitudes. One need not thirst for the Water of Life in vain. Whosoever will may come and partake freely.

167 Looking Unto Jesus

"Looking unto Jesus the author and finisher of our faith . . ." (Heb. 12:2).

Someone went to visit a great painter while he was working in his studio. To his great amazement he saw attached to the easel of the artist various costly precious stones in many colors. In answer to his question why they were there the artist answered: "I need them for stimulating and strengthening my eyes. When I look only at the colors of the paint, it is just as if at last my feeling for color and shade weakens. But the brilliance of these wonderful stones is like a restrengthening of my eyesight."

It is good to read and search the Scriptures. But let us never forget that if the eye of our soul is not to become faint or weak, it continually must be refreshed, strengthened, and encouraged by the wonderful glory and splendor of Him who is the living Soul of the Bible.

His Love

168 Christ Pulling at Our Hearts

"Remember that pretty parable given by one of our ministers, of the boy's kite. He made it fly aloft: it rose up so high that he could no longer see it. Still he said he had a kite, and he held fast by it. "Boy, how do you know you have a kite?" "I can feel it pull," said he. This morning we feel our Jesus pull. He draws us with a far greater force than a mere string. He is gone into Heaven, and he draws us after him. O Lord, draw us with greater power than ever."

—Spurgeon

169 Constraining Love

"The Gospel of our Lord and Savior, Jesus Christ, has never lacked earnest devoted workers. There have been teachers and preachers at home, and missionaries and evangelists abroad, who counted not their lives dear to themselves in order that they might work for Christ, but never has St. Paul been surpassed or even equalled as a devoted and laborious servant of our

Lord. What was the secret of His wonderful perseverance and indomitable courage? No matter how reviled and troubled, no matter the dangers and difficulties he had to encounter, bound and imprisoned—nothing daunted Him. He waved on one side the taunts of critics and the sneers of heretics, and went on with his work as though nothing had happened. How did he do it? What was the secret of all his enthusiastic work and marvellous courage?

Now, if we had only the Acts of the Apostles to refer to we might find it very difficult to answer that question; but in his Epistles we have the record of his thoughts as well as his actions. We have, as it were, the history of the Apostle's inner life. And as we read his Epistles and think his thoughts after him we begin to see the motive-power of his life. In a word, it was the love of Christ that constrained him. "For whether we be beside ourselves, it is to God; or whether we be sober, it is for your cause. For the love of Christ constraineth us . . ." (2 Cor. 5:13, 14).

170 He Understands

A young mechanic became involved in some trouble with his employer on the question of money that was due him. A friend reasoned with him, upon learning the name of the lawyer to whom he had gone for consultation. "Why, I could direct you to a score of better lawyers," said his friend. "That man is only a commonplace fellow."

"That may be true," replied the mechanic, "but he understands my case as no one else would be able to understand it. He used to work at my trade himself."

Jesus Christ attracts the man who is in need of help, because he knows all about human sorrows. He was once in the place of the sorrowing one himself.

171 Endurance of Christ's Love

General Garibaldi met a Sardinian shepherd one day, in sore trouble because a lamb had strayed away from the fold. Garibaldi summoned men, and, provided with lanterns, they went hither and thither to find the lost one. They all grew tired of the search and returned to their tents. Next morning, Garibaldi's servant, finding his master had not risen at the usual hour, entered the tent and found him asleep, exhausted after his long walk; but Garibaldi, upon awaking, turned back the covering of his bed and revealed the missing lamb. How tireless is our Savior in his search for those who have wandered and strayed. He seeks until He finds (Matt. 18:10-13).

172 Noontide of Eternal Love

"Mercy and truth are met together: righteousness and peace have kissed each other" (Ps. 85:10).

The person, the love, and the work of Christ afford matter for eternal meditation and joy. Here shine spotless justice, incomprehensible wisdom, and infinite love, all at once. None of them darkens or eclipses another; each one gives a luster to the rest. They mingle their beams, and shine with united splendor. The just Judge, the merciful Father, and the wise Governor—no other object gives such a display of all these perfections. Nowhere does justice appear so awful, mercy so amiable, nor wisdom so profound, as in a crucified Christ! The cross of Christ was the noontide of everlasting love; the meridian splendor of eternal mercy!

173 The True Shepherd

" 'The sheep follow him, for they know his voice; and a stranger will they not follow, for they know not the voice of strangers' (John 10:4, 5). I remember hearing a brother tell how he disproved the notion that sheep only know the shepherd by his dress. When in Palestine he asked a shepherd to allow him to put on his clothes. Then he began to call the sheep, but never a one would come, not even a lamb. The most sheepish of the flock had sense enough left to know that he was not the shepherd, and even the youngest kept aloof, heedless of the stranger's voice. He might have called till he was hoarse, but they would not come. So God's people know their Lord, and they know the kind of food which he gives them."
—Spurgeon

174 How Much Christ Loves Us

"Herein is love, not that we loved God, but that He loved us, and sent his Son to be the propitiation for our sins" (1 John 4:10).

The love of Christ appears in his amazing sufferings for sinners. That love is immense, unsearchable! The inexpressible wrath of God fell from heaven upon Him, as a tremendous thunderstorm, from which there could be no flight, no shelter; so that it entirely crushed His human nature; and the extremity of pain and anguish dissolved the bond between his inmost soul and body. He was brought into the blackest regions of death and darkness (and his love brought Him there), that the sinner might be brought to the regions of light above. His love, his sufferings, were beyond parallel, and from the one you may well take the dimensions of the other. O my soul, see thy Savior agonizing in the garden, bleeding on the cross; and weep tears of gratitude and joy! Oh! On that cross, what love was displayed! Every thorn was a pencil, and every groan was a trumpet, to publish abroad His love to man!

Could we with ink the ocean fill,
Were the whole earth of parchment made,
Were every single stick a quill,
Were every man a scribe by trade:
To write the love of God alone,
Would drain the ocean dry;
Nor would the scroll contain the whole,
Though stretch'd from sky to sky!

His Power

175 The Ever-Present Christ

Some years ago a Parisian artist set up his studio in a cab. He drove from place to place, painted the scenes in the street, and into all these pictures of modern Parisian life introduced the Christ. Even Paris was startled at his daring. In the midst of the follies, jostled by the merry and frivolous crowd, stood Christ—His eyes searching, sorrowful, pleading! The painter, too, painted Him, not in His Eastern dress of long ago, but in modern costume. It was the ever-present Christ he meant to represent: it was the message that Christ is in Paris and London today, as He was in Jerusalem two thousand years ago; and painting Christ thus in the heart of the frivolous throng, he recalled it to that which alone can glorify life, the power of love and sacrifice.

176 Rock of Safety

In a storm one dark night some sailors were thrown by the sea upon a rock, to which they clung for their lives. Their first feeling was one of joyful gratitude. They were on a rock. Their second emotion was a sickening fear, for the tide might rise, and the storm and waves sweep over the rock and carry them away to death in the raging sea. Just then a flash of lightening overtook the darkness, and by its lurid glare they saw that the rock was covered with samphire, a plant which always grows above the level of the tide. Then were they greatly glad, for they were assuredly safe. So is it in our wildest storms, if we cast upon the rock Christ Jesus. If God loves us we shall live, for the love involves the life—life here, life everlasting.

177 The Revolutions Effected by Christ

Napoleon, when dying at St. Helena, said to his comrades, "When I am dead my spirit will return to France to throb with ceaseless life in new revolutions." It was a great exaggeration to say the least! But when our Lord died His Spirit did literally come again to the earth, and in His people, by His Spirit's power, and in His Word, He is constantly working revolutions. He is born into hearts and peoples by the Holy Spirit.

178 Achilles' Heel

It is reported by the Greek poets that the mother of Achilles the Grecian captain was warned by the oracle and dipped her son, as a child, into the River Lethe, thus providing an impenetrable armor for protection during the Trojan War. Paris, Achilles' archenemy, knowing of this fact, realized the only place he could attack his foe would be the heel, that by which his mother held him while immersing her son in the river. Ultimately, Paris attacked and shot Achilles in the heel and killed him.

For the believer, there is a whole armor to protect us from Satan's attacks. We must put on each piece with prayer and God has promised to protect us, even down to our Achilles' heel (Eph. 6:10–18).

179 Man's Inabilities

Man's ability and sufficiency is always short of where he should be. It is very much like a bed sheet that is too short. When it is pulled up close to your head, your feet become uncovered, and likewise visa versa. This picture reveals the inadequacy of man's efforts. Christ desires us to trust Him alone for our sufficiency (Prov. 3:5, 6).

His Return

180 The Return of Christ

Years ago, a great crowd was waiting on the streets of Edinburgh to greet Gladstone, who was going to speak at the Exchange. In the crowd was a man, upon whose heart the Holy Spirit had been working tenderness and interest in Divine things. Suddenly, as with a flash of penetrating light, the thought flashed into his soul, "One of these days they will be gathering to meet the coming Christ. Will you be ready?" The thought would not let him rest. He went home, and found the Son of God as his Savior.

181 When He Comes

A man visiting a certain elementary school informed a class that he would give a prize to the pupil whose desk he found to be the cleanest and most organized when he returned. "But when will you return?" some of them asked.

"That I cannot tell," was the answer.

A little girl, who had been noted for her disorderly habits announced that she intended to win the prize.

"You!" her schoolmates jeered; "why, your desk is always a mess."

"Oh! but I will clean it the first of every week."

"But what if he should come at the end of the week?" someone asked.

"Then I will clean it every morning."

"But he might come at the end of the day."

For a moment the little girl was silent. "I know what I'll do," she said decidedly; "I'll just keep it clean."

So it must be with the Lord's servants who would be ready to receive the prize at his coming. It may be at midnight, at cock-crowing, or in the morning. The exhortation is not, "Get ye ready," but, "Be ye ready."

His Suffering

182 Christ in the Dying Hour

The following illustration is by Charles Spurgeon: "There is a young girl in heaven now, once a member of this church. I went with one of my beloved deacons to see her when she was very near her departure. She was in the last stage of tuberculosis. Fair and sweetly beautiful she looked, and I think I never heard such syllables as those which fell from that girl's lips. She had had disappointments, and trials, and troubles, but all these she had not a word to say about, except that she blessed God for them; they had brought her nearer to the Savior. And when we asked her whether she was not afraid of dying, 'No,' she said, 'the only thing I fear is this, I am afraid of living, lest my patience should wear out. I have not said an impatient word yet, sir; I hope I shall not. It is sad to be so very weak, but I think if I had my choice, I would rather be here than be in good health, for it is very precious to me; I know that my Redeemer liveth, and I am waiting for the moment when he shall send his chariot of fire to take me up to him.' I put the question, 'Have you not any doubts?' 'No, none, sir; why should I? I clasp my arms around the neck of Christ.' 'And have not you any fear about your sins?' 'No, sir, they are all forgiven; I trust the Savior's precious blood.' 'And do you think that you will be as brave as this when you come actually to die?' 'Not if he leaves me, sir, but he will never leave me, for he said, I will never leave thee nor forsake thee' " (Heb. 13:5).

183 Lost along the Way

A young lady named Bridgette left her homeland of Ireland. When she left, she was given a high recommendation for her work as a housekeeper. The valued paper was packed with her belongings as she boarded a boat for America. Along the way, her valued possession was lost. Upon her arrival, she solicited the advice of a friend who provided the following written proposal: "To the general public: Bridgette had a good reputation upon leaving Ireland, but lost it along the way."

This misunderstanding of the friend truly revealed what can happen when a person relies on his own abilities, not on the sufficiency of Christ (2 Cor. 12:9).

184 The Patient Christ

Perhaps most of us fail more frequently in the matter of patience than in any other department of Christian life. But we do not fail for lack of example in Him who is at once our Model and our Savior. Peter calls attention to the patience of Jesus in the second chapter of his first Epistle. He says there that ". . . Christ also suffered for us, leaving us an example that ye should follow his steps: who did no sin, neither was guile found in his mouth: who, when he was reviled, reviled not again; when he suffered, he threatened not; but committed himself to him that judgeth righteously; who his own self bare our sins in his own body on the tree, that we, being dead to sins, should live unto righteousness: by whose stripes we are healed" (2 Pet. 2:21-24). Christ was able to keep his patience through all because his faith in God was unwavering and he saw ahead the victory which was sure to come. We, too, should trust God, and have our eye on the prize which is at the end of the race. It is only the man who is sure he is going to win who can remain patient under every trial.

Humility

185 No Reputation

The use of the Greek word *knenóō* in Philippians 2:7 is of great theological importance. It refers to Jesus Christ emptying Himself at the time of His incarnation, denoting the beginning of His self-humiliation of "being found in fashion of a man" (Phil. 2:8a). This can be explained in Christ taking the "form of a servant" and "was made in the likeness of man." Imagine if you were asked to relinquish something beautiful for something quite undesirable. Christ, though remaining equal with God, made this sacrifice willingly. His love overflowed for mankind in becoming this "servant" and giving His life. As Romans 5:7 states "scarcely for a righteous man will one die: yet peradventure for a good man some would even dare to die." Christ paid the price knowing our sinful state. Though His earthly peers gave Him no good reputation, for the believer, His sacrifice makes Him our heavenly king.

—Spiros Zodhiates

Master

186 Christ the Supreme Teacher

It was a famous saying of Cicero that Socrates brought philosophy from heaven to earth, introducing her to private houses and public squares, and to the daily life of mankind. It might be said with far greater truth and force that Jesus Christ did this with heavenly love. Before he came, the words "foreigner" and "enemy" were synonymous, but he taught a brotherly love that was to remove all barriers of race, and men and nations also were to love their neighbors as themselves. Were the teachings of Jesus to be fulfilled, earth would become heaven, for all sin and hate would be forever banished.

Propitiator

187 The Faithful Advocate

A faithful advocate can never sit without a client in a courtroom. Nor does a true advocate even darken the court itself without a hope that something true and honest will result. A goldsmith may attain to lofty status as long as there are those who deal in precious metals. An advocate, in much the same manner, is a limb of friendship. As observed by a famous past lawyer, a Roman named Cecero who was killed by a man he had defended, was once accused of the murder of his defendant's father because "certainly he that defends an injury is next to him that commits it."

However, we are dealing with Christ, the great Advocate, who does not side with us because of who we are whether great or lacking in character, but because he loves us. We have everything to lose when we do not trust One so honest and true.

In today's society, much is said of crooked and selfish advocates, but we have one who sticks closer than a brother—Jesus Christ, the Righteous.

188 In My Place

In the French Revolution, a young man was condemned to die by the guillotine, and was put in prison until his name would be called for execution.

There were many who loved and cared for this young man, but none more than his own father. When the time came and the names were called, the father, whose name was the same as his son's, went to the executioner's stand instead of his son. In this he revealed the ultimate of his love.

Christ showed the ultimate of His love by dying in the place of sinners. His death paid the price that God required so that sinners could be given eternal life.

189 The Devil and the Advocate

The story is told of an old gardener, who was a rough, though sometimes gentle man. He was questioned one day as to his unorthodox behavior. His reply was with an analogy of his life struggle. He said, "A few days ago the devil came to tempt me. He was a crafty sort, much like a lawyer debates. When I could no longer argue with him, I asked the nature of his actions towards me. His reply was concerning my soul [which he desperately desired]. I answered to him explaining that Christ has received my soul, 'lock, stock, and barrel.' If the devil wanted my soul, he must talk to my Advocate, Jesus Christ." ". . . And if any man sin, we have an Advocate with the Father, Jesus Christ the righteous" (1 John 2:1b).

190 Expedient Absence

"It is better for us that Christ should be in heaven than with us upon earth. A woman had rather have her husband live with her than go to the Indies; but she yields to his absence when she considers the profit of his traffic." The figure is well selected. Let us dwell on it awhile, and think of the amazing profit which this journey of our best Beloved is bringing in to us. He is pleading in the place of authority: what an enrichment to us to have an Intercessor at the throne of grace, through whom every true prayer is accepted! He is ruling on the seat of empire, arranging all providences for the success of His church: what a gain to have our Head and Leader raised above all principalities and powers! He is preparing a place for his people: what a blessing to have such a Forerunner, Representative, and Preparer! Moreover, by His departure we have received the Holy Spirit, of whose divine value what pen shall write! He is with us and in us, our Instructor, Quickener, Purifier, and Comforter.

Even upon these few points we are great gainers by His bodily absence; but there is much more. If our Lord judged it to be expedient that He should go, then expedient it is in the highest sense, and therefore let us solace ourselves in His present bodily absence from us "till the day break, and the shadows flee away" (Song 2:17).

Provider

191 Repeating the Promises

Jesus had regard to the human need of his disciples when he reminded them of his promises. Just how much they owed to these frequent reminders we can not know. Nor do we know how much we owe to the open Word, where we may go day by day and be assured that "He has promised."

Cold reason might say that we have no need to read again and again what he has said. But it is the experience of every heart that, before long, as the way narrows, and thick clouds shut out the light, we need to hear his voice saying, "Lo, I am with you alway" (Matt. 28:20). The mother bending over her child repeating, "I love you; I will take care of you!" tells it nothing new, and yet how those words calm and cheer the troubled little heart. So, "as one whom his mother comforteth" (Is. 66:13), he means that we shall be reminded of his love over and over again.

192 God Will Provide

Mr. Spurgeon, speaking of his grandfather's experience, says that when the family cow died, and the poor pastor's children were left without their staff of life, the grandmother asked, "What will you do now?" The grandfather replied, "I cannot tell what *we* shall do, but I know what God will do. God will provide for us. We must have milk for the children." The next morning there came 20 pounds for him. He had never made application to the fund for the relief of ministers, but on that day there was 5 pounds left when they had divided the money, and one said, "There is poor Mr. Spurgeon down there in Essex; suppose we send it to him." The chairman said, "We had better make it 10 pounds, and I will give 5 pounds." Another 5 pounds was offered by another member, if a matching amount could be raised to make it up to 20 pounds—which was done. "They knew nothing about my grandfather's cow," says Spurgeon, "but God did, you see, and there was the new cow for him. And those gentlemen were not aware of the importance of the service they had rendered."

193 The Great Equalizer

"The rich and poor meet together; the Lord is the Maker of them all" (Prov. 22:2).

The difference of high and low, rich and poor, is only calculated for the present world, and cannot outlive time. In the grave, at the day of judgment, and in heaven, there are no such distinctions. The grave takes away all civil differences. Skulls wear no wreaths nor marks of honor. "The small and the great are there, and the servant is free from his master" (Job 3:19). The poet alludes to this, when he says:

Tis here all meet,
The shivering Icelander and sun
  burnt Moor;
Men of all climes that never met
  before;
And of all creeds, the Jew, the
Turk, and Christian.
Here the proud prince, and
  favorite yet prouder,
His sovereign's keeper, and
  the people's scourge,
Are huddled out of sight.

Christianity

194 Christian Teachers and Their Families

There is an old proverb: "The shoemaker's wife is always the worst shod." The families of many very busy Christian teachers suffer woefully for want of remembering "He first findeth his own brother" (John 1:41).

195 Table of Religion

The commonplaces of religion are the most important. Everybody needs air, light, bread and water. Dainties are for the few; but the table which our religion sometimes spreads for them, is like that at a rich man's feast—plenty of rare dishes but never a bit of bread; plenty of wine and wine glasses, but not a tumbler-full of spring water to be had.

196 Following Men Instead of Following God

We are all apt to pin our faith on some trusted guide, and many of us, in these days, will follow some teacher of negations with an implicit submission which we refuse to give to Jesus Christ. We put the teacher between ourselves and God, and give to the glowing colors of the painted window the admiration that is due to the light which shines through it.

197 Putting God Off

Are we not ever in danger of giving the very choicest of our love to the dear ones of earth, lavishing on them the precious juice which flows from the freshly-gathered grapes, and putting God off with the last impoverished and scanty drops which can be squeezed from the husks?

198 Remaining Strong in Uneventful Times

It is a great deal easier to be up to the occasion in some shining moment of a man's life, when he knows that a supreme hour has come, than it is to keep that high tone when plodding over all the dreary plateau of uneventful, monotonous travel and dull duties. It is easier to run fast for a minute than to grind along the dusty road for a day.

Many a ship has stood the tempest, and then has gone down in the harbor because its timbers have been gnawed to pieces by white ants. And many a man can do what is wanted in the trying moments, and yet make shipwreck of his faith in uneventful times.

Like ships that have gone down at sea,
When Heaven was all tranquility.

Soldiers who could stand firm and strike with all their might in the hour of battle, will fall asleep, or have their courage ooze out at their fingers' ends, when they have to keep watch at their posts through a long winter's night.

199 Struggles of Life

The past struggles are joyful in memory, as the mountain ranges—which were all black rock and white snow while we toiled up their inhospitable steeps—lie purple in the mellowing distance, and burn like fire as the sunset strikes at the peaks.

200 Setting Sun and Believers

"As the setting of the sun," says Salter, "appears of greater magnitude, and his beams of richer gold, than when he is in the meridian, so a dying believer is usually richer in experience, stronger in grace, and brighter in his evidences for heaven, than a living one."

201 Kings and Priests unto God

One of the royal captives taken by Alexander was asked by his conqueror how he desired to be treated. He said, "Like a king." Alexander then asked had he nothing else to request of him. "No," replied he, "everything is comprehended in the word king." Pleased with the response, he gave him back more than he had taken from him with the sword.

Believers are "kings and priests unto God." But how seldom does their faith in Him who has conquered them by His grace rise to such a height as to lead them to ask for favors which only belong to heirs of His royal kingdom! God loves to hear His children ask for large favors, and in their deepest humility they have a right to enjoy the loftiest relationship, and to believe that as they bear a royal name their Father will not refuse to grant them royal gifts. The cry, ". . . Make me as one of Your hired servants" (Luke 15:19) may be changed into the prayer, "Treat me as an heir of Your own glories."

202 Belief Typified

"I had been absent from home for some days," a Christian writer relates, "and was wondering, as I again drew near the homestead, if my little Maggie, just able to sit alone, would remember me. To test her memory, I stationed myself where I could see her, but could not be seen by her, and called her name in the old familiar tone, 'Maggie!' She dropped her playthings, glanced around the room, and then looked down upon her toys. Again I repeated her name, 'Maggie!' when she once more surveyed the room; but, not seeing her father's face, she looked very sad, and slowly resumed her employment. Once more I called 'Maggie!' when, dropping her playthings, and bursting into tears, she stretched out her arms in the direction from where the sound proceeded, knowing that, though she could not see him, her father must be there, for she knew his voice."

203 Transforming the Commonplace

The first change wrought by Christianity upon architecture was the transference of the basilica into the Christian church. The basilica was the gathering place of the Romans; here they transacted their business, here they held their tribunals, and engaged themselves in the ordinary duties of life, and it was the basilica which the early Christians consecrated to the service of God. The act is full of suggestion. It recalls us to the supreme fact that religion does not lie separate from the ordinary duties of life, but is here to consecrate them, and to teach us how we may use them in the service and worship of God. It teaches us also that Christianity has come into the world not to destroy, but to fulfill.

204 The Pharisee's Ideal

Here is an excerpt from the sermon, *On Self-Examination*, by Dr. B. H. Streeter:

". . . Now the parable of the Pharisee and the publican is one of the most popular stories in the Gospels. It cuts straight to the heart of everyone, and when we are thinking of Christianity in a sentimental mood it is one of the first things that occurs to us. When it comes to real life it is different. The publican, or his equivalent, in the life of today we fight a little shy of, unless indeed he happens to have a good social position and an income of ten thousand a year [a respectable salary in 1924]. And the Pharisee's strictness of religious observance is not particularly popular nowadays, and very few people think much the better of a man for that; but in so far as the Pharisee is the man who lives a decent, moral, respectable life, and looks down on others, I suppose we may as well admit that we are all of us Pharisees. We are all of us people who are content to live a reasonably blameless life, doing a little good this way and that as we go along, and although we pardon little slips, we draw the line at people who fall below a certain standard.

"The point I am trying to make is this, that the ideal which most of us set before ourselves is to do no harm, to commit no special sin, and do as much good as we can without serious inconvenience or expense. The soldier of Christ is one who is sworn to lifelong battles, lifelong aspiration. His life is given him, like his rifle, as a weapon to use. Our life is not given us to do some good with, but to do all the good we can, that we may leave the world in any way we can better than we found it.

"The question which we commonly ask ourselves in self-examination, or at any rate in ordinary life, is, given our lives, how are we to live comfortably, pleasantly, and do as little harm as possible? But the question which Christ asks is: Given your life, what good are you going to do with it? And it makes all the difference to our conception of sin whether we estimate the successes and failures, whether of ourselves or other people, from the one standpoint or the other . . ."

205 The Things We Know

Percy Austin in his sermon, *The Certain Christianity,* explains the difference between the Christian and a non-believer:

". . . the difference between the true Christian and one who is not a Christian is not simply that one believes certain things that the other does not believe. It is that one knows something that the other does not know, he has entered into something which the other has not entered, and there is a far greater difference between the two positions than is always obvious on the surface or to the superficial gaze.

"Now if this be a true summary of the case, it follows that there should be certain things about which the Christian can speak with the note of confident, and even dogmatic, assurance. There are many domains of thought, even in the realms of religion, where that note is not justified and where its presence is of the gravest disservice to truth. Where, then, is it justified? What are the things concerning which the Christian can say 'I know'? For our purpose we take just two.

"First, the fact of Redemption, of pardon and peace with God. The New Testament assures us that the man who believes in Jesus Christ has his sins forgiven and enters thereby into a new experience of reconciliation and peace with God. Now a true Christian is not simply one who believes the truth of that; he is one who *knows* it. True, he may very inadequately understand it. His theory of the Atonement, if he has a theory at all, may be vague, crude or even grotesque. Nor is he always on the same level of conscious realization of the new spiritual experience. He has his ups and downs, days of cloud as well as days of sunshine. But he *knows,* however imperfectly he may himself understand it, that faith in Jesus Christ has made things vitally different in the deeper realms of the soul's life. He may not express himself in theological terms, or even in the language of the New Testament, but he is sure of the reality of the personal experience.

"Second, the fact of fellowship. The Christian is one who *knows* the reality of soul communion. Here again he may very inadequately understand it. There is a mystery of spiritual fellowship as there is a mystery of redemption. We do not and cannot clearly understand how the human spirit, under all the hampering limitations of the flesh, can yet reach forth to conscious fellowship with the Spirit Divine; but the reality of the experience is beyond question. It is not always vivid. Sometimes the believing soul knows the Emmaus Walk or the vision of the Transfiguration Mount; at other times spiritual things seem far away and almost unreal. But the reality is there beyond the possibility of question to any soul that has once entered into it — a reality to which the experience of the saints in all ages bears glad testimony."

206 A Question of Ownership

When we want to describe certain very disagreeable people, we say that they act as though they own everything. Perhaps not many of us are disposed to be thus in our relationships with each other, and yet it is a common fault. Nothing is plainer than the teaching of the Bible on the subject of our indebtedness to God. He gives nothing, though he entrusts us with many things. Yet there is a common feeling that it is our business, and ours alone, as to how we make use of that which has been left in our hands. In other words, we act as though we owned things.

Suppose, if, when you leave your car with the mechanic to have some minor repairs done, he should use it for his personal driving. Suppose the dry-cleaner should take the shirts that you bring him to have cleaned, and wear them going about his own affairs. It would, at least, cause some friction between you and your mechanic or dry-cleaner, as the case might be. When you are about to decide how you shall use this opportunity, or that talent, remember that the Owner has some rights that ought to be considered.

207 "If I Were a Christian"

"If I were a Christian," a man was saying the other day, as he viewed critically a faulty church-member,

"I would certainly try to live up to my obligations."

"If you would live up to your obligations, you would be a Christian," was the somewhat startling reply. The average man who holds himself aloof from the church seems to forget that the same God who created the Christian created him also, and that, in the strictest sense, God is the Father of them both. The fact that he goes into an alien land to live out his life, and deprives his Father of his service altogether, does not free him from accountability. It does not even warrant him in making a favorable comparison between himself and the son who remains at home and renders imperfect service to the one to whom he owes so much.

208 What the Temple Is For

Suppose, when that beautiful chapel of yours was completed, the trustees had said: "From now on we are going to see that this temple is kept clean, and that nothing unworthy ever enters its doors." So the house was kept clean and free from dust, but it was never opened once for service. No hymns of prayer or praise ascended here, and never a soul found Christ within its walls. Wouldn't we say that these men had been untrue to their trust? The temple should be kept clean, it is true, *but it was built for service.* So, Christians, let us make sure that we are not using the temple of this body to his glory, simply because we are keeping it strong and pure. It was built for service.

209 Allow Jesus to Come on Board

John Pulsford says: "The vessel in which we are passing over the sea of mortal life is always driven by contrary winds till the Lord embarks. All voyagers who know the pleasantness of having Christ on board and the certainty of getting safe to land under Him, pray Him with all their hearts to abide with them. All days may seem alike, but the monotony of going on is different from the monotony of drifting. We must always keep in mind the courage-bringing fact that it is the will of God that we arrive in port."

210 In Tune with God

Mr. Marconi, famous for inventing radio technology, once constructed a receiver that would only respond to a special transmitter. If the transmitter radiated eight hundred thousand vibrations a second the receiver would only take from the same rate of vibration. In the same way, the familiar tuning-fork will only respond to another tuning-fork of precisely the same musical tone. This is the principle of assured answer to prayer. If I am right with God, tuned to his purposes and will, I cannot ask in vain. "If ye abide in me and my words abide in you, ye shall ask what ye will and it shall be done unto you" (John 15:7). God's response to our petitions follows our response to His commands. "Delight thyself also in the Lord and He shall give thee the desires of thine heart" (Ps. 37:4). Affinity of soul with God is assurance of His hearing us.

211 Christianity a Life

American coins have on one side their value stamped "One cent," "ten cents," "one dollar," and on the other side "In God we trust." So a man may be a busboy, a mechanic, a salesman, a member of Congress, or even President of the United States, and yet in every case a Christian, a true believer. Milton said of Queen Christina: "She may abdicate the throne, but can never lay aside the queen." And we may renounce our calling, but our Spirit-life never. The Christian is independent of position or rank, it is the man himself.

212 Christianity and the Child

A recent traveler in China remarks on the fact that all the time he was there, some two and a half years, he never saw a single monument or tombstone marking the grave of a child. This is very remarkable, remembering the people's ancestor and grave worship. The whole countryside is a densely populated cemetery, and yet no tokens of the burial of children. Buddhism and Confucianism ignore the child; only Jesus took them in His arms and said, "Of such is the Kingdom of Heaven" (Matt. 19:14).

213 Homely Christianity

A certain "prophet" thought to render God a perfect service, and to do this, believed it necessary to journey to Mount Sinai, for there he might hear God's voice and learn the secret of holiness. After long toil he reached the mountain, and waited vainly for the special vision of God. One day he found a bed of moss and violets. Then he remembered that at home his child had offered him some violets quite similar to those on Mt. Sinai. This taught him that God was as much evident in his daily routine life as at the Holy Mount, and he turned homeward to live with God where God had placed him.

214 One with Christ

Mr. Spurgeon once showed a brother minister a crumpled piece of papyrus paper covered with Arabic characters. "That," said he, "is Gordon's signature." When expected supplies did not at once arrive from Britain, Gordon used these as current coin, and so mighty was his name in all the Sudan that they were everywhere accepted as good payment. His name pledged the honor and faithfulness of his country and people. Would that we were so identified with our Lord that our actions were recognized as that of our Master, and our word a pledge of His.

215 Christ Always First

The late Principal Cairns, though one of the most popular platform speakers of his day, was truly a lowly heart. At public meetings he constantly refused the place of honor in the procession to the platform, holding back, and saying to others: "You first, I follow." It came to be one of his trademark mannerisms. On his deathbed he was overheard to be saying, "You first, I follow"; and those who listened knew that it was to the Christ who had ever been chief and first and leader of his life that this was spoken.

216 The Beauty of Holiness

There is no path in life so dark but that the Christian graces, growing in the garden of the heart, may make the soul like an oasis in the desert. A former keeper of the Point Pinas Lighthouse, near Monterey, California, was a woman. When Mrs. Fish entered upon the duties of her office, she found the lighthouse a dreary abode, situated as it was far from any neighboring houses upon the gray ocean sands. She at once began transforming it into a more homelike spot. Within she added warm draperies, rare china, and other dainty furnishings. Without she enclosed a large garden, and made it a brilliant, fragrant spot. About its boundaries she planted the native cypress, which is found nowhere else in the world. Behind these sheltering trees she made a broad, velvety lawn, and planted tea-roses, geraniums, and other fragrant flowers. On the warm, sunny days that come in such quick succession there, this garden, only ninety feet above the sea, and overlooking the vast blue Pacific, is one of the prettiest, most romantic, and sightly places on the coast. But more careful than of all else was Mrs. Fish to the great light entrusted to her care. Punctual to the moment the lamp always sent its rays across the water, and as punctually it was extinguished when the stronger light of day appeared.

217 Keep the Lights Bright

"Let your light so shine before men." (Matt. 5:16).

The keeper of the lighthouse at Calais was boasting of the brightness of his lantern, which can be seen ten leagues at sea. A visitor said to him, "What if one of the lights should by chance go out?" "Never! Impossible!" he cried, horrified at the thought. "Sir," he said, pointing to the ocean, "yonder, where nothing can be seen there are ships going by to all parts of the world. If tonight one of my lamps went out, within six months would come a letter, perhaps from India, perhaps from America, perhaps from some place I never heard of, saying, 'Such a night, at such an hour, the light of Calais burned dim, the watchman neglected his post, and vessels were in danger!' Ah, sir, sometimes in the dark nights, in stormy weather, I look out to sea, and feel as if the eyes of the whole world were looking at my light. Go out? Burn dim? Never!"

218 Christian Influence

Too often, we as Christians fail to realize how influential our lives can be on the lives of other people, including other Christians. We should live our lives with a daily goal of producing faith in others. John Bunyan, the renowned author of *Pilgrims Progress* conveys the idea of influence quite beautifully with this quote: "Christians are like the several flowers in a garden that have each of them the dews of heaven, which, being shaken with the wind, they let fall at each other's roots, whereby they are jointly nourished and become nourishers of each other."

Christians should remember that our spiritual growth and strength not only comes from regular bible study and prayer, but also from using the talents and spiritual gifts that God gives us to encourage and equip others.

219 Christ Living in Us

It is said by Dr. W. Milligan, that "Christ must not only be on us as a robe, but in us as a life, if we are to have the hope of glory."

220 To Win a Crown

The Reverend H. W. Webb-Peploe once said, "You must take possession of Christ for salvation, but to win a crown Christ must take possession of you."

221 Blackout!

Dennis E. Hensley writes:

"When I was a newspaper reporter, I did a feature on training procedures for Air Force pilots. One flight condition a pilot must understand is hypoxia or 'oxygen starvation.' Students are paired off in an altitude simulation chamber. With oxygen masks on, they are taken to simulated conditions of 30,000 feet. Then one student removes his mask for a few minutes and begins to answer simple questions on a sheet of paper. Suddenly, their partners force the oxygen masks on the uncovered mouths and noses of the people who are writing. After a few gulps of normal air, each writer is astounded at what he sees on his paper. The first few written lines are legible, but the last few lines are unreadable. One minute earlier, the participant was absolutely sure he had written his answers in perfectly legible script. In reality, he was on the verge of losing total consciousness. Remarkably, he didn't even know he was blacking out.

"Similarly, people can be spiritually starved. They may not know anything is wrong, but unless someone explains how to obtain the 'breath of life,' those disconnected from God will never gain spiritual 'consciousness.'"

222 The Parable of the Potter

Jeremiah 18:4—"And the vessel that he made of clay was marred in the hand of the potter: so he made it again another vessel as seemed good to the potter to make it."

The late D. D. F. MacDonald wrote an excellent illustration on this subject, and it reveals to us how Christians are the "clay" which is constantly being molded and shaped by the greatest Potter:

"He takes the lump of clay, plants himself close by two wheels which are connected in such a way that by revolving one with his foot he sends another wheel revolving with great rapidity. On this upper wheel the wonderful work of evolving the beautiful productions of his ingenious art is carried out. With one hand he holds and with the other hand he molds, until, with amazing speed, the urn, the water-jar, or the gracefully-shaped vase is fashioned. If all goes well and we are told you may stand long enough before you see anything go wrong, the product of the day's labor is set aside to be afterwards placed in the furnace and baked, and so grow from an intention in the potter's brain into a finished work in the potter's hands, whether that work be one of homely usefulness or a work more suited to give the eye pleasure as it rests upon its beauty.

"And, as we gaze thoughtfully upon the man at work, watching for the flaw that mars his task, at last we see him pause, for something evidently has gone wrong, and the work that was nearing completion is swiftly crushed back again into a lump. It is not flung aside as so much waste and useless matter. He had power to do this. The potter can do as he pleases with the clay, but he presses it back to its first condition of formlessness and then begins anew to work out the same design or perhaps another of proportions less ample and better suited to work up the quantity of clay in his hand."

Remember, our Potter is a perfect Creator. Any mistakes or flaws in the molding process of our Christian lives is of our own doing. These "flaws" occur when we refuse to allow Christ to mold us into the image He has designed for us; yet, as MacDonald correctly states, he never flings us aside, but continues the process of molding us into the image of Christ-likeness.

223 Stretching the Soul

It's a good story which was told many years ago by R. Lee Sharpe. And a short but big sermon it was, too! Let's relate it mostly in Mr. Sharpe's own language: "I was just a child. One spring day Father called me to go with him to Mr. Trussel's blacksmith shop. He had left a rake and a hoe to be repaired. And there they were, ready, fixed like new. Father handed over a silver dollar for the repairing. But Mr. Trussel refused to take it. "No," he said, "there's no charge for that little job." But Father insisted that he take the pay, still extending the dollar. If I ever live a thousand years, I'll never forget that great man's reply: "Ed, can't you let a man do something now and then—just to stretch his soul?"

That short but big sermon from the lips of that humble, lovable blacksmith has caused us to find, again and again, the great joy and quiet happiness which come from a little "stretching of the soul." Doing little favors, perhaps mere trifles in themselves—making life a little brighter for those we meet— not expecting a return of any kind, this is "stretching the soul."

224 The Cure for Nerves

A lady who was troubled with her nerves went to a famous doctor about her condition. To her astonishment, he gave her his prescrip-

tion: "Go home and read your Bible an hour a day, then come back to me a month from today." At first, she was angry, but later decided that she felt so miserable that she was willing to try anything.

A month later she went back to the doctor a different person, and asked him how he knew that was just what she needed. "Madam," he replied, pointing to a well-worn open Bible lying on his desk, "If I were to omit my daily reading of this Book, I would lose my greatest source of strength and skill."

225 When You Can't Get Enough

Have you ever gone to a restaurant which had a salad or food buffet and asked yourself if it was "all you can eat?" Some places even go as far as to say "all you care to eat." There have been many times that we have enjoyed those unlimited trips to fill our plates again and again.

Think about God's love and His grace. It is much the same way. We have been saved and have been rescued from sin and its eternal punishment, and now can rejoice in the fact that we can realize God's love and grace on a continual basis. There is no end to His sufficiency in time of trouble and struggle in our Christian walk (1 Cor. 10:13; 2 Cor. 12:9).

Jesus said, "I have come that they might have life, and that they might have it more abundantly" (John 10:10b). As believers, we can make many trips to the overflowing bounty of God's grace (Col. 3:16a), which is truly more than enough and more than we can obtain!

226 Another Way to Serve

A young man accepted for the African missionary field reported at New York for passage, but found on further examination that his wife could not stand the climate. He was heartbroken, but he prayerfully returned to his home and determined to make all the money he could, to be used in spreading the Kingdom of God over the world. His father, a dentist, had started to make, on the side, an unfermented wine for the communion service. The young man took the business over and developed it until it assumed vast proportions. His name was Welch, whose family still manufactures grape juice. He has given literally hundreds of thousands of dollars to the work of missions.

Think of ways which you can serve God despite your human frailties. God wants our willing hearts!

227 Accompanying With Sympathy

H. R. Haweis says: "To accompany well you must not only be a good musician, but you must be mesmeric, sympathetic, intuitive. You must know what the singer wants before he tells you, must feel which way his spirit sets, for the motions of the soul are swift as an angel's flight. Unless you can do this you haven't enough music in you to know that you are a failure. The Christian is called to serve and to have the mind of Christ (Phil.

2:5) and as Paul wrote, 'Be ye followers of me, even as I also am of Christ' " (1 Cor. 11:1).

228 Surpassing Angels

"For ye are all the children of God, by faith in Christ Jesus" (Gal. 3:26).

The privileges of the children of God by adoption are wonderful. Angels are celestial beings; but you have privileges which they cannot possess. Your adoption connects you with the Lord Jesus, by ties more close than those by which He is connected with angels. God is yours, in a fuller sense than He is theirs. You have a place in a covenant, which they cannot occupy; feelings at the communion table in which they cannot participate; and a song of praise which they cannot sing. It is true that they have no experience of your sorrows; but they know not the comforts of that mercy which heals the brokenhearted, nor the renovating power of repentance unto life. There is not a blessing in the great salvation which He will deny you, nor a moment of your being which is not marked by His bounty. "If children, then heirs; heirs of God and joint-heirs with Christ" (Rom. 8:17).

229 Mimic

Père Carbasson brought up an orangutan, which became so fond of him that, wherever he went, it was always desirous of accompanying him. Whenever therefore he had to perform the service of his church, he was under the necessity of shutting it up in his room. Once, however, the animal escaped and followed its master to the church: where silently mounting the sounding board above the pulpit, he lay perfectly still till the sermon commenced. He then crept to the edge, and overlooking the preacher, imitated all his gestures in so grotesque a manner, that the whole congregation were unavoidably urged to laugh. The minister, surprised and confounded at this ill-timed levity, severely rebuked his audience for their inattention. The reproof failed in its effect; the congregation still laughed, and the preacher in the warmth of his zeal redoubled his vociferation and his action; these the ape imitated so exactly that the congregation could no longer restrain themselves, but burst out into a loud and continued laughter. A friend of the preacher at length stepped up to him, and pointed out the cause of this improper conduct; and such was the arch demeanor of the animal that it was with the utmost difficulty he could himself keep from laughing, while he ordered the servants of the church to take him away.

A crude example for the Christian, but yes, there are those who watch our lives so closely that they often imitate our actions. We must be careful what we are doing as we are also required to imitate Christ with our lives. We should be as Paul when he wrote: "Be ye followers of me, even as I also am of Christ" (1 Cor. 11:1).

230 Moving Day

Croft M. Pentz relates: "When one moves, you soon realize all the things you have accumulated, which you don't need. There is so much you kept, which is of no value, and you must throw out. In the Christian life, there are so many things we keep in our life which are needless, and must be thrown out. Stop and think for a moment of the things you have in your Christian life that are of no value—then throw them out."

231 What Sinks Ships?

Someone has pointed out that it isn't the ship in the water but water in the ship, which sinks ships. A ship can ride out the most severe storm so long as it isn't capsized or punctured so that water gets inside. There may be a great external threat, but if the water can be kept out, the ship will remain afloat.

It's just so with the spiritual life of a Christian. We are in the world, but not of the world. All around us, and often very close to us, there are immoral and unspiritual elements which, if allowed to penetrate our defense, will surely "sink" us. Those elements must be kept out at all costs.

We must be strong to keep the world out of our hearts and lives. John says, "Love not the world, neither the things that are in the world" (1 John 2:15), and then identifies those things more closely as the "lust of the flesh, the lust of the eyes and the pride of life." The problem isn't the Christian in the world, it's the world in the Christian. Whatever takes our eyes off Christ, discourages us from serving Him in the church, or compromises our spirituality and morality in any way, can destroy us. "O soul be on thy guard; ten thousand foes arise."

232 Deeds Not Words

A converted cowboy put it very well when he said, "Lots of folks that would really like to do right, think that serving the Lord means shouting themselves hoarse praising His name. Now I'll tell you how I look at that. I am working for Jim here. Now if I would do nothing but sit around the house here telling what a good fellow Jim is and singing songs to him, I would not suit Jim. But when I buckle on my straps and hustle among the hills and see that Jim's herd is all right, not suffering for water and feed, or being driven off the range and branded by cow thieves, then I am serving Jim as he wants to be served." Let that be our philosophy, too, when the temptation is to talk too much, even for Christ (1 John 3:18).

233 Sing and Be Happy

A young boy complained to his father that most of the church hymns were boring to him—too far behind the times, boring tunes, meaningless words. His father put an end to the discussion when he said, "If you think you can write better hymns, then why don't you?" The boy went to his room and wrote his first hymn. This was in 1690; the teenager's name was Isaac Watts. "When I Survey the Wondrous Cross" and "Joy to the World"

are among the almost 350 hymns written by him.

Feeling bored? Do something great! Let the world remember you for 300 years!

234 People Are Watching

A preacher told of eating lunch in a restaurant and seeing the manager eating lunch from a nearby fast food establishment. What did the manager's choice say to the people who watched? I would think, "Don't eat here . . . the food across the street is better."

People are watching you. They see how you live. They hear you talk. They see your priorities in the things you buy and the way you dress. They observe the places you go. And they know the company you keep. You are a "walking billboard." Does your advertisement say "follow me to Christ," or does it lead people across the street?

"Let your light so shine before men, that they may see your good works, and glorify your Father which is in heaven" (Matt. 5:16).

235 Kicking a Habit

The following story is by Stuart Briscoe:

I well remember a young man who was a member of a group that my wife and I took to Holland for a conference. He had a problem with smoking. Every evening he used to go alone to a quiet canal for his evening cigarette. The boy was absolutely addicted and had been since he was twelve years old. In fact, he smoked so heavily that he had to manufacture his own supplies.

One night I talked to the group about the words of Jesus when he stated, "You will know the truth, and the truth will set you free" (John 8:32). Then I showed that when the Lord said the truth would be emancipating, He was referring to Himself, for he added, "So if the Son sets you free, you will be free indeed" (John 8:36). Obviously He was using the term truth as a description of Himself. I tried to show the young people that whatever was binding them in their Christian experience, the Lord through His indwelling life could and would set them free.

Unknown to me, there was a hungry boy listening. He was hungry to be rid of that habit that was his master. He heard that a Christian is a person who has a power greater than any other power within him. Therefore, he knew that for him to claim to be a Christian but at the same time to be dominated by a lesser power than the Spirit of God was a contradiction. So he evaluated his grave clothes and knew that they had to go.

As usual, he went down to the canal. But for the first time he went there longing to be set free. He did an unusual thing. He took out his cigarettes and threw them into the canal, one at a time. As each cigarette fell into the water, he repeated the words that he believed with all his heart, "So if the Son sets you free, you will be free indeed." He testifies to this day that

the Lord had the victory over this thing.

Naturally, he still had many battles over this problem. Many times he longed for a calming, soothing smoke. The Lord hadn't taken away his desire, and the Lord hadn't given him a new strength of willpower. Every time he claimed the promise of God, however, and each time he counted on the adequacy of his Lord, he was set free.

236 Blunders Can Have Great Value

The March 13 issue of *Coin World* carries exciting news for coin collectors. The Philadelphia mint struck a number of 1995 pennies with a faulty die. What's so exciting about a "boo-boo" at the mint? It makes those coins with the out-of-focus words "Liberty" and "In God" valuable items for collectors. Early estimates are that the penny could be worth somewhere between $175 and $225. That amounts to quite a return on a paltry one-cent investment!

The story that has excited numismatists everywhere made me think of the way God views you and me. Things as petty as a "bad-hair day" make some of us turn on ourselves in harsh judgment. Then there are the really serious problems that come as cancer, a child's death, or bankruptcy. For others, they come as a jail sentence, a divorce, or a homosexual lifestyle. The hard thing is getting anyone to see these flaws and failings as having positive value. How can pain bring a reward? How can embarrassment be good? How can doing something outside the will of God have a positive outcome?

One of the most spiritual and committed Christians I know will tell you in a heartbeat that he owes it all to alcoholism! When he threw that account of things at me, I must have gone pale. So he explained how it was hitting bottom on account of the bottle that got his attention, broke through his barrier of lies, and forced him to seek God. Now that makes sense, doesn't it?

If you have ever had your heart broken, you can never laugh at another person's pain. If you have failed miserably at something that was incredibly important to you, you can never be happy over a disaster in someone else's life. If you have ever been wrong about anything, you realize you have no right to gloat about an error you see in someone else's theology. If you have ever taken your personal sin seriously, you will find it impossible to be arrogant and judgmental about another's transgression of God's will. And if you have received and been grateful of God's grace, you will learn to be gracious with people around you.

There's a key ingredient in all this, of course. Since not every life crisis has a positive outcome, it must be that only those persons who react in faith witness a happy ending to what started as a near-certain disaster. Otherwise there is only grief, bitterness and anger. Surrendering all to the Lord is the only way to transform lead into gold, pain into joy, and defeat into victory. Your most glaring flaw is God's most likely opportunity for your redemption.

—Rubel Shelly

237 *Without Folds*

There is a significant word in the Greek New Testament which is used to describe a person who truly exhibits sincerity in their Christian life. The word is *haplotēs,* which literally means without folds. This is best illustrated by examining a simple sheet of paper. As you fold down the edges or if you were to crumple the page, you will notice that in trying to straighten it out, there is still evidence which is permanently ingrained into the texture of the paper.

A person that is truly sincere will have evidences of "no folds." In the New Testament, this type of person is described as faithful, pure and benevolent (Eph. 6:5; Col 3:22). Also, it is used to describe a generous giver who has no ulterior motives (2 Cor. 9:13). Are you a person "without folds" in your character? In the workplace, are you the type of worker who respects authority for the right reasons? When God looks at you does He see your sincerity?

—Spiros Zodhiates

238 *Scripture's Diagnosis*

There is a Greek word used only once in the New Testament and yet what a practical word it is for today's Christian. It is the word *diagnōsis* and yes, the English word is a derivative. It means discernment or something that is distinguished. In Acts 25:21, it was used by Luke, the author, to describe Festus' discussion with King Agrippa concerning the Apostle Paul. When Festus spoke of Paul's scheduled meeting with Agrippa, he used the word translated "hearing" (KJV). Paul then followed shortly after with his defense address in the presence of Agrippa. It is unusual to describe what Paul was about to speak as a "hearing," but in the Christian's life it is very appropriate.

We are daily bombarded with attacks on our faith. Christians must be well prepared to face the scrutiny and "diagnosis" of the world (1 Pet. 3:15).

How will you react to the examination of the world? Will you find that you are not prepared? Will you find that your preparedness is founded in self-reliance? Self-diagnosis should occur first before the world begins its "hearing" about your faith.

—Spiros Zodhiates

239 Glory to God

A native Hindu convert, who had originally belonged to one of the lowest castes, thus addressed a number of his countrymen, among whom were some of the superior castes. The words form a delightful comment on 1 Corinthians 1:26-29:

"I am by birth, of an insignificant and contemptible caste; so low, that if a Brahmin should chance to touch me, he must go and bathe in the Ganges for the purpose of purifica-

tion; and yet God has been pleased to call me, not merely to the knowledge of the Gospel, but to the high office of teaching it to others. My friends, do you know the reason of God's conduct? It is this. If God had selected one of you learned Brahmins, and made you the preacher, when you were successful in making converts, bystanders would have said it was the amazing learning of the Brahmin, and his great weight of character, that were the cause; but now, when anyone is converted by my instrumentality, no one thinks of ascribing any of the praise to me: and God, as is His due, has all the glory."

240 Poor, yet Rich

The following is a passage from the will of the author of a well-known commentary on the Bible: "I have now disposed of all my property to my family; there is one thing more I wish I could give them, and that is the Christian religion. If they had that, and I had not given them one shilling, they would be rich; and if they had not that, and I had given them all the world, they would be poor."

241 Truth of Christianity

"I give my dying testimony," said Dr. John Leland, after a long and exemplary life devoted to the service of the Gospel—"I give my dying testimony to the truth of Christianity. The promises of the Gospel are my support and consolation. They alone yield me satisfaction in my dying hour. I am not afraid to die. The Gospel of Christ has raised me above the fear of death; for 'I know that my Redeemer liveth'" (Job 19:25).

242 Beauty and Deformity

A gentleman had two children: one a daughter, who was considered plain in her outward appearance; the other a son, who was considered handsome. One day, as they were playing together, they saw their faces in a looking-glass. The boy was charmed with his beauty, and spoke of it to his sister, who considered his remarks as so many reflections on her lack of it. She told her father of the affair, complaining of her brother's rudeness to her. The father, instead of appearing angry, took them both on his knees, and with much affection gave them the following advice: "I would have you both look in the glass every day: you, my son, that you may be reminded never to dishonor the beauty of your face by the deformity of your actions: and you, my daughter, that you may take care to hide the defect of beauty in your outward appearance by the superior lustre of your virtuous and amiable conduct."

243 Francis Xavier's Example

Francis Xavier at times received, in the prosecution of his missionary labors, the most mortifying treatment. Preaching in one of the cities of Japan, some of the multitudes made sport of him. One man, more wanton than the rest, went to him while he addressed the people, feigning that he had something to communicate in private. Upon his approach, Xavier, leaned his head to learn what he had to say. The scorner thus gained his object, which was to spit freely upon the face of the missionary, and thus insult him in the most public manner. The missionary, without speaking a word, or making the least sign of anger or emotion, took out his handkerchief, wiped his face, and continued his discourse, as if nothing had occurred. By such an heroic control of his passions, the scorn of the audience was turned into admiration. The most learned doctor of the city, who happened to be present, said to himself, that a law which taught men such virtue, inspired men with such unshaken courage, and gave them so perfect a victory over themselves, could not but be from God.

244 Good Manners in High Places

When Pope Clement XIV (Ganganelli) ascended the Papal chair, the ambassadors of the several states represented at his Court waited on him with their congratulations. When they were introduced, and bowed, he returned the compliment by bowing also; on which the master of the ceremonies told his Highness that he should not have returned their salute. "Oh, I beg your pardon," said the good Pontiff, "I have not been Pope long enough to forget good manners."

245 American Indian and Englishman

Shortly before the war between the English settlers and the Pennsylvania Indians broke out, one of the former was standing at his hut door when an Indian came by and desired a little food. He answered he had none for him; he then asked for something to drink, and received the same brief reply. Not yet discouraged, he begged for a little water; but the man only answered, "Get you gone for an Indian dog!" The Indian fixed his eyes for a little time on the Englishman, and then went away. Some time after, this man who was fond of shooting, pursued his game till he was lost in the woods. After wandering awhile, he saw an Indian hut, and went to it to inquire his way to some plantation. The Indian said, "It is a great way off, and the sun is near going down; you cannot reach it tonight, and if you stay in the woods the wolves will eat you up: but if you have a mind to lodge with me, you may." The Indian boiled a little venison for him, gave him some rum and water, and then spread some deerskins for him to lie upon; having done this, himself and another Indian went to lay at the other side of the hut. He called the man in the morning, telling him that the sun was up, and that he had a long journey to get to the plantation, but that he would show him the way. Taking their guns, the two Indians went forward, and he followed. When they had gone several miles, the Indian told him he was within two miles of the plantation: he then stepped before him, and said, "Do you know me?" In

great confusion, the man answered, "I have seen you." The Indian replied, "Yes, you have seen me at your door; and I will give you a piece of advice: when a poor Indian that is hungry, and thirsty, and faint again asks you for a little meat or drink, do not tell him to get gone for an Indian dog."

246 *Living and Doing*

A brief and simple, but very expressive eulogy was pronounced by Martin Luther upon a pastor at Zwickau, in 1522, named Nicholas Haussmann. "What we preach," said the great reformer, "*he* lives." A good woman who had been to the house of God was met on her way home by a friend, who asked her if the sermon was done. "No," she replied, "it is all *said;* it has got to be *done.*"

247 *Malice Refuted*

Rowland Hill, when once shamefully attacked in a public paper, was urged by a friend to take legal action to which he replied, "I shall neither answer the libel, nor prosecute the writer: 1) Because in doing the one I might be led into unbecoming violence. 2) Because I have learned from long experience that no man's character can be eventually injured but by himself."

248 *Christ or the World?*

Rev. Adoniram Judson, missionary in Burma, relates as follows:

"A Karen woman offered herself for baptism. After the usual examination, I inquired whether she would give up her ornaments for

Christ. It was an unexpected blow. I explained the spirit of the Gospel, and appealed to her own consciousness of vanity. I then read to her the Apostle's prohibition, 1 Timothy 2:9. She looked again and again at her handsome necklace, and then, with an air of modest decision, took it off, saying, 'I love Christ more than this.' "

249 Fighting against Friends

In a sermon which Mr. Williams once delivered, a striking effect was produced by the following anecdote, which he applied to his favorite topic of Christian union: "I recollect on one occasion conversing with a Marine, who gave me a good deal of his history. He told me that the most terrible engagement he had ever been in was one between the ship to which he belonged and another English vessel, when, on meeting in the night, they mistook each other for a French man-of-war. Many persons were wounded, and both vessels sustained serious damage from the firing. But when the day broke, great and painful was their surprise to find the English flag hoisted from both ships, and that through mistake they had been fighting the previous night against their own countrymen. They approached and saluted each other, and wept bitterly together. Christians sometimes commit the same error in the present world—one denomination mistakes another for an enemy; it is night, and they cannot see to recognize one another. What will be their surprise when they see each other by the light of another world, when they meet in heaven, after having shot at one another in the midst of the present state?"

Church

250 That Family Feeling

". . . you have come to . . . the assembly of the firstborn . . ." (Heb. 12:22, 23).

A young lady who had broken the grip of drug addiction both by medical help and new relationships in the church said, "I thank God every day for His forgiveness, and His mercy in delivering me from the habit that was killing me. And I also am grateful I finally have a family. I came from a broken home and never knew the love of a father or mother but you in the church have given me everything I missed."

That is what the church should be. A family. Not a family closed to all but the unsoiled, but a family to those most in need. Parents do not stop loving their children when they stray. In fact, parents who keep loving erring children—rather than feeling sorry for themselves for the embarrassment their children's misdeeds have caused—will likely see those children one day grow strong.

251 The Church Needs Today

More tithes and fewer drives.
More action and less faction.
More workers and fewer shirkers.
More backers and fewer slackers.
More praying and less straying.
More of God's plans—less of man's.
More burden-bearers and fewer tale-bearers.

252 Sectarian Pride

Among the treasures of the Museum in Constantinople there is one which outdistances them all in intense though painful interest. In one of the main halls there lies a block of stone some three feet square. Black with age, and without carving of any kind, the incautious visitor might well pass it with but a careless and uninterested glance. When carefully examined, however, it is found to have some words engraved upon it by which it is possible to identify it. Here then, as the inscription disclosed, is the very stone set up in the Temple of Jerusalem, between the Gentile and the Jewish court, warning the Gentiles that if they dared to pass into the sacred place they would instantly be put to death. That stone, therefore, lying thus in the Museum of Antiquities, stands for all the exclusiveness and intolerance which blighted the ancient world. Christ as He passed in and out must often have looked upon it and read its inscription with heavy heart. He came into the world for the very purpose of removing it, and all that it represented of exclusiveness, bitterness, inhumanity, and religious

92

bigotry and pride. It was to Him, as to all whom He has emancipated, "a stone of stumbling and a rock of offence" (1 Pet. 2:8).

Since that day until now, however, His Church has never ceased to re-erect this stone, to inscribe upon it in His very name the language of cruel bigotry, and by its ignorance of His Spirit to retain the worst passions of Judaism.

253 The Altar of Sacrifice

Within the church the central position is occupied by the altar. It stands in the most prominent place, and to this there is attached a great meaning. The altar, or communion table, stands there to remind us that there can be no true worship without sacrifice, and that sacrifice is the central fact of worship, and should be of our lives. Our true object then in entering the House of God is not to hear a sermon—the pulpit ought not to occupy the central and dominating position—it is to offer unto God the sacrifices of praise and acceptable worship. "Come into His courts and bring an offering with you" (Ps. 96:8) does not refer merely to material things. The chief offering is the offering of ourselves unto God, and without this no other form of offering, however splendid, will make it acceptable unto Him. It will be noticed, also, that our offerings—those which we give for the support of the ministry and of the church—when received, are placed upon the altar. And they are placed there to remind us that they are an acknowledgment that our possessions are His. If one could read the history of each coin given in God's House, it would be found how many beautiful acts of sacrifice they represent.

The altar is there, too, to remind us that no life can be lived in the Spirit of Christ which is not sacrificial. Christ sacrificed Himself for us (Eph. 5:2). We must "lay down our lives for the brethren" (1 John 3:16).

254 Drifting into It.

A lady brought her little girl to a teacher that she might learn music. The child came up week after week without knowing her lesson, and finally the teacher appealed to the mother. "Does your daughter practice?" she asked. "No," replied the mother, "and I won't make her do it; I'd rather she would drift into music sort of naturally." Needless to say, she never drifted into it. I am afraid that there are people who come into the church with pretty much the same ideas. They make the start and then never give themselves any more concern. They expect to drift into sainthood.

255 Sin of Self-Righteousness

A young woman once contemptuously informed an old preacher that she was as good as lots of church-members.

"I know it my sister," he replied, shaking his head sadly, "and no one regrets more than I do that we have so many unworthy people in the church."

256 Contentious Peacemakers

Perhaps it has been true at times that the only way to get peace was by means of war; more often, however, the remedy has proven far worse than that which it strove to banish. There is a story told of a man who was awakened one night by the sound of a gunshot in his room. On inquiring the cause, his servant replied that there was a rat in the room, and, fearing it would awaken his master, he shot it.

Here is logic surpassed only by that of the brother who is willing to throw the whole church into a turmoil for the sake of getting rid of something that he fears may cause dissension.

257 Victory Without Leaders

After the battle of Lookout Mountain, when the Federal troops cleared the heights with a dash that was unstoppable, General Grant sent to General Wood and asked, "Did you order that charge?" He said, "No." To Hooker and Sheridan the same inquiry was put and from them the same response was received. The fact was that the men were filled with such enthusiasm that nothing could have stopped them. They leaped to the fray, defying danger and death, and when the victory was gained, were filled with glad wonder at it. When the Church of Christ is filled with enthusiasm for the conquest of the world it will go forward, whether earthly leaders give the word of command or not. It will hear His command Who

has promised His presence unto the end of the age, and will do wonders in His name.

258 The Church and Philanthropy

Long ago, a ship was wrecked upon the reef of an island in the Pacific. The sailors, escaping to land, feared that they might fall into the hands of the head-hunting natives. One man climbed a bluff to look around. Turning to his mates, he began to shout joyously, "Come along, we are all right; *here's a church!*" The shipwrecked men felt it was safe to go where a Christian church spread its cross—that they would find shelter, and help, and all kind attention at the hands of people who loved God. The Church of Christ should ever be the ready helper of the sad, the sinful, the despairing. Love to God can only prove itself by love to man.

259 Listening for the Spirit's Speech

We go to Church sometimes, with itching ears, having no thought of the Spirit at all, to hear what *the preacher* says. If he should furbish up some old error, on which the blood of souls had rested, and bring it forth as a new-discovered truth, he gets our admiration and attention; he is "so able," or so "original," or so "advanced." If he should speak God's truth, however plainly and earnestly, but with a cracked voice and awkward gestures, we come away disappointed. It was not the truth, but the manner of address we thought about, as if a hungry man should be satisfied with the skillful way in which a cook sets down empty dishes before him. It would cure more evils than we think of, if we would heed this word: "What *the Spirit* saith."

260 The Church as God's Garden

Nature has her wild flowers, and they have their own loose, lawless beauty. Yet the finest effects in form and color, and fragrance, are only to be found under careful cultivation. Wild roses are no argument against the value of gardening; for even cultivated flowers, if left to themselves, will revert little by little to their wild, rude state. And so outside the Church of Jesus Christ there are good and noble, and in some senses morally winsome souls, and yet it is true that for the full cultivation of Christian character, we need the Garden of the Lord—Christ Jesus by His Spirit being the Chief Gardener. Even the wild flowers, in whatever measure they possess true beauty and perfume, get it from His secret influence, though they know it not. In the realm of spirit it is as true as in nature and history, He upholdeth "all things by the word of His power" (Heb. 1:3).

261 The Unknown Treasure

A gentleman who owned a small estate wished to sell it. He sent for a real estate agent and asked him to produce an advertisement of the estate. When the advertisement was read to him, he said: "Read that again." The agent read the description of the estate once more, whereupon the owner of the property said: "I do not think I will sell. I have been looking for an estate like that all my life, and I did not know that I owned it."

Well, there are church members just like that. All the flowers that bloomed for them were the fragrant blossoms of truth. All the blessings that smiled upon them were gifts of their church. All the memories of childhood and motherly love trailed around her altars. Yet, some earthly advantage or convenience was force enough to snap the bonds. Now they are backslidden. "Father, forgive them; for they know not what they do" (Luke 23:34).

262 The Dead Church

A painter was once given the commission to paint a picture of a dead church. What was expected was probably the picture of an ivy-clad ruin—perhaps a relic of Norman times, such as are seen here and there upon an English landscape, or the picturesque remains of some Gothic cathedral such as are seen in France or Italy. The painter, however, had a spiritual conception of his task and painted a picture that was rather a sermon. He put on canvas the inside of a cozy, well-appointed church: upholstered pews, a large organ, a finely-chiseled altar were there, and an audience whose appearance indicated culture and prosperity. Then, at the corner near the exit, he painted the picture of a box bearing the inscription "FOR MISSIONS," and, right before the slot, a large cobweb. An apt picture of a dead church indeed; for a congregation that has nothing for missions is dead, even though it may pay its preacher $75,000 a year.

263 Christian Unity

Bishop Simpson gives the following illustration in which he compares the church to a canopy of trees:

"I was walking some weeks since in a beautiful grove. The trees were some distance apart, and the trunks were straight and rugged. But, as they ascended higher and higher, the branches came closer and closer together, and still higher the twigs and branches interlaced and formed a beautiful canopy. I said to myself, 'Our churches resemble these trees. The trunks near the earth stand stiffly and widely apart. The more nearly towards heaven they ascend the closer and closer they come together, until they form a beautiful canopy under which the sons of men enjoy both shelter and happiness.'"

264 Dead Church Members

Pay close attention to this illustration by Spurgeon and see how his analogy accurately describes many churches of the 1990's: "Have you ever read *The Rime of the Ancient Mariner?* I dare say you thought it one of the strangest imaginations ever put together, especially that part where the old mariner represents the corpses of all the dead men rising up to man the ship—dead men pulling the rope, dead men steering, dead men spreading sails. I thought what a strange idea that was. But do you know, I have lived to see that time. I have gone into churches, and I have seen a dead man in the pulpit, a dead man as a deacon, a dead man handling the plate, and dead men sitting to hear."

265 A Defective Church

The following illustration is by D. L. Moody: "A father took his little child out into the field one Sabbath, and he lay down under a beautiful shady tree, it being a hot day. The little child ran about gathering wild flowers and little blades of grass, and coming to his father and saying: 'Pretty! pretty!' At last the father fell asleep and while he was sleeping the child wandered away. When he awoke, his first thought was 'where is my child?' He looked all around, but he could not see him. He shouted at the top of his voice, and all he heard was the echo of his own voice. No response! Running to a little hill, he looked around but all he heard was his own voice. Then going to a precipice at some distance, he looked down, and there upon the rocks and briers, he saw the mangled form of his loved child. He rushed to the spot, and took up the lifeless corpse, and hugged it to his bosom, and accused himself of being the murderer of his own child. While he was sleeping his child had wandered over the precipice. I thought as I heard that, what a picture of the Church of God! How many fathers and mothers, how many Christian men are sleeping now while their children wander over the terrible precipice a thousand times worse than that precipice, right into the bottomless pit of hell? Father, where is your boy tonight?"

266 Church Atmosphere

Do not some professors cause sinners to loiter by their own loitering? A man taking a seat at the Tabernacle came to the minister and said, "Sir, do I understand that if I become a seat-holder I shall be expected to be converted?" "Yes," was the reply, "I hope you will, and I pray that it may be so. Do you object?" The answer was, "O sir, I desire it above everything." Was not the man hastened by the general feeling of hopefulness which pervaded the church? Assuredly there is much in the atmosphere which surrounds a man. Among warm-hearted Christians it is hard for the careless to remain indifferent.

—C. H. Spurgeon

267 Church Members with Bad Attitudes

C. A. Eaton has this to say about fussy church members: "When a man enlists in the army he takes on sacred obligations. If in the midst of a battle he were to quit fighting because the drill sergeant did not call him by his right name, he would not be shot. I do not think he would even be hanged. They would simply throw him into a ditch, away from the sight of noble men. But a full-grown man will unite with the Christian Church, assuming the most sacred, binding and exalted obligations in the world. On the slightest pretext he will quit. Perhaps the minister has not recognized him on the street, one of the deacons failed to call him by name in the church, he is asked for money, or he does not like the choir. Any trivial pretext will do. Immediately he disregards every solemn obligation. If you were to tell him that his sin is worse than perjury, he would be insulted. Yet it is. If you were to tell him that his disloyalty in this regard is more despicable than the disloyalty of a traitor to his country, he would not believe you. Yet it is."

268 The True Church

H. W. Beecher says that "some churches are like lighthouses, built of stone, so strong that the thunder of the sea cannot move them . . ." The light that shines from these churches is the light of Christ shining through his believers. Sinners are not reached solely through the church's ceremony, pomp, beautiful music or largeness—they are reached through the Christlikeness of its individual members.

269 Judging the Church

Spurgeon tells a story of an American fruit-grower who once tried to persuade a friend to taste apples from his orchard. The friend did not accept the offer, and the fruit grower was offended. The friend frankly told the man that he had once picked up and tasted one of the apples that fell over on the other side of the wall that bordered the orchard and admitted that he had never tasted such a sour apple in his life. Relieved, the grower then explained that he had put those sour apples across the fence to discourage children from stealing from his orchard, which in reality contained some of the sweetest apples to be found in that part of the country. Many people today make the same mistake of judging a church by one "bad apple."

270 Unity Leads to Success

Moody uses a story about Gen. Ulysses S. Grant to compare his war success secrets to church success. History tells us that during the Civil War, when Grant's army had just been chased into a Virginia wilderness, he held a council meeting among his co-commanders and sought their advice. Generals Sherman and Howard led the majority opinion among the commanders to retreat. Grant listened to this advice, and sent everyone back to their headquarters, but shocked everyone the following morning by ordering an offensive on the enemy to begin at daylight. The commanders all faithfully obeyed Grant's orders, and they captured the city of Richmond—capitol of the confederacy, which severely broke the backs of the Confederate troops. Moody says that Christians "should advance in solid column against the enemy; let us lift high the standard, and in the name of our God let us

work together, shoulder to shoulder, and keep our eye single to the honor and glory of Christ."

271 The Church as a Priestly Body

The late Bishop of London, A. F. Winnington-Ingram, describes the church as a "priestly body" in his sermon The Chief Shepherd: "The Church is said to be in the Bible the Body of Christ. Therefore, it is a priestly body. The laity of the Church are holy because they are part of the body of the Great High Priest Himself. 'They are baptized unto Christ Himself' (Rom. 6:3, 4) as St. Paul says. And priests who are ordained are organs of the priestly body with special functions, no layman can dare to assume, [such as] the celebration of the Holy Communion . . ."

272 Formalism in the Church

Formalism was rampant in the Jerusalem of Jesus' time, as it is in many churches today. Perhaps the Pharisees were the most meticulous formalists the world has ever seen. Christ rebuked them, and called them the children of the devil, because they established their worthless traditions on an equal footing with the word of God. They zealously attempted to adhere to the laws of Moses, when in reality, they blatantly misunderstood Moses' spirit. They also made every attempt to publicly display their zeal in the synagogues and the streets. Jesus called them exactly what they were—hypocrites!

But, unfortunately, formalism still thrives in many churches today. J. Ossian Davies, in his sermon *The Self Doomed City,* calls a formalist one "whose religion is a decorated skeleton . . . [who] does more to demoralize [Christianity] than ten righteous men can do to elevate it." Let the Pharisees be an example to us as we determine whether our church ceremonies uphold or weaken the cause of Christ.

273 Who Will Teach?

There was once a church staff looking for teachers for children—preschoolers and youth. And some adults said, "I don't want to leave the good fellowship and study in my adult class." But the drug pusher on the street said, "Not even the threat of jail will keep me from working with your children." And some adults said, "I don't have the time." But the pusher, the pornographic book dealer, and movie producer said, "We'll stay open whatever hours are necessary every day to win the minds of the kids. Some adults said, "I'm unsuited, untrained and unable to work with children." But the movie producer said, "We'll survey, study and spend millions to produce whatever turns kids on."

So the adults stayed in their classes, enjoyed the fellowship, absorbed the good Bible study, and weren't tied down on the weekends. And when Sunday came, no one was there to teach the children. They were assured that someone would surely come to teach them some Sunday soon. But no one ever came, and the young children soon quit coming because they had gone to listen to others who cared about what they did and about what went into their minds.

274 "Dump Ministry"

Doug Forbes observes:

"In parts of New England, we still have to take our trash to the local dump. When I lived in Maine, I rarely saw three people together at once. But Saturday at the dump was a different story! All day long the dump had a steady stream of cars taking care of one of life's necessary bits of business. From this observation came our 'Dump Ministry!'

"When our church held a special event, we took turns out at the dump handing out colorful flyers. We worked in teams so that we could encourage each other. In one day we reached approximately three-quarters of all the homes in our town. So, if you have a dump, God has given you an inexpensive way to publicize your next church activity, youth event, or concert. Give it a try, and next Saturday, I'll see you at the dump!"

275 Top Five Excuses for Church Absences

1. I work so hard all the week that when Sunday comes . . .

2. When I was a kid, I was made to go to church three times a week, and so now . . .

3. Company came to our house just as we were getting ready.

4. I came twice and not a soul spoke to me.

5. I don't have anything suitable to wear.

276 Washington as a Good Example

George Washington's pastor once said of him: "No company ever kept him away from church. I have often been at Mount Vernon on the Sabbath morning when his breakfast table was filled with guests. But to him they furnished no pretext for neglecting his God and losing the satisfaction of setting a good example. Instead of staying home out of fancied courtesy to them, he used constantly to invite them to accompany him."

277 Another Good Example Set by Washington

J. H. Vincent reports that early on in the Revolutionary War, Washington issued the following order: "That the troops may have an opportunity of attending public worship, as well as to take some rest after the great fatigue they have gone through, the general in future excuses them from fatigue duty on Sundays, except at the shipyards or on special occasions, until further orders. We can have but little hope of the blessing of Heaven on our arms if we insult it by our impiety and folly."

278 A Sunday Keeping Baker

A baker, who had long been accustomed to attend to his business on the Lord's day, on which day he obtained a large portion of the support he earned for his family, having had his attention drawn to religion,

and felt its power and conviction, became desirous of associating with a body of Christians; who, however, declined to receive him, unless he abandoned his practice of working on Sunday. The struggle in his mind was long and painful, but he finally yielded to the claims of duty; and, by refusing to work on the Lord's day, offended many of his customers, who stopped buying from him. His decision to not work on Sunday reduced him to great poverty. His Christian friends urged him to persevere, assuring him that God would not forsake him. He was enabled to do so, and Providence intervened on his behalf. His customers gradually returned to him, and eventually he was favored with a larger share of business than had ever before come his way.

279 A Factory Owner's Story

"After I was convinced of my sin," said an English businessman, "I continued to work my mills and sell meal and flour on the Lord's day as usual. But in this practice I soon became very uneasy, being continually followed by those words, 'Remember the sabbath day, to keep it holy' (Ex. 20:8). I at last determined, whatever might be the consequence, to give it up. Accordingly my mills were stopped; I ground no more, and I informed my customers that I would no longer serve them on the sabbath, and hoped they would come on a Saturday evening. Some pitied me; others said they would go to other shops; and almost all thought I should soon break my strange resolution.

"The next Sunday they came as usual, but were all refused. Their displeasure was general, and they went to other millers. The next week, however, many of them came on a Saturday evening, and were served; and in a short time, all, or as many as I had before, returned; and now, so far from being poorer, on account of this determination to keep the sabbath, which many of them said would be my ruin, I am this day at least one thousand pounds richer than I was before I made this resolution."

280 A Punctual Attendant

A woman who was always used to attending public worship with great punctuality, and took care to be always on time in her arrival, was asked how it was she could always come so early. She answered, very wisely, "It is a part of my worship never to disturb the worship of others."

Commitment

281 Having the Courage of One's Convictions

If you want to find three young men who had the courage of their convictions, you should get acquainted with Shadrach, Meshach, and Abed-nego, whose memory is treasured up in the book of Daniel. Those young men did not take the time to consider what was offered them when they refused to worship the golden image. They knew they would not change their minds, and might as well have the execution performed sooner rather than later. It looked bleak for them at the moment. After they had made their defiant answer, Nebuchadnezzar seemed to go wild with fury. His face was distorted with anger, and he shouted the command that they should heat the furnace seven times hotter than it was usually heated. The soldiers were called and commanded to bind the brave young men and cast them into the burning fiery furnace. And the soldiers gathered them up in their garments as they were, and carried them along, with great boldness, no doubt, and show of strength and authority, and cast them head first into the seething hell of flame. But though the furnace was so hot that it slew the soldiers that cast them in, the three young heroes walked unharmed in the midst of the fire. Not only were they unharmed, but a fourth figure, one of such glorious appearance that the king said of him that he was "like a son of the gods" (Dan. 3:25), walked with them in cheering fellowship through all their fiery trial. God is as faithful to give comfort of His presence to people who have the courage of their convictions today as in the days of Daniel and his friends.

282 He Crawls to Church

Al Maxey says: "There is a brother in Christ in Nigeria who is badly deformed; his legs are withered. Unable to walk or afford transportation, he crawls to the worship assemblies! In order to bring his Bible, he either balances it on his head or pushes it on the ground in front of him! Here is a man who knows the value of commitment to the Lord. When the saints assemble he is there!"

283 Consecration

"Will you please tell me in a few words," said a Christian woman to a minister, "what you think 'consecration' means?" Holding out a blank sheet of paper, the minister replied, "It is to sign your name at the bottom of this blank sheet and let God fill it in as He wills."

284 Give the Key to the Master

Years ago, I am told, an old organist sat at his bench playing the instrument for the final time. He was a good organist and had served the church faithfully and well. Now a new organist was to come and the old organist wanted to step aside with dignity and grace. He struck the last chord, closed the instrument, locked it, and placed the key in his pocket. He then made his way to the rear of the church.

There, eagerness flashing in his eyes, the young organist was waiting for him. He asked for the key and, after a moment's pause, he raced to the organ, opened it, and began to play. The old organist had played with precision the notes before him, but this new organist played with a depth of soul and feeling that brought tears even to the eyes of the retiring organist. Reports of his artistry spread by word of mouth, and soon people came from miles around to hear him strike the keys of the console.

This new organist was a master at his craft; to that, the ear and the soul would abidingly attest. He was, in fact, none other than Johann Sebastian Bach. As the old organist left the church he thought to himself: "Just suppose I had not given the master the key!"

We do not know what spiritual music these sermons of ours have in them, but we do know that they shall be what He wants them to be, if we simply give the Master the key.

285 An Accurate Testimony

There was a young man once in the office of a western railway superintendent. He was occupying a position that four hundred boys in that city would have wished to get. It was honorable, and "it paid well," besides being in a line of promotion. How did he get it? Not by having a rich father, for he was the son of a laborer. The secret was his beautiful accuracy. He began as an errand-boy, and did his work accurately. His leisure time he used in perfecting his writing and arithmetic. After awhile he learned to telegraph. At each step his employer commended his accuracy, and relied on what he did, because he was just right. And it is thus with every occupation. The accurate boy is the favored one. Those who employ men do not wish to be on the lookout, as though they were rogues or fools. If a carpenter must stand at his journeyman's elbow to be sure that his work is right, or if a cashier must run over his book-keeper's column, he might as well do the work himself as employ another to do it in that way; and it is very certain that the employer will get rid of such an inaccurate workman as soon as he can.

As Christians in the workplace our attitude should always be to live the Christian life, not just to speak about it. People who do not know the Lord may have only the chance to watch us being Christians in order to find out what the Christian life really means (Phil.

1:27; Heb. 13:5). Don't miss the opportunities that God gives us in our everyday lives to witness for Him.

286 Stand Where the Fire Has Been

Out on the prairie after a dry, sunny day, the owners of a log hut may be contentedly gazing over the miles and miles of long grass, when suddenly a dark cloud appears upon the horizon, and behind it a fierce, fiery glare. Although still a long way off, there can be no doubt as to what it means—the prairie is on fire.

Driven by the wind, the fire is seen approaching at the rate of fifteen miles an hour or more. What can stay its course? Nothing, absolutely nothing. It is true that a firebreak exists around the little settlement, but this is for an ordinary grass fire and is no shelter from this oncoming destructive flame. Men and animals, terror-stricken, flee from it for their lives. No time for thinking is left. What can be done? Is there no escape, no deliverance? Must all perish? Hold! There is one—and only one—way of escape. What is it? How is it accomplished? It is by means of the very element pursuing them and threatening them! Hurriedly a match is struck and the grass at their feet is lighted. Swiftly flies this new fire ahead, consuming all before it, leaving the ground, blackened and bare. Into this burned place, or the terrible fire behind reaches them, men and animals pass over to safety! We ask why they are safe, and the answer is, there is nothing left to consume! The fire having gone over the place once, it cannot do so the second time and so they stand where the fire has been, secure from the devouring fire which now rages around them but cannot touch them!

As believers, we should so burn the knowledge of the Word of God into our lives that the turbulence of outside world influences will have no affect (1 John 2:15-17).

287 Influence

Your influence is like your shadow. It may not always fall where you want it. Therefore, you need to be especially careful to see that wherever it falls, it will have a "good" effect on all. You may not be able to control the shadow, but you can control the one who casts the shadow. Make your influence count for God. Be not deceived! Others are being influenced by your example right now, this very hour.

288 To Know God or to Be Known by Man

Commenting on the influence an elderly minister left on his life, legendary baseball player Babe Ruth said:

"Most of the people who have really counted in my life were not famous. Few ever heard of them, except those who knew and loved them.

"I knew an old minister once whose hair was white and whose face shone. I have written my name on thousands and thousands of baseballs in my life; he wrote his name on just a few simple hearts. How I envy him! He was not trying to please himself and win the plaudits of the world. So fame never came to him.

"I am listed as a famous home-run hitter. Yet, beside that humble, obscure minister, who was so good and wise, I never got to first base!"

289 Are You Really Free?

John 8:31–47.

During World War II, June 1, 1945, the crew on a B-29 suffered a direct hit from a flak shell from Tokyo. Half of the big plane's nose was shot away. The pilot, strapped in his seat, was dead. The co-pilot, his left arm hanging uselessly and blood streaming over his body, tried to control the aircraft. All of the gauges were inoperable. He did not know his speed, direction, or altitude. He was flying blind. To bail out, with the enemy below, meant sure death. When the situation seemed hopeless, two American P-61 Black Widow Night Fighters suddenly appeared on the horizon. They flew alongside the badly damaged bomber and nudged it back safely to Iwo Jima.

In 1984, almost forty years later, the crews of the planes met for a reunion in Long Beach, California. They recalled the day when death seemed so near, and comrades in arms came along beside them and delivered them to safety.

There is spiritual truth in this story. Persons without the Lord are flying blind, with death as their destination. We must come along beside them and guide them to safety.

290 Yield to the Great Architect's Plan

The following illustration is by J. R. Miller and it deals with the subject of surrendering one's self to Christ: "An architect complains that many of his clients come and ask him to design a house for them, only for him to discover that they have already designed it for themselves. What they really want is his sanction of their own plan, and the satisfaction of seeing him draw on paper what they have exactly in mind. It is in very much the same fashion that we often go to the Great Architect with our lives. We ask Him for wisdom and guidance, but we have already planned how we will build our fortunes and shape our course; and it is not His way we are seeking, but His approval of our way."

291 Don't Look Back

The control of the backward look is one of the chief secrets of personal power. Lloyd George liked to tell of an old doctor of his acquaintance who left at death this message: "Throughout life I think I have always closed the gates behind me!"

The successful man has an eye not only for the openings of opportunity, but also for the closings of settled questions.

292 *Are Our Lights Shining?*

A man was killed at a railroad crossing one summer evening in 1891. His relatives sued the railroad, claiming negligence on the part of the watchman. During the ensuing trial, the watchman was called to the witness stand. The prosecuting attorney asked him several questions.

"Were you on duty at the crossing at the time of the accident?" "Yes sir, I was." "Did you have a lantern?" "Yes sir, I did." "Did you wave your lantern in warning?" "Yes sir, several times."

Having answered in the affirmative to every question, the watchman helped the railroad win its case. An officer of the railroad came to see the watchman later to thank him for giving evidence in favor of the railroad. The officer inquired, "Tell me, Mr. Jarvis, were you nervous during the questioning at the trial?" The watchman replied, "Yes, I feared every moment that he would ask, 'Was the lantern lit?' "

Anyone can go through the motions of outward religiosity. We can wave our lanterns wildly, but it accomplishes nothing if we do not light them! The night is dark. Many lost souls have no hope but us. Are our lights shining?

Compassion

293 *The Peril of Souls*

A party of young men were strolling along the beach at a fashionable concession area, watching with idle interest the fantastic gestures of some boys who were apparently engaged in frivolous horseplay in the surf not far away. Suddenly one of the young men threw off his coat and dashed into the water.

"Men!" he shouted to his companions, "those boys are not playing, they are asking for help. Don't you see they are drowning?"

The knowledge that lives were in danger had, in a split-second, changed indifference into the most intense solicitude. Let the church once realize that men are really dying without Christ, and it will have been enlisted—heart and soul—in the cause of missions.

294 *Worthy of the Cost*

What is it that the church has been ordered to carry into all the world? Is it something sufficiently precious to warrant the risk and expenditure? Suppose that tonight, in the still hours, someone comes knocking at your door. With difficulty you rouse yourself, and, going to the window, look out. A woman is standing at the door.

"What do you want?" you question impatiently.

"Oh," she replies, "I want you to carry this package to a friend of mine, who lives over on the other side of town."

"What! at this hour?" you answer. "There is no light and an awful storm is raging. What is in the package, that I should brave such dangers in order to deliver it?"

"Well," she answers, reluctantly, "it is a bouquet—"

You do not wait for her to finish. Your indignation is kindled, and you are ready to call the woman a lunatic. Suppose, on the other hand, she comes to ask you to carry some sovereign remedy to a dying man? Her plea, instead of rousing your indignation, will stir you to the best that there is in you. The storm and the darkness and the danger will count for nothing, when you are a bearer of that which means life to another. Brethren, when the church realizes that men without Christ are lost, and that the gospel has power to save and redeem them, it will need no more bugle-blasts to arouse it to its duty and to its opportunity.

295 *Looking for Trouble*

"He must have been looking for trouble," a young man said not long ago when the fact was mentioned that the good Samaritan seemed to have been so well equipped for taking care of the wounded traveler. Whether he can be said to have been actually looking for trouble, this much we know—he was ready for it.

There is a wholesome lesson to be found here. A fund of sympathy is a good thing, but there are cases where something else is needed. The Samaritan might have felt sorry for the unfortunate man, and not have been able to help him.

"I never know what to do for anyone who is sick or in trouble," a lady said. She had never tried to learn. She might have carried oil and wine along the way with her, but she had never taken the trouble to thus equip herself. Another confesses that, while she is often deeply concerned about her unsaved acquaintances, she does not know enough about the Bible to attempt to talk with them. The man who realizes God's purpose in His creation looks for trouble to the end that he may relieve it. He not only looks for it, but he makes himself ready to meet it.

296 The Costliness of Sympathy

One of the most common fallacies is that sympathy is a very cheap commodity, that it may be bestowed in place of something more tangible. Smooth words may serve this purpose, but genuine sympathy, never. When we feel the need of others most deeply, we are least likely to be assuring them of our

sympathy. It is because men have possessed the genuine sympathy for humanity that they have placed themselves and their possessions upon the altar. "Your husband is a man who seems to have much sympathy for his fellowman," someone said to a lady recently. "Yes," was the curt reply, "and they have cost him the price of a house since I have known him."

297 Sympathy and Help

Dr. James Simpson, the discoverer of chloroform was of so keenly sensitive a nature that from his earliest student days he was possessed by the ardent longing to alleviate the agony of those who were under the dread necessity of undergoing the surgeon's knife. One time, after seeing the awful suffering of a woman during an amputation surgery, he left the classroom resolved to abandon the profession of a doctor altogether. However, he did a much wiser thing: he remained in it, and never rested until he discovered the great remedy which since then has saved millions from unspeakable torture of pain. His sensitive sympathy had become a blessing to the race.

298 Blessing Ourselves by Helping Others

John Keeble once said: "When you find yourselves overpowered with melancholy, the best way is to go out and do something kind to somebody or other." Thousands who today are sitting daily in the gloom of a self created misery, would soon lose it if they began to care for others. One quaint writer says concerning this, "When I dig a man out of trouble, I turn the hole he leaves behind him into a grave in which I bury my own trouble."

299 Cheer Him

A terrible fire was raging, and many attempts were being made to save a child who stood frantic at the top window. One man, braver than the rest in making a bold venture, was about to fail, when someone in the crowd cried, "Cheer him, cheer him!" The people obeyed the command, and cheered loudly, and, inspired by the shouts of encouragement raised on all sides, the man redoubled his efforts and rescued that which he sought to save from the flames. Do you know any Christian worker who is trying by all means in his power to snatch "brands from the burning," and to save immortal souls? *Cheer him,* and then see how your kindly sympathy helps him to work on with fresh courage and renewed energy.

300 Twice to the Rescue

A young English aristocrat, discovering an inviting pond, found it irresistible and, shedding his clothes, jumped into the refreshing cool water for a pleasant swim. Unexpectedly seized by fierce cramps, he was unable to swim back to shore. Desperately, he cried for help. Another young man working in a field nearby heard the noise and rushed to the pond as quickly as possible. Seeing the youth slipping

beneath the surface, he jumped in and saved him.

The next day the young fellow who came to the rescue was approached by the father of the boy he had saved. A rich man, he wanted to show his gratitude. Eventually his conversation coaxed from the rough hewn young man an expression of his hidden desire to study medicine, so the grateful father promised to pay for him to go to medical school. He went, and he excelled.

According to Peter Marshall, some years later Winston Churchill became gravely ill with pneumonia in Africa and, knowing of the wonder drug penicillin, asked for Dr. Alexander Fleming, the discoverer of penicillin, to come to his aid. So Fleming came by express flight, administered the drug and saved Churchill's life—for the second time! For he had saved him in the pond years earlier.

301 A Generous Clergyman

The biographer of the Rev. Philip Skelton, an Irish clergyman, informs us that his salary, arising from the discharge of his ministerial duties and from tuition was very small; and yet he gave the larger part of it away, scarcely allowing himself to appear in decent clothing. Returning one Sunday from church, he came to a cabin where an awful fire had occurred. Two children had been burned to death, and a third showed but faint signs of life. Seeing the poor people had no linen with which to dress its sores, he tore his linen from his back—piece by piece—for their use, and cheerfully submitted to the inconvenience to which it exposed him. Sometime after this, when a scarcity of food was felt around him, he sold his library, though his books were the only companions of his solitude, and spent the money in provisions for the poor. Some women hearing of this, sent him fifty pounds, that he might again retain some of his most valued works; but while he gratefully acknowledged their kindness, he said he had dedicated the books to God, and then applied the fifty pounds also to the relief of his poor.

302 An Old Gentleman's Liberality

When the money to build Bethlehem hospital was being collected, those who were employed to solicit donations went to a small house, the door of which being half-opened, they overheard the master, an old man, scolding his servant because she had thrown away a match without using both ends. After diverting themselves some time with the dispute, they presented themselves before the old gentleman, and stated the reason for their visit; though from what had just passed they entertained very little hopes of success. The supposed miser, however, no sooner understood their business than he stepped into a closet, from where he brought a bag, and counted out 400 guineas, which he presented to them. No astonishment could exceed that of the collectors at this unexpected occurrence; they expressed their surprise, and told the old gentleman that they had overheard his quarrel with the servant.

"Gentlemen," said he, "your surprise is occasioned by a thing of very little consequence. I keep house and save money in my own way; the first furnishes me with the means of doing the other. With regard to benevolent donations, you may always expect most from prudent people who keep their own accounts." When he had thus addressed them, he requested them to leave without the smallest ceremony, to prevent such ceremony, he shut the door, not thinking, probably, so much of the 400 guineas which he had just given away, as of the match which had been carelessly thrown into the fire.

303 A Servant in London

It certainly is expected of all who have received favors from others to manifest their gratitude in return, and to show kindness, when opportunity presents itself, to those who have conferred benefits. It is gratifying to record instances of this kind. During the severe Panic which many years ago plagued the great bankers and merchants of London, a man who had lived some years in the service of his master, who was connected with a banking house, when things were at the worst, sent a note to the gentleman to this effect: "Sir, I formerly lived some years in your father's family, and a few in your own. I saved 700 pounds. Can it be made of any use to you? If it can, it is yours; take it."

Today, we benefit from many blessings, both from God and from men; but what is our attitude towards benefitting others with the excess of our blessings?

304 Sir Philip Sidney's Nobleness

This eminent man was governor of the town of Flushing, and general of the Horse under his uncle, the Earl of Leicester. His valor, which was esteemed great, and not exceeded by any of his age, was at least equalled by his humanity. After he had received his death-wound, at the battle of Zutphen, and was overcome with thirst from excessive bleeding, he called for drink, which was soon brought to him. At the same time a poor soldier, dangerously wounded, was carried along, who fixed his eager eyes upon the bottle just as Sir Philip was lifting it to his mouth. Sir Philip immediately presented it to him, with the remark, "Thy necessity is greater than mine."

Conscience

305 The Possession of a Happy Conscience

George H. Morrison, one of the most prominent preachers and theological writers to ever come out of Scotland eloquently states:

". . . Conscience not only makes cowards of us all: it overshadows our society. He who walks with an uneasy conscience because he is unworthy or unfaithful is an unfailing source of social upheaval. I need not remind you how the Gospel insists upon wholeheartedness. "Whatsoever thy hand findeth to do," it says, do it with thy might (Eccl. 9:10). And it insists on this not only because all honest labor makes the doer happy, but because—so interwoven are our lives—it brings happiness and peace to others too. Here is a man, for instance, who comes home at evening after a day of honest, manly toil. He has done his work, faced his difficulties, resisted temptation when it met him. Such a man, when evening falls, not only enjoys serenity himself; he also spreads serenity around him. He feels a kinship with the children's merriment. There is that *in* him which augments the merriment. His wife has been toiling patiently all day—there is nothing to reproach him there. His happy con-

science is a source of peace not only to himself, but to everyone with whom he comes in contact. Contrast with him another man who has squandered the precious hours of the day, who has not faced his work as a man should, who has yielded weakly to solicitings: such a man when he goes home at evening is not only unhappy in himself, he is also a source of unhappiness to others. He is almost certain to be irritable. He is very likely to be quarrelsome. On bad terms with himself, he is ready to be on bad terms with everybody. Like those widening ripples on the lake which the stone makes when cast into its stillness are the outward goings of the heart. None is so ready to foment a quarrel as he who has a quarrel with his conscience. None is so angry with the innocent as the man who is angry with himself. Half of those brutalities which shock us when the drunken ruffian beats his wife are but the outward sign of that dumb rage which the poor wretch feels against himself. . . ."

306 When Conscience Speaks

When the oyster lies at the bottom of the sea, it is even more interesting than when it lies at the bottom of a dish. As the tides roll over and around it, the oyster

112

opens its shell, so that the cool water may refresh its cramped body and bring to it the food it needs. For the oyster is a living animal, which not only gets hungry but knows when it is time to eat. But when the shell opens, there is great danger. The body of the oyster is all jelly. The hungry fish which swarm around it are as fond of oysters as we. However, the oyster cannot see, nor hear, nor smell, nor taste. It can only feel. In consequence it does not know anything has happened to it until it finds a friend there to protect the helpless oyster. Did you ever see in your oyster stew one of those red, tiny crabs? When your teeth came upon it you were dubious as to whether to swallow or to lay it aside. Well, you may do about that as you please; but you should know that the tiny crab is the best friend of the oyster. When the shells are open, the crab slips in to have a home for itself. Consequently, when the fish comes along, the crab, seeing it, stirs; then the shell closes and the oyster is safe.

The soul cannot hear, see, or smell sin. What it feels of it, is rather sweet—at first. Now there is something in the soul that has a tender touch. It is conscience. That speaks when your soul is about to be grasped by the teeth of sin. And many a bitter hour you will avoid, if you heed it.

307 Elasticity of Conscience

The elasticity which many respectable people, who are honest about most matters, show in regard to the appropriation of public property to their personal uses has often been remarked. When such people are deceived and duped in their thievery, all are willing to laugh. On the posts of one of the old beds in the Washington mansion in Mount Vernon are small glass knobs with sockets drilled into them, which fit like spikes, but are not fastened to the bed. Before sections of rooms in Mount Vernon were roped off to keep visitors from touching the room's contents, it was perfectly natural for visitors to place their hands upon the knobs, and those who did so immediately discovered that they could be taken off. The next step of some visitors was to slip them quietly into their pockets and carry them away as relics of the sacred place. Although an attendant was employed to watch this room, there were so many visitors that it was impossible for him to prevent such pilfering, and the glass knobs had to be replaced two or three times a week during the busy season, but it cost very little trouble and expense. A factory near Pittsburgh turned them out for thirty cents a gross, and the superintendent was in the habit of ordering a barrel of them every spring. There are several thousands of these glass knobs scattered over the world, in museums and private collections of mementos and historical relics. Many more are doubtless concealed for reasons of conscience and fear of discovery, but the guilty persons need have no concern. The original knobs that belonged to the bed are safely hidden in a vault.

308 An Awakened Conscience

The man who commits sin and imagines he can go his own way and be happy if only his sin is not discovered, makes the fatal mistake of leaving his conscience out of the account. No man can tell when conscience will rise up and shake the accusing finger in his face, and make him condemn himself. This was illustrated when a young thief who had stolen a package of diamonds worth over $1,000 walked into the West Twentieth Street Police Station, in New York City, and confessed himself a thief in order to save a girl who was held for the crime. That mysterious thing we call conscience would not let him sleep or enjoy his stolen goods in peace, but took him by the throat and marched him to jail for his misdeeds. It was like the case of the men who were about to stone the woman to death for adultery, and Jesus said to them: "He that is without sin among you, let him first cast a stone at her" (John 8:7). And John, recording the incident, says: "They which heard it, being convicted by their own conscience, went out one by one" (8:9).

309 Conscience as Clearness

Bernard once said that, "Conscience is the clearness of eternal light and the mirror of the majesty of God."

310 The Stolen Lamb

Thomas Drew had a large family. There was a time when he loved his Bible, attended his church, and endeavored to instruct his children in the fear of God.

Finding work became difficult, and Thomas struggled hard against poverty and sickness. His trials were very great: and instead of taking those trials to the Lord in prayer, he sunk into a low state, little short of desperation. This was Satan's opportunity. When Thomas was reduced to this condition, and he feared that his wife and children would be famished, he meditated and planned a step at which he would have formerly shuddered: he resolved on stealing a lamb from the flock of a neighboring farmer. This, after many inward struggles was accomplished, and that too without detection. The lamb was killed, and brought home. To the inquiries of his wife, Thomas gave an evasive answer, and part of the stolen provision was cooked for supper. The poor woman called her husband from the loom when it was ready, and he was about to follow his usual custom of asking a blessing; his tongue faltered, and he could not do it; but snatching up the dish from his astonished family, he went with it to the farmer's house, and confessed his guilt.

"My life," said he, "is yours, or if you spare it, I will try to pay you for the lamb." The farmer was touched at his tale of misery, and the voluntary confession of the theft. He told the poor fellow to take the dish and its contents back to his cottage, and freely forgave him of what he had done.

311 An Assyrian Monarch

Phul, the Assyrian monarch, who spent the latter part of his life in excesses, when he came to die, exclaimed, "Oh! If I had thought I should have died as I do, I would not have lived as I did." This was the language of despair, and might be expressed without any conviction of the deceitfulness and desperate wickedness of the human heart. The distress which follows when conscience testifies against our sins must not always be considered as true Christianity. How many called Christians have felt the same, if they have not uttered the same words.

312 The Orphan School

A mechanic in London, who rented a room very near the Orphan Working School, was unhappily a determined infidel, and one who could confound many a thoughtless Christian with his philosophical reasonings on religion. He, one day, however, said to another man, "I did this morning what I have not done for a long time before; I wept." "Wept?" said his friend; "what caused you to weep?" "Why," replied the infidel mechanic, "I wept on seeing the children of the Orphan Working School pass; and it occurred to me, that if Christianity had done nothing more for mankind, it had at least provided for the introduction of these ninety-four orphans into respectable and honorable situations in life."

Contentment

313 Mistaken Values

There is a beautiful picture, by Doré, of a woodland scene, with its solemn growth and undergrowth, its warm, brooding twilights, its glimmer of broken sunbeams, and with a still pool in which a male deer is beholding itself as in a glass. The buck is admiring its beautiful antlers, but complains bitterly that nature has given it legs so slender and disproportionate. Shortly afterwards the creature, hearing the deep baying of the hounds, makes off in terror, and finds that, whereas its beautiful antlers delay its speed and threaten its capture, its safety is secured by the slim legs which enable it to fly as swift as the wind. The picture, which illustrates a fable of La Fontaine's, illustrates also how we foolishly admire the ornamental, and despise the useful, and how often our estimate of values is mistaken.

314 Contentment Glorifies God

Cheerfulness serves charity, fills the soul with harmony, makes and publishes glorifications of God.

315 The Secret of Contentment

The small boy who admitted that he had several times had all he could eat, but never yet all that he wanted, finds his counterpart among children of a larger growth. While there is such a thing as desiring great possessions for a noble purpose, such instances must always be painfully rare. The capacity of the millionaire and the multimillionaire for eating and drinking is no greater than that of the poor man. He can only wear so much clothing. He must acknowledge that he has long ago had all he could make use of, but the greed of getting has not abated. Paul says in 1 Timothy 6:8: "Having food and raiment, let us therewith be content." And he might have added: If you are not content with that, you never will be.

316 Abundant Life

One of the sweetest assurances that Jesus ever gave to his followers was that he had come not merely to save men, not merely that they should have life, but "that they might have it more abundantly" (John 10:10). Look upon some narrow, self-centered life, where the first question is always that of self-gratification, and then look at the life that is pouring itself out on the world, a stream of blessing, and you will begin to catch his meaning: "For whosoever will save his life shall lose it: and whosoever will lose his life for my sake shall find it"

(Matt. 16:25). Our Lord came to teach us a more excellent way. The saving soul can never know the meaning of abundant life.

Hear the parable of the vinedresser. There is a vine, living and bearing leaves enough to feed its body, and that is all. There are no clusters of fruit to bless those who come to it. The vinedresser looks at it. It is alive, but that does not satisfy him. Of what profit is it that the vine be kept alive, if it is to live on in this meager fashion? See, he begins to cut away here a limb and there a limb; and when he leaves the vine it seems to be impoverished indeed from having given up so much of itself. But let us return at the time of harvest. Look at the weight of great, purple clusters under which it bends. "Ah! this is life," we say; "it is abundant life."

O men, women, learn this lesson. When the Master of the vineyard comes down to take away that which you cherish as a part of yourself, he has come not in anger: he has come that you may have life, and that you might have it more abundantly.

317 The Preciousness of Joy

Robert Louis Stevenson says: "By being happy we sow anonymous benefits upon the world which remain unknown to ourselves, or, when they are disclosed, surprise nobody so much as the benefactors. A happy man or woman is a better thing to find than a five-pound note. He or she is a radiating focus of goodwill; and their entrance into a room, is as though another candle has been lighted. We need not care whether they could prove the forty-seventh proposition; they do a better thing than that, they practically demonstrate the great Theorem of the Liveableness of Life." Yet how few realize that gladness of soul is a binding duty, a solemn command from God's Word to God's people, and that joy is among the first fruits of the Spirit.

318 The Surprise of Joy

Dr. Kane tells us that once, in his dreary journey through Polar ice, he was so overcome by a trivial accident, that he wept in spite of himself. It was when, after months of wandering amid awful frozen desolations, he came suddenly upon a violet blooming at the base of an iceberg—one gleam of lovely life amid eternal solitary death. Many a Christian worker has been similarly touched and gladdened by the sight of one soul blessed and saved amidst general barrenness. The missionary's first convert, a star in the night of heathenism, the teacher's first scholar led to the Savior. These have given joy and melting emotion that seemed a swift foretaste of heaven's own bliss.

319 Luther's Prayer

In the last will and testament of this legendary reformer occurs the following remarkable passage: "Lord God, I thank Thee, for that Thou hast been pleased to make me a poor and indigent man upon

Earth. I have neither house, nor land, nor money to leave behind me. Thou hast given me wife and children, whom I now restore to Thee. Lord, nourish, teach, and preserve them, as Thou hast me."

320 Secret of a Quiet Mind

The following anecdote is taken from one of our old English moralists: "I know a man that had health and riches, and several houses, all beautiful and well furnished, who would be often troubling himself and his family to move from one of them to another. On being asked by a friend why he moved so often from one house to another, he replied, 'It was in order to find contentment in some of them.' But his friend, knowing his temper, told him, if he would find contentment in any of his houses, he must leave himself behind, for contentment can never dwell but with a meek and quiet soul."

321 An Italian Bishop

An Italian bishop struggled through great difficulties without repining, or betraying the least impatience. One of his intimate friends, who highly admired the virtues which he thought it impossible to imitate, one day asked the prelate if he could communicate the secret of being content. "Yes," replied the old man; "I can teach you my secret with great facility; it consists of nothing more than making a right use of my eyes." His friend begged of him to explain himself.

"Most willingly," returned the bishop. "In whatever state I am, I first of all look up to heaven, and remember that my principal business here is to get there; I then look down upon the earth, and call to mind how small a place I shall occupy in it, when I die and am buried; I then look abroad into the world, and observe what multitudes there are who are in all respects more unhappy than myself. Thus I learn where true happiness is placed; where all our cares must end; and what little reason I have to repine or to complain."

322 A Good Woman in London

Mr. John Newton tells the story in an anecdote of a very poor and aged woman, who manifested great submission to the will of God. She was one day attempting to cross a road in London, when a cart that was passing threw her down, and broke one of her thigh bones. She was carried into a house, and several people expressed their kind concern on account of the accident; but she replied, "I thank you for your pity; but all is very well, and I hope I have not one bone in my body that is not willing to be broken if such be the Lord's will."

Creation

323 Observation of the Universe

Long before the Voyager space probe or the recent launching of the high-tech Hubble Telescope/Satellite, Professor Barnard, of the famous Lick Observatory had been engaged for many years in the task of photographing the Milky Way galaxy. He once estimated that his camera would reveal no less than five hundred million stars in the heavens, or rather, that part which he was examining. What stupendous force it gives to the Psalmist's saying, "When I consider thy heavens . . . what is man?"(Ps. 8:3, 4).

324 Keen Observation of Creation

Wordsworth relates that at the age of fourteen he noticed how the boughs and leaves of the oak darken and come out when seen against the sunset. "I recollect distinctly," he says nearly fifty years afterwards, "the very spot where it first struck me. It was on the way between Hawkshead and Ambleside, and gave me extreme pleasure. I saw how much of natural effects and beauties were unnoticed by the poets, and I made a resolution in some degree to supply the deficiency."

325 God and Creation

Carlyle once said: "Creation lies before us like a glorious rainbow: but the Sun that made it lies behind us hidden from us. Nature is the living visible garment of God."

326 Evolution and the Creator

Says a modern scientist dealing with the study of biology: "The whole field of the microscope is crowded with moving bodies that incessantly shoot backwards and forwards, or twirl and spin in ceaseless activity. Where does all this active life come from? It was there that the theory of spontaneous generation took its last stand; it was here that it made its most desperate resistance, here also it has been most signally defeated. Science now reiterates the dictum that there can be no life without antecedent life. Starting, from no matter how complex a substance, once kill all the germs it contains and supply it with air freed from germs, and no life will ever appear. Life involves a Creator."

327 Creation vs. Evolution

The late Dean Burgon hated the theory of evolution, and contended against it on all occasions. It was he who cried in a sermon: "O ye men of science, give me back my ancestors in the Garden of Eden, and you may keep yours in the Zoological Gardens."

328 The Self-Made Model

The great astronomer, Kirchner, had a friend who denied the existence of a God. One day he called on the astronomer. When he saw in the corner of his room a very beautiful celestial globe, he inquired who had made it. "It's not mine," said Kirchner, "and I don't think anybody made it. It must have come there by chance, and of its own accord." "Ridiculous!" said his friend. "Why," rejoined Kirchner, "you cannot believe that this little, imperfect piece of workmanship sprang into existence of itself? How then can you imagine that the glorious heavens, which this merely represents, could have sprung into being of their own accord?"

329 God Strike Us with Lightning!

Lightning and thunder can be pretty scary at times, but even they have a purpose. In everything there is some good!

When a storm comes, and the lightning and thunder is flashing and crashing around us, we hope it will soon pass. But, would you believe, lightning has a purpose? Plants would die if it weren't for the lightning! In order for the plants to grow, they need food from the air and the ground. The air is filled with a food we can't see, a gas called nitrogen. The plants can't use it until it becomes nitrates. What turns nitrogen into nitrates? Lightning! When the lightning flashes in the sky, the electricity makes the change. If there were no lightning, there would not be enough nitrates, and all the plants would die.

Isn't it amazing that what scares us, God uses to do something good? It's time God struck us with lightning so we will begin to do what He expects of Christians!

330 No Replicas

There is one sense in which we are truly alone in the world. There is no one else exactly like us. No one knows the world like we do. No one has heard what we have heard or seen what we have seen.

Our daughter, Emily, says no one knows how things taste to her. Whenever we try to convince her to eat a new food, we tell her just how good it tastes. But, she reminds us that we don't know how food tastes on her taste buds. Of course, she is right. No one does know except her. No one else knows exactly what it is like to be us, have our experiences, our feelings, our memories. Only we know the life we have had. Only we know how things taste to us. She is right. In one sense, we are alone in the world.

So, I don't believe God will take away all of our aloneness, because to do that would be to take away the final thing which distinguishes us from others. Our own wounds, our own perspectives, our own tastes are what make us unique. We can talk about these. We can tell each other how we feel. However, we cannot give away what has made us unique. We can discover, however, how to share our aloneness with each other.

—Stephen Melton

Criticism

331 Praise, Too Late

Mr. Wyke Bayliss, writing on David Cox the artist, says: "It would be an endless as well as graceless task to cite from the reams of newspaper articles in which he was assailed. It is sufficiently known that the writers of the Press were all too late in their discovery of his transcendent genius to do more than crown his head with laurels, just a little time before he lay it down for his last sleep beneath the turf of the village churchyard, steeped in the sunshine or shadowed by the clouds he so loved to paint."

332 Indifference to Slander

The following illustration is by Mr. Spurgeon: "It often happens, when the devil cannot ruin a man by getting him to commit sin, he attempts to slander him; he sends a hawk after him, and tries to bring him down by slandering his good name. I will give you a piece of advice. I know a good minister, now in venerable old age, who was once most villainously lied against and slandered by a man who had hated him only for the truth's sake. The good man was grieved; he threatened the slanderer with a lawsuit, unless he apologized. He did apologize. The slander was more believed than if he had said nothing about it. And I have learned this lesson—to do with the slanderous hawk what the little birds do, *just fly up.* The hawk can not do them any hurt while they keep above him—it is only when they come down that he can injure them. It is only when by mounting he gets above the birds, that the hawk comes sweeping down upon them, and destroys them. If any slander you, do not come down to them; let them slander on."

333 Little Things Are Not to Be Despised

When the hot air-balloon was first invented, a matter-of-fact gentleman asked Dr. Franklin contemptuously, "What is the use of it?" The doctor answered it by asking another question and answering it, "What is the use of a new-born infant? It may become a man." So we are not to despise the weak believer, the weak Church, the weak and watered-down religious society. If it has life it will grow.

334 Grumblers

Some really good men and women simply cannot wait for a chance to say something disagreeable. There is something very strange about the man whom you never heard say a good word about anybody, but whom you have often heard say many critical things about many people.

335 Endurance in the Face of Criticism

When a bitterly cruel review of Wordsworth's poetry had appeared, one of his friends wrote him a letter of hearty sympathy and regret, and to this the poet replied: "Trouble not yourself upon the present reception of my poems: of what moment is that compared with what I trust is their destiny! To console the afflicted: to add sunshine to daylight by making the happy happier: to teach the young and gracious of every age to see, to think, and to feel, and therefore to become more actively and securely virtuous. This is their office, which I trust they will faithfully perform, long after we (that is, all that is mortal of us) are mouldering in our graves."

336 Wrongful Criticism

Ruskin says: "In Art the envious and incompetent have usually been the leaders of attack, content if like the foulness of the earth they may attract to themselves notice by their noisomeness; or, like its insects, exalt themselves by virulence into visibility."

337 Destructive Criticism

Leslie Stephen has this to say about damaging criticism: "When naturalists wish to preserve a skeleton, they bury the animal in an anthill and dig him up after many days with all the perishable matter fairly eaten away. That is the process that great men have to undergo. A vast multitude of insignificant, unknown and unconscious critics destroy what has no genuine power of resistance, and leave the remainder for posterity."

338 Discouraging Criticism

The poet Byron was so sensitive to criticism, that one time, after hearing a friend say that an established literary critic had called his poetry "all Grub Street," he was so wounded, that for a long time after he could not bring himself to write a line; and, one morning opening a drawer where the neglected manuscript lay, he said, "Look here, this is all Mr. S—'s Grub Street."

339 Exposing Criticism

Wirtz, a great Belgian painter who now has a gallery in his honor at Brussels, was, in his day, considered by many to be mad. The critics both abused and laughed at him. He used to send his odd fantastic pictures to the Salon year after year, but they were always returned: the judges would have nothing to say to him. After he gained possession of a genuine Rubens, the malicious idea occurred to him to put his own name to it and send it up to the Salon. The judges taking it for his own sent it back! Then followed the exposure that might have been expected, and Wirtz began to smile as did many others. Shortly after this, came his rightful recognition and installment in public honor.

340 Critics

The following poem is by Walter Learned:

"When I was seventeen I heard
From each censorious tongue,
'I'd not do that if I were you,
You see you're rather young.'

"Now that I number forty years
I'm quite as often told,
Of this or that I shouldn't do,
Because I'm quite too old.

"O carping world! If there's an
  age
Where youth and manhood keep
An equal poise, alas! I must
Have passed it in my sleep."

341 Good Critics

"To be a good critic a man must have all the essential elements of a good author; and yet, while we have but few good authors, even the solitary places and the wastes teem with critics."

342 The Cynic

A cynical old man is bad: but a cynical young one is a great deal worse. The cynical young man is probably shaming: he is a humbug, not a cynic. But the old man probably is a cynic, as heartless as he seems.

Crucifixion

343 *The Sheltering Cross*

There are some who come to the Cross in the early part of their lives, and who, in relinquishing themselves to its protection in the dew of their youth, are saved from much of the world's suffering and shame. There are some who never come at all, whose natures seem too shallow to need, or too worldly to desire, its cleansing and redeeming fires. But there are others who wander far, who taste life's bitterness, who grope and sigh for rest, who in lonely hours cry with bitter cry for an answer to the burning questions of the brain. They wander far in lone and perilous ways, but at last they come to the sheltering Cross of Christ. Tired, and with a sigh they sink down before it, and, as weary children, stretch forth their hands in humble faith and, accepting its deliverance, find rest.

344 *The Banner of the Cross*

There are many interesting things about flags. The white flag is the sign of peace. After a battle parties from both sides often go out to the field to rescue the wounded or bury the dead, under the protection of the white flag. The red flag is a sign of defiance, and is often used by revolutionists and communists. In the United States

Navy it is a mark of danger, and shows a vessel to be receiving or discharging her powder. The black flag is the sign of piracy. The yellow flag shows a vessel to be in quarantine, and is the sign of contagious disease. A flag at half-mast means mourning. If the President of the United States goes on board a ship, the American flag is carried in the bow of his barge, or hoisted at the main vessel on board of which he is. Our Christian flag is the banner of the Cross. It means that the church is in the world to save souls, and no church ought to ever pull that banner down. Summer and winter, weekday and weekend, it should always be kept afloat by the disciples of Jesus.

345 *Christ's Divine-Human Love*

Each man of all the race may be quite sure that he had a place in that Divine-human love of Christ's, as He hung upon the cross. I may take it all to myself, as the whole rainbow is mirrored on each eye that looks.

346 *Clinging to the Cross*

The vine which trails along the ground, and twines its tendrils around any rubbish which it may come upon is sure to be trodden

125

under foot. If it lift itself from the earth, and fling its clasping rings around the shaft of the Cross, its stem will not be bruised, and its clusters will be heavier and sweeter. The tendrils which anchor it to the rubbish heap are the same as those which clasp it to the Cross.

347 Freedom from Sin through Jesus' Death

The chains of sin can be got off. Christ looses them by his blood. Like a drop of corrosive acid, that blood, falling upon the fetters, dissolves them, and the prisoner goes free, emancipated by the Son.

348 Glory and Shame Manifested in Jesus' Death

There blends, in that last act of our Lord's—for His death was His act—in strange fashion, the two contradictory ideas of glory and shame; like some sky, all full of dark thunderclouds, and yet between them the brightest blue and the blazing sunshine.

349 Jesus Is Still the Light of the World!

All His life long Christ was the light of the world, but the very noontide hour of His glory was that hour when the shadow of eclipse lay over all the land, and He hung on the Cross dying in the dark. At His eventide 'it was light,' and 'He endured the Cross, despising the shame' (Heb. 12:2); and the shame flashed up into the very brightness of glory, and the very ignominy and the suffering were the jewels of His crown.

350 The Spreading of the Gospel Fire

The coals were scattered from the hearth in Jerusalem by the armed heel of violence. That did not put the fire out, but only spread it, for wherever they were flung they kindled a blaze.

Death

351 *Life Is But a Vapor!*

"Every day is a little life, and our whole life is but a day repeated. Those, therefore, that dare lose a day are dangerously prodigal; those that dare misspend it, desparate."

—Bishop Hall

352 *"Caretakers, Not Proprietors"*

Dr. W. J. Dawson gives this unique anecdote on the purpose of our short life spans: "Find something that is purely your own creation, something for which you are indebted to no one, either for the idea, or the material, or the pattern or the execution, something that you have gained neither by inheritance, nor gift, nor appropriation from the past or the present, something that would have been yours if the world had never existed—find that, and you may call it your very own; but you will no more find it than you will find snowflakes in the sun. No, we are all caretakers, not proprietors, entrusted for a few years with that which death will quietly remove from our hands."

353 *"Be Ye Also Ready"*

The Scripture declaration that in the midst of life we are in death had never a more striking illustration than in a thunderstorm on the Hudson, where a young officer of the Twenty-Second Regiment, militia, was sitting writing a letter in the YMCA tent. There were several long tables in the tent, at which the men were accustomed to sit and write. Corporal McDonald and ten others sat at the table nearest the entrance. The young corporal had arranged to celebrate the close of the tour of camp duty on the following Saturday by getting married, and when the tent was struck by lightning, leaving its mark on the floor and furniture, he was writing to his fiancee. The letter was complete, and its last words were: "Yours until death." The date was to follow, but when the expectant bridegroom had written "State Cam—" the flash came and the pen stopped. The tour of duty was over—taps had been sounded—the lights were out. The best way to be ready to die is to live with reverent fidelity to duty. None of us ought to leave anything undone for last hours which may never be consciously known to us.

354 *The Short Life of Man*

When the gospel was first preached to the Saxons of Northumbria by Paulinus, and King Edwin sat in council with his chiefs and wise men to consult whether they should give up their idols and believe the Lord Jesus Christ, one of the councillors arose and spoke the following words: "In winter, O king, when thou art sitting in thy hall at supper, with a great fire, and thy nobles and commanders around thee, sometimes a little bird flies through the hall, in at one window and out at another. The moment of his passage is sweet to him, for he feels neither cold nor tempest; but it is short, and from the dark winter he vanishes into the dark winter again. Such, O King, seems to me the short life of man; for we know not whence we came or whither we go. If therefore this new doctrine can teach us anything certain, let us embrace it." And so Edwin and his people came out of the dark winter of paganism into the glorious light of the gospel, and became Christians.

355 Preparation for Death

"Be ye also ready" (Matt. 24:44).

A Lady once said to John Wesley, "Suppose you knew you were to die at twelve o'clock tomorrow night, how would you employ the intervening time?" "Why, just as I intend to spend it now. I would preach this evening at Gloucester, and again at five o'clock tomorrow morning. After that, I should ride to Tewksbury; preach in the afternoon; meet the societies in the evening; then repair to friend Martin's who expects to entertain me; converse and pray with the family as usual; retire to my room at ten o'clock; commend myself to my heavenly Father; lie down to rest; wake up in glory!"

356 Jesus Took the Sting for Us

One recent summer, a bee was drawn into the open window of a car traveling down the road. The bee was upset, and so was a boy in the car, who had previously suffered a severe reaction from a bee sting. But before things got out of hand, the boy's father caught the bee in his hand and tossed it back out the window. Then he pulled the car over to comfort his son.

The boy, however, was now desperately worried that his father would die from the bee sting. "Oh, no," said the father, showing him that his hand was only slightly swollen. "The sting won't hurt me like it would you, so I took the sting for you."

And that is just what Jesus did for us: He took the sting of death for us, and now that sting is gone. "O death, where is thy sting? O grave, where is thy victory? The sting of death is sin . . . But thanks be to God, which giveth us the victory through our Lord Jesus Christ" (1 Cor. 15:55-57).

357 Dying Is No Loss for the Christian

We lose nothing worth keeping when we leave behind the body, as a dress not fitted for home, where we are going.

358 Fear of Death

There is a widespread unwillingness to say the word "Death." It falls on men's hearts like clods on a coffin—so all people and languages have adopted euphemisms for it—fair names which wrap silk around his dart and somewhat hides his face.

359 Jesus Is Our Pilot in Time of Death

Thinking of the past, there may be a sense of welcome lightening from a load of responsibility when we have got all the stress and strain of the conflict behind us, and have, at any rate, not been altogether beaten. We may feel like a captain who has brought his ship safe across the Atlantic, through foul weather and past many an iceberg, and gives a great sigh of relief as he hands over the charge to the pilot, who will take her across the harbor bar and bring her to her anchorage in the landlocked bay, where no tempests rave any more forever.

360 River of Life

The life of men and of creatures is like a river, with its source, and its course, and its end. The life of God is like the ocean, with joyous movements of tides and currents of life and energy and purpose, but ever the same and ever returning upon itself.

Decisions

361 Getting Advice and Taking It

"It seems strange that nothing could have been done for her," someone was saying of a woman who had just died. "I have been told that she consulted some of the most eminent physicians in the country."

"Oh, yes; she consulted them," was the reply. "The trouble was that it ended there. She never took the advice they gave her."

The same is true of a good many of us. It isn't that there has been a lack of advice, but rather a refusal to take it.

362 Lot Went with Him

When Abraham went out to Canaan, we are told that "Lot went with him" (Gen. 12:4). There came a time, no doubt, when Abraham devoutly wished that Lot had stayed in Mesopotamia. Even now, when a man resolves to change his plane of living, somebody is pretty sure to conclude to go with him. A father, who became a Christian after the age of fifty, was alarmed to find that, during his years of reckless living, his young son had been following him. The son had gone still further away, and all of the father's efforts to bring him back were of no avail.

On the other hand, there is comfort in the thought that, if we are climbing upward, we will be sure to inspire other souls to do the same thing. And I believe that, when we reach the better country, we will find those who date their start in the upward way to the moment when we folded our tents and set our faces toward Canaan.

363 Unheeded Warnings

Heed the words of admonition by Henry Ward Beecher: "A man would not go into a plague hospital and inoculate himself with the plague when he knew that ninety-nine of every hundred that took it would die; but you do! No man seeing twenty or thirty men attempting to walk along the face of a cliff, and all falling over and perishing, would follow them; but you do! No man seeing the flame and the furnace heat of the building, and one fireman falling through, and another, hearing the word, "Stand Off!" would go in; but you rush in, even though others perished before you. Here are men that think they can go down into the house of death, amid the lures of corruption there, and come out unscathed; you are rotten already! Men think they can play the part of a rascal and be prosperous in life; the halter is around their neck! They think that they can drink, and cast off the danger; they are on the broad road, and not far from infamy! O, slow of heart to believe the testimony of mankind, the testimony of your own experience, and the solemn word of God!"

364 Bury It

A man who took pride in his openness once told John Wesley, "Mr. Wesley, I pride myself on speaking my mind; that is my talent." "Well," Wesley replied, "the Lord wouldn't mind if you buried that!"

365 Choosing

J. Spencer gives an illustration about a father of three sons who, in order to test their discretion, gave each of them an apple that had some part of it rotten. The first son ate all of his apple—even the rotten part. The second son threw his entire apple away, because he knew part of it was rotten. But the third son cut out the bad part of the apple, and ate the rest; consequently, he appeared to be the wisest. Spencer says that many people in this Age of Grace, for lack of better judgment, "swallow down all that is presented, rotten and sound altogether; others throw away all truth, because everything delivered unto them is not truth, but surely they are the wisest and most discreet, that know how to try the spirits whether they be of God or not—how to choose the good and refuse the evil."

366 Early Decisions for Christ

According to J. Morley Wright, Griffith John, the famous missionary to China, became a Christian at the age of eight. Mr. John was quoted as saying, "Had I not taken that step then, I doubt whether I should ever have been a missionary, if a member of a Christian Church at all."

367 Immediate Decisions

Spurgeon tells the story of a young man who openly confessed his decision to trust Christ. This decision sorely offended his father, who advised him, "James, you should first get yourself established in a good trade, and then think of the matter of religion." "Father," said the son, "Jesus Christ advises me differently; He says, 'Seek ye first the kingdom of God'" (Matt. 6:33).

368 Inevitable Decisions

There is a solemn choice in life. Life and death, light and darkness, truth and lies are set before us. At every instant the cry comes for us to choose one or the other, and the choice of one involves the putting away of the other. And we must choose. That is one of the certainties of life. There is no such thing as offering one hand to God and another to evil; one hand to the self-sacrifice of Christ, and the other to the coveteousness of the world. You cannot serve God and Mammon. You cannot follow Jesus at home, and your own pleasure in your outward life. Your life, whether you like it or not, becomes of one piece.

369 Fixed Impressions

On the subject of photography, Charles Deal says: "The photographer at the first has no security of the picture which he has taken. He cannot be said, in any true sense, to possess it. It is true, the impression is made upon the sensitive plate, but in its first condition, for all practical purposes, it is useless. The slightest exposure to the light would mar it hopelessly. It must be taken into the darkened room, and there, by being immersed in chemical solutions, it becomes fixed and assumes a permanent form. Just so is it with the thoughts which enter the mind. They are volatile and fugitive unless permanently fixed in the chambers of the mind by steadfast meditation."

370 Personal Liberty

In one of his lectures, John Ruskin reminisced about an incident of his childhood which his mother was fond of telling him. "One evening when I was yet in my nurse's arms, I wanted to touch the tea-urn, which was boiling merrily. It was an early taste for bronzes, I suppose; but I was resolute about it. My mother bade me keep my fingers back; I insisted on putting them forward. My nurse would have taken me away from the urn, but my mother said— 'Let him touch it, Nurse.' So I touched it,—and that was my first lesson in the meaning of the word "liberty." It was the first piece of liberty I got, and the last which for some time I asked for.

371 Resist Evil Beginnings

When you stand and look at the sweeping flames of a prairie on an autumnal day, stretching leagues away, or at night, throwing a lurid light into the broad heaven above, you do not suppose that those vast flames were put there. The negligent hunter, after his evening meal, sat smoking his pipe; he knocked a spark out of it, and it kindled, and grew, and he watched it, thinking that he might at any moment subdue it by the stroke of his boot; but it escaped him, and ran, and spread here and there and everywhere, and swung on, and the wind caught it and nourished it, and it laughed and roared and cracked as it sped along, growing wider and more fierce, consuming harvest, fence, hut and hovel. It took care of itself after it was once kindled. It had in itself multiplying power. Evil always has: put it out early!

—H. W. Beecher

372 Begin Again

Waste no tears
Upon the blotted record of the
    lost years,
But turn you the leaf, and smile,
    oh smile to see
The fair white pages that remain
    for thee.

Is it not great to know that we can always begin again?

373 Saved as a Sinner

When the late Duke of Kent, the father of Queen Victoria, was expressing, in the prospect of death, some concern about the state of his soul, his physician endeavored to soothe his mind by referring to its high respectability, and his honorable conduct in the distinguished situation in which Providence had placed him, when he stopped him short, saying, "No; remember, if I am to be saved, it is *not as a prince, but as a sinner.*"

374 Self-Renunciation

"Jesus only." (Matt. 17:8).

A story is told of a Chinese potter, who being ordered to produce some great work for the emperor, tried long to make it, but in vain. Finally, driven to despair, he threw himself into the furnace, and the effect of his self-immolation on the ware, which was then in the fire, was such, that it came out the most beautiful piece of porcelain ever known. So in the Christian ministry, it is self-sacrifice that gives real excellence and glory to our work. When self in us disappears, and only Christ is seen, then will be our highest success alike in our own lives and in the moving of our fellow men.

Macaulay tells us in his brilliant article on Southey's *Bunyan,* that James II sat for his portrait by Varelst, the famous flower painter. When the performance was finished, his Majesty appeared in the midst of a bouquet of sunflowers and tulips, which completely drew away attention from the central figure, so that all who looked at it took it for a flower piece. Let not the lesson be lost on us. It is as criminal to hide the Christ beneath gorgeous illustrations as it is to ignore Him altogether. He must be supreme. *We* may, and ought to cover *our* faces before Him; but we must never put a veil, no matter how exquisite its texture may be, over His glorious countenance.

Another story is told of a man who visited a friend and was taken on a tour of his garden. The visitor, while walking through the garden, could not help but notice a plentiful crop of a very troublesome weed. The visitor asked the gardener how he came to have so much of the weed. The gardener said, "My neighbor was absent from his house three months last year, and let his garden run wild; it was just at that time when that particular weed was running to seed, and the wind blew the blasted seeds over here. It would have paid me to have hired a man to clean his garden for him, but then, you see, I did not think of it in time." So, to go on unchecked, the seeds that spring from them will blow over into our own garden, and produce there confusion and every evil work.

375 The Cross of Self-Denial

"If any man will come after Me, let him deny himself, and take up his cross, and follow Me" (Matt. 16:24).

An American was once taken prisoner in an Islamic nation. During his captivity he amused himself by sketching. His enemies saw his handiwork. As they gazed at his skillful and curious productions it struck them that they might turn his talent to profitable account. He was promised liberty, on condition that he would design a new mosque. He agreed to the proposal. An elegant and substantial building was planned. At first it pleased them, and the hour of his emancipation seemed near. Some keen eye, however, made a discovery. It was found that the mosque was drawn in the shape of the cross. Disappointed and angry, they put the architect to death. Thus do some reject the gospel. They are well pleased with the plan of salvation, until they discern in it the cross of self-denial.

376 *The Worth of the Soul*

A converted Jew pleading the cause of the Missionary Society through whose instrumentality he had been brought to a knowledge of Christ, was opposed by an educated gentleman, who spoke very critically of the objects of the Society, and said, "He did not suppose they would convert more than a hundred altogether." "Be it so," returned the Jew; "you are a skillful calculator—take your pen now, and calculate THE WORTH OF ONE HUNDRED IMMORTAL SOULS!"

Discernment

377 *A Powerful Warning*

On a rural American railway there was a particular level crossing where many serious accidents had happened, even though elaborate warnings had been posted nearby the track. At last one of the local officials came up with the idea of having a sign posted on which was written in bold letters that everyone could see, "**STOP! LOOK! LISTEN!**" and from that time accidents became almost unknown. This is God's threefold warning to every man and woman in danger of soul-destruction. **Stop!**—think on your ways! **Look!**—to the Cross on which the Savior died to put away sin. **Listen!**—as God says "Believe and be saved."

378 *Why This to Me?*

"Why this to me?" a child of God is likely to ask when some fell blow of grief comes down. Sometimes God's children renounce their obedience to Him when they feel the blow. Oh, that we might view all earthly griefs from the standpoint of eternity!

In the city of Pottsville, PA., the broken end of a high voltage wire was lying upon the pavement, along which the engineer of the electric plant, Mr. Hildebrand, was walking, unmindful of the fact. A person by the name of Mr. Schlitzer saw the danger and yelled to warn him. Picking up a stone, he threw it and hit Mr. Hildebrand on the chest. He looked up and avoided the wire just as he was about to step on it. With tears streaming down his face he thanked Schlitzer for saving his life.

The chastening rod is hard, as when a baby dies or a father; or when poverty pinches. However, what our eyes fail to see those of God perceive: the danger ahead. Only by abiding in God can we meet and defeat it. Every grief that strikes us is an invitation from the Father in heaven to lean hard.

379 *Aware Too Late*

Thomas Carlyle (1795-1881) loved his wife. She loved to help her husband in his writing career. But she became ill with cancer and was confined to bed. Though he loved her dearly, Carlyle was so busy writing that he rarely found time to stay at her bedside.

The day of her burial it rained and the mud was deep. After the funeral, Carlyle returned home, deeply shaken. He went into his wife's bedroom, sat down on a chair beside her bed, realizing he had not spent enough time with her in her illness.

From the bedside table he picked up her diary and began to read.

One line smote his heart: "Yesterday he spent an hour with me and it was like being in heaven. I love him so." He turned the page and this time his heart was broken, for she had written, "I have listened all day to hear his steps in the hall, but now it is late and I guess he won't come today."

Carlyle threw the diary to the floor and rushed back to the cemetery in the rain. Friends found him face down in the mud at the newly made grave. He was weeping, saying over and over, "If I had only known! If I had only known!"

380 Narrowness a Virtue

In these days, when compromise is applauded and accommodation is often promoted, it may be well to recall that some things just don't work that way. Take, for instance, the pilot of an airliner who is heading for a distant city across the ocean. His radio-compass has 360 potential headings, but only one will point him to his destination.

And when he nears the airport, no broad-minded approach will do. His passengers don't want him to debate with the control tower over the various runways—they want him to listen closely to the man in charge and obey his instructions implicitly.

The Bible is our compass and guide in life. Allow yourself to follow the direction.

Doctrine

381 Why Theology Is Needed

On the subject of sound doctrine, James M. Campbell says: "Between doctrine and life there is an inseparable connection. Beliefs are creative forces; they are the things by which we live, as the very etymology of the word 'belief' indicates. As a man believeth in his heart, so is he [Prov. 23:7]. The strong Christians of the past have been nourished upon the great doctrines. Theological gruel can never make strong men. Diluted theology will always result in diluted religion; shallowness of thought will always issue in shallowness of character. Milk is for babies, strong meat is for men. The writer of the Epistle to the Hebrews makes this complaint respecting those to whom he was writing: "When by reason of time ye ought to be teachers, ye have need again that some one teach you the rudiments of the first principles of the oracles of God, and are become such as have need of milk and not of solid food" [Heb. 5:12]. Here we see the harmfulness of feeding too long upon doctrinal milk. It prolongs the state of religious babyhood, and keeps in the kindergarten those who ought to be teachers of others. That this is the effect of the watered-down theology of the present day is painfully evident. . . ."

382 Definite Teaching as to Sin

Delivering publicly a charge to a newly-ordained minister, Robert Hall said to him: "Be not afraid of devoting whole sermons to particular parts of moral conduct and religious duty. It is impossible to give right views of them unless you dissect characters and describe particular virtues and vices. The works of the flesh and the fruits of the Spirit must be distinctly pointed out. To preach against sin in general, without descending to particulars may lead many to complain of the evil of their hearts, while at the same time they are awfully inattentive to the evil of their conduct." How wise is this; we need to be specific as to home-sins, and pulpit-sins; for to lay bare definite evil, is half way towards its removal. No preaching was ever more pointed and personal and practical than that of our Lord Jesus Christ, and those who heard Him knew He meant themselves if no other.

383 Immortality of the Soul

One day the German poet, Goethe, when in his old age, was riding home to Weimar accompanied by his friend Eckermann, and conversing on the immortality of the soul, they turned by Tiefurt into the Weimar road, and stopped at a spot from whose outlook they had a most majestic view of the setting sun. The poet remained for some moments in perfect silence, and at last said with mystic emphasis, "Though setting, the sun is nevertheless always the same sun. I am convinced that our spirit is of a nature quite indestructible, and that its activity continues from eternity to eternity." Thus, true philosophy ever affirms the Scripture declaration, "It is appointed unto men once to die, but after this—" (Heb. 9:27). Personality, responsibility, intensified and quickened life follow the transition we call death.

384   Holding Fast

A magician will put a coin in a man's palm, and shut his hand upon it and say, "Are you sure it is there? Open your hand." It is not there. That is how many people lose their assurance of God's salvation. They thought they had it: the last time they looked at it, it was there. Why is it not there now? Because they do not brace up mind, heart, and will to think about God and Christ continually, every day of their life, and so the truths we believe, slip away, before we know they are gone. It is not without reason that even to a preacher Paul should say, "Fight the good fight, *lay hold* on eternal life" (1 Tim. 6:12).

385   Eternal Life in Christ

On opening an Etruscan tomb, it was found to be occupied by the skeleton of a king. After thousands of years, he still wore, amid the gloom and ghastliness of the grave, a remainder of his former state of majesty. A rough fillet of gold had been placed around the skull—a mocking satire on his present condition, was a memorial of his previous greatness. Such a crown man wears in his hopes of immortality. Like indestructible gold, they have survived the fall and its spiritual death, though they are only vestiges of his departed glory. Of himself, and until quickened by Him who is the Resurrection and the Life, he cannot wear them as his crown; but when the Son of God raises the soul from its death; then He brings life and immortality to light, and life, kingly and eternal, becomes his blessed and abiding possession.

386   Eternal Security of the Believer

Wall Street is wonderfully well looked after by detectives. Money in all forms is plentiful there, and the aim of the police is to prevent those huge and paralyzing thefts which are the work of a moment, and are seldom traced. Many years ago, twenty men from the Detective Bureau, selected for one particular qualification—their knowledge of thieves and their ways—were the guardians of Wall Street. These men had made a study of the faces of the most important thieves of the world. As soon as one of those noted criminals appeared in Wall Street he was sure to be recognized by one or more of the twenty. Even though he may not have committed a crime for which he had not been punished, his very presence in the precinct where money and valuable securities were the only commodities at hand, was a suspicious circumstance, and he was quickly driven outside the sacred limits. The dead line on the north was Fulton Street, and on the west, Broadway. The thief had to stay behind the dead line. So our God has His "dead line," beyond which even the malignity of Satan cannot go. "Thus far and no further." He will permit him to assail, but the precious treasure of our soul shall never be robbed from us. He "will not suffer you to be tempted above that ye are able" (1 Cor. 10:13). "I have prayed for thee" (Luke 22:32). None shall "pluck them out of My hand" (John 10:28, 29). These keep the great footpad of the universe at bay, and secure our absolute safety in our Lord.

387 The Doctrine of Christ's Deity

Once two men, both brilliant and learned in the world's ways and wisdom, had a discussion concerning Jesus Christ. They did not think that He was what Christians take him to be—God in the flesh, the bearer of the world's sin, crucified and risen from the dead. But He was to them a most interesting man, excelling all others in interest and fascination. One of these men was Robert Ingersoll, an atheistic lawyer, the other Lew Wallace, an atheistic general. Robert Ingersoll

suggested that a splendid romance could be written with Jesus as a subject—a tale of the Christ; and Lew Wallace took the hint.

Accordingly he studied the life of Christ in the book of God's Word, the Bible, and in the book of God's people, the living Church of the Son of God. The result of the study was a thorough change of the atheist's views. He read and read. He thought and thought, and one day there burst from his lips and heart the confession of the Roman captain, who, beneath the blasted, darkened skies of Calvary confessed: "Truly this man was the Son of God" (Mark 15:39). Instead of feeding infidel fancy that Jesus is merely a most interesting character, the ensuing book *Ben Hur, a Tale of the Christ,* eventually developed into a major motion picture, feeds the faith of every reader, generation by generation in the eternal deity of the Lamb of God.

388 Look for the Blood

Whenever we are hearing a new teacher and a new message, let us look for the sign of blood. Jesus says of Himself that He had come "to give His life as a ransom for many" (Matt. 20:28). Beware of any prophet who does not say as much of Christ!

There was a Frenchman by the name of Lepaux, who wanted to create a new religion. It was not long when he complained to the statesman Talleyrand of his ill-success. The statesman replied: "That you have difficulty in introducing your new religion, does not surprise me. But I believe I can show you how to succeed . . . The way to succeed in teaching religion is: Go and perform miracles; heal the sick of every variety; raise the dead; then be crucified and rise up again from the grave on the third day. When you shall have done all this, you may succeed." No doubt, the philosopher went back somewhat thoughtful.

Talleyrand was right. The core and strength of the Gospel is the death of atonement suffered by Christ for us. If the test of blood is not met, the message may sound attractive; but it is a new gospel—with salvation left out of it.

Faith

389 *"The Master Has Said It"*

A school teacher gave to three of his pupils a difficult problem. "You will find it very hard to solve," he said, "but there is a way." After repeated attempts, one of them gave up in despair.

"There is no way!" he declared. The second pupil had not succeeded, yet he was smiling and unconcerned.

"I know it can be explained, because I have seen it done."

The third worked on, long after the rest had given up. His head ached and his brain was in a whirl. Yet, as he went over it again and again, he said without faltering, "I know there is a way, because the master has said it."

Here is faith—that confidence that rests not upon what it has seen, but upon the promises of God.

390 *Unwarranted Faith*

A man that had proven to be a failure at everything that he undertook, finally decided that it was his mission to preach. After he had begun his work he came home one night and offered up, in the presence of his wife, a prayer, in which he outlined rather minutely what he thought the Lord ought to do. "I know the Lord will answer that prayer," he said confidently to his wife. When the good woman seemed to dissent, he was very indignant, and questioned her excitedly, "Have you no faith in God?" "Yes," was the calm reply, "I've got too much faith in Him to suppose that he is going to trust you to run His business for him." This is a distinction we do not always make. The faith that does not trust God except when he lets us have our own way is a poor start.

391 *Unwavering Faith in God's Word*

When George Müeller was working to build up his orphanages in Bristol; when he had the beginnings of his buildings, but very few orphans; and again when afterwards he needed yet larger buildings for the work he felt had to be done, he was one day on his knees in prayer to God, and he opened his Bible to Psalm 81:10: "Open thy mouth wide and I will fill it." The truth of this promise seized and mastered his soul, and he declared from that time he had expected great things from God, had asked great things, and had not been disappointed. The Father honored the faith which so honored him.

392 Light in Sorrow's Darkness

During the last days of Daniel Webster's life, he was very restless and sleepless. From the window where he lay he could see the Union flag which floated from the masthead of a vessel just outside in the harbor. The captain of the ship, hearing that the great statesman was cheered by the sight of it, and that his nights were often sleepless, not only left the flag there at night, but hoisted up a lantern beside it, so that during the long wakeful hours the same sight might still be there to cheer and inspire. God has given a banner to us who fear Him, that it may be displayed, not hidden. Let us hold high our flag of faith and hope, and joy in God, and hoist the light of truth beside it, that even in the dark and gloom of men's sin and sorrow, they may see it, and be cheered to glad hope and high effort thereby.

393 Seeing Through a Glass, Darkly

It was Paul the apostle who spoke of faith, which is the eye of the soul, as seeing through a glass, darkly. Let us see what he meant. There was a boy whose family was very poor. He received no gifts at Christmas time, but he spent what time he could looking in the store-windows at the pretty things other boys could have, but he could not. One day he was run over by a car and taken to a hospital. One of the nurses brought him a toy, a troop of toy-soldiers. As he touched them,

this is what he said, "There isn't any glass between."

Now the ways of God often seem dark to us. We are poor when we know that we should give lovingly and liberally when we are prosperous. A new stroke of trouble comes when we are still panting from the weight of an old burden. We are sick when work has never been more plentiful. We cannot understand God's ways; but we know He does. "We see through a glass, darkly" (1 Cor. 13:12).

Some day our body will be wrecked by the stroke of death. There will be fears on our part, and tears on the part of others. But our first amazing discovery upon opening our eyes to heaven's light will be: "There isn't any glass between."

394 The Beautiful Simplicity of Faith

One of the best things about faith is its being so simple. The skeptics who know too much to believe are but wise in their own conceit. It has been well said that the Gospel is a stream in which lambs can wade, but in which elephants must swim. Children can grasp the simple fact that they are lost in sin but saved in Christ, and the wisest of men must marvel at the depth of wisdom revealed in Christ. Here is how one woman found out how simple a thing faith is.

This woman told a soul winner that was eager to lead her to Christ that she would like to believe but could not. The minister replied: "Mrs. Franklin, how long have you been Mrs. Franklin?" The answer was "Oh, ever since the minister asked me, 'Will you have this man to be your lawful wedded husband?'"

"You said," the minister interrupted, "'I hope so,' or, 'I'll see.'" "Indeed no," rejoined the woman, "I said, 'I will.'"

"Well," the minister insisted, "why not give God the same answer when he asks you the question: 'Will you take my Son, Jesus Christ as your Savior?'" "Oh, is that all?" the woman asked. Her relief came at once when she understood that Jesus gave salvation and that He would do all else, provided He was received as Savior. Faith is an act of the will to receive Christ as Savior. That, in turn, means two things: the forgiveness of sin and the death of sin.

395 Filial Faith

A German botanist, who was traveling in Turkey, saw a rare flower hanging from an inaccessible precipice. Desirous of possessing it, he first offered ten piastres, then twenty, then half-a-sovereign, and, finally, one pound, to a tempted but hesitating boy near him, if he would be slung over with a rope and cut the plant. The boy, struck with a new thought, said, "Wait a moment, and I will go for my father to come and hold the rope; then I will willingly go down and get it." So, if God our Father is our Friend, and Christ is our Savior, all is well, and we know we need not fear evil.

396 Faith Without Works

A child once was greatly distressed by the discovery that her brothers had set traps to catch the birds. Questioned as to what she had done in the matter, she replied:

"I prayed that the traps might not catch the birds."

"Anything else?"

"Yes," she said, "I then prayed that God would prevent the birds from getting into the traps."

"Anything further?"

"Yes, I went out and kicked the traps all to pieces."

This child seems to have mastered the doctrine of the futility of faith without works.

397 Faithful Performance of Common Duties

Philip Henry, one day upon visiting a tanner, found him so busy tanning a hide, that he was not aware of his approach until he tapped him on the shoulder. The man was startled by Mr. Henry's unexpected arrival and exclaimed, "Sir, I am ashamed you find me here." "Nay," replied Mr. Henry, "may the Lord Jesus when He comes find me discharging, with the same faithfulness and zeal, the duties of my calling."

398 Belief Possible

D. L. Moody says: "God has put the matter of salvation in such a way that the whole world can lay hold of it. All men can believe. A lame man might not perhaps be able to visit the sick; but he can believe. A blind man, by reason of his infirmity, cannot do many things; but he can believe. A deaf man can believe. A dying man can believe. God has put salvation so simply that young and old, wise and foolish, rich and poor, can all believe if they will."

399 Cast-Iron Faith

"If you believe in God," wrote Robert Louis Stevenson, "where is there any more room for terror? If you are sure that God, in the long run, means kindness by you, you should be happy." Fighting a losing battle with death, he wrote: "The tragedy of things works itself out blacker and blacker. Does it shake my cast-iron faith? I cannot say it does. I believe in an ultimate decency of things; aye, and if I woke in hell, should still believe it." Let us thank God for the faith of this great author, who in his dying days was often heard singing the following song:

If to feel in the ink of the slough,
And sink of the mire,
Veins of glory and fire
Run through and transpierce
  and transpire,
And a secret purpose of glory in
  every part,
And the answering glory of
  battle fill my heart;
To thrill with the joy of girded
  men
To go on forever and fail and go
  on again,
And be mauled to the earth and
  arise
And contend for the shade of
  a worm and a thing not seen
  with the eyes:

With the half of a broken hope
  for a pillow at night;
That somehow the right is the
  right
And the smooth shall bloom from
  the rough:
Lord, if that were enough?

400 Cut the Cords!

Moody once told a humorous story of two heavily intoxicated men who on one night went down to their boat to return to their homes across the bay. They got in and began to row. They rowed hard all night, wondering why it was taking them so long to get to the other side of the bay. When the sun came up, and as the two became more sober, they discovered that their mooring-line had never been loosened, and that their anchor had not been raised. This story is quite funny, but it is sad to say that many people are trying to get to heaven in similar fashion. As Moody says, "They cannot believe, because they are tied to this world. Cut the cord! Cut the cord! Set yourself free from the clogging weight of earthly things, and you will soon go on towards heaven."

401 Christian Faith

John Ruskin had this to say about faith: "You have seen, it may be, an antique, Italian painted window, with the bright Italian sunshine glowing through it. It is the special excellence of pictured glass that the light which falls merely on the outside of other pictures is here interfused throughout the work, illuminating the design, and investing it with a living radiance. . . . Christian faith is a grand cathedral, with divinely pictured windows. Standing without, you see no glory, nor can possibly imagine any. Nothing is visible but the merest outline of dusky shapes. Standing within, all is clear and defined; every ray of light reveals an army of unspeakable splendors."

402 The Definition of Faith

It was a good answer that was once given by a poor woman to a minister who asked her, "What is faith?" She replied: "I am ignorant, and I cannot answer well, but I think it is taking God at His word."

403 Absolute Trust

Dr. J. R. Miller says: "It is often given as a wonderful proof of confidence in a friend that once when the great Grecian emperor, Alexander, was ill, it was told to him in a letter that his physician intended to give him poison under the form of medicine. The emperor put the note under his pillow. The physician came, poured out the potion, and gave it to him. The emperor looked his friend full in the face, drank the contents of the goblet, then handed him the letter. It was a beautiful trust. We are to have similar confidence in the will of Christ for us. We are never to doubt His love nor His wisdom."

404 Saving Faith

"Listen here!" said a Christian sailor, when explaining to a ship-mate at the wheel, "Listen here—it isn't abstaining from swearing and the like; it isn't reading the Bible, nor praying, nor being good; it is none of these; for even if they would answer for the time to come, there's still the old score; and how are you to get over that? It isn't anything that you have done or can do; it's taking hold of what Jesus did for you; it's forsaking your sins, and expecting the pardon and salvation of your soul, because Christ let the waves and billows go over Him on Calvary. This is believing, and believing is nothing else."

405 The Heroism and Faithfulness of Christ

Seldom has there been a more heroic sacrifice than that made by seven nuns at Roberval, Quebec, when, on the 6th of January, 1897, their convent was found to be on fire at six o'clock in the morning. When the alarm was given, the nuns bravely undertook the task of rescuing the young girls who were in attendance at their school. From floor to floor of the doomed building they rushed through blinding smoke and lurid flame, and not until everyone in their care was warned of the danger and safely out of the building did they turn to the task of saving their own lives. It was then too late, and, overcome by the heat and smoke, seven of the heroic sisters gave up their lives. Such a deed arouses our sympathies and touches our hearts to admiration and tenderness. Yet these women held their students as a sacred charge, and duty and love alike united in leading them to this heroic sacrifice. But Christ came to die for our poor race when we were sinners, and though men rejected him, and hated him, and persecuted him even to the cross, he prayed for them in his dying moments and gave his life to redeem them. The world does not furnish a parallel for such a sacrifice. We may be sure that he who gave himself to die upon the cross for us when we were sinners will never desert us when we are trying ever so feebly to please him. Well does Isaiah say, "Faithfulness is the girdle of his reins" (Is. 11:5).

406 The Danger of the Fog

A fine ship went down on the Black Rock, near the entrance to the harbor of Halifax. The ship was strong and she had a fine cargo, and was manned by a faithful captain and crew, but the fog that gathered around the ship was so dense that the sailors could scarcely see their hands before their faces. There is an atmosphere about us which rises from the slough of sin that often clouds the mind and heart with its fog of temptation. Perilous indeed is our situation in such a case if we depend upon our own vision. But there is a Pilot to whom we may yield the wheel, who can see through all the fogs which gather about a human life, and guide the ship to safety.

407 The Keen Perceptions of Childhood

When Dr. Nansen was on his famous journey to the North Pole, and the time had long passed when his wife had expected to hear from him, the suspense became so terrible that her family decided it was best for her that her husband's name should never be mentioned around her. But with her little girl it was most difficult to use any silencing persuasion. She wished to talk of her father constantly, until her baby perceptions were made to see that at every mention of his name her mother suffered acutely. Month after month passed by, and little Liv kept her promise bravely until one morning, on meeting her mother in the garden, she ran up gleefully, exclaiming: "Papa's coming home! Papa's coming home!" Tears and remonstrances had no effect on the child, and, not half a dozen hours after her confident assertion, word ran along the telegraph wires all over Europe that Dr. Nansen and his companion were landed safe and sound in Norway. Of course this may only have been an interesting coincidence, but we know that in a spiritual way childhood's perceptions are very keen and sensitive. It is the childlike mind to which we need to bring ourselves. There is a world of meaning in Christ's selection of a little child as a model for worshipers, and his declaration that we must come to him in the spirit of a child in order to receive the blessings which he alone can bestow upon us.

408 An Inquirer's Dream

One night, an inquirer, long under deep conviction, but still unsaved, dreamed that he was walking along the edge of a terrible precipice, and fell over it into a horrible abyss. As he was falling he grasped a little branch of some bush that was growing half-way down. There he hung, and cried for help. He could feel the branch giving away. He looked into the dark yawning gulf beneath, and again cried out for help. Looking up, he saw, in his dream, Christ standing on the edge, and saying, "Let go of the twig and I will save you." Looking at the terrible abyss below, he could not. He cried again; and again came the same answer. Finally, he felt the branch slipping, and in the utter desperateness of despair, he let go of the branch, and instantly the arms of Jesus were about him, and he was safe. He awoke. It was only a dream of the night; yet, from the vividness and instruction of its imagery, he was enabled to let go every false confidence, and rely only on the true.

409 Lash Yourself to Jesus

Loose things on the deck of a ship will be blown or washed overboard when the storm comes. There is only one way to keep them firm, and that is to lash them to something that is fixed. It is not the bit of rope that gives them security, but it is the stable thing to which they are lashed. Lash yourself to Christ by faith, and whatever storm or tempest comes you will be safe, and stand firm and immovable.

410 Leaning on the Savior

The trust with which we lean upon the bruised reeds of human nature is the same as that with which we lean upon the iron pillar of a Savior's aid.

411 Trust Christ

The final condition will be the perfection of human society. There all who love Christ will be drawn together, and old ties, broken for a little while here, be reknit in yet holier form, never to be parted more. The all-important question for each of us is how may we have such a hope, like a great sunset light shining into the western windows of our souls. There is the answer: Trust Christ. That is enough. Nothing else is.

Family

Parents

412 A Memory That Saved

What a blessing to the prodigal was the memory of his father's house. However wretched and barren the world was here, at home there was bread enough and to spare. The memory of a Christian home and of Christian parents has proven a beacon-light to many a doubting soul. In a company of naive young people, a young man was speaking sneeringly of religion. The old ideas of God and heaven and hell were worn out, he declared. They were old-fashioned, and the world had outgrown them. A young woman, who had known the skeptic's mother, took him aside and said:

"You were not telling the truth awhile ago. You believe that there is a God, and that he used to hear your mother's prayers. And you will not dare to deny that you think of her as being in heaven at this moment."

The young man was deeply affected.

"You are right," he said. "I cannot be a skeptic when I remember my mother's Christian life."

413 Parental Example

A man going from his house to the stable one snowy morning, heard a voice behind him, "I'm coming along, too, papa," and, looking behind, saw his little son lifting his little feet and planting them carefully in his father's footsteps. So do the children imitate their parents. "No man liveth unto himself." Our children walk in our footsteps; so let us take heed how we walk.

414 Children are Following Your Example

Dr. Johnson tells a story of a worthy father, who was one day hiking his way along a mountain side, and his child called out, "Take care, father; take a safe path, for I am coming after you." If older Christians, while hiking along the rugged mountain of life, would only remember that young Christians and children are following them, how much more cautious would they be concerning the paths they choose to take.

415 A Father's Love

There was a father who had a stubborn son who ran away from home with a large sum of money. Some time afterwards, the old man was told that this boy had returned to London, and was very ill in a house

148

of ill-repute. The father thought, "Shall I go to see him there?" Finally, with a detective, he went. He was horribly disgusted when he entered the house, and more so at the companion with whom he found his son. But when he looked upon the bed, and saw the young man asleep, he noticed his eyelash tremble, and then there came from under it a tear. This moved the father's heart, and he said, "I am his father; he is my child!" The old man put from his mind his disgust at the whole surroundings, and awaking his son, looked tenderly upon him saying, "My poor boy, will you come home?" The wretched youth whispered, "Father, if you can forgive me, take me away from here!" It was a sad coming home, but all the way the old man said, "He is my boy!" and the youth said, "It is my father!"

416 *A Parable for Parents*

Dr. W. B. Riley was once spending a vacation with a Scottish sheep herder. Noticing one day that the herder was uncommonly quiet, Dr. Riley asked him why. The herder replied, "I lost 65 of my best lambs last night. Wolves got in." Dr. Riley then asked how many of the older sheep were killed. The herder looked at him in surprise and said, "Don't you know that a wolf will never take an old sheep as long as he can get a lamb?" This finely illustrates the devil's clever effort to get our young people into his clutches!

417 *Devoted Father and Son*

Among the multitude of persons who were selected for execution under the second triumvirate of Rome, were the celebrated orator Cicero and his brother Quintus. Quintus found means to conceal himself so effectively at home that the soldiers could not find him. Enraged at their disappointment, they put his son to torture, in order to make him discover the place of his father's concealment; but dutiful affection was proof against the most exquisite torments. An involuntary sigh, and sometimes a deep groan, were all that could be extorted from the youth. His agonies were increased; but, with amazing fortitude, he still persisted in his resolution of not betraying his father.

Quintus was not far off; and it may be imagined, better than can be expressed, how his heart must have been affected by the sighs and groans of a son expiring in torture to save his life. He could bear it no longer; but, leaving the place of his concealment, he presented himself to the assassins, begging of them to put him to death, and dismiss the innocent youth. But the inhuman monsters, without being the least affected with the tears either of the father or the son, answered that they must both die; the father because he was sentenced to death, and the son because he had concealed the father. Then a new contest of tenderness arose who should die first; but this the assassins soon decided, by beheading them both at the same time.

418 A Dying Father

A young man, neglecting the advice given him by his best friends, wandered in the paths of vice. When his father lay on his deathbed, the son approached him, and instead of being scolded for his improprieties, his father treated him with affection, and only desired that every day he would retire, and spend a quarter of an hour alone: this he promised faithfully to do. After a while it became tedious to him to spend even so short a time by himself, and he began to inquire for what reason his father could require so singular an act. It suggested itself to his mind, that it could only be intended to bring him to a state of consideration, with a view to a change in his character. The impression produced on his mind by this reflection was deep and wholesome, and the change in his life great and lasting.

419 Playing with the Children

It is said that Henry IV of France required his children to call him papa or father, and not sire, which was the new fashion introduced by Catherine de Medicis. He would frequently join in their amusements; and one day, as he was walking on his hands and knees with his son on his back, an ambassador suddenly entered the apartment, and surprised him in this unkingly attitude. The monarch, without changing his position, said, "Monsieur l' Am-

bassadeur, have you any children?" "Yes, sire," he replied. "Very well, then," said the monarch, "I shall finish my race around the chamber."

420 Gratitude for a Holy Mother

Richard Knill, the great missionary and evangelist returning to England after forty years, fell asleep in his old home. He did not, however, sleep very much. He found his father gone, his mother gone, all gone, except his brother. In the early morning a ray of sunlight came in and rested on the very spot where his mother had said to him more than once, "Richard, my boy, kneel, that your mother may pray with you." It now all came back to him with a great rush of memory, and he got out of bed and on the very spot—wept and prayed? No! He knelt down and blessed his God for such a mother who had started him in such a course, and whose memory had been as a guiding and guardian angel all his life.

421 A Godly Mother

A clergyman concluding a sermon to youth, took occasion to impress upon parents the duty of parental faith, and illustrated its power in the following manner: "Many years ago, a little circle met around the couch of an apparently dying baby boy; the man of God, who led the devotions, seemed to forget the sickness of the child, in his prayer for his future usefulness. He prayed for the child, who had been consecrated to God at his birth, as a man, a Christian, and a minister of the word. The parents laid hold of the horns of the altar, and prayed with him. The child recovered, grew towards manhood, and ran far in the ways of folly and sin. One after another of that little circle ascended to heaven; but two, at least, and one of them the mother, lived to hear him proclaim the everlasting gospel. 'It is,' said the preacher, 'no fiction; that child, that prodigal youth, that preacher, is he who now addresses you.'"

422 A Mother's Love

The following poem is by Abby S. Hinckley:

She softly sings, and paces to
  and fro,
Patient, unwearied, bearing in
  her arms
The fretful, sickly child, with all
  his harms,
Deformed and imbecile, her love
  and woe.
Croons with caressing intonation,
  low,
Some sweet, old minor melody
  that charms
The ear that listens and the
  sufferer calms,
And her own sorrow soothes
  with silver flow.
Oh holy tenderness of motherhood!
Most pitiful and patient to the
  child,
Foolish, unlovely, seemingly
  defiled
By powers of death and darkness.
  The All Good

Alone so loveth and remembereth,
And like a tender parent pitieth.

423 My Mother Never Tells Lies

Some women and their children met at the house of a friend in the city of St. Louis, for an evening visit, when the following scene and conversation occurred: The child of one of the women, about five years old, was guilty of rude, noisy conduct, very improper on all occasions, and particularly so at a stranger's house. The mother kindly reproved her. "Sarah, you must not do that." The child soon forgot the reproof, and became as noisy as ever. The mother firmly said "Sarah, if you do that again I will punish you."

But not long after, Sarah "did that again." When the company were about to separate, the mother stepped into a neighbor's house, intending to return for the child. During her absence, the thought of going home recalled to Sarah's mind the punishment which her mother told her she might expect. The recollection turned her rudeness and thoughtlessness into sorrow. A young lady who had observed Sarah's countenance and had learned the cause for this sorrow, in order to pacify her, said, "Never mind, I will ask your mother not to whip you." "Oh," said Sarah, "that will do no good. *My mother never tells lies.*"

The writer who communicated the above for the *St. Louis Observer,* adds, "I learned a lesson from the reply of that child, which I shall never forget. It is worth everything in the training of a child, to make it feel that its *mother never tells lies.*"

424 A Minister's Mother

A Christian minister many years ago stated, that during the evening worship service, when the first permanent impressions were made on his mind, his godly mother was detained at home. She spent the time devoted to public worship in secret, yet fervent prayer for the salvation of her son; and so fervently did she pray, that she fell on her face, and remained in passionate supplication till the service had nearly closed. Her son, brought under the deepest impressions by the sermon of his father, went into a field after the service and there prayed most fervently for himself. When he came home, the mother looked at her son with a manifest concern, anxious to discover whether her prayers had been heard, and whether her son had initiated the all-important inquiry, "What shall I do to be saved?" In a few days the son acknowledged himself as being a Christian. His salvation experience laid the foundation of an excellent ministerial career.

Children

425 A Little Child Shall Lead Them

A most touching sight was witnessed at Ellis Island, when a Swiss hatter and his child arrived from France, and were detained on a complaint lodged by the man's wife, who had come to this country two years ago. There had been a cruel misunderstanding between herself and her husband, and in their estrangement she had obtained a legal separation and come away, and now sought to obtain custody of her child. The wise and kindhearted commissioner of immigration brought the estranged parents together in one of his rooms, and the little girl, who had not seen her mother for two years, threw herself into her arms, crying: "Mama, you mustn't go away any more, but must come and live with Papa and me." Both parents were visibly affected by this childish appeal for a reconciliation, and the commissioner, believing that the parents should be reunited, if only for the sake of the child, urged them to mutual forgiveness. His appeals, reinforced by those of the little girl, were successful—they concluded to bury the past, a clergyman was called to reunite them in marriage, and the little girl led them away to a new life on American soil. It was a new fulfillment of the old prophecy which says: "A little child shall lead them" (Is. 11:6).

426 Martin Luther and the Children

Martin Luther, writing in the year 1518, remarks, that when the children say, "Hallowed be thy name," the Father asks, "How can My honor and name be sanctified among you, seeing that all your hearts and thoughts are inclined to evil, and you are in the captivity of sin, and none can sing My song in a strange land?"

Then the children speak again thus: "O Father, it is true. Help us out of our misery; let Thy kingdom come, that sin may be driven away, and we be made according to Thy pleasure, that Thou alone mayest reign in us, and we be Thy dominion; obeying Thee with all the powers of body and soul."

427 Mr. Wesley and Children

Dr. Leifchild in his diary relates the following anecdote:

"Mr. Wesley, whose rising fame was great among religious people, came to preach at the little chapel in the town of Barnet. Upon arriving, he drove to my father's house, as that of the principal Methodist in the place. When the door of his carriage was opened, he came out arrayed in his canonicals. Childlike, I ran to lay hold of him, but my father pulled me back; upon which, extending his hand, he exclaimed, 'Suffer little children to come unto Me, and forbid them not, for such is the kingdom of God'" (Luke 18:16).

428 Grace in Little Children

We often hear sceptical remarks about the astonishing manifestations of Divine grace in very young children. But there are many cases where this early experience has been authenticated by a long subsequent life of earnestness, consis-

tency, and usefulness. We shall limit ourselves to one example. In modern Church history there is scarcely a name more eminent and honored than that of Nicolaus Ludwig, Count of Zinzendorf. His praise is in many churches, for through him, true Christianity was revived in almost all the churches of European Christendom; and the cause of missions will always regard him as a servant of the Lord raised up especially to remind Christ's disciples of the Master's great command, "Go ye therefore, and teach all nations" (Matt. 28:19). "In my fourth year," he says, "I began to seek God with all earnestness, according to my then childish ideas. Especially was it from that time my constant purpose to be a faithful servant of the crucified Jesus. The first deep impression on my heart was made by what my mother told me about my sainted father, and his great love to the suffering Savior. I remember hearing then the stanza: 'Thou art our dear Father, because Jesus is our Brother.' These words impressed me very much during my fourth and fifth years: for I thought, that accordingly everyone had a right to walk with the Savior as with a brother." We can see in these experiences of the young child the peculiarity which distinguished him afterwards as a Christian and theologian; nor is the depth and reality of this experience at all affected by the childish form in which it manifested itself, as, for distance, his writing letters to the Savior, and throwing them out of the window, in the assured confidence that the Savior would receive and read them (wherein he certainly was not mistaken). But how powerfully do we find the central idea of his subsequent life (as a man, a theologian, and organizer of a Church) impressed upon his heart at the tender age of four years! Intense love of a crucified Savior and fellowship with Him as an elder Brother! Was this the teaching of man or of God?

429 Pomponius Atticus

This distinguished Roman man, the friend and correspondent of Cicero, when delivering a funeral oration for his mother, declared that, though he lived with her 67 years, no reconciliation ever took place between them, because there never occurred any difference to render it necessary.

430 A Boy, Caught in a Lie

A noble father had devoted great attention to the moral and religious education of his son, who had maintained a spotless reputation for veracity until the age of 14, when he was detected in a deliberate untruth. The father's grief was great, and he determined to punish the offender severely. He made the subject one of prayer; for it was too important, in his opinion, to be passed over as a common occurrence of the day. He then called his son, and

prepared to inflict the punishment, but the fountain of the father's heart was broken up, and he became overtaken with emotion. For a moment the lad seemed confused. He saw the struggle between love and justice in his parent's heart, and broke out with all his usual ingenuousness, "Father, father, whip me as much as you please; but don't cry." The point was gained. The father saw that the boy's character was sensibly affected by this incident. He grew up, and became one of the most distinguished Christians of America.

Children should remember that their parents love them, and the recollection should induce them to do whatever they are instructed to perform.

431 Alexander the Great

Olympias, the mother of Alexander, was of so very unhappy and morose a disposition, that he could not employ her in any of the affairs of government. She, however, narrowly inspected the conduct of others, and made many complaints to her son, which he always bore with patience. Antipater, Alexander's deputy in Europe, once wrote a long letter to him, complaining of her conduct; to whom Alexander returned this answer: "Do you not know that one tear of mother's will blot out a thousand such letters?"

Fear

432 I'm Not Discouraged!

A man stood to watch a ball game between two young teams. As he walked toward the bleachers, he asked one of the players, "What's the score?" The young fellow replied, "We're behind 18 to nothing." "Well," the man said, "I must say you don't look discouraged." "Discouraged," the player said with a puzzled look, "Why should we be discouraged? We haven't had our turn to bat yet."

The army of Israel faced a giant, but a young man named David thought, "I haven't had my turn," and he won! The twelve disciples saw 5,000 hungry people and said, "Send the crowds away, so they can buy some food." But Jesus thought, "I haven't had my turn yet!" The angry mob had Pilate seal the tomb where Jesus was buried, but God knew, "I haven't had my turn yet!"

The church is ready to "go to bat" and, like others who have placed their trust in God, we will win! Remember these words of Jesus; "I will build my church, and the gates of Hades will not overcome it" (Matt. 16:18).

433 Why the Christian Should Not Be Afraid

In a factory where the employees were, during a good deal of the time, left to themselves, some of the men paid very little attention to the rules. It was only when it was known that the inspector was about to make one of his rounds that they took care to keep the rubbish out of the way and their worktables in order. One man, however, was an exception to this. There was never a time when his corner was not in proper condition. He took pains to keep it so. Some of the men laughed at him. They said he was afraid of the inspector. And yet he was not. He knew that his coming meant commendation. He was the only man in the shop who did not tremble to hear the inspector's footstep. We have a way of speaking of the day of final reckoning as being an awful day, and yet let us remember that it will be a day of reward as well as a day of judgment. Unbelievers may sneer at the man who sets his house in order and keeps it that way, and say that he is afraid of death. The fact is that he is the one man who has nothing to be afraid of.

434 Protected by Christ

During the retreat of the Allied forces after the battle of Mons, a French officer fell wounded in front of the trenches. The enemy's shrapnel was bursting all around him where he lay entirely unprotected. Seeing his danger, a fellow soldier crawled out from the trench and dressed his wounds as best as he could; then, placing himself in a protecting attitude, he whispered, "Don't fear. I'm between you and the shells. They've got to hit me first." This is literally true of us and Christ. What is the meaning of Calvary? This, that Christ whispers to us, "I'm between you and the death your sins have brought on." We live—now in fellowship with God, hereafter in His presence, because Jesus bent over us and caught the death that would have been ours.

435 Fear Caused by Inaction

A soldier in one of the regular batteries of the army of the Confederacy, had displayed conspicuous bravery in a dozen engagements while serving with his gun as a cannoneer. At the battle of Chickamauga he was assigned the duty of a driver only, and instead of participating in the excitement of loading and firing, had nothing to do but sit quietly on his horse, and watch the havoc created around him by the enemy's shot. He soon became seized with a terror which completely unmanned him, and after the battle, implored his commanding officer to send him back to his gun. His courage leaked away when he had nothing to do.

436 Eccentricity of Fear

Fear generally affects persons when death is threatened, in an inverse ratio to the value of their lives.

In battle an officer upon whom the fate of a command depends will risk his life generously unmoved by a sense of fear, while a shirk whose life is of no importance to the engagement, will skulk in the rear and dodge all danger.

437 Groundless Fear

Did you ever sail over a blue summer sea towards a mountainous coast, frowning, sullen, gloomy; and have you not seen the gloom retire before you as you advanced; the hills, grim in the distance, stretch into sunny slopes when you neared them, and the waters smile in cheerful light that before looked so black when they were far away? This is a parable of life.

438 Fear of Insufficient Resources

It is said that General M'Clellan always had more troops in the Revolutionary War than he knew what to do with and was always calling for more. Secretary Stanton one day said of him, "If he had a million men he would swear the enemy had two million and then he would sit down in the mud and yell for three!"

439 Self-Composure in Prayer

Two things are said to be unknown to Thomas A. Edison, the great inventor—discouragement and worry. His associates have claimed that his freedom from these afflictions came from the fact that he possessed absolutely no nerves. One day, one of his associates had to report to him the failure, in immediate succession, of three experiments involving enormous expenditure of money and labor. But the inventor simply smiled at the recital. The associate, worn out with the nervous strain of his long workday, and disheartened by his disappointment, said impatiently: "Why don't you worry a little about it, Mr. Edison?" "Why should I?" was the inventor's reply. "You're worrying enough for two." The victory which overcomes the world is our faith; if we rely upon God and trust him unwaveringly, it will give us a self-composure and a peace that shall be free from worry.

Fellowship

440 Fellowship with Christ

A young man who was highly ambitious, and who believed that he had made an important mechanical discovery, found himself in such dire straits that he was forced to accept the position of a common laborer in a large factory. He hoped to get together sufficient means to enable him to perfect the invention that would give him fame and fortune. His work, however, was so exhausting that he could scarcely keep awake, much less study after his daily tasks were finished. Once or twice the wish had come to him that he might have the opportunity of discussing the matter with the owner of the mill, but there was small hope that he would ever be able to meet the great man.

One day he was notified that he would be expected to go to work in another part of the factory. "The work is a good deal harder than what you are doing now," his informant told him, "but the boss saw you the other day and picked you out as the only man in the room fitted for it." For a moment the young man's heart grew faint within him. Harder work than he was doing now! How could he do it? His strength was now being used to the limit. Still there seemed to be nothing he could do to prevent the change, so the following morning he went with the superintendent to his new place. As he entered the room, he saw a noble-looking man inspecting one of the machines.

"Yes, that is the boss," the superintendent whispered, answering his questioning look; "he always comes and works beside the man that takes this job." The young man could scarcely realize the good fortune. Here was the opportunity he had not dared to hope for, and he had come so near turning away from it. How many have learned a similar lesson! They have gone fearfully to some heavy task, saying, "I am not able," to find in it a new and close fellowship with Him whose life was that of a servant. The Master always comes and toils beside the servant who takes up some heavy task for His sake.

441 Walking with Christ

While men have doubtless been saved when they were very near death, what can compensate for the loss of years that might have been spent here in the companionship and service of Christ? Several years ago two young men spent their vacation at a little resort far up in the mountains. While stopping at the

158

hotel, they met a quiet old man who several times asked them to accompany him in his walks. Finally one of them, George Bennet, consented to go. The other declared that he had come to the mountains to have a good time and not to wander about with "old-timers." George came back enthusiastic over the trip he had taken. Even this did not influence his friend, so George went again and again without him. The day before their departure, however, he accepted the old man's invitation. They had gone but a short distance when he discovered that the plain-looking old man was none other than a celebrated botanist whom he had long desired to meet. That day he saw the world with a new vision. As the walk came to an end, the look of enjoyment faded out of the young man's face. "Oh! To think what I have missed," he exclaimed. "I shall never cease to regret that I walked all these days by myself, when I might have been walking with you."

My brother, that is one argument in favor of your immediate acceptance of Jesus Christ. Many a man who has put off coming till the best part of his life has been spent, is saying with deep regret, "To think that I might have been walking with Him all these years!"

442 Trusting for Power

John Wesley writes in his diary: "My brother Charles among the difficulties of our early ministry used to say, 'If the Lord would give me wings I would fly.' I used to answer, 'If the Lord bids me fly I would trust him for the wings.'" If God wants us to do something, He will provide the help to do it. Partnership with His spirit is ever trusting Him to supply all our needs.

443 Knowing God

John Bunyan had a blind child who was his constant companion, and of whom he was very tenderly fond—"he would not let the wind blow on her." She never saw her father's face, could only dimly recognize his marvelous genius, and was sadly incapable of reading his immortal book. Yet did she not know him? If any one in this world knew him it was his little blind daughter. She saw right into his heart, knew him as no critic, biographer, or historian ever knew him. Our knowledge of God is much of the same quality and kind. He is the light that no man approacheth unto. Yet we know the touch of His hand, the love of His heart, the power of His strengthening presence. This is eternal life, to know God in Jesus Christ.

444 Bond of Union

The old Theban regiments fought with such desperation upon the field of battle because it was the principle of Theban military science that those who stood next to each other in the rank should always, if possible, be bosom friends. Let us, in our great battle of life, learn the secret of affection and mutual trust.

445 The Give and Take of Life

A very remarkable thing once happened in Minnesota, on the Great Northern Railroad. A company of men working on the road were suddenly startled by seeing fully half a mile of the track lifted from the road-bed and thrown into a ditch. In some places the track was thrown six feet from the road-bed, and down a steep embankment. The men say it was done so quickly that they could hardly realize what had happened. It looked as if some supernatural power had lifted the track from the ground and hurled it aside. The weather had been intensely hot, and it is supposed that the rails had not been given sufficient room to expand with freedom. In dealing with iron or steel one must take into consideration the give and take of the metal under heat or cold. In this case a passenger train was flagged barely in time to save a wreck. The human heart under restraint, yet lacking the spirit of worship and the freedom of love, is like a constrained piece of steel. There is certain to be an explosion. In fellowship with Jesus Christ there is provision for the expansion and contraction of the soul.

446 Communion with God

One of the most pathetic things in life is the number of people to whom life is all commonplace and barren of oases—where they retire from the desert sands and hold secret communion with the Heavenly Father, drawing strength from sources that the world knows not of. On Broadway, in New York City, there stood a church whose doors were always open during the busy hours of the day. One day an old woman was noticed to leave the mass of hurrying humanity and ascend the steps of this church. Her face was the picture of misery and desolation, but not the desolation of poverty. Within all was silent, vast; a boundless gloom lay over everything, broken here and there by the yellow flicker of a low-turned gas lamp. Above in the gallery, the organist was pouring forth a soft flow of improvisation that in its gentle harmony seemed to breathe forgiveness upon a few far-separated figures kneeling below. The old woman took her place among them and knelt there for a while. Then she arose and passed out into the street, and the light falling upon her face revealed a countenance of perfect peace.

447 Lumpers or Splitters?

Willis Owens writes:

"The oldest specialty in the field of biology is the science of classification known as taxonomy. Taxonomists are the biologists who give organisms their scientific names. In addition, they group organisms into a hierarchy (or categories) designed to organize the vast array of living things into an orderly system. However, there is some disagreement among taxonomists due to a basic difference in approach.

"Some taxonomists operate on the premise that if two organisms share a few major characteristics, they should be placed into the same group. These individuals are referred to as 'lumpers.' A second approach to taxonomy proposes that if two organisms differ in any significant way they should be placed into separate groups. These people are called 'splitters.' In actual practice, taxonomic systems usually represent a compromise between these two extremes.

"When a Christian begins to consider the question of whom he should fellowship with, he becomes more or less a spiritual taxonomist. He is trying to make a decision as to which persons should be included in his group. Once again, we find some are 'lumpers' and others are 'splitters.' Some believe in extending fellowship to anyone who believes in a Supreme Being or power. Others accept anyone who calls himself a Christian, including those who deny the virgin birth and resurrection. Then there are those who fellowship with individuals who are living in moral decadence and who state publicly they do not believe it is wrong (c.g., homosexuals). These people are 'lumpers.'

"On the other hand, there are 'splitters.' They do not believe in fellowshiping with anyone who disagrees with them on any point. They exclude from their fellowship people who use different versions of the Scriptures, people who believe it is wrong to support institutions from the church treasury, and many others with whom they actually share the same views in reference to the basic tenets of the Christian religion. This approach has wreaked havoc among those of us who claim to be committed to the restoration of New Testament Christianity.

"Surely there is a middle ground of appropriate fellowship somewhere between the extremes of 'lumpers' and 'splitters.' I concur with the view that the seven 'ones' of Ephesians 4 are the clearest biblical identification of the essential tenets of Christian faith which should serve as the basis of fellowship.

"Avoiding the pitfalls of lumping and splitting, let us hold fast to the Word of God and be humble followers of the One who alone knows the heart of each person and who only has the final right to receive or exclude a human being from God's grace."

448 The Nature of Christian Fellowship

"Christian fellowship," writes Dr. D. O. Mears, "from its very nature and necessity, assumes that we must meet together at the mercyseat. A church without a prayer meeting is like an individual who never prays—cold and formal."

Forgiveness

449 If We Confess Our Sins

Jesus plainly stated that he came to save sinners. The man who refuses to be called a sinner puts himself beyond the possibility of salvation.

A wealthy industrialist was traveling in California in search of better health; while spending a few days in an inland town, he learned that in this village there resided a man who owed him a large sum of money. The young man had come here after an unsuccessful career in the East, and was beginning to prosper in a small way.

"The young man seems to have been trying to help himself," said the rich man, "and I am going to destroy the note I hold against him." The note, however, was miles away among his papers, and he realized that he might not live to return. Not knowing the exact amount of the note, he sent his private secretary to the young man, to make inquiry concerning it, and to offer to give the debtor a receipt against it; thus protecting him from proceedings that might in future be entered against him, should the capitalist die before he reached home. To the surprise of the secretary, the young businessman put on an indignant manner and denied the debt.

"When I owe your employer it will be time enough for you to be talking to me about forgiveness," he said.

The debt remained unforgiven and the heirs of the rich man insisted upon the collection of the note. This was done, to the ruin of the man who remained unforgiven because he was not willing to admit that there was anything to forgive.

450 Holding a Grudge

One day a visitor leaned on the old fence around a farm while he watched an old farmer plowing with a mule. After a while, the visitor said, "I don't like to tell you how to run your business, but you could save yourself a lot of work by saying, 'Gee' and 'Haw' to that mule instead of just tugging on those lines." The old farmer pulled a big handkerchief from his pocket and wiped his face. Then he said, "Reckon you're right, but this animal kicked me five years ago and I ain't spoke to him since."

The moral of the story seems obvious: A grudge is harder on the one who holds it than the one it is held against. The Apostle Paul said that we are to forgive any man if we have a quarrel against him. Just like Christ forgave us, we are to forgive each other (Col. 3:13). Friend, if God and Christ can extend mercy

162

to you for your sins, surely you can be merciful to those who offend you.

451 The Price Of A Grudge

". . . if ye forgive not men their trespasses, neither will your Father forgive your trespasses" (Matt. 6:15).

Jesus said that an individual who refuses to forgive others will lose the assurance of divine mercy and the joy of fellowship with God. An unwillingness to pardon another is a grievous sin, and many have paid a heavy price for failing to heed the Lord's admonition.

Some time ago a middle-aged woman sought to be reunited in marriage with her former husband. She told her pastor that they were both Christians when they established their home, and that they had been blessed with two sons. Then one day they quarreled, and harsh words were spoken. Each was too proud to ask the other's forgiveness, and the bitter feelings finally led to a divorce. Neither had found a new mate; and now, 25 years later, with one son dead and the whereabouts of the other unknown, this woman learned that the only man she had ever loved was in the hospital. She went to see him, and with tears they forgave one another. At their request, the pastor gladly remarried them right there in the hospital room. As he left after performing the ceremony, he thought of the price they had paid because of their unwillingness to forgive. The prayers of both had been powerless, they

could not experience the joy of their salvation, and their sons had suffered because of a broken home. Although the husband and the wife had been reunited, the wasted years could never be recalled.

Anybody who harbors an unforgiving spirit is cheating himself of fellowship with God. The beauty of a Christlike character, and the best joys of life. The Christian cannot afford to pay the price of bearing a grudge!

Since the Lord your debt did pay,
Saved your soul in grace one day,
You with charity should live,
Always ready to forgive!

452 But I Cannot Get Out!

Jim N. Bartlett gives the following story in relation to the bondage of sin: "When people tell me that they have been in sin so long that God could never forgive them, it reminds me of the time I picked up an older Christian lady and drove her in the back seat of my two door car to church. When I opened the door to help her she discovered she was stuck and unable to get out. My youngest daughter, who was in the back seat with her, pushed while I pulled, but still we were unable to get her out of the car. 'But I cannot get out, Brother Bartlett,' she cried out after a long struggle. 'That is okay Sister,' I replied; 'if I can just reach behind you and unhook your coat from the window roller, we will get you out.'

"If a person would reach behind and simply unhook the snags of sin and turn it all over to God then truly the sinner could 'get out' of sin. Jesus is the way out and through Him there is an escape from sin, and its torments."

453 Forgiving Because Forgiven

"Life's cruel thrusts and stinging wounds cut deep—I can't forget.
I know not if I can forgive, dear Lord, they hurt and fret.
But when I think how I have sinned and oft have wounded Thee,
Repentant, then I too, forgive, as Thou forgavest me!"

—Gertrude Dugan

454 On Which Side Are You?

Calvary's Hill had three crosses. Christ on the center cross, dying for the sin of mankind. On one side was the Cross of Reception—a sinner who received the shed blood of Christ as payment for his sin; how close he was to that Sacrifice! On the other side, the Cross of Rejection—a sinner who rejected Christ's payment; how far he was from God's Sacrifice!

In the middle was the Cross of Redemption. The Cross of Reception shows the grace and mercy of God, even though it was a last-minute salvation. It could also be called the Cross of Repentance. Christ told him, "Today shalt thou be with Me in Paradise," (Luke 23:43). That sinner didn't deserve forgiveness and salvation. None of us do.

You are on one side of the Cross of Christ. Are you on the Cross of Reception? This is the cross of Rejoicing. The other side is the Cross of Eternal Remorse and Regret—unless you switch over.

—David E. Matthews

455 Archbishop Cranmer's Forgiving Spirit

Archbishop Cranmer appeared almost alone, in the higher classes, as the friend of truth in evil times, and a plot was formed to kill him. The providence of God, however, so ordered it, that the papers which would have completed the plan were intercepted, and traced to their authors, one of whom lived in the archbishop's family, and the other he had greatly served. He pulled these men aside in his palace, and told them that some persons in his confidence had disclosed his secrets, and even accused him of heresy. They loudly condemned such villainy, and declared the traitors worthy of death; one of them even added, that if an executioner could not be found, he would direct the execution himself. Struck with their dishonesty, after lifting up his voice to heaven, lamenting the depravity of man, and thanking God for his preservation, he produced their letters, and inquired if they knew who had written them. They then fell on their knees, confessed their crimes, and implored forgiveness. Cranmer mildly expostulated with them on the evil of their conduct, forgave them, and never again alluded to their treachery. His forgiveness of injuries was so well known, that it became a by-word, "Do my Lord of Canterbury an ill turn, and you make him your friend forever."

456 Praying for Our Enemies

Mr. Herring, one of the Puritan ministers, was eminently distinguished for Christian meekness, and for love to his greatest enemies. Dr. Lamb, a violent prosecutor of the Puritans, and especially of this good man, being on a journey, unhappily broke his leg, and was carried to the inn where Mr. Herring happened to be staying for the night. Mr. Herring was called on to pray that evening in the family, when he prayed with so much fervor and affection for the doctor as to surprise all who heard him. Being afterwards asked, why he manifested such respect to a man who was so utterly unworthy of it, he replied, "The greater the enemy he is, the more need he hath of our prayers. We must prove ourselves to be the disciples of Christ by loving our enemies, and praying for our persecutors."

On another occasion, Archbishop Laud having said, "I will pickle that Herring of Shrewsbury," the good man meekly replied, "If he will abuse his power, let it teach the Christians the more to use their prayers, that their enemies may see they have a God to trust in, when trampled upon by ill-disposed men."

457 A Little Girl Overcoming Evil

A very little girl, who often read her Bible, gave proof that she un-

derstood her obligations to obey its precepts. One day she came to her mother much pleased to show her some fruit which had been given to her. The mother said the friend was very kind, and had given her a great many. "Yes," said the child, "very, indeed; and she gave me more than these, but I have given some away." The mother inquired to whom she had given them, when she answered, "I gave them to a girl who pushes me off the sidewalk, and makes faces at me." On being asked why she gave them to her, she replied, "Because I thought it would make her know that I wanted to be kind to her, and maybe she will not be so rude and unkind to me again." How admirably did she thus obey the command in Romans 12:21 to "overcome evil with good!"

458 Two Christians Forgiving Each Other

Two good men on some occasion had a hotly contested dispute; and remembering the exhortation of Paul in Eph. 4:26: ". . . Let not the sun go down upon your wrath," just before sunset, one of them went to the other, and knocking at the door, his offended friend came and opened it, and seeing who it was, became stricken in astonishment and surprise; the other, at the same time, cried out, "The sun is almost down." This unexpected salutation softened the heart of his friend into affection, and he responded, "Come in, brother, come in." What a happy method of conciliating matters, of redressing grievances, and of reconciling brethren!

459 Forgiving an Enemy

While Wishart, the celebrated reformer, was engaged in relieving the temporal wants of the inhabitants of Dundee, during the prevalence of the plague in that city, and daily preaching to them the way of salvation, Cardinal Beaton bribed a wicked priest to murder him. On one occasion, Wishart had finished his sermon, the people were retiring, and the preacher was descending from the pulpit, when his keen eye noticed that Weighton, the priest, had a drawn dagger concealed under his gown. He immediately spoke to him, and deprived him of the murderous weapon. The priest fell on his knees, confessed his intention, and begged his forgiveness. The people were greatly enraged at the conduct of the priest, and would have had him killed, had not the reformer taken him in his arms and said, "Whatsoever hurts him shall hurt me; for he hath done me no mischief, but much good, by teaching me more heedfulness for the time to come."

460 Sigismund's Enemies

Some courtiers reproached the emperor Sigismond, that instead of destroying his conquered foes, he admitted them to favor. "Do I not," replied this illustrious monarch, "effectually destroy my enemies, when I make them my friends?"

Gifts

461 Diamonds and Corn

Generally speaking, there is no comparison to be made between the value of a diamond and that of a grain of corn, yet all depends on the disposition you make of the corn. Put both of them away, and at the end of a hundred years the grain of corn will still have no money value, while the diamond's value, running up into the hundreds of dollars, will be undiminished. At the end of a thousand years the same thing will be true. But suppose, instead, we bury the grain in the warm, moist earth, and year after year throughout the centuries let it go on producing and reproducing. In that time it will have produced a store that the whole earth could hardly contain. Its production represents a money value that makes the diamond's price not more than an atom in comparison. To have saved the grain of corn would have been to lose all it was capable of producing. "Except a corn of wheat fall into the ground, and die, it abideth alone" (John 12:24). To save your gift from God may seem to be a prudent thing, but let me tell you that in the end it will mean loss.

462 Utilize Your Gift to the Fullest

"As every man hath received the gift, even so minister the same one to another, as good stewards of the manifold grace of God" (1 Pet. 4:10).

In her book, *Today's Good Word*, Ethel B. Sutton tells of a young British soldier who was blinded in battle. He was an accomplished musician and spent much of his time in the hospital playing the piano for the wounded. He always put his heart into his playing, hoping the music would encourage the men. One day when he finished a number, someone clapped energetically. The soldier asked, "Who are you?" He was astonished when the man replied, "I am your king!" The king had come to encourage those who had been wounded for their country. Without realizing it, this young man had been using his talent to entertain the king.

Peter says, "Each has received a gift." It may not seem like much when compared with what others may possess, but utilize it "in serving one another." When it is used, we may be sure there is always an audience of at least one—our Lord. Do what you can. You may not get much attention. You may not win an award—you may not be mentioned in the bulletin, but God notices it.

When Jesus was teaching in the temple, he went and sat opposite of

167

the treasury and watched the people as they contributed their money (Mark 12:41-44). There was one who caught the eye of Jesus but she wasn't noticed by anyone else. The reason, her gift was too small; but in the eyes of Jesus, it was bigger than all the others.

When you use your gift faithfully—whether it is an encouraging word, a pat on the back, visiting the lonely, generous giving of money, making a phone call, providing transportation—whatever it may be, remember, you're playing for the King.

Giving

463 Give Quickly

The benevolent Dr. Wilson once discovered a clergyman at Bath who was sick, poor, and had a large family. In the evening he gave a friend fifty pounds, requesting him to deliver it in the most delicate manner, and as from an unknown person. The friend said, "I will wait upon him early in the morning." Dr. Wilson then said, "You will oblige me, sir, by calling directly. Think of what importance a good night's rest may be to that poor man."

464 Nothing Lost

"With what measure ye mete, it shall be measured to you" (Mark 4:24).

During the summer a clergyman called on a lady who had a very fine collection of roses. She took him out to see them—white roses, red roses, yellow roses, climbing roses, and roses in pots, the colorful giant of battles and the modest moss rose—every species he had ever heard of, were there in rich profusion. The lady began plucking, right and left. Some bushes with but a single flower she plundered. The clergyman remonstrated. "You are robbing yourself, dear madam." "Oh, no! Do you not know that the way to make a rosebush abundantly produce healthy roses is to pluck its flowers freely? I lose nothing by what I give away," she explained. This is a universal law. We never lose anything by what we give away.

465 Giving to God

A servant in a house once said to a gentleman visitor who was notoriously mean: "What shall I tell the master that you gave me, sir, when he asks me?" The tightfist was cornered, and though very reluctant to do it, felt compelled to give the servant something. But it is no mere trick when our conscience says: "What shall we say when the Master asks us at the judgment, 'How much have you given of time and influence, as well as money, for His kingdom and glory?'" May we be able to give a satisfactory answer both now and then!

466 All the Difference

When St. Theresa was laughed at because she wanted to build a great orphanage, and had but three shillings to work with, she answered: "With three shillings Theresa can do nothing; but with God and three shillings there is nothing that Theresa cannot do."

467 Give the Best You Have for Jesus

It does not matter how little your offering is, if it is given in the right spirit. A legend tells us how once a little boy in church had no money to place among the offerings on the altar, so he gave a rosy apple—the only gift he had to offer. Presently, when the pastor emptied the offering plates, he found there an apple of pure gold. The simplest gift in the eyes of God is as pure gold.

468 Giving from the Right Motive

It is related that when Andrew Fuller went into his native town to collect for the cause of missions, one of his old acquaintances said, "Well, Andrew, I'll give five pounds, seeing it's *you*." "No," said Mr. Fuller, "I can take nothing for this cause, seeing its *me*"—and handed the money back. The man felt reproved, but in a moment he said, "Andrew, you are right. Here are ten pounds, seeing it is for the *Lord Jesus Christ.*"

469 Giving through Living

A pig was lamenting his lack of popularity. He complained to a cow that people were always talking about the cow's gentleness and kind eyes. He admitted that cows give milk and cream, but maintained that pigs give more. He asserted that pigs give bacon and ham and bristles, and that people even pickle their feet. He demanded the reason for such lack of appreciation. The cow thought for a while and then said, "Maybe it's because I give while I'm still living."

Each of us has a calling from God for this life. Our efforts should be to produce for Him while we live (Phil. 1:21).

God

470 *Knowing His Voice*

One night in a river town in southern Ohio, there was a fearful storm, which suddenly raised the river and sent a flood sweeping over the town. It was at the hour when the people were returning from the Sunday evening service. Friends were separated in the darkness and a number of lives were lost. A little girl, who had become separated from her friends, was saved in a way that seemed nearly miraculous. Her father, who had gone in search of her, wandered about, calling her, with little hope of making himself heard, even if she were near. Suddenly he felt her little hands clasping his.

"I heard him calling, 'Come this way! I am here!'" she said afterward, when questioned about the matter.

"But how did you know it was your father calling you?" someone asked.

"How did I know?" she returned, wonderingly. "I think I ought to know my father's voice. I've been with him enough."

The child's reason was certainly sufficient. It was only by association that she could have become so familiar with his tone that she would know it even when she could not see. Jesus said of his sheep, "They know my voice." Those who know his voice in the midst of the world's distracting turmoil are those who have been much with him.

471 *"In the Beginning God"*

Does one duty ever take the precedence over another? It is the old question over which the rabbis disputed. "Which is the first and greatest commandment?" The question was, after all, a legitimate one. Even among unmistakable obligations there are those which have the right to rank first.

The man who builds a house cannot leave out the framework, but before that must come the foundation. Roof and framework and foundation are all essential, but imagine the result if he attempts to reverse the order and begin with the roof! Jesus did not condemn thrift and carefulness about material concerns, but he did say, "Seek ye first the kingdom of God" (Matt. 6:33). Someone has noted it as a significant fact that the first words of the Bible, taken alone, set forth the same thing. "In the beginning God" (Gen. 1:1). When a man puts God first in considering that which claims his time and talent, and in mapping out his plans, he will not be unfaithful to any other obligation.

171

472 He Is Waiting for You

A little girl had been away all day with the family of a neighbor; they were late in their return, and instead of reaching home before dark, as they expected, it was almost midnight when they arrived at the house.

"I will get out first and awaken your father," one of the gentlemen said to the little girl. "Awaken him!" said the child; "my father won't have to be awakened. He is waiting for me."

Men out of Christ, do you imagine that it is only through continued beseeching that you can gain the ear of God? Let me tell you, your Father does not have to be awakened. He is waiting for you.

473 Conscious of God

Tennyson, walking with his niece over the breezy downs at Freshwater, began talking of God's presence, and told her that he was as sure of it as were the disciples when they had the Christ with them on the road to Emmaus. His niece replied that she thought the presence of God would be awful to most people, but he replied, "I should be surely afraid to live my life without God's presence." The truly awful thing is to be without God, to be in the deepest sanctuary of our being terribly alone. And yet how many seem to battle in order to banish God—He is not, in all their thoughts.

474 Carlyle on God

"Time and space are not God; but creations of God: with Him it is an universal Here: so it is an Everlasting Now."

475 God in the Little Things

Writing on the grass of the field Dr. Macmillan says: "Its exquisite perfection enables us to see how God cares for helplessness and lowliness. In studying it, we seem to get behind the veil within which the Creator works in secret: we come into contact as it were with Him who is invisible. Each blade whispers to us, 'The place whereon thou standest is holy ground,' (Ex. 3:5) and we reply, 'Surely the Lord is in this place' " (Gen. 28:16).

476 God Revealed

In some parts of Southern France when the lavender is in bloom the perfume penetrates everywhere. It steals into the houses through every crack and cranny, and has no need to announce its presence. If God possesses us, His love will be shed abroad in our hearts as a penetrating fragrance, and of that revelation of God as of our Master it will be said, "It was noised that He was in the house" (Mark 2:1). Christians fragrant with the grace of God repeat the Incarnation.

477 The Peace of God

Wordsworth describes St. Mary's lake as being so utterly calm that the "swan floats double, swan and shadow." God's peace is so calm and eternal that while all the needs of all His creatures find their answer and response in Him, nothing disturbs His deep serenity.

478 *The Character of God*

Dr. Henry Scott-Holland speaks of the mystery of God's character in the following anecdote from his sermon *The Unfolding Mystery:*

"Is there anything so fascinating as the gradual and manifold disclosure of an inexhaustible secret? And our secret is manifold; it is inexhaustible; because it is the secret of a Personal Character, and that Character the Character of God. A character is always a secret, a mystery. We can never say exactly what it is going to do, however well we know it. Even among ourselves we have to wait on circumstances or emergencies, on the variety of the environing situation, to reveal to us what is already our precious possession—the soul of the beloved. It is ours; we are knit to it by indissoluble bonds; we are identified with its innermost being. Yet, love it as we may, we have not got to the bottom of its hidden wonders; we have heaps and heaps to learn yet. A thousand little incidents that occur will evoke a thousand new aspects of this loved soul, which are all new; and all surprises. Even the very commonest details of the daily round will open up fresh capacities that we had not suspected. We can never quite say what it is that will be said or done; and when the act or the word comes, we salute it with the delight that is given to things that are quite new. The closer and more intimate our love, the fresher abides this delight."

479 *Which Direction?*

A young man was walking along a country road. Along came a farmer driving a wagon. Without asking permission, the young man jumped upon the wagon and said, "I'm going to ride along with you to Louisville." The farmer just looked at him and said nothing. They rode for ten miles. The young man began to feel uneasy. He turned to the farmer and said, "I say, old pop, how much farther is it to Louisville?" The farmer replied, "If you keep in the direction you are going, it is about 25,000 miles, but if you want to get off and walk back the other way, it is about sixteen miles—six miles from where you jumped on."

Sometimes in life we just jump on for a ride without really finding out where the ride is going to take us. God has a ride mapped out for us already as we follow His divine will. Are you going in the right direction?

480 *The Master Key*

There are many locks in my house and all with different keys, but I have one master key which opens all. So the Lord has many treasurers and secrets all shut up from carnal minds with locks which they cannot open; but he who walks in fellowship with Jesus possesses the master key which will admit him to all the blessings of the covenant; yea, to the very heart of God. Through the Well-Beloved we have access to God, to heaven, to every secret of the Lord.

481 Bending the Standard

"No prophecy of the scripture is of any private interpretation" (1 Pet. 1:20).

The story is told of a small village that had a clock in the town square. At some time in the past, the glass had been broken out of the face of the clock, and now the villagers took it upon themselves to set the clock according to their own watches. Consequently, the hands of the great clock were constantly being changed, and no one really knew what the correct time was.

An even greater error is made when men bend the Scriptures to agree with their own opinions. Scripture must be compared with Scripture, and accepted as the final word of God; otherwise confusion will prevail and men will be led astray.

Faithful

482 God Meets the Need of the Soul

Expert scientists declare that iron in some quantities is to be found in every country, not only in the form of ore, but that it enters into the composition of all soils. Gold, too, is to be found, but only in a few countries. Someone once declared that, after careful examination, we should find that these were bestowed where most needed for the people's comfort. Plenty of iron, because it is necessary for man's use continually; gold in immeasurably less degree, because its main purpose is lustre, ornament, luxury. So the gifts absolutely essential for man's salvation and soul sustenance are to be found all over God's Word, and that, too, without money and without price. Deep need is met by Divine abundance of generosity.

483 God Never Changes

On going abroad at night, and gazing at the stars, we note that every hour changes their position. The one that on its first appearance shone above our heads is now sinking in the west, while those we saw mounting just above the horizon, have climbed to the top of the sky—the whole host appear to be marching on, one orb only, the Pole Star, excepted. Around that they seemed to roll, as the pivot on which the whole firmament turns. What it appears to be, God is. Among all beings there is One fixed, immovable, unchangeable. He alone can say, "I am the Lord, I change not" (Mal. 3:6), and therefore speaking of Him, the prophet says, "Behold the Lord's hand is not shortened that it cannot save; neither is His ear heavy that it cannot hear" (Isa. 59:1).

Loving

484 God's Bounty

A Roman Emperor once gave a magnificent banquet, and at an agreed signal the roof opened and a shower of roses descended on the guests. It was regarded as a singularly beautiful and original pro ceeding, and has helped to immortalize the Emperor. But when God pours upon earth the refreshing rain, could our eyes but be opened, we should see that He pours down on field and garden, forest and plain, not only roses, but golden grain and fruit for the sustenance and delight of mankind. The King of kings is ever entertaining us at His providential banquet of blessing and beauty too.

485 God's Care for the Least

"A good man came to ask counsel in what to him was a terrible emergency: bankruptcy, accompanied with possible dishonor, seemed to stare him in the face. He had been talking over his own affairs—and in an interval of the conversation he took me, a child, on his knee, and enquired all about my childish concerns, what books I had read, what places I had been at, what games I liked best, and before all was over he took out his knife and mended a broken whistle for me. The pressure of his own affairs did not prevent his being interested in a child. I can look up through an experience like that, and understand how the Lord, who cares for all the worlds of space, cares for the least, and has numbered the very hairs of my head."

486 Love in Other Words

Valentines Day is the time of year that most people think of love: first for a family member, a friend, another relative, or just people in general. Think of the things we do to show our love. We take the time to send flowers or a card, but often that is as much as is done. And even for a child to really know what true love is, we have to say the words, "I love you"; yet we often mix those words with a toy or a special gift. But sometimes our actions and words seem superficial because it is hard for us to purely know what true love is.

If you want to see a real example of how actions matched the word spoken, just take a look at Jesus. He told us in His Word that He loves us, then He stretched out His hands and showed us, by dying on the cross of Calvary. He promised us the Holy Spirit to guide us in our Christian walk (John 16:13). Salvation is offered to anyone who will receive His gift (Rom. 5:4-8). All this love, freely given in word and deed— what a perfect example for us.

The next time you say "I love you," remember how Christ matched His words with the cross.

Omniscient

487 No Hiding

Mr. Mac and my daddy used to work together, making hay, harvesting grain, and cutting and hauling cross ties. They had a wagon load of Mr. Mac's cross ties, and were on the way to market with the load. They had stopped at the little stream to let the horses drink when Daddy noticed a decayed place in the end of one of Mr. Mac's ties.

"Mac," he said, "did you want to put this tie with the decayed place in your load? The inspector will deduct from the price you get for the load." Mr. Mac picked up a handful of mud and daubed it into the decayed place to cover it quite effectively. On they went to the market. The inspector looked the load over and rejected the whole load.

Do our lives stand inspection? Jesus said, "There is nothing covered that shall not be revealed: neither hid, that shall not be known" (Luke 12:2).

—Robert C. Sieg

488 True or False?

A rich merchant died, leaving a large fortune. He had but one son, who had been sent when quite a lad to an uncle in India. On his way home, after an absence of some years, the young man had been shipwrecked; and though it was believed he had been saved, still no certain tidings reached his father, who, meanwhile, died rather suddenly, leaving his large fortune to the care of an old friend, with strict instructions not to give it up to any claimant until certain conditions had been complied with. At the end of a year, a young man appeared who said he was the heir; then a second, and finally a third. The guardian, who knew that two out of the three claimants must be imposters, made use of the following stratagem: He gave each rival a bow and arrow, and desired them to use the dead man's picture as the target, and to aim at the heart. The first nearly hit the mark; the second pierced the heart; but the

third claimant burst into tears, and refused to dishonor his father's memory by injuring the portrait of one whom he venerated so highly. The guardian was quite satisfied with the result of his device, and at once welcomed him as the rightful heir and his old friend's son.

2 Timothy 1:7 says, "For God hath not given us the spirit of fear; but of power, and of love, and of a sound mind." This speaks of the wisdom we receive from God for everyday decisions. As we walk with Him, He will reveal to us through the Holy Spirit how to make wise decisions (John 16:13). Let us look to Him and we will, like the guardian in our story, be able to rightfully discern truth.

Omnipotent

489 A Better Answer

A young man went away from home to embark in a modest enterprise. His capital was small, but it represented the earnings of many years. He had won the esteem of his employer, and, as he was about to leave, the merchant said to him, "Don, if you ever get into a tight place, let me know of it. I will be glad to help you." For awhile the young man prospered; then came a misfortune. This was followed by others in such rapid succession that he began to see before him bankruptcy and ruin. He thought of his old employer, and at last resolved to write to him and ask for help. He had not the courage to ask for the whole amount, but hoped the small sum he asked for would enable him to somehow retrieve his fortunes. He waited eagerly for an answer, but no answer came. He knew that the merchant was at home, and that he was not a man who ever procrastinated about what he intended to do. Don's heart grew sick. Tomorrow his creditors would seize upon his possessions. There seemed to be no way of escape. As he sat wrapped in his gloomy thoughts, the door opened and his old employer stood before him.

"My boy," he said, "I received your letter, and while you said you wanted money, I made up my mind that you needed me. I have been to see your creditors, and they understand that my entire fortune is behind you."

His friend had kept his promise, but he had answered in a way that the petitioner had not dared to hope. Brother, if your Lord has given you exceeding great and precious promises, do not allow yourself to fear that he will not fulfill them. God does not always give his loved ones what they ask, but he never fails to supply their needs.

490 God's Promises

God's Word is full of promises as the heavens are full of stars. All of them are payable on demand, according to the conditions named. They are made freely, and paid fully. Mr. Spurgeon calls it, "a checkbook of the Bank of Faith." We do not have checkbooks for ornament or for meditation, but for use. Some promises are payable on demand; but long-time promises of God are as sure of payment as those in demand. Some are payable here, some hereafter. Heaven's security is as good as God can make it.

491 Just One Day at a Time

One of God's aged saints fell and broke her hip. As she lay discouraged in a hospital bed, she asked the doctor, "How long will I have to stay here?" The wise doctor replied, "Just one day at a time!"

God deals with His children on a day-by-day basis: "As thy days, so shall thy strength be" (Deut. 33:25); "Give us this day our daily bread" (Matt. 6:11).

Just for today, my Savior,
Tomorrow is not mine;
Just for today, I ask Thee
For light and health divine;
Tomorrow's care I must not bear;
The future is all Thine.

492 What's Your Hindrance?

How nimbly does the little lark soar up singing towards heaven in a straight line, whereas the hawk which is stronger and swifter of flight, mounts up gradually. The bulky body and wing span hinder a direct ascent and requires both the help of the air and scope of its wings to advance its flight. The small bird, on the other hand, cuts through the air with only resistance and needs very little movement of the wings for propulsion. It is much the same way with the Christian life. As believers "soar" together to accomplish God's will for their individual lives, oftentimes their strength (physical or spiritual) may become a hindrance to another. Meanwhile, another may exhibit a life with no incumberances and others benefit from his example. Many are proud of the spiritual "burdens" they bear, but what better choice could there be to be one whose reliance is solely resting on the Lord.

Sovereign

493 God's Sovereign Control

When Napoleon was contemplating his great march to Moscow he explained his plans to a lady in a very haughty and boastful manner. "Please be reverent," said the lady, "for man proposes, but God disposes." "Madam," said the proud emperor, "I will propose and dispose too." But he forgot the King of kings who is on the great throne. And in a few months he was in retreat from the burned city, and engaged in that awful battle with frost and snow that wrecked his army, his prestige, and eventually sent him as a defeated exile to the prison of St. Helena. Man proposes, but, still, God disposes.

494 God Will Not Forsake Us

"Oh that one could believe that God is almighty!" Luther would exclaim when everything seemed to go against him. "If God be for us," Paul says in Romans 8:31, "who can be against us?"

Oh, where is our faith when the storm clouds gather and lightning flashes? Is God's promise to Joshua, "I will not fail thee nor forsake thee" (Josh. 1:5), not made to us also?

A minister was in distress. His congregation knew nothing of it. His deacons knew nothing of it. But God knew all about it; for he had told Him in prayer. While he sat in his study-room, praying, the door opened and a woman stepped in. Every stitch of this woman's apparel gave her the appearance of being stricken with poverty, but in the most strange way she quoted the words of God to Elijah: "Behold, I have commanded a widow woman there to sustain thee" (1 Kgs. 17:9). Saying this, she put $250 on the table and vanished. And he never saw her again.

495 The Clock of Providence

There is a clock with which Providence keeps time and pace, and God himself sets it, so that everything happens with divine punctuality. Israel came out of Egypt on the self-same night in which the redemption was appointed, and afterwards wandered in the wilderness till the hour had come when the iniquity of the Amorites was full. Our time is always come, for we are in selfish haste; but our Lord when on earth had His set times and knew how to wait for them. God is never before His time, and never too late. We may well admire the punctuality of heaven.

Our trials come in due season, and go at the appointed moment. Our fretfulness will neither hasten nor delay the purpose of our God.

We are in hot haste to set the world right, and to order all affairs: the Lord hath the leisure of conscious power and unerring wisdom, and it will be well for us to learn to wait. The clock will not strike till the hour; but when the instant cometh we shall hear the bell. My soul, trust in God, and wait patiently when he says, *"My time is not yet come"* (John 7:6).

496 God's Lantern of Warning

"Did you ever go down a country road," asks Dr. Bob Jones Sr., "and see a sign, 'This Land Posted?' Or down the road farther, 'Stay Out of This Field?' God does a similar thing in the Bible. Many roads lead men to hell, but God has posted every one of them. You are tempted to steal. God won't stop you; but He wrote above your road, *"Thou shalt not steal."* You are tempted to kill; and you can do it if you want to. You can pull a trigger or thrust a dagger into somebody's heart; but God posted the road, *"Thou shalt not kill."* At each dangerous place on life's highway God puts a red lantern; and if you go to ruin, you go over God's lantern of warning."

497 A Lantern in the Dark

The following illustration is by Herman W. Gockel:

It was a cold winter's night. Five-year-old Bobby held his father's hand tightly as they walked along a dark footpath which led to a neighboring farmhouse. It was evident that Bobby was afraid—afraid of the pitch-black darkness which stretched out endlessly before him. Finally, looking at the lantern in his father's hand, he whimpered, "Daddy, I am scared! The light reaches only such a little way!" The father tightened his grip on the little boy's hand and answered with confident assurance: "I know, son. But if we just keep on walking, we will see that the light keeps on shining all the way to the end of the road."

What a fitting parable for the Christian pilgrim as he leaves another day behind him and places his feet on the unknown road which lies ahead! To our Heavenly Father you and I are little Bobbies—sometimes confident, but sometimes frightened by the inky darkness of the road before us. How often, in the blackness of our night, have we whimpered that the light which God has given us "reaches only such a little way!" And how often have we found that, if we just kept on walking in the light which He has given us, His light would keep on shining, illuminating each new step as we would take it. God has not given His believers a battery of klieg lights which light up each detail of the road which lies ahead; but He has given us a lantern in the darkness which, if we take heed to it, will illumine our entire pathway—step by step.

"Thy word is a lamp unto my feet, and a light unto my path" (Ps. 119:105). There is no darkness which cannot be pierced by that lamp. And in the light of that lamp we can take each new step with confidence. There may be vast stretches of the road ahead which we cannot see, but the lamp of God's Word assures us that those stretches, just as the step which lies before us, will be illumined by His love. "If we walk in the light, as he is in the light, we have fellowship one with another, and the blood of Jesus Christ his Son cleanseth us from all sin" (1 John 1:7). The light of God's lamp is the light of His love. His love, revealed to us in Bethlehem, on Calvary, and again in Joseph's garden, is the guarantee of our security.

"He that spared not his own Son, but delivered him up for us all, how shall he not with him also freely give us all things?" (Rom. 8:32). Surely, if we will just keep walking in His light, He will be with us—all the way.

498 *In God's Hands*

An old story concerning Martin Luther is well worth repeating in these days of uncertainty and fear. In one of the great crises of his life, when he was standing firmly and alone for a conviction that he refused to surrender, he was confronted furiously by a powerful opponent. Did he realize, asked that opponent, what he was doing and what power he was defying? Did he expect any force worth mentioning to take up arms and come to his help?

"No," said Luther quietly, "I do not expect that." "Then where will you be?" thundered the dignitary who had come to challenge him. "Where will you be?" And to that Luther answered in words that seem to go to the very heart of things, "I shall be where I have always been—in the hands of Almighty God."

499 *Later Than They Think*

The story is told of a man who rushed into a suburban railroad station one morning and, almost breathlessly, asked the ticket agent: "When does the 8:01 train leave?" "At 8:01," was the answer. "Well," the man replied, "it is 7:59 by my watch, 7:57 by the town clock, and 8:04 by the station clock. Which am I to go by?" "You can go by any clock you wish," said the agent, "but you cannot go by the 8:01 train, for it has already left."

God's time is moving forward hour by hour, minute by minute. There are multitudes who seem to think that they can live by any schedule they choose and that, in their own time, they can turn to God. But His time is the right time. Now it may be later than they think. Soon it may be too late. "Behold, now is the accepted time; behold now is the day of salvation" (2 Cor. 6:2).

Gospel

500 Attention to the Gospel

H. Bonar relates:

"Suppose you were attending to hear a will read, where you expected an inheritance; would you employ the time in criticizing the manner in which the lawyer read it? No; you would be giving all attention to hear if anything had been left to you. So you ought to hear the Gospel.

"The Gospel comes to the sinner at once, with nothing short of complete forgiveness as the starting point of all his efforts to be holy. It does not say, 'Go and sin no more, and I will not condemn thee'—it says at once, 'Neither do I condemn thee; go and sin no more'" (John 8:11).

501 The Law and the Gospel

"The Law shows us our sin," says an old writer, "the Gospel shows us a remedy for it. The Law shows us our condemnation, the Gospel shows us our redemption. The Law is the word of despair, the Gospel is the word of comfort. The Law says, Pay your debt; the Gospel says, Christ has paid it. The Law says, You are a sinner, despair and you will be damned; the Gospel says, Your sins are forgiven; be of good comfort, you will be saved. The Law says, Make amends for your sin; the Gospel says, Christ has made it for you. The Law says, Your Father in heaven is angry with you; the Gospel says, Christ has pacified Him with His blood. The Law asks, Where is your righteousness, goodness, and satisfaction? The Gospel says, Christ is my righteousness, goodness and satisfaction. The Law says, You are bound and indebted to me; the Gospel says, Christ has delivered you from them all. He that believes not God's word believes not God Himself. The Gospel is God's word; therefore he that believes not the Gospel believes not God Himself."

502 The Gospel, Not Merely a Message of Deliverance or Theology

The gospel is not merely a message of deliverance, it is also a rule of conduct. It is not merely theology, it is also ethics. Like some of the ancient municipal charters, the grant of privileges and proclamation of freedom is also the sovereign code which imposes duties and shapes life.

503 The Gospel Represented in the Smallest Duties

The greatest principles of the gospel are to be fitted to the smallest duties. The tiny round of the dewdrop is shaped by the same laws that mold the giant sphere of the largest planet. You cannot make a map of the poorest grass field without celestial observations. The star is not too high nor too brilliant to move before us and guide simple men's feet along their pilgrimage.

Grace

504 Grace Abides

There is a pair of famous bronze gates in the city of Florence, which Michaelangelo, in a burst of admiration, declared were fit to be the gates of Paradise. They are panelled with noble figures and dainty pictures. Once they were gilded, and Dante referred to them as "The Golden Gates." But the centuries have worn off the gold—so that hardly a particle is left now. Still the fine masterly work of the artist abides in the solid bronze, looking none the less impressive in its severe simplicity. So while the years may wear away many meritorious accomplishments and much of the glitter of the natural life, the graces firmly ingrained in our soul by the Great Master of all Arts and Hearts will abide. No change can touch these, for "though our outward man perish, the inward man is renewed day to day" (2 Cor. 4:16).

505 Sufficiency of Grace

Careless drivers often push their automobiles beyond their designated capabilities, and the poor vehicle chugs and chugs until the motor finally dies. Daring and foolish engi-neers will put too much pressure on their boilers, or try to force more power from an engine than it can provide. But our Master guarantees that tasks shall be balanced with the precise strength we possess. He knows our frame: He remembers that we are dust (Ps. 103:104). He will not be less merciful to us than the merciful man is to his beast. He knows the exact pressure we can stand, for He has made us; He knows the utmost load we can lift, and will not suffer us to be tried, tested, above what we are able (1 Cor. 10:13). He is a Faithful Creator, be-cause He is an abiding Sustainer.

506 Transforming Grace

A traveler describing an ancient volcano which he visited, tells of a cup-like hollow on the mountain summit full of lush vegetation, and that, where the fierce heat had once burned, lay a still, clear pool of water, looking up like an eye to the beautiful heavens above. How many a man, who before conversion was a fiery death-dealing volcano of sin, has by the grace of Jesus become gentle and beautiful, reflecting in his measure the heavenly peace and loveliness.

Greed

507 Prosperity Can Be Dangerous

Spurgeon says: "Ships never strike on rocks out in the great deeps. Children, perhaps, may fancy that a shallow sea is the safest, but an old sailor knows better. While he is off the Irish coast the captain has to keep a good look out, but while he is crossing the Atlantic he is in far less danger. There he has plenty of sea room, and there is no fear of quicksands or of shoals. When the sailor enters the Thames he encounters first one sand bank and then another, and he is in danger, but out in the deep water, where he finds no bottom, he is but little afraid. So, mark you, in the judgments of God. When he is dealing out affliction to us it is the safest possible sailing that a Christian can have. 'What,' says one, 'trial safe?' Yes, very safe. The safest part of a Christian's life is the time of trial. 'What, when a man is down do you say he is safe?' Yes, for then he need fear no fall; when he is low he need fear no pride; when he is humbled under God's hand then he is less likely to be carried away with every wind of temptation. Smooth water on the way to heaven is always a sign that the soul should keep wide awake, for danger is near. One comes at last to feel a solemn dread creeping over one in times of prosperity. 'Thou shalt fear and tremble because of all the good that God shall make to pass before thee' [Jer. 33:9], fearing not so much lest the good should depart as lest we should make an ill use of it, and should have a canker of sloth, or self-confidence, or worldliness growing up in our spirits. We have seen many professed Christians make shipwreck, in some few instances it has been attributable to overwhelming sorrow, but in ten cases to the one it has been attributable to prosperity."

508 The Really Good Things

J. H. Jowett has an illustration that probably hits too close to home for most of us. His subject is that of materialism, and its effect on Christianity:

"The really good things, the big things, are inside and not outside the man. The big thing is not luxury, but contentment; not a big house, but a big satisfaction; not accumulated art treasures, but a fine, artistic appreciation; not a big library, but a serene studiousness; not a big estate, but a large vision. The big things are not 'the things that are seen, but the things that are not seen' (2 Cor. 4:18). 'Seek peace and ensue it' (1 Pet. 3:11). 'Seek the things that are above'

(Col. 3:1). 'Seek ye first the Kingdom of God and His righteousness' (Matt. 6:33). Such are the goodly pearls."

509 Seek Eternal Things

Isaac Edwardson has this to say on the subject of comparing material things with those that are spiritual in nature:

"Part of our work in life is to learn values and to estimate the worth of doubtful things. We walk by faith and faith may be mistaken. But to the eyes of faith each new experience sooner or later reveals its inward worth and nature. We acquire, discard and cherish; and the things that we retain are those which can endure the light of the presence of God. And these are the things which are eternal."

510 Greed of Gold

According to Greek mythology, Midas, the Phyrgian king, asked a favor of the gods, and they agreed to grant him anything that he desired. The king decided to make the best of their offer. He asked that whatever he touched in the future be turned into gold. The wish was granted, but the consequences were severe! He placed his hand upon a rock, and immediately it became a huge chunk of priceless gold. He laid his hand on his staff, and it, too, became a rod of precious gold. At first the king was overcome with joy, and he returned to his palace as one of the most favored kings. He sat at his dinner-table, and every item of food that he touched turned into solid gold. Then he realized that this foolish wish would cause him to die in the midst of his newly-found riches, and he fearfully remembered these ominous words: "The gods cannot take back their gifts." He then begged the gods to restore him to the coarsest, vilest food, and deliver him from the curse of greed. Although this particular tale is a mere fable, we see this story manifest itself everyday in the lives of many people in our increasingly materialistic world. God often does bless people with wealth, but he expects this wealth to be used for his service. How sad it is to see people who are never satisfied with what God has already blessed them with!

511 Burning up the Bread of Life

In a storm on Lake Erie, the steamer ran out of fuel, and was compelled to throw small sacks of flour out of the cargo into the furnaces in order to keep up steam. A carload of flour was burned in this way before the steamer came into the port. Of course everybody will agree that it was much better to burn up a carload of flour than to allow a whole shipload, as well as the officers and crew, to sink to the bottom; but how different it would be if a captain should, out of indifference or carelessness, burn his cargo to make steam for his voyage! Yet that is what we are doing in American citizenship when we sacrifice our principles and permit our state governments to allow thousands of our citizens to ruin themselves in taverns and liquor stores in order that we may get revenue from a licensed partnership in the liquor traffic. And the individual citizen who denies his conscience burns up the bread of life in the furnace of political party prejudice or greed of gold.

512 The Love of Money

"Ye cannot serve God and mammon." (Matt. 6:24).

Robert Hall once wrote the word "God" on a small slip of paper, showed it to a friend, and asked whether he could read it. He replied, "Yes." He then covered the word with a coin, and again asked, "Can you see it?" and was answered, "No." He did this to show his friend how easy it is for the world to shut out of the mind a sight and sense of God. The love of riches may so fill the mind that there is no place in it for the great God of the universe. In the view of such a mind, a coin is larger than God.

513 All That Glitters Is Not Gold

A Frenchman who came to the U.S. from Paris met with a very sad mishap. He brought with him to this country 10,000 francs, which was all his fortune. He met a seem-ingly friendly Spaniard at his boarding-house, and the Frenchman trusted the Spaniard enough to loan him his money. The Frenchman accepted from the Spaniard five gold bricks as collateral for the loan, but when the Spaniard went away, and the Frenchman took his bricks to a jeweler to assess their monetary value, he was sadly informed that they were composed of copper, tin, and zinc, without one particle of gold. The despair of the poor Frenchman when he discovered that he had been swindled out of all his little fortune was very sad to behold. But how many are deceived in a similar manner. Men and women invest all their time and talent in glittering and delusive treasures which promise happiness and peace, but one needs to realize that they are only a base alloy. Many who are deceived in this fashion are crying out that life is not worth the living, and we see stories in the news media every day of those who have wickedly put an end to their lives because they had not the courage to rise out of their defeats. But those who live genuine lives, doing the will of God with honest hearts, and seeking always to please him, do not find life a cheat. These people find life worth the living, and have heaven added as a crown of glory which never fades away.

Heaven

514 Love Prepares Us for Heaven

H. Van Dyke says that, "There is only one way to get ready for immortality and that is to love this life, and live it as bravely and faithfully and cheerfully as we can."

515 Earthly Things Are Ordinary

"Ordinary human motives," claims Alexander Maclaren, "will appeal in vain to the ears which have heard the tones of heavenly music; and all the pomp of life will show poor and tawdry to the sight that has gazed on the vision of the great white throne and the crystal sea."

516 Heaven Compared to Earth

The British poet Alfred Lord Tennyson once went to South Kensington to visit Norman Lockyer, and see the heavens through a very fine telescope. After looking for a long time at the marvels of the night sky, Tennyson turned away from the telescope with the remark, "After seeing that, one does not think so much of the County families." This is only the modern poet's way of echoing the ancient inspired bard's saying, "When I consider thy heaven's—what is man?" (Ps. 8:3, 4).

517 Heaven's Perfect Rest

At Cadiz above the House of Refuge is carved the inscription, "This is my rest; here will I dwell." The ear misses the familiar word of the Psalm, "forever." A visitor looking up one day at the words, noticed the omission, and the tour guide, who happened to be near, with a smile explained the reason. "This house" he said, "is the rest of the poor, but not forever." So there is no perfect, absolute rest for us here on earth, but we can rest in the Lord, and await patiently for His return, and for the rest that remains and abides for the people of God.

518 Face to Face

A remarkable incident occurred recently at a wedding in England. A young man of large wealth and high social position, who had been blinded by an accident when he was ten years old, and who won university honors in spite of his blindness, had courted and won a beautiful bride, although he had never looked upon her face. A little while before his marriage he submitted himself to a course of treatment by experts and the climax came on the day of his wedding. The day came, and the presents, and the guests. There were cabinet ministers and generals and bishops and learned men and a large number of fashionable men and women. William Montagu Dyke, dressed for the altar, his eyes still shrouded in linen, was driven to the church by his father, and the oculist met them in the vestry. The bride, Miss Cave, entered the building on the arm of her white-haired father, the admiral, who was all decked out in the blue and gold lace of the quarterdeck. So moved was she that she could hardly speak. Was her lover at last to see her face—the face that others admired, but which he knew only through his delicate fingertips? As she neared the altar, while the soft strains of the Wedding March from Lohengrin floated through the church, her eyes fell on a strange group. Sir William Hart Dyke stood there with his son. Before the latter was the oculist in the act of cutting away the last bandage. William Montagu Dyke took a step forward, with the spasmodic uncertainty of one who can not believe that he is awake. A beam of rose-colored light from a pane in the chancel window fell across his face, but he did not seem to see it. Did he see anything? Yes! Recovering in an instant his steadiness of mien, and with a dignity and joy never before seen in his face, he went forward to meet his bride. They looked into each other's eyes, and one would have thought that his eyes would never wander from her face.

"At last!" she said. "At last!" he echoed solemnly, bowing his head.

That was a scene of great dramatic power and no doubt of great joy to both the bridegroom and his bride. It is a suggestion of what will happen in heaven when the Christian, who has been walking through this world of trial by faith, shall awake in the likeness of his Savior, and see Him no longer through a glass darkly, but, as Paul says, *"face to face"* (1 Cor. 13:12).

519 *The Heart Is Home*

"I will dwell in the house of the Lord forever." (Ps. 23:6 NASB).

There's no place like home, be it ever so humble. Natalia Solzhenitsyn, wife of the exiled writer and Nobel Prize winner Alexander Solzhenitsyn, must have been muttering these words as she returned to Moscow after 18 years in exile. She promised that her husband would soon follow. "This is what we have been living for all these years in exile: the return home," Mrs. Solzhenistyn said at Moscow's Shremetyevo Airport after arriving from the United States.

There is something in the human heart that always wants to go home—the place from which it came. God has given us a "homing device" like that of a pigeon, and it is only natural to respond: "This is what we have been living for all these years in exile: the return home."

—Purnell Bailey

Hell

520 No Friendship in Hell

When we fall into the outer darkness, we do not go in bands and companies—each man must fall by himself. And this same lonesomeness will mark the judgment of each soul. "Thou must go forth alone," is the hardest part of the verdict pronounced upon the impenitent sinner.

521 How Far Is It to Hell?

The following illustration is by T. David Sustar:

Tears were streaming from the evangelist's eyes as the Spirit of God directed him toward three young men on the back row. The message that night had been on the "The Horrors of Hell." The man of God had made a passionate plea, attempting to rescue any soul bound for that awful place. As he approached the trio, he was about to ask them to please come to the Lord and confess their sins. Before he could utter a word, one of them smirked and said, "Huh, preacher, how far is it to hell, anyway?" The other two laughed and they all turned and exited quickly from the church. The evangelist told me he heard the squeal of the tires as they pulled out on the highway and sped away. His broken heart followed them as far as possible, hoping they would return. Others, however, did respond and a number of people were praying around the altar.

The prayer was soon interrupted by a state trooper's knock on the front door of the church. His question paralyzed the congregation. "Do any of you know three young men?" and he went on to describe what they were wearing. The people responded that they did and wondered aloud why he asked. The officer sadly unfolded the story. Just two and one-half miles down the road, at the big bend, their car had left the road and split in half around a large oak tree. The people hurried to their cars. When they arrived, they found three dead bodies lying beside the road. It was two and one-half miles to hell for those young men!

I suppose that none of us realize how close death is to us. It stalks our every step and waits around every corner. God's Word says it would be thus, "It is appointed unto men once to die, but after this the judgment" (Heb. 9:27). In reality, I suppose we're all just one breath away from judgment. At any moment, we could meet all the facts of our life, which will dictate where we spend eternity.

Isn't it great to know that sins forgiven will allow us to stand with joy before the judge of the universe, Jesus Christ?

Heroes

522 *Luther in His Closet*

Vitus Theodorus, one of the German Reformers, once said: "I cannot enough admire the cheerfulness, constancy, faith, and hope of Luther, even in these trying times. He constantly feeds these good affections by a very diligent study of the Word of God. Then, not a day passes in which he does not employ in prayer at least three of his best hours. Once I happened to hear him at prayer. Oh, what spirit, what faith was there in his expressions! He petitioned God with as much reverence as if he were in the Divine presence, and yet with as firm a hope and confidence as he would address a friend. 'I know,' said he, 'that Thou art our Father and our God; therefore I am sure that Thou wilt bring to naught the persecutions of Thy children; for shouldest Thou fail to do this, Thine own cause being connected with ours, would be endangered. It is entirely Thine own concern; we, by Thy providence, have been compelled to take a part; Thou therefore wilt be our defense.' While I was listening to Luther praying in this manner, at a distance, my soul seemed to burn within me, to hear a man address God so much like a friend, and yet with so much gravity, and reverence; and also to hear him, in the course of his prayer, insisting on the promise contained in the Psalms, as if he were sure his petitions would be granted."

523 *John Knox and Mary, Queen of Scots*

"You interpret the Scriptures in one way," said Mary to Knox, "and the Pope and the cardinals in another; whom shall I believe, and who shall be judge?" "You shall believe," replied Knox, "God, who plainly speaketh in His word; and farther than the word teacheth you, you shall believe neither the one nor the other—neither the Pope nor the Reformers—neither the Papists nor the Protestants. The word of God is plain in itself; if there is any obscurity in one place, the Holy Ghost, who is never contrary to himself, explains it more clearly in other places, so that there can remain no doubt but unto such as are obstinately ignorant."

191

Holy Spirit

524 The Promise of the Comforter

During World War II, a contingent of American troops in Normandy who were holding a few German soldiers as prisoners received a message that relief was on the way. They were holding their own at the greatest cost; provisions were low, and they felt that they could not hold out much longer. What cheer the message brought! They were not alone. They were allied to a great power that was at their service. But the prisoners did not rejoice; they had no part in the blessings of their captors. So the Comforter comes to help the children of God alone, and they alone rejoice in the promise of his coming.

525 The Comforter

Mr. J. Burns gives the following illustration of an artist's painting with a very uplifting message: "A picture of deep pathos, carrying its own tender suggestion to the heart, appeared in the Academy of 1897. It was painted by Byam Shaw, and entitled *The Comforter.* In the interior of a room, upon a bed, there lies a form, the face of which is not seen, only a hand lying upon the silk counterpane with a wedding-ring upon the finger. By the side of the bed there sits a young man, his elbow leaning upon the bed, his head supported by his hand, his face drawn with grief. In his loneliness he sits there while his beloved, with slow and painful breaths, sighs out her little store of life. The picture gives the impression of stillness; pitiful tragedy is working itself out within. But the young man, as he sits there in his unutterable anguish, is not alone; the Comforter has come. Seated beside him is a white figure, unseen to the young man, and in that silent room of death there is another watcher."

526 Our Guide

It has been said that when John Bunyan was in Bedford Jail, some of his prosecutors back in London had heard rumors that he was often allowed to leave the prison; so they sent an officer to Bedford to discuss the matter with the jailer. This officer was to arrive at night. On this particular night, Bunyan was at home with his family, but for some reason, he was so restless, that he told his wife that, although the jailer had given him permission to stay till morning, something was telling him he should go back to the jail immediately. He did so, and the jailer, uninformed of the impending arrival of the London officer, was slightly perturbed by Bunyan's coming at such an unreasonable hour. But early in the morning the messenger came, and interrogated the jailer, asking, "Are all the prisoners here?" "Yes," said the jailer. "Is John Bunyan here?" "Yes." "Let me see him." He was called, and appeared, and all was well. After the messenger was gone, the jailer said to Bunyan, "Well, you may go in and out any time you think is proper, for you know when to return better than I can tell you."

527 Sin against the Holy Spirit

"But he that shall blaspheme against the Holy Ghost hath never forgiveness, but is in danger of eternal damnation" (Mark 3:29).

Just what is this unpardonable sin that Christ mentions? This passage of the Bible has often been misunderstood, but H. W. Beecher gives an excellent explanation for this:

"This is not a sin which one can commit by accident, and without knowing it. 'The unpardonable sin' is not a single act, but a comprehensive state of mind: that is, a sin which applies to the whole condition to which a man has brought himself by repeated perversions, and in which you may say his moral condition is broken down.

"No man ever becomes dissipated at once. No man, no matter what his experience may be, can become utterly dissipated in a week—and still less in a day or an hour. But a man can, by days, and weeks, and months, and years, become so dissipated as to have broken down his whole bodily constitution; as to have sapped and sucked dry the brain; as to have impaired every nerve; as to have over-strained every organ. Every part of a man's body may be utterly destroyed by dissipation.

"Now, there is a dissipation of the soul which corresponds to the dissipation of the body. It comes on by the perversion of a man's reason; by the perversion of his judgment in respect to things right and wrong. It is a gradually accumulating process. It is not a single act. It is the comprehensive result of a long series of various acts."

528 You Can't Do It!

An old man once said, that it took him forty years to learn three simple things. The first was that he could not do anything to save himself; the second was that God did not expect him to; and the third was, that Christ had done it all, and all he had to do was to accept the accomplished fact. When it comes to Holy-Spirit filled living and the grace of God, always keep this little saying in your hearts and minds:

You can't.
God never said you could.
He can; He always said he would!

Honesty

529 Native American Honesty

An American Indian, visiting his white neighbors, asked for a little tobacco, and one of them, having some loose tobacco in his pocket, gave him a handful. On the next day, the Native American came back, saying he had found a quarter of a dollar among the tobacco. After being told that he could keep the quarter, he replied, pointing to his breast: "I got a good man and a bad man here; and the good man say, 'It is not mine, I must return it to the owner;' the bad man say, 'Why, he gave it to you, and it is your own now.' The good man say, 'That not right, the tobacco is yours, not the money;' but the bad man say, 'Never mind, you got it, go buy some drink. The good man say, 'No, no, you must not do so;' so I don't know what to do, and I think to go to sleep; but the good man and the bad keep talking all night, and trouble me; and now I bring the money back, I feel good."

530 The Abomination of Lying

Lying is at the bottom of a whole list of vices. As long as any man is willing to face the truth and to confess it, there is hope of his recovery from sin. Always and everywhere "the truth will set you free" (John 8:32). Men loathe the liar. God's presence is not for him. The lake of fire is the liar's doom.

A twelve-year-old boy was an important witness in a lawsuit. One of the lawyers, after cross-examining him severely, said, "Your father has been telling you how to testify, hasn't he?" "Yes," said the boy. "Now," said the lawyer, "tell us how your father told you to testify." "Well," said the boy modestly, "father told me the lawyers would try to entangle me in my testimony; but if I would just be careful and tell the truth, I could tell the same thing every time."

Needless to say, right prevailed, with that boy as witness of the truth.

531 The Honest Waterman

Years ago, Thomas Mann, who was well known in London as the "honest waterman," was pledged to hold himself in readiness at an hour specified every day. The gentleman for whom he undertook to wait, and to whom he was well known, was prevented from using his boat for three weeks, at the end of which time, upon his offering to pay, agreeably to the condition, Mann replied, "No, sir, only for the first two or three days; I afterwards learned by inquiry that you would not want me, so I ceased to wait, and I will not take your money."

532 An Honest Employee

A person who dined at a restaurant in a London borough, was lamenting that he had lost, on the preceeding day, a five-pound note, of which he did not know the number. A waitress, who served the table, said she had found the note, and immediately restored it. The customer begged her (with great difficulty) to accept one pound as a reward of her honesty and candor. Does the reader possess enough of her spirit to conceive of the pleasure which this waitress felt when she returned the note?

533 A Russian Cottage Owner

The following interesting anecdote occurs in a German work, entitled, *A Picture of St. Petersburgh:*
In a little town, five miles from St. Petersburgh, lived a poor German woman. A small cottage was her only possession, and the visits of a few shipmasters, on their way to Petersburgh, her only livelihood. Several Dutch shipmasters having supped at her house one evening, she found, when they were gone, a sealed bag of money under the table. Someone of their company had no doubt forgotten it, but they had sailed over to Cronstadt, and the wind being fair, there was no chance of their going back. The woman put the bag into her cupboard, to keep it till it should be called for. A full seven years, however, elapsed and no one claimed it; and though often tempted by opportunity, and more often by want,

to make use of the contents, the poor woman's good principles prevailed, and it remained untouched.

One evening, some shipmasters again stopped at her house for refreshment. Three of them were English, the fourth a Dutchman. Conversing on various matters, one of them asked the Dutchman, if he had ever been in that town before. "Indeed I have," replied he, "I know the place all too well; my being here cost me once seven hundred rubels." "How so?" "Why in one of these wretched hotels, I once left behind me a bag of rubles." "Was the bag sealed?" asked the old woman who was seated in a corner of the room, and whose attention was aroused by the subject. "Yes, yes, it was sealed, and with this very seal here at my watch-chain." The woman knew the seal instantly. "Well, then," said she, "by that seal you may recover what you have lost." "Recover it, mother? No, no, I am much too old to expect that—the world is not quite so honest—besides, it is full seven years since I lost the money;—say no more about it, it always makes me melancholy."

Meanwhile, the woman slipped out, and soon returned with the bag. "See here," said she; "honesty is not so rare, perhaps as you imagine;" and she threw the bag on the table.

534 An Honest Jeweler

A gentleman one day conversing with a jeweler upon the dishonest practices of people in his line of business, was thus addressed by him: "Sir, I served my apprenticeship with a man who did not fear God, and who, consequently, was not very scrupulous in the charges which he made to his customers. He would frequently call me a fool, and tell me I would someday die homeless, when in his absence, I would deal with customers fair and honestly. Eventually, I started my own business, and have been so successful, I have never suffered any financial difficulty; while my unscrupulous instructor, who used to chide me for my honesty, became so helpless in his financial circumstances, that he came to me to ask for money: and eventually it was he, himself, who died homeless."

535 A Repentant Thief

As a gentleman of London entered his house, he found a well-dressed female sitting on the stairs, who asked pardon for the liberty she had taken, saying, that hearing the alarm of a mad dog, she had taken refuge in his house, and had almost fainted. On hearing her story, the gentleman gave her refreshment, then she recovered and walked off, thanking him for his civility. In the evening his wife noticed that her gold watch was missing, which she had left hanging at the head of her bed; the servants said no person had been in the room since they had made up the bed, when they were certain the watch was there. It was therefore concluded that this female was the thief.

Fifteen years afterwards, the guard of the York mail coach arrived with a small parcel, saying that a gentleman had given him five shillings to deliver it. On opening the parcel, it was found to contain the lost watch, and a note from a female, saying, that as the gospel had changed her heart, she desired to return the watch to its rightful owner.

536 A Penitent Servant.

A young woman, who was in service at a large inn in England, observed a traveler drop from his pocketbook a pound note. She picked it up, and consulted with her fellow servants, whether she should return it to the owner. They laughed at her scruples, and told her to keep it; which she agreed to. In the course of time, she was settled in the world, having married a successful businessman; and the occurrence of the theft appeared to be forgotten. But after she had been married a few years, she fell into a deep decline. In this state, she was awakened to a sense of her sins. She became, through grace, a sincere penitent; and was deeply impressed with the value of true Christianity. She sometimes felt its comforts; and found that peace of God in the mind which passes all understanding.

537 An Honest Merchant

A story is told of an English merchant known for his integrity. This businessman was considered as careful and shrewd as any businessman when it came to making bargains, but when they produced greater advantage than he expected, he returned to his friends, as a gratuity, the surplus of his honest computation. In this manner, during his mercantile career, several thousand pounds were restored. When he was asked, if he thought his friends would have treated him in the same manner, if the favor of the bargain had been on their side, his reply was—"With the conduct of others I have nothing to do. It is my duty to do. It is my duty to regulate my own [business] by the rules of equity, as they appear to me."

Hope

538 Peace in God

Some years ago there was an earthquake in California which the silver-miners who were working deep down beneath the surface knew nothing about. The tremors and agitation stopped far above them, and only when they came up from their work did they hear of what had been alarming the people above. Our life may be so "hid with Christ in God" (Col. 3:3) that we may be joyously oblivious of much that sadly troubles worldly men. We may be so sheltered in God that nothing can disturb our deep, calm peace in Him. "In me ye might have peace" (John 16:33). is no empty solace, but an assured promise of practical help.

539 Anxiety Is Not Healthy

A man planted two rose bushes on either side of his house. The bushes were equally strong and healthy, but after a time the one grew and prospered, the other withered and died. Then the man discovered that the living one was on the sunny side of the house. Live on the sunny side of the street.

540 The Saving Power of Hope

The following illustration is from George Herbert Morrison:

". . . we are often saved by hope from losing faith. Think, for instance, how often that is true of our Christian hope of personal survival. When his friend Arthur Hallam died, Tennyson was plunged into the depths. It seemed as if the foundations were destroyed and the moral universe had fallen in ruins. And then, as one may read in *In Memoriam,* morning broke with the singing of the birds through the shining Christian hope of immortality. Nothing could be more dreary than the inscriptions on old pagan tombs, but pass to the catacombs and everything is different: they are radiant with trust in God. What millions have been saved from loss of faith in the hour when the heart was desolate and empty by the burning hope of a blessed immortality. 'My soul, hope thou in God' (Ps. 42:5). His name is love, and love demands *forever.* . . . When life is desolated by the hand of death so that faith in Fatherhood is very difficult, multitudes have been upheld and comforted by the saving power of hope.

"Now, it is very beautiful to notice how our Savior utilized that saving energy. Think how often He began His treatment by kindling the flame of hope within the breast.

One might take the instance of Zacchaeus, that outcast from the commonwealth of Israel. He had been taught there was no hope for him, and he believed it till the Lord came by. And then, like the dawn, there came the quivering hope that his tomorrow might differ from his yesterday, and in that new hope the saving work began. Often hope is subsequent to faith. The Scripture order is 'faith, hope, charity' (1 Cor. 13:13). But it is equally true, in the movements of the soul, that hope may be the forerunner of faith. And our Lord, bent on evoking faith, that personal trust in Him which alone saves, began by kindling hope within the breast. That is how He often begins still. He does not *begin* by saying, 'Trust in Me.' He begins by kindling these hopes of better things that are lying crushed in every human heart. Despair is deadly. It is blind. It cannot see the arm outstretched to help. Our Lord begins with the quickening of hope."

541 *The Better Day That Is Coming*

The Christian's hope for the overthrow of war and selfishness in the earth and the coming triumph of the Christian spirit is beautifully set forth by the English poet, Lewis Morris:

There shall come out of this noise
  of strife and groaning
A broader and a juster brotherhood,
A deep equality of aim, postponing
All selfish seeking to the general
  good.

There shall come a time when
  each shall to another
Be as Christ would have him—
  brother unto brother.

542 *The Great Anchor*

The body of a suicide victim, whose story is infinitely pathetic, was taken out of the North River in New York. The dead man was a graphic artist, musician, and linguist. He was fifty-seven years old at the time of his death. After he had graduated from a German university he went to Puerto Rico to seek wealth. Fortune smiled on him, and he sent home flowing accounts of the great printing business he was conducting. At the height of his prosperity he fell in love with a beautiful woman who soon became his wife. His marriage was a happy one, but only eight years afterward, she died. With her death his power to work and plan seemed to cease. From that moment fortune seemed to desert him. He lost his zest in his work and finally failed in business. Two years later he came to New York and was advised by a friend to teach languages, for he spoke German, English, French, Spanish, and Italian, with great fluency; but he lacked that appetite for life and nerve of purpose that make men succeed. Finally, without money and without heart, he filled his pockets full of stones and leaped overboard into the North River. The thing he lacked above everything else was the great anchor of faith and hope in Christ. His heart was anchored in his love for his wife, and when that cable parted he drifted. If his soul had been buoyed and held steady by a sublime faith in Christ and the immortal life, he could have gone on, with a chastened heart, but with a serene and dauntless spirit.

543 My Father's Will

(Matt. 19:29) A devout old man was one day walking to the sanctuary with a New Testament in his hand, when a friend met him, and said, "Good morning, Mr. Price." "Good morning," replied he; "I am reading my Father's will as I walk along." "Well, and what has he left you?" said his friend. "Why, He has bequeathed to me a hundredfold more in this life, and in the world to come—life everlasting!" This beautiful reply was the means of comforting his Christian friend, who was at that time in sorrowful circumstances.

544 An Inquirer

A gentleman in the inquiry room rose from the side of a man to whom he had long been speaking, and begged of one well advanced in years to take his place, saying that he could not get the inquirer to see salvation. As requested, the aged man took his seat. "What is wrong?" he said. "Wrong! *Everything* is wrong. My soul is lost, and I have only found it out now." "Are there no people known to you whom you can believe, whatever they say to you?" "Yes," said the sorrowful one. "Just as you believe them, will you now believe in God? God says

in his word, 'Come unto Me, all ye that labor and are heavy laden, and I will give you rest.'"(Matt. 11:28). "I wish to see it for myself," said the man. His aged guide was taking out his glasses to read the words, but this would not do. "Give me the book so I can read it for myself." With his finger fixed on the spot, he read them over and over and over again. "God, I take you at Your word," he cried. Before they parted, his friend asked him, "How is it now?" "My burden is gone," he said.

545 A Word Spoken in Haste

A young traveler was going around the countryside in search of peace in his life. As he entered the depot a porter taking his luggage, said, "Where are you going?" He answered: "To hell; away with you." A minister overheard the answer and was startled. Seated near the young man in the train carriage; he entered into a conversation with him, and at length said, "When do you expect to arrive at your journey's end!" He answered that he did not know, as it was beyond the sea. The minister said, "I meant the place you told the porter you were going, upon entering the carriage." The young man answered, "Perhaps it may be so."

So many in this world have no hope for eternity and their answers to life's questions are often filled with confusion and uncertainty. For the believer, however, Christ is their hope and has all the answers (1 Tim. 1:1).

546 *The Visitor's Secret*

"The riches of the glory of this mystery . . . which is Christ in you, the hope of glory" (Col. 1:27).

The only son of a widow runs off to sea when quite a lad. She must needs work for her living, and takes lodgers in her little home. After years have passed, a bronzed and bearded sailor comes to her door for accommodation, which she gladly affords at an agreed price. She has no idea who has come to dwell beneath her roof—it is a secret, a mystery.

By-and-by, one day as they are sitting at the midday meal, a remark, a gesture, startles her; she looks hard into the stranger's face, recognizes him, and, with a cry, rushes into his arms and weeps out on his bosom her joy: "My son, my son, what deceived my old eyes, that I didn't know thee!" That is the glory of the mystery, which breaks in smiles and kisses.

Then he says, "Mother, how hard life has gone with you; your hands are hard with toil. But see, I have plenty of money, and you shall go shares in all. I will take a nice little home, and you shall live there, to keep it as long as you live, and never have to do a stroke of hard toil." That is the riches of the glory of the mystery.

So at your conversion Jesus came into your heart to abide. Too long He has been unrecognized; but of late you have been made aware of the nature and worth of your heavenly Friend. The mystery has broken in light. Henceforth, realize that all his riches are yours, to be shared and enjoyed; that all your needs may be fully met, even to the abundance of His unsearchable riches; and that there may be an end for ever to all the weary sense of inability and incompetence to meet the inevitable demands of daily living. Christ is in you; let His life within reach out its hands to the life of glory above.

—F. B. Meyer

547 *The End of the Day*

"At Evening Time it Shall be Light" (Zech. 14:7)
When the crimson sky at the setting sun
Proclaim to the world that thy work is done,
May you walk serenely through the twilight gray,
Go Home and rest at the end of the day.

548 *"What Comes After Death?"*

I remember a pioneer officer of the law in New Mexico in wild frontier times. He had risked his life again and again. He had gone out to track down and arrest and bring in many a murderer, many an outlaw. And this is what he said to a preacher, "I am not afraid to die! You know I am not afraid to die. I have risked my life many and many a time. and I am not afraid to die—but O God, what comes after death? That is what frightens me—this is what I am afraid of.

549 *"Your Boy Is Alive!"*

At the death of his son Willie, Lincoln was convulsed in sorrow. In an effort to console him, Dr. Francis Vinton said, "Your boy is alive in heaven!" "Alive! Surely you mock me!" "No," said the minister. "It is accepted by many as a most comforting doctrine of the church and founded upon the words of Christ Himself." For a moment the President repeated incredulously, "Alive! Alive!" Then his sorrow abated.

Globe-girdling joy will come when the following prophecies are fulfilled and death is vanquished: "He will swallow up death in victory; and the Lord God will wipe away tears from off all faces" (Is. 25:8). The "sorrow and sighing shall flee away" (35:10).

Humility

550 *The Humility of Christ*

Spurgeon says: "Never was there a poorer man than Christ; he was the prince of poverty. He was the reverse of Croessus—*he* might be on the top of the hill of riches, *Christ* stood in the lowest vale of poverty. Look at his dress, it is woven from the top throughout, the garment of the poor! As for his food, he oftentimes did hunger; and always was dependent upon the charity of others for the relief of his wants! He who scattered the harvest o'er the broad acres of the world, had not sometimes wherewithal to stay the pangs of hunger? He who digged the springs of the ocean, sat upon a well and said to a Samaritan woman, 'Give me to drink' (John 4:7). He rode in no chariot, he walked in his weary way, foot sore, o'er the flints of Galilee! He had not where to lay his head. He looked upon the fox as it hurried to its resting-place, and he said, 'Foxes have holes, and the birds of the air have nests; but I, the Son of man, have not where to lay my head.' He who had once been waited on by angels, becomes the servant of servants, takes a towel, girds himself, and washes his disciples' feet! He who was once honored with the hallelujahs of ages, is now spit upon and despised! He who was loved by his Father, and had abundance of wealth of affection, could say, 'He that eateth bread with me hath lifted up his heel against me' (John 13:18). Oh, for words to picture the humility of Christ."

551 *A Noble Reverence*

In the House at Bonn occupied by Beethoven there still is preserved the piano upon which the great master played, and which he used in the composition of his great music. Years ago, an American girl visited the shrine. She waltzed airily to the instrument and began playing a careless tune; and then, turning to the custodian, said, "I suppose you have many visitors here every year?" "A great many," was the reply. "Many famous people, no doubt?" said she. "Yes, Paderewski came recently." "I suppose, of course, he played on the piano?" said the girl, her fingers still thrumming the keys. "No," said the custodian, "he *did not consider himself worthy.*"

This is the reverence of the great in soul. The flippant enter the hallowed places, the sanctuaries of the world, with light laughter and careless jest; they feel nothing in their shallow souls, and reduce everything to the flippant and commonplace; but the high-souled enter with bared heads, they take the shoes off their feet, they stand awed and in silence. *"They do not consider themselves worthy."*

552 Elisha's Humility and Ambition

The friendship between Elijah and Elisha is a beautiful story of a strong love growing up between an old man and a young one. Elijah was no doubt often the guest in the home of Elisha's father, who was a rich farmer. One day Elijah came through the field, past where Elisha was plowing, and, throwing his mantle over the boy's shoulders, walked away as fast as he could. Elisha knew very well what that meant. It was the call of God to be a prophet. He settled up his affairs at once and went forth with Elijah. As Elijah's transition drew near, Elisha begged that the mantle of the man of God might fall upon him. He had such reverence and love for Elijah that; he longed to be like him, and to be able to go on doing his work when he should lay it down. The humility as well as the elevation of a noble soul is revealed in this longing to carry on the work of the Lord in the spirit of his friend.

553 The Humility of Greatness

Humility belongs to true greatness. Science wins its way by humbly sitting at the feet of nature. Man becomes great by opening mind and heart with the simplicity of a child to win knowledge from all quarters.

Sir Arthur Sullivan has said of Charles Dickens that he was a most delightful companion. "Apart from his high spirits and engaging manner," the musician adds, "one might have two special reasons for this. On the one hand he was so unassuming he never obtruded his own work upon you." It is said that the great novelist would revel in enjoyment with younger men, and one would never have known from his conversation that he was an author; that is, he never discussed himself with his associates, but he gave himself up with the most natural sincerity of interest to the conversation of younger men. He would treat their feeblest trivialities as if they were the wittiest remarks, or the ripe meditations of a matured judgment.

554 The Highest Lesson

Andrew Murray wrote the following anecdote on humility: "The highest lesson a believer has to learn is humility. Oh, that every Christian who seeks to advance in holiness may remember this well! There may be intense consecration and fervent zeal and heavenly experience, and yet, if it is not prevented by dealings of the Lord, there may be an unconscious self-exaltation with it all. Let us not learn the lesson—the highest holiness is the deepest humility; and let us remember that it comes not of itself, but only as it is made a matter of special dealing on the part of our faithful Lord and his faithful servant."

555 No Shouting for Him

Johana Omari says: "I want to be like the little donkey our Lord chose to ride on to enter Jerusalem. They laid their robes on it and shouted, but the shouting was all for the Lord Jesus whom he was carrying. As believers, we often praise the method or the messenger of Christ, when all the world needs to see is Christ" (Eph. 1:6, 7, 12).

556 A Wife's Humility

"Blessed are the meek: for they shall inherit the earth" (Matt. 5:5).

A drunkard husband spending the evening with his jovial companions at a tavern boasted that if he should take a group of his friends home with him at midnight and ask his Christian wife to get up and cook supper for them, she would do it without complaint. The crowd considered it a vain boast and dared him to try it by a considerable wager. So the drunken crowd went home with him and he made the unreasonable demands of his wife. She obeyed, dressed, came down, and prepared a very nice supper just as quickly as possible and served it as cheerfully as if she had been expecting them.

After supper one of the men, a little more sober than the others, asked her how she could be so kind when they had been so unreasonable, and, also when they knew she did not approve of their conduct. Her reply was, "Sir, when my husband and I were married, we were both sinners. It has pleased God to call me out of that

dangerous condition. My husband remains in it. I tremble for his future state. Were he to die as he is, he will be miserable forever; I think it my duty to render his present existence as comfortable as possible." This wise and faithful reply affected the whole company. The husband thanked her for the warning, and became a serious Christian and a good husband.

557 The Will of the Father

Take a minute and examine the importance of Christ's birth and His life on this earth. Consider what splendor He left in heaven with the Father. To live among sinful men in a sinful world, yet as a sinless man He carried out God's plan. Because Jesus was God, He was humbly willing to fulfill the will God had established (Phil. 2:5-10). Christ's focus was clear on this earth although man could not understand. His disciples questioned His direction, the Pharisees and religious leaders of the day questioned His authority, and those who followed Him around the countryside failed to understand His motives. With all this adversity and misunderstanding that Christ experienced, He remained faithful to God's will.

How little it is that can begin to distract and deter us from God's purpose in our lives. Even in his birth, Christ was in accordance with God's plan though Herod would have had Him killed. Reliance on God should be our aim of all times. To do this we must be as Christ—renouncing our flesh and pride and man's concerns and cling to God (1 Pet. 5:6-9).

558 Why Did Jesus Take upon Himself Human Nature?

A little girl dressed in dungarees walked into a pet shop and asked whether they had a puppy with a lame leg. She had a dollar with which she wanted to buy it. The salesperson of the pet shop was surprised that the little girl wanted to buy a lame puppy. She asked, "Why, don't you want to buy a puppy that can run around and play?" "No, I want a lame one." Finally, she pulled up one leg of her dungarees and showed her brace, saying, "I don't walk so good either." The little girl with a lame leg identified herself with a lame puppy.

The Lord Jesus became a man, taking upon Himself a human body with its frailties in order to identify Himself with us in our bodily weaknesses (Heb. 4:15).

559 Reaching the Summit by Way of the Valley

The Christian is to find exaltation by humility. Christ advised his hearers, when they went to a great dinner, not to go early and get into the best places, but to go in modestly and take a humble seat; and then if it was proper for them to have the higher place, the host would honor them by public invitation to the better seat. It is by being, and not by seeming to be, that one really comes to be exalted. Christ emptied himself of all reputation, laid aside his glory and his riches, and came to the earth to be born among the lowly in the manger of an inn stable; but it was the way toward exaltation, for Paul says: "God also hath highly exalted him, and given him a name which is above every name: that at the name of Jesus every knee should bow, of things in heaven and things in earth, and things under the earth; and that every tongue should confess that Jesus Christ is Lord, to the glory of God the Father" (Phil. 2:9-11). We, too, shall come to our highest through sacrificing ourselves in humility for the blessing of others.

560 The Lowest Friendship

In Eastern lands the story is told of the great Shah Abbas, who delighted in mingling in disguise with the common folk of his realm. Once, dressed in wretched rags, he descended to the lowest level of the palace, where one of his humblest servants sat tending the furnace. Each enjoyed the other's company, and by and by the furnace tender shared his lunch of black bread and water with his companion. This led to many another visit, and a deepening friendship, though the servant had no idea of his new friend's identity.

At last, the shah revealed his identity, and waited, ready to grant whatever petition the servant might make. But the other sat silent, gazing on him with love and wonder. "Haven't you understood?" asked the shah. "I can make you rich and noble. I can give you a city. I can appoint you as a great ruler. Have you nothing to ask?"

"Yes, my lord, I understood," the furnace tender replied. "But what is this you have done, to leave your glorious surroundings, to sit with me in this dark place, to partake of my coarse fare, and to care whether my heart is glad or sorry? Even you can give nothing more precious. On others you may bestow rich presents, but to me you have given yourself; it only remains to ask that you never withdraw this gift of your friendship" (Mark 10:45; Gal. 2:20; Eph. 5:2, 25).

Hypocrisy

561 Contradictory Testimony

If you do not recommend Christ by your life, you need not expect that your words will carry conviction with them. A young female voice student was very enthusiastic over her music professor, and went about among her friends telling them what a good teacher he was and advising them to sign up for his voice classes. That would have been all very well but for the fact that the young woman's musical performances were atrocious. They spoke of just the opposite to efficient teaching. It may have been that her teacher was not responsible for her mannerisms, but because of them his reputation certainly suffered.

562 The Cost of a Good Reputation

A young man, who had been active in Christian work, went to a distant city to take a position. Some time afterward a friend, calling on him, mentioned his former work in the presence of some of his new acquaintances. The young man looked annoyed, and when he and his friend were alone, he said: "I didn't intend that these people should know about my church work."

"I am sure your record wasn't one to be ashamed of," his friend rejoined.

"Oh, no," was the answer, "but I did not want them to expect so much of me." The fact was that he had made up his mind to lower the standard of his Christian living, and did not want those with whom he associated to expect anything better of him.

There is a warning in the incident. While it costs something to win a good reputation, it also costs something to hold fast to it. If there ever comes a time when you feel that you would prefer that those around you do not know that you profess to be a Christian, you need to question yourself closely as to the reason. Peter, who denied his Lord, first sought to have it appear that he belonged, not to the disciples, but to the crowd.

563 What Is Your Business?

"What is your business?" or, "What are you driving at?" is the question that shapes everything about our lives. It forms our habits, chooses our friends, and determines the road we will take. If you meet a man with his fishing-rod on his shoulder, you do not need to ask him what he is seeking. You do not wonder if he is not going out to pick grapes. I believe that each one of us carries about us that which proclaims the object that we have in view. A man who goes into the mines dressed like a miner, and with a pick on his shoulder, may say that he is merely going to look at the scenery, but nobody will believe him. So, if we are dressed in the garments of the world and persist in hanging about its quarters, the fact that we call ourselves Christians is not going to carry much weight with it.

564 The Real Thing

Have you noticed the new design of the $100 bill? The Treasury Department tells us that counterfeit bills have become such a problem, a completely new design was necessary to combat the copycats. The new bill looks so much different from the old, it can easily be mistaken for "play-money," however it contains a high-tech watermark, and other features that should prove difficult to duplicate. Counterfeit dollars have always been in circulation in this country; yet, no one has ever refused real money just because counterfeit money is abroad. Nothing can be more foolish than the excuse which some people give for not becoming Christians. They say

that so many professors of Christianity are hypocrites that therefore they will stay out altogether. While there is now and then a counterfeit life, it remains true that the life of Jesus is ever the same divine and holy career, and for every counterfeit Christian there are many whose lives ring out true every time. Men would not counterfeit $100 bills if real bills of that denomination were not abundant and valuable; so men would not counterfeit Christianity if it were not so precious a thing.

565 Some Other Way

Years ago, some scoundrels in Philadelphia were trying to get rich by furnishing foreigners with a shortcut to citizenship. It has been shown that fraudulent naturalization papers were sold to newly-arrived citizens at $17 a head. Sad as it is to have our citizenship corrupted in that way, it is sadder yet to have people come into the church, and cause others to believe that they are truly Christians, when they have had no genuine change of purpose or transformation of spirit. Christ says whoever climbs up some other way is a thief and a robber (John 10:1). Christ only is the true door; through him we may go in and out and find pasture.

Judgment

566 Sin's Awakening

There is a well-known picture by the artist Rude entitled *C'est l'Empereur!* It represents the grey dawn of the early morning with opposing armies near. A sentinel has been placed on the outskirts, and upon his watchfulness the safety of the sleeping army depends. But, faithless and careless, he has allowed himself to fall asleep. Napoleon passing along, sleeplessly vigilant, discovers him, and taking his musket stands sentinel through the night. In the dawn the sleeper awakes, and to his horror beholds the Emperor on guard. The nature of the awakening is forcibly expressed, one can almost hear the hoarse whisper in the soldier's throat. There is always the awakening to be reckoned with when conscience is lulled to sleep. The gray dawn comes, and the hour of reckoning (Mark 13:35–37).

567 What We Deserve

What would an employer think of one of the men in his service if he would assume the same attitude concerning his work that we do about our professed service of the Lord? Can you imagine a bookkeeper saying that he thinks his employer ought to show him special favors because he has been at his post every day for a week? We say, certainly not; that is simply a part of what he agreed to do when he took the position. Indeed, he could not expect to keep the position if he failed to do these things. Not long ago a man said that he had served the Lord faithfully for three years, but he found that he did not get anything for it. His neighbor, who made no pretensions at being a Christian, had better luck in business and had prospered generally more than he had. It was said that his "service" had consisted in going to church when everything was favorable. Well, it also has been said, that if the Lord saw enough in his Christianity to entitle him to the hope and privileges of a Christian, he ought to have been humbly thankful, instead of asking for a premium.

568 According to Our Own Doing

"I don't believe that God would create a soul and bring it down to everlasting hell in the end," someone says. No, my friend, He never did. Look at the man who has just died from alcoholism or a drug overdose. Does it seem strange to you that God would create a physical body and then wreck it like that? "But God did not do it," you say. "The man defied the laws by which he might have preserved his life." So it is with the man who chooses the destiny of the wicked.

On one particular night a man leaped from a large Cincinnati bridge over the Ohio River, and was drowned. One of his friends heard of his intention, and begged him to stay at home; another caught him and tried to hold him as he mounted the bridge. A policeman even plunged into the water and gave his life trying to keep the man from drowning. The man's determination baffled all of them. Let me tell you that the sinner who goes down to everlasting death does so in spite of all that God and man could do to keep him from it. He has rejected the pleadings and warnings of his friends, and even pushed aside the outstretched hand of the Christ who died to save him. "He that pursueth evil, pursueth it to his own death" (Prov. 11:19).

569 The Double Judgment

In the English Law Courts there are two broad divisions, the Civil and Criminal. In the Criminal Court, the man is tried, and he has to be declared innocent or guilty. In the Civil, cases are tried, not people; whether a deed was just or unjust. So is God's two-fold judgment by-and-by. The unbeliever, like the criminal, will be on trial in person, and will hear his guilt and doom pronounced by the Judge. The believer, accepted in Christ, will never come into judgment, but is passed from death unto life; nothing shall be laid to his charge. But his works shall be tried, with a view to his reward, and whether gold, silver, precious stone, or wood, hay, and stubble.

570 Human Judgment

The female English novelist who wrote by the pseudonym George Eliot once said: "The touchstone by which men try us is most often their own vanity."

571 Judgment of Journalists

The next time you hear politically-conservative commentators talk of a "liberal bias" among members of the news media, remember what Thomas Carlyle said of the media over one hundred years ago: "Journalists are now the true kings and clergy."

572 Mistaken Judgment

"You find it hard to give a man credit for being possessed of sense and talent, if you hear him make a speech at a public dinner, which approaches the idiotic for its silliness and confusion. And the vulgar mind readily concludes that he who does one thing extremely ill, does nothing well. But the man who fails in one thing is by no means a fool in all: in his own realm he may be a genius and a success."

573 Startling Judgment

"About a quarter of a century ago," says Dr. A. T. Pierson, "an infidel got up on one of the heights of the Catskill Mountains, and in the presence of some athiestic companions defied the God of heaven to show Himself in battle. He swung his sword to and fro, and challenged the Almighty to meet him in single combat. The Almighty paid no attention to him, of course, but He just commissioned a little gnat, so small that it could scarcely be seen by a microscope, to lodge in his windpipe and choke him to death."

574 Trying to Escape Judgment

In a Polish Jew's burying place there are a number of stones having no names or other inscriptions upon them. The idea is that at the last day the angel of eternal life will call the sleepers reading the names upon the stones, the good to inherit bliss, the wicked to suffer. If the stone is however without a name, the sleeper may be passed over.

575 Ordained from the Foundations of the World

According to Carlyle: "Justice was ordained from the foundations of the world, and will last with the world and longer. For Justice and Reverence are the everlasting central laws of this universe against one, God and one's self for enemies and only the Devil and Dragon for friends, is not that lameness like few?"

576 Heaven's Justice

The following lines of poetry are by Shakespeare:

May one be pardoned, and retain the offence?

In the corrupted currents of the world,
Offence's gilded hand may shove by justice:
And oft 'tis seen the wicked prize itself
Buys out the law: but 'tis not so above:
There is no shuffling: there the action lies
In his true nature."

577 Imperfect Justice

"Before the awful throne of Zeus," said Hesiod, "*Dikē* [right, justice] stands and weeps whenever the earthly judge decides wrongly." "No wonder then," adds a caustic critic, remembering some of the judgments of rural magistrates, "that our modern sculptors represent Justice on town halls with a bandage on her eyes; she has seen so much injustice, she has gone weeping blind!"

578 No Substitute for Justice

Speaking on the question of International Copyright Laws, the poet James Russell Lowell said: "To steal a book I have bought is theft; to steal a book I have made—what is that? There is one thing better than a cheap book; that is a book honestly come by." And then he added this memorable golden sentence: "No successful substitute for justice has ever been discovered—nothing with the lasting quality of justice."

579 Unswerving Justice

A band of conspirators against the Roman State were brought before Brutus, and among them to his dismay were found two of his own sons. With the unswerving justice of a Roman he condemned them to death with the others, and they were executed before his eyes.

580 God's Judgments

God's judgments (Ps. 36:6.):

Are often unfathomable. We cannot discover the foundation, cause or spring.

Are safe sailing. Ships never strike on rocks in the great deeps.

Conceal great treasure, and work great good. Great deep, not a salty and barren wilderness, is one of the greatest blessings to the world.

Become a highway of communion with God.

581 Unseen Evidence

A very interesting telephone case was decided in Sweden. A business man in Stockholm, Mr. Kugelman, had entered into a business arrangement with a certain banker, the affair having been arranged during a telephone conversation. As the business did not pay the profit Mr. Kugelman expected, he absolutely refused to come to a settlement and was consequently sued by the banker. When the case appeared in court the dealer insisted that the bank had no written security from him, and no witnesses to prove the transaction took place. It was, however, shown to the intense amusement of both court and spectators, that the telephone at the bank was provided with two receivers, and everything transpiring through the

telephone could therefore be heard and legally proven. The dealer lost his case.

The universe of God is a whispering gallery where nothing is lost out of being. Unseen evidence is kept of all the deeds of human life. After a while the books are to be opened.

582 Too Late!

"And the door was shut" (Matt. 25:10).

In an ancient Catholic church there is a curious picture carved in wood. It represents an altar with a communion rail in front. On one side there is a pilgrim with his staff, who, evidently had been rushing on to get there in time, but he was too late; the gate was shut, and the priest had gone home. On the other side is an image of the devil, sitting comfortably on a chair, and in the act of saying to the pilgrim, "Too late! Too late!" and appears as if he enjoyed saying, "Too late!"

583 Everlasting Punishment

A venerable minister once preached a sermon on the last judgment. On the next day some thoughtless men agreed that one of their number should go to him, and, if possible, draw him into a discussion. He went accordingly, and began the conversation, saying, "I believe there is a small dispute between you and me, and I thought that I would call this morning and try to settle it." "Ah!" said the good man, "what is it?" "Why," he replied, "you say that the punishment of the impenitent will be eternal, and I do not think it will." "Oh, if that is all," he answered, "there is no dispute between you and me. If you turn to Matthew 25:46, you will find that the dispute is between you and the Lord Jesus Christ, and I would advise you to go immediately and settle it with Him."

Kindness

584 Linked Together

A few years ago at the Seattle Special Olympics, nine contestants, all physically or mentally disabled, assembled at the starting line for the 100-yard dash. At the gun, they all started out, not exactly in a dash, but with a relish to run the race to the finish and win.

All, that is, except one boy who stumbled on the asphalt, tumbled over a couple of times and began to cry. The other eight heard the boy cry. They slowed down and looked back. Then they all turned around and went back. Every one of them. One girl with Down's syndrome bent down and kissed him and said, "This will make it better." Then all nine linked arms and walked together to the finish line. Everyone in the stadium stood, and the cheering went on for several minutes. People who were there are still telling the story. Why?

Because deep down we know this one thing: What matters in this life is more than winning for ourselves. What truly matters in this life is helping others win, even if it means slowing down and changing our course.

Paul wrote: "Brethren, If a man be overtaken in a fault, ye which are spiritual, restore such an one in the spirit of meekness; considering thyself, lest thou also be tempted. Bear ye one anothers burden's, and so fulfill the law of Christ" (Gal. 6:1,2).

585 Strength and Gentleness

In the Ninety-first Psalm there is something splendid in the way the singer mingles his thought of God's majesty and power and strength to defend and protect those who trust him with the other thought of the graciousness and gentleness of the Divine love. One moment his thought is on the fortress with its great stone walls, and sentinels standing at every corner, and soldiers with bow and arrow, or huge stone or javelin, with which to face all comers. Listen and see the fort rise before your eyes: "I will say of the Lord, he is my refuge, and my fortress: my God; in him will I trust. Surely he shall deliver thee from the snare of the fowler" (Ps. 91:2, 3). And then, quick as thought, the psalmist turns from the majesty and power of God and thinks of his gentleness of heart, thinks of the caress of the Spirit, softer than a mother's kiss, and he bursts forth in thankful praise and confidence: "He shall cover thee with his feathers, and under his wings shalt thou trust" (v. 4). In our thought God's power and his gentleness ought always to go together.

In our own lives, too, gentleness should always keep pace with strength.

586 The Hospitality of the Poor

It has been said that the greatest hospitality and helpfulness shown in our cities come from the poor, who divide their insufficient means and share it with someone else who is poorer than they. The hospitable soul is brought into close touch with the God who declares that it is more blessed to give than to receive. The poor widow woman in Zarephath made a good investment when she divided her last handful of meal and oil with Elijah. The meal-barrel and oil-cruse became temples of the Lord, and they were not wasted, but abounded in comfort for many a long day. It will be a neighborly world when that spirit possesses all hearts. The first great practical influence which Christianity has among men is to make them good neighbors.

587 Christ's Reward for Kindness

A kindhearted merchant bought a cottage and a piece of wasteland for a garden, which he gave in life-rent to an elderly and poor man whom he respected for his Christian worth. The whole property cost about a hundred pounds. He thought of nothing but kindness, and hoped for nothing to gain. Fifteen years passed and two things occurred: the merchant was reduced to poverty and the old man died. The cottage and ground returned to their original owner. But its value had in the interval multiplied by ten: so he who had given away a hundred received back a thousand. It may serve as a parable of what is the reward given yonder to little deeds of service performed here. Not in this life, but in the life to come is the promise given, that even a cup of water given in the name of a disciple shall not lose its reward.

588 Be Kind to the Elderly

When Queen Victoria first came to the throne many of the court officials came to wish her well. Among the number was an old man who was a little lame, and in his excitement he partly stumbled up the steps. The queen sprang forward and helped him; she forgot for a moment that she was Queen, and only thought how youth might help old age. Prove yourself always ready to do a service for the old and infirm.

589 How to Conquer an Enemy

In 1736, Benjamin Franklin was chosen clerk of the General Assembly of Pennsylvania—his first promotion, as he calls it in his narrative. The choice for the position was to be voted on by the public annually, and the year following a new member made a long speech against his re-election. We copy what Franklin relates on this occasion, because it is every way characteristic:

"As the place was highly desirable for me on many accounts,

I did not like the opposition of this new member, who was a gentleman of fortune and education, with talents that were likely to give him in time great influence in the House, which indeed afterwards happened. I did not, however, aim at gaining his favor by paying any servile respect to him, but after some time took this other method. Having heard that he had in his library a certain very scarce and curious book, I wrote a note to him expressing my desire of perusing that book, and requesting that he would do me the favor of lending it to me for a few days. He sent it immediately, and I returned it in about a week with another note, strongly expressing my sense of the favor. When we next met in the House, he spoke to me—which he had never done before—and with great civility; and he ever after manifested a readiness to serve me on all occasions, so that we became great friends, and our friendship continued to his death. This is another instance of the truth of an old maxim I had learned, which says, 'He that has once done you a kindness will be more ready to do you another than he whom you yourself have obliged.' "

Franklin shows us how much more profitable it is prudently to remove, than to resent, return, and continue adverse proceedings.

590 Command of Temper

The Duke of Marlborough possessed great command of temper, and never permitted it to be ruf-fled by little things, in which even the greatest men have been occasionally found unguarded. As he was riding one day with Commissary Marriott, it began to rain, and he called to his servant for his cloak. The servant, being embarrassed with the straps and buckles, did not come up to him. At last, it raining very hard, the Duke called to him again, and asked him why he did not bring his cloak. "You must stay, sir," grumbled the fellow, "if it rains cats and dogs, till I can get at it." The Duke turned around to Marriott, and said very coolly, "Now I would not be of that fellow's temper for all the world."

591 The Story of the Stones

There was a man who went to hear George Whitfield preach, and he went with his pocket crammed with stones. As Whitfield preached, he first took out one stone, and threw it behind him; and then another stone, and threw that down; until at last there was not a stone left except the one in his own breast— his heart, and even that was loosening and softening. And presently that stone changed too, and became a fountain of waters, giving glory to God in tears of sorrow, instead of remaining a hard stone of resistance. Now it may be that, if under the pretense of throwing stones at King David, we are really angry with the Bible, and want to throw stones against the Lord God Himself—it may be that we shall empty our pockets, and throw this stone down—this objection down, and that criticism down, and the other objection down—and presently there be nothing left but our heart, and that not so stony as it was, because it has been growing softer and softer with every foolish and perverse quibble thrown aside. Our own heart is changing. And if the first action of the new heart be to make itself like a fountain of sunny and invigorating waters; and it is well even to have to weep a little, if by-and-by, through the softness that you have thus experienced, you obtain joyful drafts of refreshing water out of the ever-flowing fountain of eternal life, that is now not far off, but within your own penitent and happy breast.

592 Power of Tenderness

A circumstance is mentioned by the naturalist Audubon, as occurring within his knowledge, of a certain individual who for many years had led the life of a pirate. On one occasion, while cruising along the coast of Florida, he landed, and was lying in the shade on the bank of a creek, when his attention was arrested by the soft and mournful note of a Zenaida dove. As he listened, each repetition of the melancholy sound seemed to him a voice of pity; it seemed to him like a voice from the past, a message from childhood's innocent and sunny hours; then it appeared like a voice of deep, sad sorrow for him, the far-off-wanderer, the self-ruined, guilty prodigal; and so thoroughly did it rouse him from his long sleep of sin, that there, on that lonely spot,

where no minister of mercy had ever stood, he resolved within himself to renounce his guilty life, return to virtuous society, and see the mercy of God—a resolution which he subsequently fulfilled, as we are assured by the narrator. There is that in the human heart which responds to the voice of gentle, pitying love, when all other agencies have lost their power; when all the thunder and lightning of Sinai itself might roll and glitter in vain. Would that there were more, among those disposed to do good, who would make full proof of the omnipotence of the spirit of kindness, pity, and love. The Spirit of Jesus must be the model of our benevolence.

593 A Soft Answer

When Sir Matthew Hale dismissed a jury because he was convinced that it had been illegally chosen to favor the defense attorney, the latter was highly displeased with him; and when Sir Matthew returned from the circuit, Cromwell told him in anger that he was not fit to be a judge; to which, all the answer he made was, "That it was very true."

594 Ecclesiastical Quarrels

A gentleman who was in the company with the late Mr. John Newton, of London, lamented the violent disputes that often took place among Christians respecting the non-essentials of Christianity, and particularly church government. "Many," he said, "seem to give their chief attention to such topics, and take more pleasure in talking on these disputable points than on spiritual religion, the love of Christ, and the privileges of His people." "Sir," said the venerable old man, "did you ever see a whale-ship? I am told that when the fish is struck with the harpoon, and feels the smart of the wound, it sometimes makes for the boat, and would probably dash it to pieces. To prevent this, they throw a cask overboard; and when it is staved to pieces, they throw over another. Now, sir, church government is the tub which Satan has thrown over to the people of whom you speak."

Love

595 Miscellaneous Quotes on Charity

"Charity is the scope of all God's commands."—Chrysostom

Erasmus said that "Charity resembleth fire, which inflameth all things it toucheth."

"It is not charity to let others have what we cannot keep."—Beecher

"Where Charity is, there doth God reside. Possess charity, and you will see Him in your own heart, seated as on His throne."—Augustine

596 Our Fellow Man

It is written of Plato that, when he did give to a poor depraved wretch, his friends very much admired that Plato, the great divine philosopher, should take pity on such a wretched scoundrel; but he, like himself, in such indistinct days as those were, made answer, "I show mercy to the man, not because he is wicked, but because he is a man of my own nature." "His answer," says Salter, "was warrantable; for, if we consider our first parents, we shall find ourselves bound by the same obligation to do good unto all men. There is neither Jew nor Greek, bond nor free, neither male nor female, in Christ Jesus." (Gal. 3:28).

597 Neglect of Brotherly Love

If you neglect to love your neighbor, in vain you profess your love for God; for by your love for God the love for your neighbor is produced, and by loving your neighbor your love for God is nourished.

598 Mutual Help

Sir Walter Scott says: "The race of mankind would perish did they cease to aid each other. From the time that the mother binds the child's head till the moment that some kind assistant wipes the death camp from the brow of the dying, we cannot exist without mutual help. All therefore that need aid have a right to ask it from their fellow mortals. No one who holds the power of granting can refuse it without guilt."

599 The Test of Brotherly Love

"Be merry with them that be merry, weep with them that weep" (Rom. 12:15). He who does not have this fellow-feeling may suspect worthily that he is not a lively member of Christ; for His body is coupled and knit together throughout every joint wherewith one ministers to another. If, therefore, we do not bear one another's burden and feel one another's misery, we are not knit together by the sinews of love; and if not knit to the body, no part of the body.

600 Brotherly Love a Measure of Love to Christ

Our love to our brethren, is, as respects ourselves and our posterity, not only the evidence, but the measure of our love to Christ. He who does not have enough love in him for a man like himself, how can he love God, whose goodness, being above our knowledge, requires a transcendency in our love? This is a sure rule, he that loves not a member of Christ loves not Christ; and he who grows in his love to his brethren grows likewise in his love to Christ.

601 Brotherhood of Man

You recognize in every nation, in every tribe, your fellow-men, your brethren. Go to Egypt, and stand among the sphinxes, the pyramids, the old and wondrous temples, and you are a stranger in a strange land, and it seems scarcely less than a ghastly dream. Go farther East; behold the ruined architecture, revive the manners and customs of the Syrian and Babylonian empires, and you seem still among a strange people. If they should rise and speak to you, their tongues would be as strange to you as yours would be to them. But let a maiden speak her love, and instantly you know that voice. The works that their hands wrought are wondrous. The affections that throb in their heart are familiar. The things that they live for

outwardly—see how widely you are separated from these! How different are their laws, their institutions, and their methods of commerce from ours! How strange to us are their political economy and their ecclesiastical system! Touch that which man fashioned and formed, and man is disjointed, and split apart by rivers, and mountains, and times, and ages; but touch the human heart, and let that speak, and all men rise up and say, "That voice is my voice." Reach but the feeling of love, and every human being says, "It is my brother; it is my sister." Strike those cords that bring out the experience of grief, and every man wails with the hoary wailers of antiquity. Man is not a unit by virtue of the fruits of his intellect and the works of his hand, but by virtue of those eternal identities of sentiment and affection which are common to all men in all nations and ages.

—Beecher

602 Love for Christ

The following poem is from the pen of Alfred Lord Tennyson:

THE HIGHER PANTHEISM
Is not the vision He? Tho' He be
    not that which He seems?
Dreams are true while they last,
    and do we not live in dreams?
Earth, these solid stars, this
    weight of body and limb,
Are they not sign and symbol of
    thy division from Him?
Dark is the world to thee: thyself art the reason why,

For is He not all but that which
has power to feel "I am I"?
Glory about thee, without thee:
and thou fulfillest thy doom,
Making Him broken gleams and
stifled splendour and gloom.
Speak to Him thou, for He hears;
and spirit with spirit can meet.
Closer is He than breathing,
nearer than hands and feet.
God is law, say the wise! O Soul,
and let us rejoice,
Law is God, say some: no God at
all, says the fool;
For all we have power to see is a
straight staff bent in a pool.
And the ear of man cannot hear,
and the eye of man cannot see;
But if we could see and hear, this
vision—were it not He?

Commenting on this particular
poem, Ernest J. Barson, in his sermon *Can Men Live Without God*
says: "If such a vision were granted
to us, would not the words of the
Psalmist once again express our
need, that 'as the hart panteth after
the water brooks, so panteth my
soul after Thee, O God'?" (Ps. 42:1).

603 The Work of His Hands

The great heart that really loves
people, that causes its owner to
shed tears over the needs of
Jerusalem, New York, or Chicago, is
all too rare. We can love our friends,
our proteges, and even our enemies, but to really yearn over people
we can not call by name and who
appear to us as one face in a great
troubled human sea of faces is another matter. Loving God and loving

people is the same thing when we
keep in mind the fact that God
made the people. The work of those
we love is never lacking in interest
to us. The following story illustrates
this. A young man is fondly gazing at
a picture that has been painted and
given to him by the woman he
loves. He has bought for it a beautiful and costly frame. Most people
would pronounce the picture common and crude, but to him it is full
of rare beauty. He sees in it the soul
of the one who conceived it. The
trouble with most of us is that we
forget that God made man. So long
as he is simply a creature of the
earth, earthy, we will pass him by as
an uninteresting clod. We need to
associate him with the great Father
to whom he belongs, before we can
appreciate him.

604 Love's Offering

Love always offers something that
is a part of itself. Suppose your
friend comes into your home just as
you are ready to dine; you go to
the corner bakery and buy him a
box of tempting things to eat, and,
leaving them with him, go into the
dining room, shut the door behind
you and sit down to your dinner.
You may have provided hand-
somely for your friend, but the
chances are that you have wounded
him by shutting him out from your
fellowship. You have been willing
to give him something, but you
have refused to share your own personal pleasures with him.

It was said of a now-deceased
multimillionaire, that while he lived

a sensual life and resented all efforts to enlist him in the service of God, he gave now and then large sums to religious enterprises. Whatever may have been the motives that prompted the gifts, we can not attribute them to the impulse of a loving heart. What God asks of you is not some splendid gift, but to be a sharer in your life, whatever that may mean.

605 Love to God and Man

The more we realize our dependence upon God, the more we shall realize our kindred with our brethren. It is as with a circle of men standing all around the circumference at a distance from each other. If each one of them takes half a dozen steps towards the center, they will stand wondrously nearer each other. As we press toward "Jesus in the midst" we draw closer to each other. The electric spark of love to Christ will combine the different elements into one. Cleaving to the one Shepherd, the sheep become one flock, held together not by the outward bonds of a fold, but by the sweet attraction that fastens all to Him.

606 Loving Devotion to Leader

After the American Civil War, General Lee, who was deeply loved of his soldiers, was one day riding in a country district when he was greeted by an old weather-beaten mountaineer. "Ain't that General Lee?" he inquired as he seized the horse's bridle. "Yes, sir," said the General. Asking his old commander to dismount—which he did—the man stood before him and said: "I am one of your old soldiers, General. I want you just to let me give three rousing cheers for Marse Robert." At the first shout Lee dropped his head with embarrassment. The next yell was choked with sobs as the old soldier dropped on his knees in the dust hugging Lee's leg, and the third died away in tears. If such devoted love were only given by every soldier of Christ to his Lord how soon victory would be seen! Yet He is our Living Leader, and will be to the end.

607 Delays of Love

Dr. Hans Richter, the great musical conductor, was in 1870 a close friend of Richard Wagner, the famous composer. One day near the end of the year Mrs. Wagner said to her husband, "I cannot think why Richter has been so idle of late, he used to be so industrious." No answer of explanation was then given, but she learned the meaning of his seemingly apparent idleness before long. On Christmas Eve, her birthday, Wagner and Richter played under her window the "Siegfried Idyll" as a surprise serenade. They had been busy composing and rehearsing it for weeks as a birthday gift for the mutually-beloved one. The seeming delay of our God and the seeming indifference to us, often cover a deep design of love and rich blessing. As Jesus did not hurry to Bethany, but stayed in the same place two days (John 11:6), so

God puts our faith and patience to the test, and then discloses a purpose of larger blessing.

Deep in unfathomable mines
Of never-failing skill,
He treasures up His bright designs,
And works His Sovereign will.

608 The Service of Love

Robert Louis Stevenson had a remarkable power of attaching hearts to himself by the very magnetism of his personality, as well as the kindness of his behavior. A recent book of remembrance of his life in Samoa tells that one day when the cook was away Stevenson told another servant, Sosimo, just to bring him a little bread and cheese for lunch to his writing-room. But to his surprise he was served an excellent meal—an omelette, a good salad, and perfect coffee. "Who cooked this," asked Stevenson, in Samoan. "I did," said Sosimo. "Well then, great is your wisdom." Sosimo bowed and humbly corrected him, "Great is my love!" It was love that gave skill and deftness to his hand, and added welcome to the feast.

609 Jonathan: The Prince of Friends

Jonathan deserves to be called the "prince of friends." He was the son of the king and the heir-apparent to the throne. Suddenly David looms upon the horizon with his beauty, his courage, and that nameless magnetism and heroism that surrounded him and marked him as the coming leader of the people. A small man would have been insanely jealous. An ordinarily wise and good man might have been expected to have nothing to do with David, though he yielded to him the crown. But Jonathan was a rare soul. He cast all ambition out of his heart, and his soul was linked to David's. Their friendship lights up the pages of a warlike and corrupt time. It was a golden thread that runs through all the later years of the story of Saul's reign. David was worthy of the friendship, and cared for Jonathan's crippled son with the tenderness of a father. Great friendships can grow up only between large and generous natures.

610 Love Never Retreats

A little English drummer-boy was brought prisoner before Napoleon. The emperor told him to sound the retreat. "I never learnt it," was the prompt reply.

Love never retreats. Love is ever accompanied by faith and hope, and in their company it always dares to pursue its course, however the odds may appear against it.

611 Our Neighbors

"Thou shalt love thy neighbour as thyself." (Matt. 19:19).

A gentleman once said to Dr. Skinner, who was asking aid for foreign missions, "I don't believe in foreign missions. I want what I give to benefit my neighbors." "Well," the doctor asked, "whom do you regard as your neighbors?" "Why, those around me." "Do you mean those whose land joins yours?" "Yes." "Well," said Dr. Skinner, "how much land do you own?" "About five hundred acres," was the reply. "How far down do you own it?" inquired Dr. Skinner. "Why, I never thought of it before, but I suppose I am half way through?" "Exactly," said the doctor; "I suppose you do, and I want this money for the Chinese—the men whose land joins yours at the bottom." Every Christian should say in a higher sense than the pagan poet, "I am a man, and nothing human is foreign to me." To a believer in Christ all men are neighbors.

612 Love Your Enemies

"I say unto you, Love your enemies, bless them that curse you." (Matt. 5:4).

When Dr. Duff read to the intelligent youth for the first time this precept of the Savior, one of them could not restrain himself from speaking out his feelings: "Oh, how beautiful!" For days and weeks he could not cease repeating, " *'Love your enemies, bless them that curse you.'* How beautiful! Surely this must be the truth!"

613 Room for Jesus

The following anecdote by Ian Maclaren should remind Christians of Matthew 25:40, 45—". . . Inasmuch as ye have done it unto one of the least of these my brethren, ye have done it unto me": "Anyone who gave a feast to Jesus in Galilee had to count on twelve disciples

also; but he would be a shrewd calculator that could now estimate the number of his following. There are those who would fain have Jesus without his friends, but the Master does not relish this invitation for He considers that if we have not love enough to afford them houseroom we can have very little for Him."

614 The Simplicity of God's Work

Moody once said, "God's business is not to be done wholesale. Christ's greatest utterances were delivered to congregations of one or two."

615 Carry the Love of Christ

"For the love of Christ constraineth us" (2 Cor. 5:14).

Carry the love of Christ with you, wherever you go. In prosperity, it will melt the heart and open the hand; in the scene of strife and debate, it will maintain a generous forbearance, and prompt a soft answer; in the season of affliction, it will make you patient and thankful, and lift the thoughts from the pain that is suffered, and the property that is lost, to Jesus as the soul's rest and portion; in the house of mourning, it will elevate the affections from the corpse, enclosed in its coffin or corrupting in its grave, to a living Redeemer on high; and, in the hour of death, it will lessen the pang with which you separate from all that is dear to you on earth, and make you willing to be absent from the body, and present with the Lord.

This will be the grand principle which will actuate the blessed, when repentance shall weep, patience shall suffer, and faith and hope shall anticipate no more. And, when you shall see your Lord as He is, your love to Him shall attain a strength and a tenderness more suited, than what it at present has, to the worth and the kindness of the Lamb that was slain. "Let us go on to perfection" (Heb. 6:1).

616 Follow Peace

"Follow peace with all men" (Heb. 12:14).

Do not offend a bad man, because he will stick at nothing to be revenged. It is cruel to insult a good man, who deserves nothing but good. A great man may easily crush you. There is none so mean who cannot do mischief. Therefore, follow peace with all men.

Of Archbishop Usher it is said that he was of so sweet a temper that he was never known to do an ill service to anyone, or to be revenged of anyone who injured him. It was said of Archbishop Cranmer, that the way to have him as one's friend, was to do him an unkindness.

When envy, strife, and war, begin
In little angry souls,
Mark how the sons of peace
    come in,
And quench the kindling coals.

617 Grandma's Glasses

A young boy was overheard asking his playmate, "Wouldn't you hate to wear glasses all the time?"

"No," came the answer, "not if I had some like my Grandma's. She always sees when people are tired or sad, and she knows just what to do to make them feel better. One day I asked her how she could see that way all the time. She told me it was the way she had learned to look at things as she grew older." After thinking for a minute, the first boy concluded, "Yeah, I guess you're right. It must be her glasses."

As Christians, we need to be like that grandmother. We should look at our neighbors as our Savior did. He always had compassion on the masses. Jesus Himself said that He came "not to be ministered to but to minister" (Mark 10:45), and He is the example we should follow. A few years ago there was a cartoon that showed a little child stumbling over some stones in the road. With a look of hurt surprise on his face, he asked his mother, "Mommy, why don't you look where I'm going?" That says it well. Our responsibility as believers is to look not only on our own things, "*but every man also on the things of others*" (Phil. 2:4).

Paul W. Pruyser said, "Next to God, man should be the highest in [our] value scale . . . it is a fact that persons who love and find fulfillment in other people will also find happiness for themselves." Yes, being concerned for the welfare of others does bring happiness. But our highest motivation should not be to get all we can out of a relationship; rather, it should be to obey our Lord and

Savior. He has commanded us to love one another, as He has loved us.

—Henry G. Bosch

618 What's in the Cage?

As Paul Harvey once told the story, S. D. Gordon, a Boston preacher, used a beat-up rusty bird cage one Sunday to illustrate his sermon. First he explained how he had come by the cage, saying when he first saw it, it contained several miserable small birds, and was carried by a boy of about 10.

Curious, he asked the lad what he was going to do with the birds, which he had obviously trapped. "I'm going to play with them . . . have some fun with them," the boy responded. "But after that?" the preacher persisted. "Oh, I have some cats at home, and they like birds," said the boy.

Compassion tugged at the minister's heart, and he asked the boy what he would take for the birds. Surprised, the boy blurted: "Mister, you don't want to buy these birds. They're ugly . . . just field birds. They don't sing, or anything." Nevertheless, Dr. Gordon persisted, and soon struck a bargain with the boy for the birds. At the first opportunity he released the poor creatures.

After explaining the presence of the empty cage, Dr. Gordon then told another story: this time about how Satan boasted that he had baited a trap and caught a world full of people. "What are you going to do with them?" Jesus asked him. "I'm going to play with them, tease them; make them marry and divorce, and fight and kill one another. I'll teach them to throw bombs at each other," Satan replied. "And when you get tired of playing with them, what will you do with them?" Jesus queried. "Condemn them," Satan answered. "They're no good anyway." Jesus then asked what Satan would take for them. "You can't be serious," the devil responded. "They would just spit on You. They'd hit you and hammer nails into You. They're no good." "How much?" the Lord asked again. "All your tears and all your blood; that's the price," Satan said gleefully.

Jesus paid the price, took the cage, and opened the door.

619 The Pit

A man fell into a pit and could not get out.

A subjective person came along and said, "I feel for you, down there."

An objective person came along and said, "It's logical that someone would fall down there."

A Pharisee said, "Only bad people fall into a pit."

A mathematician calculated how he fell into the pit.

A news reporter wanted the exclusive story on his experience.

An IRS man asked if he was paying taxes on the pit.

A self-pitying person said, "You haven't seen anything until you've seen my pit!"

A charismatic said, "Just confess that you're not in a pit."

An optimist said, "Things could be worse."

A pessimist said, "Things will get worse."

Jesus seeing the man, took him by the hand and lifted him out of the pit.

620 True Love for God

Sue's parents were very wealthy. They attended no church. A friend of Sue invited her to a church service. She accepted the Lord. When telling her parents, they told her if she attended this church again, she would have to leave home. Being only 16 years old, it was a hard decision. Sue went to church again. Her parents asked her to leave home. She packed several bags and was leaving. Suddenly, her parents called her back, saying, "If you love God this much, we want to know Him too."

—Croft M. Pentz

621 Failure to Love Him

Roy Osborne says, "The love of God is the product of how much we search for Him, how much we seek Him . . . if we are going to be called into question at the judgment day, it will be for failing to love Him, not for failure to follow some ritual command."

622 I Saw a Sermon

The following account is told by Rudi Risher:

"It happened in Munich, Germany. I got out of my warm bed, looked through the window covered with 'ice ferns' at the new deep snow. I debated whether I should go to the worship service or stay at home and read the Bible. I would have to walk half a block in the cold to catch the bus. Finally I decided to go, but only because I had to lead the singing.

"While I was riding the bus, I looked through the window and recognized two people trying hard to make their path through the deep snow. Mr. Trollman was a man in his eighties, who had lost his eyesight. His only guidance was his 78 year old wife, who was lame in one foot. Because they could not afford to ride the bus, they walked three miles every Sunday to church. They were driven by their love for the Lord.

"I was not able to do anything but blush, ashamed of myself. I thought of the duty which had motivated me—of the weak faith and love I had shown. Without their knowledge and without a word, this old couple had taught me that love for God is the true motive for attending worship services."

623 Real Love

A little boy declared that he loved his mother "with all his strength." He was asked to explain what he meant by "with all his strength." He said: "Well, I'll tell you. You see, we live on the fourth floor of this tenement; and there's no elevator, and the coal is kept down in the basement. Mother is busy all the time, and she isn't very strong; so I see to it that the coal bin is never empty. I lug the coal up four flights of stairs all by myself. And it's a pretty big bin. It takes all my strength to get it up here. Now, isn't that loving my mother with all my strength?"

Marriage

624 Sanctity of Marriage

"She who willingly lifts up the veil of her married life has profaned it from a sanctuary into a vulgar place."

—George Eliot

625 An Armenian Prince

The historian Xenophon states, that when Cyrus had taken captive a young prince of Armenia, together with his beautiful and blooming wife, of whom he was remarkably fond, they were brought before the tribunal of Cyrus to receive their sentence. The warrior inquired of the prince what he would give to be reinstated in his kingdom; and he replied, that he valued his crown and his liberty at a very low rate, but that if the noble conqueror would restore his beloved wife to her former dignity and possessions, he would willingly pay his life for the purchase. The prisoners were dismissed, to enjoy their freedom and former honors; and each was lavish in praises of the conqueror.

"And you," said the prince, addressing his wife, "what did you think of Cyrus?" "I did not observe him," she replied. "Not observe him!" exclaimed her husband, "upon whom, then, was your attention fixed?" "Upon that dear and generous man," she replied, "who declared his readiness to purchase my liberty at the expense of his life."

626 Bishop Cowper

Bishop Cowper's wife, it is said, was very afraid that her husband would endanger his health by an excess of study. When he was compiling his celebrated dictionary, she got into his study, during his absence, and collected all the notes he had been writing for eight years, and burned them; and when she had acquainted him of the fact, assured with the feeling of kindness in which even this improper act originated, he only remarked, "Woman, thou hast put me to eight years' study more."

Mercy

627 What We Need Most

"What we need most is mercy. Justice would ruin us."

628 Christian Nurture

A nursery worker about to plant a number of young saplings, some straight and some crooked, thus reasoned with himself—"These straight saplings will no doubt grow up to be fine trees without much attention on my part; but I will see if, by proper training, I cannot make something of the crooked ones also. There will be more trouble with them, no doubt, than with the others; but for that very reason I shall be the better satisfied should I succeed."

629 God's Mercy

John Newton claims: "For my own part, if my pocket was full of stones, I have no right to throw one at the greatest backslider upon the earth. I have either done as bad or worse than he, or I certainly should if the Lord had left me a little to myself; for I am made of just the same materials: if there be any difference, it is wholly of grace."

630 Growth in Grace

Alexander Maclaren says: "The only way by which we can grow nearer and nearer to our Lord is by steadfastly keeping beside Him. You cannot get the spirit of a landscape unless you sit down and gaze, and let it soak into you. The cheap tripper sees the lake. You cannot get to know a man until you summer and winter with him. No subject worth studying opens itself out to the hasty glance. Was it not Sir Isaac Newton who used to say, 'I have no genius, but I keep a subject before me'?"

631 Don't Send Justice

In a prayer meeting, a man stood up and prayed, "Lord send justice. All we need is justice. Please give us justice!" Then another man stood up and prayed, "Please don't, Lord! Give us mercy. We need mercy, not justice!" Scripture plainly teaches us that it is God's mercy that He has given with His grace that we should be thankful for (1 Cor. 15:10).

632 The Shoemaker's Dream

The following story is told by Darrell Stout:

One night a cobbler dreamed that the next day Jesus was coming to visit him. The dream seemed so real that he got up very early the next morning and hurried to the woods, where he gathered green boughs to decorate his shop for the arrival of so great a Guest.

He waited all morning, but, to his disappointment, his shop remained quiet, except for an old man who limped up to the door asking to come in for a few minutes of warmth. While the man was resting, the cobbler noticed that the old fellow's shoes were worn through. Touched, the cobbler took a new pair from his shelves and saw to it that the stranger was wearing them as he went on his way.

Throughout the afternoon the cobbler waited, but his only visitor was an elderly woman. He had seen her struggling under a heavy load of firewood, and he invited her, too, into his shop to eat; he saw to it that she had a nourishing meal before she went on her way.

As night began to fall, the cobbler heard a child crying outside his door. The child was lost and afraid. The cobbler went out, soothed the youngster's tears and, with the little hand in his, took the child home.

When he returned, the cobbler was sad. He was convinced that while he had been away he had missed the visit of his Lord. Now he lived through the moments as he had imagined them: the knock, the latch lifted, the radiant face, the offered cup. He would have kissed the hands where the nails had been, washed the feet where the spikes had entered. Then the Lord would have sat and talked to him.

In his anguish, the cobbler cried out, "Why is it, Lord, that Your feet delay? Have you forgotten that this was the day?" Then, soft in the silence a voice he heard: "Lift up your heart for I kept my word. Three times I came to your friendly door; three times my shadow was on your floor. I was the man with the bruised feet; I was the woman you gave to eat; I was the child on the homeless street."

633 The King's Seat

Alexander the Great once found a private in his army fainting and sick with the cold air around him, and had him carried and seated down in his own royal seat in his tent by a fire. The soldier, coming to his senses, suddenly sprang to his feet amazed and began to apologize. Alexander smiled to the young soldier and said, "Don't you know that your Macedonians live after another manner under your kings than your enemies the Persians do. For them it is death to sit in the king's chair; but to you, it became life."

As believers, we have a hope that as our strength fails, Christ reminds us of His care. The world and Satan have an unruly kingdom which to be followed will mean certain separation from God. But to be enlisted in God's army, is to know the joy of His merciful care for us.

Money

634 Money Cannot Fully Pay

Carlyle was once quoted as saying, "Cash never yet paid one man fully his desserts to another, nor could it, nor can it, now or henceforth to the end of the world."

635 Debt

Remember this little quote the next time your mailbox is bombarded with "preapproved" credit card offers: "Debt is a good deal like the old-fashioned wire mousetrap. The hole to get in is four times as big as the one to get out."

636 Money Glorified

In the *Window in Thrums,* Mr. Barrie describes how Jamie sent home to Jess, his mother, his weekly savings, and how, home from London on a holiday, he left in her lap a five-pound note (whistling the while to hide his feelings), and he adds: "I do not know the history of that five pound note, but well aware am I that it grew slowly out of passions many things for this great hour. His sacrifices watered his young heart and kept it fresh and tender. Let us no longer cheat our consciences by talking of filthy lucre. Money may always be a beautiful thing. It is we who make it grimy." This, also, is the testimony of Jesus. Two mites dropped into the treasury-box, with a heart's love added to it, are of fabulous value in His sight. The altar sanctifies this as well as all other gifts. Money can be made Divine, in Christlike benevolence and generosity.

637 Selling the Soul for Money

The late Jay Gould, the self-made millionaire, declared of himself and his financial methods: "I was born and bred so low down that I have always been on the rise at every point in my career; and accordingly, every man's hand that I have met has been against me. I cannot remember ever to have had a good turn done to me. I am not surprised, for I have had to shove down every man I ever met. I have made my own fortune, and in doing so I have had to ruin thousands." His life was an abandonment to mere money-making, and when he died a secular paper wrote of him as "the tiger of finance."

638 Money Overvalued

Years ago a journalist instituted inquiries into the personal lives of America's millionaires. He found that though their fabulous fortunes dazzled the imagination, they nearly all had a large share of the sobering ills of life. One who had made his wealth out of provisions was, by a kind of physical satire, a martyr to ill humor. Another who had weakened his eyes by fearful overwork lived in fear of total blindness. Another was such a martyr to "nerves" that he was obliged to shun all society. Others had cruel domestic tragedies which poisoned their truest life. And yet, again, their devotion to money-making had taken away all zest for the real enjoyment of life's highest and best things. They had forgotten that quality is more than mere quantity, that a man's life does not consist in "*the abundance of the things he possesses*" (Luke 12:15). Bulk is not necessarily blessing.

Obedience

639 Faith and Obedience

A visitor, passing through a certain department of a large shop, noticed a set of regulations written on a blackboard. He also noticed that, in several particulars, every man in the shop was disregarding them. He questioned the foreman concerning the matter. At first the man was reluctant about answering him. Finally he said, "Those rules were written by one of the firm. He has neither wisdom nor judgment. If we should follow his directions, we would ruin a good part of the work." The men took their own way because they lacked faith in their commander. However else we may characterize it, failure to obey is simply lack of faith.

640 Exact Obedience

An employer once discharged a capable servant because, as he said, the man obeyed and more too.

"He was continually doing things that I never told him to do," he complained. A friend who heard of the matter went immediately and employed the discharged man, remarking that it would be refreshing to have an employee who would go beyond his orders. All went well for a time, when one day the man was ordered to take some boxes from one side of the warehouse and put them in the furnace room under the factory. The man carried out the order, and, seeing that there were boxes on the other side of the room, he removed them also. Some of the latter contained explosives, and as a result the factory was demolished. If we understand that God knows more about us than we do ourselves, we must be content to let him set the limits. Men who have attempted to improve upon the commandments of God have invariably found that the sequel was disaster.

641 Unimportant Commands

When we talk of commands that are not important we virtually speak critically of the wisdom of those who sent them to us. The importance of any edict or message lies not so much in what it contains as in who sent it. A mailman brings you an envelope: you open it and find written upon a scrap of paper an order to go to a certain place at a certain time. The importance of that message to you will depend upon the name attached to it. If the signature is that of an irresponsible or an unimportant person, you will quickly discard the message. If, on the other hand, the name is that of your employer, or it is signed by some other person who has the right to give you orders, the aspect of the case is changed. So in your Christian life, if there are unimportant things, be sure they are not those of divine ordering. You may not see how obedience to this or that command can have to do with your salvation, but that is not the important point. Who gave the command? The signature will determine its importance.

642   Obedience Is Better Than Success

The agent of a powerful and wealthy business firm saw an opportunity to make a great profit for the company by deliberately breaking one of their strictest rules. He disobeyed orders and carried through his scheme. Contrary to his expectations instead of being commended he was reprimanded, and warned never to do it again, or else endure the consequence of immediate dismissal. His disobedience happened to pay on that occasion, but it might have been as disastrous as it was fortunate. It is our responsibility to obey our Master's commands apart from results, leaving those to Him, and knowing that disobedience is a capital crime against Him.

643   Blessing Through Obedience

The doctor demands entire obedience from his patient in all that pertains to medicine, diet, rest, exercise, etc. The patient's friends may wish for him to take a little of this or a little of that, and the pa-

tient himself may wish it, but the doctor's orders override these. Why? Not because the doctor loves to lord it over people, but his care for his patient's health demands it, and the more he cares for them the more relentless will he be. All our Lord's orders for us are doctor's orders, the orders of the great physician to whom our soul's health is His supreme desire. It is Divinest love speaking in the imperative mood and saying, "Thou shalt not," and giving the reason "Do thyself no harm."

644   Implicit Obedience

General Scott was once overruled by President Lincoln in his judgment as to evacuating a fort. When, however, the old General heard the order, he replied, drawing himself up to his full height, "The Great Frederick used to say, 'When the king commands, all things are possible.' It shall be done."

645   Withholding Obedience

For six hundred years the greater part of the Ottoman Empire was nominally under the authority of a central ruler called a Khalif, a "Successor" or "Substitute." At first the authority was real and powerful: the Khalif appointed the governors of all the provinces from Spain to the borders of India and removed any of them at his pleasure. But the empire was too large to hold together around a central pivot for any length of time, and gradually various local governors made themselves virtually independent, although they generally professed the utmost devotion to the Khalif and paid him *every honor except obedience.*

646 *Literal Obedience*

It is said that many years ago a distinguished minister of the gospel, who had been a great athlete in his youth, on returning to his native town soon after he had been ordained, encountered on the main street an old companion whom he had often fought and thrashed in his godless days. "So, you've turned Christian, they tell me, Charley?" said the man. "Yes," replied the minister. "Well, then, you know the Book says, if you're struck on one cheek, you're to turn him the other. Take *that;*" and with that he hit him in the face with a stinging blow. "There, then," replied the minister quietly turning the other side of his face toward him. The man was brute enough to strike him heavily again. Whereupon the minister said, "And *there* my commission ends," pulled off his coat, and gave his antagonist a severe thrashing, which no doubt he richly deserved. But did the minister keep the command of Christ? He obeyed the letter of the rule; but did he not violate the principle, the spirit, of it?

Hear the other story, and compare. It is told of a celebrated officer in the army that, as he stood leaning over a wall in the barrack yard, one of his cadets mistaking him for a comrade, came softly up behind him, and suddenly struck him on the back of the head with a strong blow. When the officer looked around, his servant, covered with confusion, stammered out, "I beg your pardon, sir; I thought it was George." His master gently replied: "And if it were George, why strike so hard?"

Now which of these two, do you think, really obeyed the command of Christ?—the minister who made a rule of it and kept to the letter of the rule, or the officer who made a principle of it, and acting on the spirit of it, neglected the letter? Obviously, the minister disobeyed the command in obeying it, while the officer obeyed the command in disobeying it.

And here we may see the immense superiority of a principle over a rule. Take a rule, *any* rule, and there is only one way of keeping it, the way of literal obedience, and this may often prove a foolish and even a disobedient way. But get a principle, and there are a thousand ways in which you may apply it, all of which may be wise, beneficial to you, and no less beneficial to your neighbor.

647 *Turned to the Wall*

Pericles told the ambassador who came to him desirous of making some changes in the Lacedemonian decree that it was against the law to take down any of the tablets upon which a decree of the people was written. The ambassador replied that there was no need to take any of the tablets down: Pericles could simply turn the other side outward. There was no law against that.

Too many treat the commandments of God in the same way. They will not deny them altogether, but they cover them up so they may not be troubled by them.

648 Every Intention

Do you ever find that when a person has been caught being disobedient how people often reply "Well, I had every intention of doing that, but—"?

Two particular words in Scripture "jump out" when a person examines Romans chapter 5. When Paul wrote about Adam's reaction to the word of God and compared that to Christ, he used the same Greek root word. The only difference is found in the preposition prefixed to the word. In Adam's case he "heard" God's words to him, but chose to disobey, never having the intention of compliance. On the other hand, when Christ obeyed His Father by going to the cross of Calvary, He knew there would be consequences. In spite of that, He had every intention of hearing and obeying (Phil. 2:5–11).

Can we say that when God speaks we have every intention of obeying His words?

Patience

649 If God Can Be Patient, Why Can't We?

The following words are the advice of George MacDonald: "Learn these two things: never be discouraged because good things get on so slowly here, and never fail daily to do that good which lies next to your hand. Do not be in a hurry, but be diligent. Enter into the sublime patience of the Lord. Be charitable in view of it. God can afford to wait; why cannot we, since we have Him to fall back upon? Let patience have her perfect work, and bring forth her celestial fruits. Trust to God to weave your little thread into a web, though the patterns show it not yet."

650 Learning Contentment

A great Italian who was renowned for his cheerful endurance of trial, when asked how he had learned such patience replied: "First, I look within me, then without me, afterwards beneath me, and last of all, above me." He looked within and saw such guilt and unworthiness that whatever blessings balanced his afflictions, they were more than he deserved. He looked without and saw those who had far many more problems than himself, and this made every complaint a piece of sore ingratitude to him. He looked

beneath and saw the earth, into which his body would soon be lowered, and when all of life's trials would be over once and for all. He looked above and saw by faith his home in Heaven, and this made the light affliction but for a moment, not worthy to be compared with the glory waiting to be revealed. The fourfold look silenced all murmuring, and produced calm submission to God's will.

651 How Pearls Are Made

A pearl is made the following way: A grain of sand is sucked in by fresh water clams with their food. Every nine months the clam throws off a milky secretion, which forms a new coating of mother-of-pearl inside the shell—white, blue, or pink. A coating of this substance forms around the intruding grain of sand, which must be a constant annoyance to the clam, and thus in the course of time the pearl is formed. So soul pearls are made by patience under trying circumstances.

652 Put on True Beauty

"Follow after patience" (1 Tim. 6:11).

Patience is the guardian of faith, the preserver of peace, the cherisher of love, the teacher of humility. Patience governs the flesh, strengthens the spirit, sweetens the temper, stifles anger, extinguishes envy, subdues pride. It bridles the tongue, restrains the hand, tramples upon temptations, endures persecutions, consummates martyrdom.

Patience produces unity in the church, loyalty in the state, harmony in families and societies. It comforts the poor and moderates the rich. It makes us humble in prosperity, cheerful in adversity, unmoved by calamity and reproach. It teaches us to forgive those who have injured us, and to be the first in asking forgiveness of those whom we have injured; it delights the faithful, and invites the unbelieving; it adorns the woman, and approves the man: it is beautiful in either sex and every age.

Patience is clothed in the robes of the martyrs and in its hand it holds a scepter in the form of a cross. It rides not in the whirlwind and stormy tempest of passion; but its throne is the humble and contrite heart, and its kingdom is the kingdom of peace.

653 Jumping to Conclusions

Al Maxey gives a splendid example of how Christians often endanger themselves with their hastiness:

"The story is told of a woman who invited all her friends over for a special dinner. Desiring to impress them, she hired a maid, a butler, and a chef. She purchased the best steaks she could find and a top brand of mushrooms to accompany them.

"When the chef noticed that the mushrooms seemed a bit discolored, the lady suggested he feed a few to the dog, since the hour was late and there was no time to purchase more mushrooms. 'If the dog eats them and doesn't get sick, they're probably alright!' The dog eagerly consumed the mushrooms and showed no signs of ill-effects, therefore the chef completed the meal and served the guests.

"Later, as the desert was being served, the maid hurried in and whispered to the lady of the house, 'Ma'am, the dog is dead!' Not waiting to hear any more, she leaped to her feet and told the guests they had no time to lose! They had eaten tainted mushrooms and must rush immediately to the hospital! Later that evening, after the lady and her guests had returned from having their stomachs pumped, she asked the maid, 'Where is the dog now?' 'Out in the front yard, ma'am,' replied the maid, 'where he crawled after the car hit him!'

"The moral of the story: It's good to investigate a matter thoroughly before leaping to hasty conclusions which may result in harsh consequences. How many times in the church have you seen people jump to false conclusions? How many times is a person's work, character, or motives questioned, or even condemned, without the benefit of investigation? How many times has someone been dismissed as a 'lost cause' all because of 'things we've heard?' Jumping to conclusions is a very dangerous practice—its victims are littered all about us!

"We must learn to examine all situations, all information, and the actions of all people fairly. Never assume you have all the facts prior to a thorough investigation of the matter. Never pass judgment until every aspect has been scrutinized, and then only with great caution. This is how we must treat others!"

654 Dreams

"Success seems largely a matter of hanging on after others have let go."

"Success . . . seems to be connected to action. Successful men keep moving. They may make mistakes, but they don't quit."

Remember: in the confrontation between the stream and the rock, the stream always wins, not through strength, but by perseverance.

—Harold Keown

655 Patience Under Abuse

When Dr. Lyman Beecher was asked why he did not reply to a letter of criticism against him, he responded by telling the following story: "One evening as I walked through a field toward my home, I encountered one of nature's most undesirable of all creatures. I had several books in my hand which I began to throw at the creature. Unfortunately, the result of my actions was a horrible smell produced by that animal—a skunk. I determined that such an animal should be left alone."

This should also be our attitude toward those who criticize or cross our path presenting undesirable characteristics to us. The negative response our flesh would like to give can only create a greater evil to our testimony. What aroma will our lives present to God? One that is a sweet smelling sacrifice should exemplify our lives, not an offensive odor displeasing to God (Eph. 5:2).

656 Courage from Suffering

The story is told in Greek annals of history of a soldier who was suffering from a deadly sickness. This sickness was so serious, doctors feared that he would soon die. The soldier was, however, a very brave man. In battle, he was always the first to charge, for he did not fear for his life. His commander saw his bravery and coordinated efforts to treat his disease. He was healed miraculously. After this change in his life, the soldier no longer sought to fight in battle. Instead, he sought a life of ease and comfort to care for his health and family he had previously neglected.

So often it is so with believers. While the fierce battle rages, we claim God's strength, and it is through his grace we are victorious and brave. When the battle is less strenuous, and we are able to "relax" spiritually, oftentimes complacency sets in. The world and our flesh become the focal point of our lives instead of seeking God's grace for every moment of our lives.

Turn your eyes upon Jesus,
Look full in His wonderful face;

And the things of earth will
    grow strangely dim
In the light of His glory and grace.

657 *Climb On!*

"He died climbing" is the simple
inscription on a monument to an
Alpine guide, who perished when
attempting the ascent of a peak.
That record is a noble tribute to a
hero. His attitude should be ours—
looking upward and pressing forward. He was pressing on in the
pathway of duty. Many a splendid
career, intercepted at the critical
juncture, might be described by
the same concise record.

"He died climbing" may be said of
many a young and ardent enthusi-
ast—of Mackay, soon cut off in
Uganda; of Bishop Hannington,
reaching the border of the same
land and martyred there; of Patter-
son, soon slain in Melanesia by is-
landers who mistook him for a
slave-catching captain. Of Henry
Martyn, who did not live to see any
of the results of his mission; of
Wycliffe, who sent forth the Bible in
England but was not permitted to
see the beginning of the Reformation—all these "died climbing."

Climb on! Climb ever! Ne'er
    despond,
Though from each summit
    gained
There stretch forth ever heights
    beyond—
Ideals to be attained!

—James T. White

Persistence

658 Excuse of a Clergyman

Bishop Blomfield, when once called to ask a vicar to reprove one of his clergy for immorality of conduct, received as an excuse the reply, "My lord, I never do it when on duty." "On duty!" answered the Bishop; "When is a clergyman ever off duty?"

659 Narrow Escapes

We should be thankful for small escapes. In this uncertain and multicolored earthly life many occasions occur when we almost hit something or nearly are hit. A miss may be as good as a mile, but it is not pleasant to think how near at times one has been to a great peril. There are also recognized misfortunes, bad enough in the bearing of them, which might have been worse—and for that amount of mitigation one ought to be thankful.

The apostle Paul, writing to the ease-loving Corinthians, who dodged all privations and persecutions if they could, said: "Of the Jews five times received I forty stripes save one" (2 Cor. 11:24). Paul also escaped death by stoning. In Acts 14, we read that Paul and Barnabas (through divine power) healed a crippled man in the city of Lystra (14:8-10). This miracle amazed the townspeople so much that they mistook Paul and Barnabas to be the pagan gods Jupiter and Mercurius, and were prepared to offer sacrifices to the missionaries. After Paul and Barnabas persuaded the citizens of Lystra not to offer pagan sacrifices to the missionaries, the Jews from Antioch and Iconium (cities from which Paul and Barnabas fled persecution earlier) came to town, stoned Paul, drug his body out of the city limits and supposed him to be dead (14:19). Perhaps he was nearly dead—but verse 20 tells us that "he rose up and came into the city: and the next day he departed with Barnabas to Derbe." God had much more work for Paul to do on this earth. This narrow escape among others prompted Paul to write "Persecutions, afflictions, which came unto me at Antioch, at Iconium, at Lystra; what persecutions I endured: but out of *them* all the Lord delivered me" (2 Tim. 3:11).

It may not be in God's plans for any of us to suffer persecution for the faith as Paul suffered, yet in the kind providence of God, interventions on our behalf have occurred, so that the power of Satan to injure us was suddenly curbed. The limit of our enjoyment may have been passed, but not of our endurance. God knows how much we can stand—not alone, all by ourselves, but by the help of His grace. The same idea seems to be indicated in the Book of Revelation where it is said, "Ye shall have tribulation ten days"; that is, not nine and one half, nor eleven days, but for a strictly limited period. "Enough is enough," both in money-making and moral suffering. To be a Christian is not leading a haphazard life on earth, but to constantly be a subject of our Heavenly Father's care and providence. Satan can pester him, but not overcome him; he may be cast down, but not destroyed. We are not in the hands of a blind fate or under the lash of an unrestrained nature. No matter what our troubles may be, God will surely intervene, in answer to prayer, when our strength is nearly exhausted.

660 Intense Application

When Dickens wrote one of his Christmas books, he shut himself up for six weeks to do it. He put his whole heart into it, and came out looking as haggard as a murderer.

661 The Christian's Race

A great horse breeder in Kentucky has had a splendid monument built over the grave of a famous race-horse. On one side of the monument there is this inscription: "Here lies the fleetest runner the American turf has ever known." The Christian race is not to the swift but to the patient. The prize is for the one that endures unto the end. "Wherefore seeing we also are compassed about with so great a cloud of witnesses, let us lay aside every weight, and the sin which doth so easily beset us, and let us run with patience the race that is set before us," (Heb. 12:1).

662 Boarding the Ship a Second Time

On a January evening in 1897, a British ship was in awful peril on the Vancouver coast near Cape Beale. For four days the captain saw neither sun nor stars on account of dense fog. One day, at noon, a shout of "Breakers ahead!" was the first warning he had of the dangerous position in which he was placed. A heavy sea was running at the time, and an attempt to weather the ship proved futile. The anchors were then let go, and, as the big ship rounded, one of the cables parted, leaving her within one hundred feet of the shore and in immediate danger of parting the other cable. Breakers were running forty feet high, and as there was no possibility, apparently, of saving the vessel, it was finally decided to launch the boats and attempt to reach shore. Several boats were capsized as soon as launched, but finally the officers and crew of thirty-three men escaped safely through the surf. The sailors spent the night under the upturned lifeboat. In the morning the weather had moderated, and as, to their great astonishment and delight, the ship still headed to her anchor, the captain and crew boarded her, and setting sail, soon escaped from the dangerous position. Let no man give up because he has been ship-wrecked and cast ashore. Board the Gospel ship again and set sail. Paul did that after his shipwreck, and God gave him a great host to bring with him into the harbor of heaven.

663 Enduring to the End

There is something pathetic in the story of the ship *Francis*, of New Bedford, Massachusetts, which was wrecked on the New Jersey coast. The ship had had a four-months voyage of fair sailing, and the captain and crew were hopeful of closing a pleasant journey in a day or so, when suddenly, in sight of land, and almost in sight of the harbor, the ship took fire and both the vessel and the cargo were destroyed. The officers and crew escaped only with their lives. It is sad to go down in sight of port. There are many such wrecks of the moral and spiritual kind—men and women who have made honorable careers, but who forfeit all their gain of a lifetime by some sad lapse into sin when almost in sight of the port of "old age." The middle-aged and the old need to be watchful as well as the young. It is the one that endures to the end that shall be rewarded.

664 Fight for Your Faith

1 Timothy 6:12—"Fight the good fight of faith . . ."

The Greek word used here for "fight" can be translated "to ago-nize," or "to take pains." Here, Paul implies that the Christian will strug-gle in promoting his faith. Believing in Christ brings inner peace and joy to the Christian, but belief does not come without conflict. Dr. D. W. Simon says that, "The struggle for faith is a noble struggle, one of the noblest; therefore fight the battle of faith if you wish to be true to your-selves, true to your own highest in-terests, not to mention the interests of your fellowmen." May we as Chris-tians always be true to God's inter-ests by never giving up the fight!

Might is right, say many; and so it is.
Might is the right to bear the burdens of the week,
To cheer the faint, to uplift the fallen,
To pull from one's own stores to the need of the famishing.

665 Great Opportunities

The late Gypsy Smith used to tell the story of his conversion as a youngster, and of his consequent earnest desire for the salvation of his Uncle Rodney. When Smith was a boy it was not considered wholly proper for a child to address his el-ders unless spoken to, and espe-cially among the gypsies was it forbidden. This would be doubly true in the case of a subject so se-rious as an adult's duty or spiritual condition. So, Gypsy simply prayed about the matter and waited for God to give him the opportunity that he so longed for.

One day the lad's uncle took note of Gypsy's worn trousers. "Laddie," said Uncle Rodney, "how do you account for the fact that the knees of your trousers have worn nearly through, while the rest of the suit is almost like new?" "I have worn the knees through, praying for you, Uncle Rodney," the boy answered. And then he added, tearfully: "I want so much to have God make you a Christian." Uncle Rodney put his arms around Gypsy in fatherly embrace and, a few moments later, fell on his knees, confessing Christ as His Savior.

Opportunities will come to speak to others about the Lord when we are sufficiently interested in their souls to wear out our possessions and ourselves in praying for them.

Prayer

666 Prayer Answered

A. T. Pierson relates the following story: "Some years ago in the great State of Minnesota, the Granary of the West, there came a scourge of grasshoppers that threatened to destroy the whole wheat crop. The Governor, who was a very devout Christian, called upon the people to observe a day of fasting humiliation and prayer for the removal of the plague. Secular papers laughed this action to scorn, and scouted the idea of an appeal to God. Spring came, the wheat appeared and the grasshopper with it, and then the secular press said, 'What is the result of your day of prayer?' But after a little while as the grasshoppers grew, there came a parasite that not merely made the grasshopper impotent to destroy the wheat, but also impotent to propagate itself. And from that day there has been no scourge of grasshoppers in the State of Minnesota."

667 The Habit of Prayer

Lord Shaftesbury wore to the last day of his life a watch given to him by his nurse, who, when he was a child, taught him to pray. "This was given to me by the best friend I ever had in the world," he proudly said. What that single woman did for the world, though occupying but an unimportant position in it, simply by teaching the child under her charge to pray, it is impossible to estimate. If parents who occupy spheres where their duties hinder them from offering any other service to God only taught their children to pray, and led them in the pursuit of holiness, they would do that which would best promote the Kingdom of God in the world.

668 The Angelus

Millet's *Angelus* has been called the most religious picture painted during the nineteenth century. Its theme is simple enough, but it is the simplicity of truth, and of a great emotion. The evening bell rings, and a man and woman, as they hear it, cease work, and together bend their heads in prayer. That is all, but the whole picture breathes with an atmosphere so rare, so tremulous with the deep mysteries of nature and of life, that prayer seems the natural action of the onlooker as well.

But the picture not only produces the emotional condition in which prayer is natural, it pierces into the heart of all worthy praying. These two humble folk pray with simple, confiding faith. They pray as children. They drop their work and turn to God with a perfect ease and naturalness, without the slightest incongruity or irreverence. Things hidden to the wise and prudent are revealed to their childlike minds. God is near. God is their Helper. There is nothing in their work which makes them ashamed to pray; there is nothing in their prayers which makes them ashamed to work. How many of us can pray thus? How many can turn from the ledger to enter the mystical gates, or from the stress of the streets to tread the silent City of God?

669 Victory in Prayer

According to G. A. Smith, "Our Lord made prayer the real battlefield of life, and there won His victory."

670 The Necessity of Prayer

Fenelon says that, "Prayer is so necessary, and the source of so many blessings, that he who has discovered the treasure cannot be prevented from having recourse to it whenever he has an opportunity."

671 The Power of Prayer

John Sergieff says: "A burning-glass only sets fire to wood, paper, or any other combustible material when we place it in such a position that the rays of the sun concentrated upon one point of the object will act upon it through their entire combined power, and thus direct on the object, as it were, the whole sun on a small scale. It is thus also during prayer, when our souls are warmed, vivified and inflamed by the wise Sun—God, when through our intellect, acting like the burning-glass, we direct upon our heart as the spiritual point of our being the mental Sun, and when it acts upon the heart with all its singleness and power."

672 Weighted Prayers

When it became known among the friends of a certain gentleman that he was going to go abroad, they came in great numbers to see him, each one with a commission for him to execute. A lady wanted him to buy her a real Paris bonnet; a scientific friend wanted a microscope, and so on with all who came to see him. When they had gone away, he looked over the list and found, to his dismay, that if he made all these purchases he would have no money with which to meet the expense of the trip. Of all the number, only one had brought the money with which to purchase what he wanted.

When the man returned, his friends gathered around him eager to see what he had brought back. To their surprise, they found that he had made but one of the purchases he had been asked to make.

"One day, as I sat upon the deck, looking over your lists, a breeze came and blew them all away except this one," he explained.

"But how could that be?" someone questioned.

"Ah!" was the reply, "his order was weighted down. It had coins wrapped up in it."

Do you see the point? Real, prevailing prayer must have your very best offering of self and substance wrapped up in it. When you pray for the relief of the poor, is your prayer anything more than words? When you somewhat emphatically instruct the Lord to convert the heathen, are there any coins wrapped up in your prayer?

673 Keep the Way Open

The CEO of a large manufacturing corporation was in the habit of going to a room on the roof of the administration building and locking himself in, that he might be free from interruptions. One day he discovered that the building was on fire. He flew to the door to find that the lock had become set, and he was unable to open it. He remembered the intercom which communicated with the room below. But, his calls were in vain. It had been many months since he had last used the intercom, and it had become so corroded with soot and dust that it was useless. How fit an illustration is this of the prayerless life. It is by daily fellowship that we keep the way open between ourselves and God.

674 Communion with God in View of Great Responsibility

In Mrs. Crawford's biography of the late Queen Victoria, she tells the following incident: After the stately and imposing Coronation ceremony in Westminster Abbey, her Majesty returned to her mother, the Duchess of Kent. When they were quite alone she said: "I suppose, mamma, it must be true that I am Queen of England?" "Yes, love, you see that you are." "Well, then, I have a request to make. I want to be alone and undisturbed for one hour." She was left alone. How she spent that hour has never been transpired. But surely we can guess. The young Queen was surely holding fellowship with the King of Kings, seeking His help for her overwhelming responsibilities. Before our Lord chose His twelve apostles, "He went into a mountain to pray, and continued all night in prayer to God" (Luke 6:12).

675 An Extraordinary Prayer

Rev. Taylor of Boston on a Sunday before a State election in which an earnest Christian man was the incumbent candidate whom he was anxious to return to office, prayed in public the following: "O Lord, give us good men to rule over us, just men, men of temperance, Christian men, men who fear Thee, men who obey Thy commandments, men who—But, O Lord! What's the use of veering and hauling and pointing all around the compass? Give us George N. Briggs for governor!" His prayer was answered on the next day.

676 Communication with God

The person who wrote that electricity was one of the "mighty agents of nature enchained by the ingenuity of man" can scarcely have contemplated in his wildest dreams the full extent of that ingenuity. For instance, he would hardly have prophesied that a sick man, far from the habitations of civilization, would cut a telegraph wire in order to obtain assistance. And yet such a thing actually occurred. The whole of the vast continent of Australia was once practically cut off from European news for nearly twenty-four hours in consequence of an interruption on the line between Adelaide and Port Darwin. Inquiries were made, and it was found that the wire had been cut by a cyclist who was taken ill while on a journey across the continent. It is not related how he set about it, but he had the satisfaction, at any rate, of getting what he wanted. God has so made the human soul that none of us need cut off communication for others in order to reach the ear of heaven. Wherever a human heart turns toward God in simple prayer the unseen wire carries the petition to the Heavenly Father's heart.

677 The Lord's Prayer

Dr. Jonas King once went to visit the children in an orphanage. The children were seated in a schoolroom and Dr. King stood on a platform before them.

"So this is an orphanage," he said. "I suppose that many of you children would tell me that you have no father or mother, were I to ask you."

"Yes, sir;" said some little voices.

"How many of you say you have no father? Hold up your hands." A forest of hands were put up.

"So you say, you have no father?"

"Yes, sir."

"Now," said Dr. King, "do you ever say the Lord's Prayer? Let me here you."

The children began: "Our Father who art in heaven—"

"Stop, children," said Dr. King; "did you begin right?" The children began again: "Our Father who art in heaven—"

"Stop again, children," said Dr. King. "What did you say? Our Father? Then you have a Father; a good, rich Father. I want to tell you about Him. He owns all the gold in California; He owns all the world; He can give you as much of anything as He sees is best for you. Now, children, never forget that you have a Father. Go to Him for all you want, as if you could see Him. He is able and willing to do all that is for your good."

678 A Holy Mother

"All things, whatsoever ye shall ask in prayer, believing, ye shall receive." (Matt. 21:22).

There was once a righteous mother named Monica, and she had a dearly beloved son who spent his youth in vanity and wickedness, and fell from the true faith into false doctrine. That righteous mother prayed for him every day with many bitter tears. Years passed, and he left her in Africa, where they lived, and went to Italy. Every hope of his recovery seemed gone, and she told her grief to the bishop. "Fear not, Monica," he said; "the child of so many prayers cannot perish." After some time she heard of him at Milan, and she went after him, now an old woman and a widow, and found him still unchanged. Daily was she to be seen in the cathedral of Milan, kneeling in prayer for her boy, and giving abundant alms to the poor, that these her gifts might rise up as a memorial before God, and obtain for her what her heart desired.

Finally, after years of long-deferred hope, her prayer was answered. One day, while her son was sitting reading in his house, a friend, an officer in the army, came in and talked to him about the holy lives of some people in Egypt, of how they lived to God alone; how they cared not for this world and its fleeting pleasures, but set their affections above on those celestial joys which alone can satisfy. When the young man heard this his heart began to tremble; he contrasted their estimate of life with his own; unable to restrain his tears, he rushed into his garden, flung himself under a tree, and burst into convulsive weeping. And when he had somewhat recovered himself, he took up the open book which he had last been reading, and his eyes fell on the words, "Not in rioting and drunkenness, not in chambering and wantonness, not in strife and envying: but put ye on the Lord Jesus Christ, and make not provision for the flesh, to fulfil the lusts thereof" (Rom. 13:13, 14). Then this man's heart yearned to tell all to his dear mother who, with perfect patience and trust in God, had continually prayed for her son from childhood, hoping against hope.

Monica did not get to see the fullness of God's long-deferred answer to her prayer here on earth, for she died soon after her son's conversion. Her son's name was Augustine, and this child of her prayers, became one of the greatest saints, bishops, and writers the world has ever produced.

679 *In the Closet*

"Enter into thy closet, and when thou hast shut thy door, pray to thy Father which is in secret; and thy Father which seeth in secret shall reward thee openly" (Matt. 6:6).

Of Mr. John Shepherd, it is recorded that he was greatly distinguished for his success in the pulpit. When on his deathbed, he said to some young ministers who were present: "The secret of my success is in these things: 1. The studying of my sermons very frequently cost me tears. 2. Before I preached a sermon to others, I derived good from it myself. 3. I have always gone into the pulpit as if I were immediately after to render an account to my Master." All who knew that devoted man would have united in expressing his secret in three words—"In the closet."

680 *Our Best Weapon!*

In the midst of a multitude of activities we must let nothing encroach upon our prayer time. The devil will allow us to be as busy as we please if only he can get us prayerlessly busy. He knows he has no counterweapon against prayer. Keep your prayer time with all diligence.

681 How Much Does a Prayer Weigh?

How much does a prayer weigh? There is a story of a grocery store owner who tried to weigh one.

A tired-looking woman came into the store and asked for enough food to make a dinner for her children. The grocer asked her how much she could spend. The frail woman answered, "I have nothing to offer but a little prayer." The storekeeper was not very sentimental nor religious, so he said, half-mockingly, "Write it on paper, and I'll weigh."

682 The Power of the Bended Knee

Birds go to sleep on their perches, but they never fall off. This is because of the tendons in the bird's legs. They are so constructed that when the leg is bent at the knee, the claws contract and grip like a steel trap. The claws refuse to let go until the knees are unbent again. The bended knee gives the bird the ability to hold on to his perch so tightly.

Isn't this also the secret of the holding power of the Christian? Daniel found this to be true. Surrounded by a pagan environment, tempted to compromise with evil, urged to weaken his grip on God, he refused to let go. He held firm when others faltered because he was a man of prayer. He knew the power of the bended knee.

From sleeping birds we can learn the secret of holding things which are most precious to us—honesty, purity, thoughtfulness, honor, char-

acter. That secret is the knee bent in prayer, seeking to get a firmer grip on those values which make life worth living. When we hold firmly to God in prayer, we can rest assured he will hold tightly to us.

—Rollin S. Burhans

683 The Cosmic Bellhop

Many of us have traveled and stayed at a hotel or inn. In many instances, the service is quite reputable as the customer is provided with exceptional amenities such as room service or bell-man service. The purpose is to make the individual as comfortable as possible without a care for anything. Just call and they will be at your service.

In many ways, this is how some perceive God and their relationship to Him. They expect that when they call to God in their time of need, but forsake Him when there is no "need." Just like the bellhop, to answer when we call. But truly, God desires a relationship beyond meeting our needs alone. The sign of a believer is found in the desire to please the Lord and fellowship with Him (1 John 3:22).

684 Always in Prayer

A number of ministers were assembled for the discussion of difficult questions; and, among others, it was asked, how the command to *"Pray without ceasing"* (1 Thess. 5:17) could be complied with. Various suppositions were stated; and at length one of the number was appointed to write an essay upon it to be read at the next meeting; which being overheard by a female servant, she exclaimed, "What! a whole month waiting to tell the meaning of that text? It is one of the easiest and best texts in the Bible."

"Well, well," said an old minister. "Mary, what can you say about it? Let us know how you understand it. Can you pray all the time?" "Oh, yes, sir!" "What, when you have so much to do?" "Why, sir, the more I have to do the more I can pray." "Indeed! Well, Mary, do let us know how it is; for most think otherwise."

"Well, sir," said the girl, "when I first open my eyes in the morning, I pray, 'Lord, open the eyes of my understanding,' and, while I am dressing, I pray that I may be clothed with the robe of righteousness, and when I have washed me, I ask for the washing of regeneration, and as I begin to work I pray that I may have strength equal to my day; when I begin to kindle up the fire, I pray that my heart may be cleansed from all its impurities. And while preparing and partaking of breakfast, I desire to be fed with the hidden manna and the sincere milk of the Word; and, as I am busy with the little children I look up to God as my Father, and pray for the spirit of adoption, that I may be His child: and so on all day. Everything I do furnishes me with a thought for prayer."

"Enough, enough!" cried the old divine: "These things are revealed to babes, and often hid from the wise and prudent. Go on, Mary,"

said he, "Pray without ceasing; and as for us, my brethren, let us bless the Lord for this exposition, and remember that He has said, *"The meek will He guide in judgment"* (Ps. 25:9). After this little event, the essay was not considered necessary.

If we pray for the Lord to fill our cups, may it be for the purpose of letting someone else share the blessing with us. A selfish prayer is lost in the air.

—W. S. Bowden

685 *A Threadbare Heart*

The late G. Campbell Morgan writes: "During the great Welsh revival a minister was said to be very successful in winning souls by one sermon that he preached. Hundreds were converted. Far away in a valley the news reached a brother minister of the marvelous success of this great sermon. He desired to find out the secret of this man's great success. He walked the long way and came to the man's poor cottage, and the first thing he said was, 'Brother, where did you get that sermon?' He was taken into a poorly furnished room and pointed to a spot where the carpet was worn threadbare, near a window that looked out upon the everlasting hills and solemn mountains and said, 'There is where I got the sermon. My heart was heavy for men. One night I knelt there and cried for power as I never had before. The hours passed until midnight struck, and the stars looked down on a sleepy world, but the answer came not. I prayed on until I saw a faint streak of gray shoot up, then it was silver—then the silver became purple and gold. Then the sermon came and the power came and men fell under the influence of the Holy Spirit.' "

686 Harmony of Prayer

A modern novelist tells us of a great bell which was made to vibrate by the note of a slender flute. The flute had no influence upon the bell, except when a certain note was sounded; then the great mass of metal breathed a responsive sigh.

So it is only when our wills are in accord with God's will that we experience an answer to our prayer, and the feeble human cry seems to elicit a divine response. There is a preestablished harmony between the voice of the Shepherd and the hearts of the sheep. "If ye abide in me, and my words abide in you, ye shall ask what ye will, and it shall be done unto you" (John 15:7).

687 Luther Praying for
Melancthon

It was about the year 1540 that Melancthon seemed in a severe illness to be approaching death; he made his will, feeling a deep persuasion that his end was coming. The story of that illness is one of the little romances of pious biography. Luther hastened in fear and alarm to the bedside of his friend; it seemed as if Melancthon was almost gone; his eyes were dim, his understanding feeble, his tongue faltering, his countenance fallen,

his hearing imperfect. Luther was in agony of intense consternation; it seems to have been one of those great moments of passion and inspiration for which the mighty reformer was so famous. "Alas!" he exclaimed, "that the devil should have thus unstrung so fine an instrument." Then he fell upon his knees, and poured out one of those passionate, irresistible prayers: "We implore, O Lord our God, we cast all our burdens on Thee, and will cry till Thou hearest us, pleading all the promises which can be found in the Holy Scriptures respecting Thy hearing prayer, so that Thou must indeed hear us, to preserve at all future periods our entire confidence in Thy own promises." Then he seized Melancthon's hand, exclaiming, "Be of good courage, Philip, thou shalt not die; trust in the Lord, who can impart new life." And while he spoke Melancthon began visibly to revive, as though his spirit came again, and he was shortly after restored to health. After his illness he wrote to his friend and biographer, Camerarius, "If Luther had not come to me, I should certainly have died. I must have died had not Luther recalled me from the gates of the grave." Luther was to precede Melancthon in the journey to the House of Life; it was in 1546, at Eislebin, the great reformer departed; his body was brought to Wittenberg, and there Melancthon pronounced his great oration by the grave of his mighty friend.

688 A Rebellious Prayer

"Let him become what he will; so he may live, I shall be satisfied." Thus prayed the father by the sick bed of a youthful and only son. He had prayed importunately for the abatement of the disease, but the child continually struggled with intense pain. A calm at last visited the sufferer. The pulse that had throbbed and fluttered beat feebly and slowly. A deathlike hue overcast the features. The physician shook his head sadly, and said there was no hope. Suddenly the father thought that perhaps God was about to take this child away, to save the child from a life of error. Should he pray God to change His purpose? There was a struggle in the parent's heart. He gazed wistfully upon the child's countenance. It was calm, beautifully calm. The cheeks that used to dimple with laughter were rigid, still, marble-like. The eye, that depth of affection into which he had loved to gaze, was unusually brilliant. The pale red lips wore those marks of sorrow that always touch a parent's heart. The longer he looked upon his idol the more lovely it seemed. All his desire and affection centered upon it. It seemed hard to give it up—hard, very hard. Tears filled his eyes, and he uttered the rebellious prayer recorded above. The child recovered. . . . "Father, will you see me to the tree?" Many years passed since the scene just described. That son had passed through an almost unparalleled course of iniquity and villainy. He had broken the sensitive heart of an affectionate and watchful mother, and brought her to a suicide's grave. He had been tried for crime, convicted, and sentenced to death. Pardon was offered him by the officers of the law, if he would reform and lead an exemplary life. But he preferred the alternative of the gallows. In vain his white-haired father attempted to reason with him. With a careless air the criminal asked if he would see him to the tree, and then went out of the prison with the sheriff, and was hung. This story is true and instructive. In our dissatisfaction with the prospective providences of God, we are in danger of having our desires granted us. It is our duty to *bear,* as well as to *do,* the will of God. All his acts towards us are acts of love. Our journey heavenward is necessarily variable. We have our Gethsemanes. Let us not forget, when praying for the bitter cup of affliction to pass, the words of our Master, "Nevertheless, not as *I* will, but as *Thou* wilt" (Matt. 26:39).

689 Be Much in Prayer

He that would be little in temptation, let him be much in prayer. Praying only for carnal things shows a carnal heart, and leaves it carnal. Prayer is a key in the hand of faith to unlock God's treasures. A family without prayer is like a house without a roof—exposed to every wind that blows, and every storm that rages. Prayer will compel a man to leave off sinning; or sinning will make him leave off praying. The greatest and hardest preparation for heaven is *within;* but the spirit of prayer can effect this. Do you profess to love anyone for whom you have never *prayed?* Prayer is heart-work. *Rhetoric* cannot pray, *with all his words;* but *faith* can pray, *even when she has no words.* In prayer it is better to have a heart without words than words without a heart. Pray not only in the *name* of Christ, but in the *faith* of Christ. *The gift of prayer* may have praise from men, but the *grace* of prayer has power with God.

690 His Life Does Not Pray

A vessel bound for Lisbon had a crew of eight men, two of whom were professors of religion. One of these two was active and earnest in his efforts to promote the spiritual good of his shipmates. The other, till near the end of the voyage, was not known as a Christian, and lived apparently as careless as any on board. After a while, it pleased God to bless the labors of the former by awakening the attention of three or four of the men to the concerns of eternity. Prayer meetings were held, morning and evening, in the forecastle, which all the crew who could be spared were invited to attend. The conscience of the backslidden professor was crushed, and, having declared that he was a member of the Church, he offered to assist his more faithful brother in the devotional services. To this objection was at once made by a young sailor, who said, "I cannot hear him pray for me. *His life does not pray.* Let him first repent of his unfaithfulness, and confess to God and his shipmates, and then we will hear him." The rebuke was felt, but produced anger rather than humiliation.

If we would have our prayers credited as sincere, our lives must be in agreement with our prayers. It is the fervent prayer of the *righteous* man that profits much (James 5:16). Our Lord is a prevalent intercessor, because He is "Jesus Christ the Righteous" (1 John 2:1). O how essential to usefulness is character!

Preachers and Preaching

691 Bold and Plain Speech

In the house of John Knox, in Edinburgh, there is a sentence of his hung upon the walls, which speaks so well of the steady strength of that hero's life, and reveals also the source where he got his strength. "From Isaiah, Jeremiah, and other inspired writers, I have learned to call a spade a spade, and a fig a fig." The prophets' courage led them to speak in words that could not be misunderstood. The prayer of Paul was fulfilled for them, "that therein I may speak boldly, as I ought to speak" (Eph. 6:20).

692 The Bread of Life

Around the turn of the century, there was a great deal of controversy over the alleged lack of cleanliness on the part of bakers. Some of the bakeries in the city of Brooklyn were closed by the State Factory Inspector on this account. It is, of course, very important for food service industries to follow the highest standards of sanitation and hygiene, and they should, indeed, require their employees to be cleanly in their habits. But how much more important it is that all who handle the Bread of Life, whether ministers or laymen, should have clean hands and pure hearts, that no infection of worldliness or sin may cling to the sacred food.

693 Poor Pay

In the "old days" not a few clergyman resembled Goldsmith's village preacher, who was "passing rich with forty pounds a year." Christmas Evans, the most eloquent of Welsh preachers, received but seventeen pounds per year for his services as pastor of several churches, located miles apart. His parishioners seem to have been marked by an insatiable appetite for sermons, and by a singular disregard for the temporal comfort of the preacher. Once, when he had preached away from home, and had received less than his expenses, an old woman remarked to the great pulpit orator, "Well, Christmas, you have given us a wonderful sermon, and I hope you will be paid at the resurrection." "Yes, yes, no doubt of that," answered the preacher humorously, "but what am I to do till I get there? And there's the old white mare that carries me, what will she do? There will be no resurrection for her."

694 Preacher as Painter

Both artist and preacher have to be seers for others, and then in turn, declarers to others, of truths liable to be overlooked. The discourse of the one, as the canvas of the other, should both so reveal truth, as to make men to say, "Yes, that is so, but I had not noticed it."

695 Inspired Preacher

The acclaimed poet, Walt Whitman is quoted as saying, "I have heard in my time all the brilliant lights of bar and platform and stall, and though I recall marvellous effects from one or other of them, I never had anything in the way of vocal utterance to shake me through and through like Father Taylor's personal electricity in his sermons, in the little old sea church in Boston, those summer Sundays just before the Secession war broke out."

696 Preach the Word

John Hall says: "Settle in your mind that no sermon is worth much in which the Lord is not the principal speaker. There may be poetry, refinement, historic truth, moral truth, pathos, and all the charms of rhetoric; but all will be lost, for the purposes of preaching, if the Word of the Lord is not the staple of the discourse."

697 The Importance of Simplicity

Austin Phelps has this to say on the danger of making sermons overly-complicated: "The most intelligent hearers are those who enjoy most heartily the simplest preaching. It is not they who clamor for superlatively intellectual or aesthetic sermons. Daniel Webster used to complain of some of the preach-

ing to which he listened. 'In the house of God,' he wanted to meditate 'upon the simple verities and the undoubted facts of religion,' not upon mysteries and abstractions."

698 Preach Jesus

"The people of this town do not want the gospel," said a disgruntled pastor who had just resigned from his position of a once-large congregation—now made up of mostly empty pews. "I have tried in every possible way to make the services attractive, but they simply will not go to church." The man thought he was telling the truth, and yet within two years after he left the flock, the old church was the center of life and interest for the entire community. Instead of empty benches, there were not enough to seat the people. What made the difference? A better preacher? Yes and no. The first man imagined the people were tired of the preaching of Christ, when in reality they were tired of the poor substitutes he had been offering them. Even worldly men who go up the temple do not go there to hear scientific discussions or flowery orations. They can get them elsewhere. "We would see Jesus," their hearts are saying. Men may grow tired of the man who steps between them and the Son of God, but they have never yet grown weary of looking at the Christ Himself.

699 Pulpit Has to Thunder

The editor of the *Louisiana Baptist* paper rightly cries, "The pulpit has to thunder . . . if the church does not raise questions of morality, no other institution will."

Therein lies our problem: Far too many preachers no longer thunder about anything! The pulpit was once the moral conscience of our nation. Remember, preacher, if you do not teach your people that gambling is wrong, it will come back to haunt you when those who have squandered their money no longer have tithes and offerings for your church! We, too, can reap what we sow. It's a terrible thing when a man of God loses his thunder!

700 Emergency Treatment

When an emergency medical technician arrives at the scene of an accident, he knows he may have only a few minutes to save a victim's life. He will waste none of those minutes in combing the patient's hair, brushing his clothes, or checking for marks of identification. He will move as swiftly as he can to the most critical wound and treat it with all of his skill.

Something similar is demanded of the minister in the pulpit. He has 20 to 30 minutes to bring life to someone within his hearing, or in which to let him remain spiritually dead.

701 Weighed in the Balances

A Lincolnshire clergyman once preached a long sermon from the text, "Thou art weighed in the balances, and found wanting" (Dan. 5:27). After the congregation had listened about an hour, some of them began to get weary, and went out; others soon followed, greatly to the minister's annoyance. Another person started, whereupon the parson suddenly stopped, and said, "That's right, gentlemen; as soon as you are weighed, pass out." He continued his sermon some time after that, but no one disturbed him by leaving.

702 Two Preachers

"What is your opinion of your two sons as preachers?" inquired a friend of Mr. Clayton, an old dissenting minister. "Well," he replied, quaintly, but pleasantly, "George has a better show in his shopwindow than John; but John has a larger stock in his warehouse."

703 Personal Preaching

A godly, faithful minister of the seventeenth century, having finished prayer, and looking around upon the congregation, observed a young gentleman just shut into one of the pews, who discovered much uneasiness in that situation, and seemed to wish to get out again. The minister, feeling a peculiar desire to detain him, hit upon the following singular expedient. Turning towards one of the members of his church, who sat in the gallery, he asked him this question, "Brother, do you regret your coming to Christ?" "No, sir," he replied, "I never was happy till then; I only repent that I did not come to him sooner." The minister then turned towards the opposite gallery, and addressed himself to an aged member in the same manner, "Brother, do you regret that you came to Christ?" "No, sir," said he, "I have known the Lord from my youth up." He then looked down upon the young man whose attention was fully engaged, and fixing his eyes upon him, said, "Young man, *are you* willing to come to Christ?" This unexpected address from the pulpit, exciting the observation of all the people, so affected him that he sat down and hid his face. The person who sat next to him encountered him to rise and answer the question. The minister repeated it, "Young man, *are you* willing to come to Christ?" With a tremulous voice he replied, "Yes, sir." "But *when,* sir?" added the minister in a solemn and loud tone. He mildly answered, "Now, sir." "Then stay," said he, "and hear the word of God, which you will find in 2 Corinthians 6:2: 'Behold, *now* is the accepted time; behold, *now* is the day of salvation.'" By this sermon he was greatly affected. He came into the vestry, after service, dissolved in tears. That unwillingness to stay which he had discovered was occasioned by the strict injunction of his father, who threatened that if he ever went to hear the fanatics he would turn him out of doors. Having now heard, and unable to conceal the feelings of his mind, he was afraid to meet his father. The minister sat down and wrote an affectionate letter to him,

which had so good an effect that both father and mother came to hear for themselves. They were both brought to a knowledge of the truth, and father, mother, and son were together received with universal joy into that church.

704 *American Backwoods Preacher*

To my other labors were added those of a chorister; for it often happens that there is not a man or woman in the congregation that can or will start a tune. It is not pleasant to be reduced to the strait of an old parson that I once heard of, who in giving out his hymn said, "I would thank some brother present to raise the tune, and then *tote* it." A dead silence ensued. It was after awhile broken by a member of the congregation saying, "I reckon you'll be dreadful sharp if you trap anybody here in that way." I therefore armed myself with three tunes, a long, short, and common metre; and when there threatened to be a "flash in the pan," from the musical inability of my audience, I would fire away with one of these. But unfortunately, sometimes I would pull a trigger, and the wrong barrel would go off; and great was my confusion, time and again, a-hitching a long metre tune to short metre words.

Pride

705 Simon Tournay's Foolish Pride

Simon Tournay affords a memorable and effective proof of the truth in Romans 1:22, "Professing themselves to be wise, they became fools." After he had excelled in all of his studies at Oxford, and had become so prominent at Paris as to be made chief doctor of the Sorbonne, he was so puffed up with foolish pride as to hold Aristotle superior to Moses and Christ, and yet equal but to himself! In his later days, however, he grew so senile as not to know one letter in a book, or to remember one thing he had ever done.

706 Saving Or Showing Off

Determination is a necessary qualification for the soul-winner, but it isn't the only one. A man, who had more determination than devotion, heard a preacher remark that the case of a certain man was hopeless. He made up his mind to show the faithless shepherd what he could do; so he worked day and night till he had induced the man to confess Christ. The convert was, however, soon disgusted with the inconsistent life of the man who had urged him to become a Christian, and fell back into his old ways. The worker had silenced the preacher, but he had not saved a sinner. The four men who brought the paralytic to Christ were not simply determined to show the crowd that when they started out to do a thing, they were not to be hindered. The fact that Christ commended their faith shows that they thought more about carrying the man than about carrying their point.

707 Giving Heed to Reproof

Years ago, a lady, who went with a party to the British Museum, expressed contempt and dissatisfaction at every thing she saw; protested it was a waste of time to continue and urged the company to hasten their departure. Finally, they politely thanked the gentleman in attendance, and were about to leave, when he detained them by the following address to their haughty companion: "When I first saw you, madam, I was struck with your beauty and interesting appearance; but you soon gave me occasion to change my opinion. I pity the man that marries you, if any one ever will; certainly I would not; and I fear for you unless some alteration takes place in your taste, manners, and habits. Madam, I wish you a good day."

Many years after, the same gentleman waited upon another company at the Museum: when they took their leave and thanked him for his polite attentions, a woman stepped forward, and expressed her gratitude in a manner more lively than the occasion seemed to require. The gentleman, rather surprised, professed himself happy in having contributed to her amusement. "Sir," said she, "my obligations to you far exceed those which you have conferred this morning." She then recalled to his memory the previously mentioned circumstance, and added, "I am that woman; and to you I am indebted next to this gentleman, who is my husband, for the happiest influence on my life and character, arising from the very pointed, but helpful reproof which you then administered."

708 A Boaster Humbled

At a dinner party, one of the company challenged any person to present a question to which he could not give a satisfactory answer. All were silent, till a worthy clergyman said, "This plate furnishes me with a question—Here is a fish that has always lived in salt water; tell me why it should come out a fresh fish, and not a salt one?" The boaster was silenced: nor was there one in the room who envied him for his feelings.

Priorities

709 *Words on Paper*

Here is a little story you may enjoy: Three boys were in school telling their teacher what their fathers did for a living. The first boy said, "My father writes words on a piece of paper and calls it a poem. He gets $100." The class was impressed. The next boy said, "That's nothing. My father writes words on a piece of paper. He calls it a song and gets paid $1000." The third body said, "My father writes words on a piece of paper, and he calls it a sermon. It takes four people to carry all the money!"

710 *Putting God's Message First*

"Reprove, rebuke, and exhort, with great patience and instruction" (2 Tim. 4:2b NASB).

We had a country parson who told the story about a young minister just out of seminary. The first Sunday in his mountain church he preached against smoking and discovered the anger of many tobacco farmers. The second Sunday the young cleric spoke out against the evils of drinking and caught the ire of those who were making a living with their whiskey stills. The third Sunday the preacher condemned with conviction the evils of gambling and found that those he had not angered already were at his heels because they raised horses for the race tracks. The next Sunday he did his best. Waving his arms with authority, he expounded on the evils of deep-sea fishing outside the boundaries of international waters. Men-pleasers have a hard time preaching the gospel.

—Purnell Bailey

711 *Do You Want My Head or My Feet?*

When Alexander Maclaren was called to the pulpit of a great Baptist church in Manchester, England, he said to the deacons, "Gentlemen, there is one matter to be settled before I take this position." "What's that?" they asked.

"Do you want my head or my feet? You can have one or the other, not both. I can run around doing this and that and drinking tea if you wish me to, but then don't expect me to bring something in my messages that will shake this city!"

How ineffectual is the pulpit ministry of many who are jacks-of-all-trades, and spread their zeal thin over an amazing multiplicity of activities, leaving little or no time for quiet waiting for God and absorbing His Word!

263

712 *Home Alone*

In this illustration, Dennis Cone paraphrases a tale once told by Martin Buber.

"An old Hasidic legend that Martin Buber liked to tell goes like this: 'All the people of the town had gathered in the synagogue on the eve of Yom Kippur. The time for the service to begin came and went, but still the rabbi did not appear. A young woman slipped out to go home and check on her small child, whom she had left alone. Entering the house she was surprised to see the missing rabbi holding her little girl. As the teacher was passing the house on his way to the synagogue, he had heard the child crying and stepped inside to see if he could help. He had held the little one in his arms until she fell asleep.'

"This story could have several applications. One would be that we should always take our children to church with us, but I would like to suggest another interpretation: that those of us who serve the church must not get so caught up in large-group public ministry that we overlook the needs of the individual, especially the little ones, like the crying child in this story."

Problems

713 Loss for the Christian Becomes Gain

There are acts of humble and beautiful devotion enacted every day in the realm of the home which, if only chronicled, would add one of the richest chapters to the book of life. How rich, for instance, would such a chapter be in instances of loyalty of wife to husband, of her faith in him, proving in his life the great buttress upon which he leans, and from which he draws support. One such instance is given in a picture by W. J. Grant, entitled *The Last Trial of Madame Palissy.* Bernard Palissy lived in the latter part of the fifteenth century, and in his experiments to recover the lost art of porcelain enamel he and his family were reduced to the greatest distress. He was convinced, although the world laughed at his efforts, that he had found the right quantities at last of a combination, and only wanted a piece of gold to mix with the other ingredients. Gold, however, he had none, and could procure none. It was at this moment that his wife came forward, and by a beautiful act of love and loyalty showed that she believed in him. Taking off her wedding ring, we see her drop it into the crucible. This act of faith, it is good to know, was not in vain. The gold which the ring possessed was all that was needed to reach a perfect success. There are many women like Madame Palissy in the world, and they are its true aristocracy.

The illustration can also be used to show how the gold of sacrifice is that which is needed to perfect life. Christ asks us to sacrifice ourselves for Him, and many find it too hard a saying. But those who take what they treasure most and drop it into the crucible find that loss is gain. Life ever after becomes glorified.

714 We Learn Love through Our Suffering

Edward B. Pusey states: "One cannot think that any holy earthly love will cease, when we shall be like the angels of God in heaven. Love here must shadow our love there, deeper because spiritual, without any alloy from our sinful nature and in fullness of the love of God. But as we grow here by God's grace, in heaven will be our capacity for endless love. So, then, if by our very suffering we are purified, and our hearts enlarged, we shall, in that endless bliss, love more those whom we loved here, than if we had never had that sorrow, never been parted."

715 Use of Trials

Spurgeon tells us that, "Often our trials act as a thorn-hedge to keep us in the good pasture, but our prosperity is a gap through which we go astray."

716 On Suffering

While the battle of Chateau-Thierry was in progress, a soldier was carried to the hospital whose face was grossly disfigured from battle wounds. By the time the surgeon was through with him his head looked like a ball of rags, with nothing but the eyes peeping out. A visitor said to him, "Poor, poor boy!" But the poor boy replied, "Don't pity me. Pity my buddies over there who have been hit where it doesn't show." "Then you don't mind," said the visitor, "your face being disfigured?" "Disfigured?" the soldier replied. "I ain't disfigured. I'm decorated." It is not likely that a child of God can escape suffering for Jesus' sake. No one can persistently resist the devil, the world, and the flesh, without arousing their hate and malice.

There is another suffering, however, which results from sin and wrong. ". . . and be sure your sin will find you out" (Num. 32:23). Hereafter, but usually already here, suffering follows in the wake of sin. Hard and thorny indeed is the bed of one who must tell himself that he has brought on suffering by his own folly. Think of the drinker; the fiend of lust! How they have to suffer! And they have deserved it! And what a badge of degradation it is!

But suffering for Jesus' sake glorifies and ennobles. Now the wounds may smart which one has received for Jesus' sake; but as decorations they shall glitter on the day of the Master's return. That will be the day of the sufferer's coronation.

717 Resource in Adversity

Towards the end of the Civil War, during the sad reverses of the Confederates, the newspapers in their besieged cities were having a difficult time finding paper on which to print their grim news. They were usually printed on the poorest straw paper, so brittle that a touch would mutilate it. When at last even this failed, the inventive genius never deserted them, for during the siege of Vicksburg its *Citizen* appeared printed on wallpaper.

718 Cast Your Burden on the Lord

A journeyman traveling by foot along a highway was passed by the driver of a pickup truck. The driver, noticing that the weary traveler was carrying a heavy backpack, stopped a few hundred feet in front of him and offered him a ride. The man accepted the offer. After driving a few miles, the driver noticed that his fellow traveler still had his load fastened to his back. "Why not put your load down and rest?" The man replied, "I could not think of doing that; it is kind enough of you to give me a ride, without allowing me to put my load upon your seat." What a silly man—like many who still cling to their burdens when bid to cast all their care on Him (1 Pet. 5:7).

719 Burden-Bearing

God knows our burden-bearing power. A little boy was helping his father to unpack some boxes of goods. His father took the parcels from the box and put them on the outstretched arms of the boy. "Don't you think you have enough of a load?" said a passerby. "Father knows best how much I ought to carry," said the boy. It showed trust and confidence. His father's love would not overburden him.

720 Giants to Fight

1. LAZINESS
2. SELFISHNESS
3. DISHONESTY
4. HATE
5. PRIDE

721 Ignoring Trouble

"Why didn't you tell her she was taking more than her share of room and encroaching upon your rights?" someone asked of a young girl who was merrily describing an old woman who had taken a seat beside her in a crowded railway car, and crammed into the small space a bird cage, a basket of apples, and bundles numerous and varied. "It wasn't worthwhile to trouble about it; we had such a little way to go together," was the reply. What a motto that would be for a life-journey! So many little annoyances are not worth noticing, so many small unkindnesses even may be passed by silently, because

we have only "such a little way to go together."

J. R. Miller

722 The Transparent Soul

It is a matter of great interest to visit plate-glass works, and inspect the casting-tables on which the heavy plate-glass used in the large store-windows is cast. Each table is about twenty feet long, fifteen feet wide, and from seven to eight inches thick. The rough plate is commonly nine-sixteenths of an inch thick, but after polishing it is reduced to six or seven sixteenths. All casting tables are mounted on wheels, which run on a track made to reach every furnace and strengthening-oven in the factory. The table having been delivered as near as possible to the melting furnace, a pot of molten glass is lifted by means of a crane, and its contents poured quickly out on the table. A heavy iron roller then passes from end to end, spreading the glass to a uniform thickness. This rolling operation has to be done by expert hands quickly, as the boiling glass, when it comes in contact with the cold metal of the table, cools very rapidly. The glass is then passed into the oven. When it is ready to be taken out of the oven, its surface is very rough. In this condition it is used for skylights and other purposes where strength is desired rather than transparency. But when intended for windows it has to go through an experience of grinding, after which it is smoothed and polished. Transparent souls are made in much the same fashion. Men must be melted down in the heat of the furnace of trial; must have many a heavy roller run over them, leveling their pride and ambition; must be strengthened in the oven of patient submission; and must be ground and polished by daily exercise in Christian duties, that at last the soul may be so transparent that whoever looks upon it shall see the face of Jesus Christ.

723 Going to Battle Well-Armed

A Rocky Mountain rancher once had a fight with a pack of half-starved mountain wolves, in which he, single-handed and unarmed, vanquished his assailants. He heard noises in the direction of his pig-pen at a late hour, and on investigation discovered that they were mountain wolves. When they attacked him he beat them off with his fists and retreated backward until he reached a well. Then he grasped the nearest wolf by the throat and flung it into the water. He was covered with blood and almost unconscious from his wounds, but he managed to dispose of four others in the same manner. He then succeeded in reaching his house. One of the saddest things ever observed is the brave fight one occasionally sees a man make against some wolfish passion or lust or evil habit, alone and unaided by Divine strength. We do not need to make this fight alone or unarmed. We may have "the whole armor of righteousness" and the strong arm of Christ to aid us in our struggle.

724 Bearing One's Own Burden

The letter of Samuel L. Clemens (Mark Twain) to the editor of the *New York Herald,* declining to accept the fund which that journal had undertaken to raise for his debt relief, is full of suggestive illustration. The beloved humorist writes:

"I made no revelation to my family of your generous undertaking in my behalf, and for my relief from debt, and in that I was wrong. Now that they know all about the matter, they contend I have no right to allow my friends to help me while my health is good and my ability to work remains; that it is not fair to my friends, and not justifiable, and that it will be time enough to accept help when it shall be proven that I am no longer able to work. I am persuaded that they are right. While they are grateful for what you have done, and for the kindly instinct which prompted you, it is urgent that the contributions be returned to the givers with their thanks and mine. I yield to their desire, and forward their request and my endorsement of it to you. I was glad when you initiated that movement, for I was tired of the fact and worry of debt, but I recognize that it is not permissible for a man whose case is not hopeless to shift his burdens to other men's shoulders."

Nothing that Mark Twain has ever written will so commend him to the honor of mankind, now and in the future, as this letter. One of the important truths that needs emphasizing in our time is Paul's declaration that "every man shall bear his own burden," when he is able (Gal. 6:5). That is just as true and as important a statement as the other made in the second verse of the same chapter, "Bear ye one another's burdens." Self-respect requires us to do to the full measure of our possibility before we accept sympathetic aid.

725 *The Courage to Remain Behind*

There is something truly splendid and great in Nansen's graceful dedication of his book, *Farthest North*, to his wife: "To her who christened the ship and had the courage to remain behind." It is always harder to christen a ship and send it forth on its long voyage, trusting it to the guidance of other hands, than it is to go with it and share its destiny. This has a possible application for us all. How often we have the opportunity to christen some good ship of thought, or effort, and send it out with our "God speed!" when duties that hold us to the narrower routine of our daily life will not permit us to share its fortunes. Let us never selfishly refuse to christen the ship, because it may not be our fortune to go as pilot or passenger.

Providence

726 *Remarkable Deliverance*

"But even the very hairs of your head are all numbered" (Luke 12:7).

The celebrated author of *Pilgrim's Progress* experienced several remarkable providential deliverances. Once he fell into the river Ouse, and at another time into the sea, and narrowly escaped being drowned. When seventeen years of age he became a soldier, and at the siege of Leicester in 1645, being required to stand sentinel, another soldier in the same company desired to take his place. He consented, and his companion was shot in the head by a musket-ball, and killed.

727 *A War Scene*

A British Lieutenant gives his account of the Siege of Copenhagen as follows:

At the siege of Copenhagen, being then a young midshipman on board HMS *Valiant,* I was particularly impressed with an object that I saw three or four days after the terrific bombardment of that devoted place. For several nights previous to the surrender of Copenhagen, the darkness of the night was ushered in with a tremendous roar of guns and mortars, accompanied by the whizzing of those destructive and burning engines of warfare, Congreve's Rockets. The dreadful effects of this destructive warfare were made visible by the brilliant lights in the city. Soon did the blazing houses and burning cottages of laborers illuminate the heavens. The wide-spreading flames, reflected the city for its destruction. When the bombardment had commenced, and every woman and child fled from the destructive shell, shot, and rocket, and from the falling and burning houses, a little child was seen running across the street for shelter—it knew not where—when a rocket, flying through the street, killed on its way the poor innocent boy. Oh, Britain! Queen of Nations, mother of such manly sons, are these thy works? After several of these horrific nights, the Danes gave up their arsenal and all it contained to the English. Some days after, walking among the ruins, consisting of the cottages of the poor, houses of the rich manufacturers, lofty steeples, humble meetinghouses, in the midst of this broad field of desolation, stood one house—all around it was a burnt mass—this stood alone, untouched by the fire, a monument of mercy. "Whose house is that?" I asked. "That," said the interpreter, "belongs to and is occupied by a member of the Society of Friends: he would not leave the house, but remained in prayer with his family during the bombardment." "Surely," thought I, "the hairs of thy head were numbered (Luke 12:7). He has been a shield to thee in battle, a wall of fire around thee; a bright and shining witness of that care our Lord and Savior has over those who follow peace. 'Blessed are the peacemakers, for they shall be called the children of God' (Matt. 5:9). Tis the example of the Prince of Peace; and all who follow Him need not, and will not fear the puny arm of man. It will be well with the righteous in those times."

728 The Iceberg

Some years ago a vessel lay calm on smooth sea in the vicinity of an iceberg. In full view the mountain mass of frozen splendor rose before the passengers of the vessel, its towers and pinnacles glittering in the sunlight, and clothed in the enchanting and varied colors of the rainbow. A party on board the vessel resolved to climb the steep sides of the iceberg, and spend the day in a picnic on the summit. The novelty and attraction of the hazardous enterprise blinded them to its danger, and they left the vessel, ascended the steep mountain of ice, spread their table on the summit, and enjoyed their dance of pleasure on the surface of the frosty marble. Nothing disturbed their security, or marred their enjoyment. Their sport was finished, and they made their way down to the water-level and embarked. But scarcely had they reached a safe distance before the loud crash of the crumbling mass was heard. The scene of their gaiety was covered with the huge fragments of the falling pinnacles, and the giant iceberg rolled over with a shock that sent a thrill of awe and terror to the breast of every spectator. No one in that party could ever be induced to try that rash experiment again. But what is this world, with all its brilliance, with all its hopes and alluring pleasures but a glittering iceberg, melting slowly away? Its false splendor, enchanting to the eye, dissolves; and as drop after drop trickles down its sides, or steals unseen through its hidden pores, its very foundations are undermined, and the steady decay prepares for a sudden catastrophe. Such is the world to many who dance over its surface, and in a false security forget the treacherous footing on which they stand. But can anyone who knows what it is avoid feeling that every moment is pregnant with danger, and that the final catastrophe is hastening on?

729 A Miraculous Escape

In the winter of 1815, a man of the name of Frost, who was employed in the mining industry, had a miraculous escape from a very perilous situation, in which he was involved by the falling in of the earth where he was at work. His voice was heard from beneath the ground in which he was entombed, and it was ascertained that his head and body were unhurt, the principal weight having fallen upon and bruised his legs and thighs. Great care was required to accomplish his release, and some of the more experienced miners were employed. A mass of earth was strangely and almost miraculously suspended over his head, where it hung like an avalanche, ready at the slightest touch to crush him to pieces at its fall. The miners, aware that his situation was one of infinite peril, would not attempt the attainment of their object by the most direct and expeditious means; slower operations were, in their opinion, essential, even though they dreaded the consequences that might attend their more protracted efforts. Had that impetuosity of feeling which, however honorable to our nature, sometimes defeats its most benevolent purposes, been alone consulted on this occasion, the poor man must inevitably have perished. They therefore proceeded with great caution and the most unwearied perseverance, from Monday, the day on which the accident took place, until the evening of the following Thursday, when they had the satisfaction of witnessing the complete success of their exertions, and the restoration of a fellow-creature to his family and the world. The man was extricated from his dreadful situation with only a few slight bruises and a broken leg, after a temporary burial of over seventy-five hours. A drop of water that fell near his head, and which he contrived to catch in the hollow of his hand, quenched his thirst, which otherwise would probably have become excessive. This fortunate occurrence no doubt contributed to the preservation of his existence. He was a Wesleyan Methodist, and his strong religious feelings supplied him with fortitude. Neither pain nor apprehension destroyed his composure, and he employed many of the hours of his premature entombment in singing those psalms and hymns with which he was previously acquainted. Under other circumstances this man would have been a hero.

730 An "If"

During the time that Charles Wesley was under the care of his brother at Westminster, a gentleman of the same family name, and of considerable respectability and opulence, wrote to Charles's father, and inquired if he had a son of that Christian name; because if he had, it was his intention to make him his heir. In consequence of this arrangement, the accounts of Charles Wesley at school were, by this unknown person, regularly discharged. The incognito, after the lapse of some time, called upon his *protegé* and inquired if he was willing to accompany him to Ireland. Charles wrote to request the opinion of his father, who left it to his own decision. The consequence, however, ultimately was that Charles Wesley remained in England. Had he gone to Ireland, the consequences it is impossible to estimate, for the person who inherited the property intended for him, and who took the name of Wesley, or Wellesley, was the first Earl of Mornington, grandfather of the Marquis of Wellesley and the Duke of Wellington. What an extraordinary interposition of Providence was this! "Had Charles Wesley," says one of the biographers of his brother, "made a different choice, there might have been no Methodists, the British Empire in India might still have been menaced . . . and the undisputed tyrant of Europe [Napoleon] might at this time have insulted and endangered us on our own shores."

731 Curious Circumstance Recorded of Louis XIV

The mother of this monarch had been almost eighteen years married before she gave an heir to the crown; and, in addition to this, had attained an age when no French princess had ever been known before to bring forth a child. From this circumstance it was that his flatterers called him *Dieu Donné,* or sent by God, as if the Almighty had miraculously imparted a fecundity to the queen which she had never before possessed, or restored it after it had been lost through age. The circumstances, however, attending the birth of this prince, although not miraculous, were certainly singular. Louis XIII had for some years ceased to cohabit with the queen, who kept her court at Paris, while the king resided at St. Germain. His Majesty happening to be one day in the capital on public business, just as he

was about to return to St. Germain, it began to rain, and continued to pour down a torrent during the whole evening. The king, unwilling to set out during the tempest, expressed a wish to sleep at the Louvre, providing the royal apartments had been sufficiently aired. On this, one of the courtiers suggested that the queen's apartment would expose him to no danger whatever. From this hint he sent a message to Her Majesty that he would be obliged to her for a share of her bed that night. The consequence was that, nine months after, to the great joy of the nation, Louis XIV was born.

732 The Finger of God: A Jewish Story

Dr. Hammond, in his treatise, mentioned an ancient story of a Jew, who, upon reading the words of Solomon, "He that hath pity on the poor lendeth unto the Lord, and that which he hath given will He pay him again" (Prov. 19:17). resolved to try whether God would be as good as his word, thereupon gave all that he had but two pieces of silver to the poor, and then waited, and expected to see it come again. But being not presently answered in that expectation, grew angry, and went up to Jerusalem to reason with God for not performing His promise. And going on his way, he found two men striving, engaged in an irreconcilable quarrel about a stone, that both, walking together, had found in the way, and so had both equal right in it; but being but one, and not capable of being divided, they could not both enjoy; and therefore, to make them friends, he having two pieces of silver, upon contract divides them between the contenders, and got the stone in exchange for them. Having it, he goes on his journey, and coming to Jerusalem, shows it to a goldsmith, who tells him it was a jewel of great value, being a stone fallen and lost out of the High Priest's ephod, to whom if he returned it, he would certainly receive a great reward. He did so, and accordingly it proved;— the High Priest took it of him, gave him a great reward, and withal sharply reproved for questioning the truth of God's promise, bidding him trust God the next time.

733 Miraculous Escape of a Drunken Sailor

A sailor named Campbell on board a boat on the Congo, a river in Africa, while in a state of intoxication, bathed in that river. When he had swam some distance from the vessel, some persons on board discovered an alligator heading towards him. His escape was considered impossible; two shots were fired at the formidable creature, but without effect. The report of the piece, and the noise on board, made Campbell acquainted with his danger. He saw the creature advancing towards him, and with all the strength and skill he possessed made for the shore, and approaching within a very short distance of some canes

and shrubs that covered the bank, while closely pursued by the alligator, a ferocious tiger sprang towards him, at the instant the jaws of his first enemy were expanded to devour him. At this awful moment Campbell was preserved. The eager tiger, by overleaping him, encountered the gripe of the amphibious monster. A conflict ensued between them; the water was colored with the blood of the tiger, whose efforts to tear the scaly covering of the alligator were unavailing, while the latter had also the advantage of keeping his adversary under water, by which the victory was presently obtained, for the tiger's death was now effected. They both sank to the bottom, and the alligator was seen no more. Campbell was recovered, and instantly conveyed on board. His danger had sobered him, and the moment he leaped on deck he fell on his knees and returned thanks to God for preserving him; and from that time he became a sober and moral man.

734 God as a Sculptor

The sculptor makes the marble image by chipping away the superfluous marble. And when you have to chip away superfluous flesh and blood, it is bitter work, and the chisel is often deeply dyed in gore, and the mallet seems to be very cruel.

735 God as a Skillful Artist

It is strange and impressive when we come to think how Providence, working with the same uniform materials in all human lives, can yet, like some skillful artist, produces endless novelty and surprises in each life.

Quotes

736 *"Judge Yourself"*

Remember this quotation by Ivan Panin the next time you are concerned with what others think about you. "Others will judge you, not by what you can be, but by what you are; but you must judge yourself, not by what you are, but what you can be."

737 *The Importance of the Simple Minded*

"God often works more by the life of the illiterate seeking the things that are God's than by the ability of the learned seeking the things that are their own."

—St. Anselm

738 *Prayer*

"The man who can pray truly is richer and more blessed than all the others."

—St. Chrysostom

739 *On Heaven*

"If ye knew what He is preparing for you ye would be too glad. He will not, it may be, give you a full draught till ye come up to the wellhead and drink, yea, drink abundantly, of the pure river of the water of life that proceedeth out from the throne of God and from the Lamb."

—Samuel Rutherford

740 *God Does Not Bless Laziness*

Jeremy Taylor says: "Whatever we beg of God, let us also work for it, if the thing be a matter of duty, or a consequent to industry; For God loves to bless labor and reward it, but not to support idleness. And therefore our blessed Savior in his sermons joins watchfulness with prayer: for God's graces are but assistances, not new creations of the whole habit in every instant or period of our life."

741 *Reverence for Christ*

"To me Christ is less an object of knowledge than of simple reverence and love. I know no reverence that goes beyond the reverence I give to Him; no love I ever knew goes beyond the love I want to offer Him; there is no loyalty that transcends the loyalty I wish to pay Him."

—Lyman Abbott

742 *Marcus Aurelius on Materialism*

"Think not so much of what you 'have not' as of what you have; but of the things which you have select the best, and then reflect how eagerly they would have been bought if you had them not. At the same time, however, take care that you do

276

not through being so pleased with them accustom yourself to overvalue them so as to be disturbed if ever you should not have them."

743 Abraham Known by Many

"Abraham is one of the most renowned persons the world has ever seen. Besides the conspicuous place he holds in the Bible history, he is introduced into the Koran of Mohammed, and is regarded by the Arabians as the father of their nation, and by the Jews as theirs. The ancient Persians pay him the highest honor, and think he was Zoroaster. In India, too, Abraham is honored by some sects as their distinguished ancestor. The people of Egypt, Chaldea, and Damascus acknowledge their obligations to this illustrious man. But what shall we say of the blessings which he received from God? His believing posterity have been multiplied as the stars of heaven. His venerable name is invested with immortal honor in the history of the church and of the world—second only to Him whose name is above every name. Canaan, the Land of Promise, was given to his natural posterity for fourteen centuries, as their peculiar inheritance. And, above all, from his seed the divine Savior in due time appeared in the flesh, to ransom, by His sufferings, death, resurrection, and glory, a multitude of immortal souls, whom no man can number."

—Mackenzie

744 A "Sunny" Temperament

"A sunny temper gilds the edges of life's blackest cloud."

—Guthrie

745 Duty

"Do but your duty, and do not trouble yourself whether it is in the cold or by a good fire."

—Marcus Aurelius

On Christian Love

746 Growth Through Love

The following quotation by Henry Drummond accurately portrays the growth of a Christian: "Contemplate the love of Christ, and you will love. Stand before that mirror, reflect Christ's character, and you will be changed into the same image from tenderness to tenderness." Augustine once said: "How shall we become lovely? By loving Him who is ever lovely."

747 "Live by Loving"

C. S. Holland writes: "Everything becomes possible to those who love. We shall be enabled to do so much if only we love. We live by loving, and the more we love the more we live; and therefore, when life feels dull and the spirits are low, turn and love God, love your neighbor, and you will be healed of your wound. Love Christ, the dear Master; look at his face, listen to His words, and love will waken and you will do all things through Christ who strengtheneth you."

748 Love Your Neighbor

Dr. Joseph Parker writes: "Seize the fleeting chance; where there is a man that you can only see today, for he will be gone tomorrow, do good to him."

The following quotations are by Ivan Panin:

"Of my neighbor, tell me only what is good; what is bad I can find out for myself."

"Only diamond cuts diamond; but the hardest heart, if cut at all, can be cut only by the tenderest."

"Love, like the sea, levels all things by covering them with itself."

Ruskin was once quoted as saying: "Not 'blessed is he that feedeth the poor,' but 'blessed is he that considereth the poor' [Ps. 4:1]. And you know that a little thought and a little kindness are often worth more than a great deal of money. This charity of thought is not merely to be exercised toward the poor; it is to be exercised toward all men."

On Tests, Trials, and Suffering

749 Affliction

Dr. Frank Bristol says that "Affliction makes and develops character. From this thorny vine burst flowers of beauty and fragrance. On this rough and gnarled tree grow the most delicious fruits. Every grace that adorns character is developed therefrom."

750 Sorrow

As G. H. Morrison so aptly put it, "Sorrow sounds the deeps, and if rightly taken makes the surface-life impossible. For sorrow lies nearer to the heart of life than joy, and to get near life's heart is always blessed."

F. B. Meyer is famous for the following quotation on sorrow: "There is no anodyne for heart-sorrow like ministry to others."

751 Strength During Tough Times

"Strength alone knows conflict. Weakness is below even defeat, and is born vanquished."

—Madame Swetchine

"To do good is to repel every enemy and to answer every sneer."

—Dr. Joseph Parker

752 Surrender to Christ

"Strengthen me, that I may be able. Give that thou commandest, and command what thou wilt."

—Augustine

" 'Thy will be done' is the keynote to which every prayer must be tuned."

—Dr. A. J. Gordon

"When God beckons you forward He is always responsible for the transport."

—F. B. Meyer

Repentance

753 *"Except Ye Repent"*

Do not imagine that you can progress into a Christian life without first turning squarely away from the world and toward heavenly things. If you were on the wrong road last year, your only salvation is in a right-about-face. Picture a man departing from Cincinnati on his way to San Francisco, turning his car toward the east instead of the west. He realizes his mistake, but does not want to turn around; and so, in spite of regrets and resolutions and protestations that he wants to go to the Pacific coast, he one day ends up confronted by the Atlantic. Conversion means turning about, and it means that you are to do the turning yourself (Luke 13:3).

754 *Sacrificed for Us*

Under the old law the blood of the sacrifice was a reminder to Israel of the awful nature of sin. When man saw it, he said, "I am worthy of death, but the loving, merciful God accepts the slain beast in my stead."

A young man went away from home to start in business. He was wild and reckless and had repeatedly called upon his father to bail him out of trouble. After several years of depravity, he returned home, to find his aged parents in the most desperate circumstances. The old farm had been sold to pay the debts he had contracted, and by hard labor his father was eking out a scanty living. Then there were on the faces of both father and mother deep lines, which told a tale of what they had suffered. The sight opened the young man's eyes and brought him to repentance. "I never realized the enormity of my sin till I saw something of what it had cost," he said. Thus has the blood of Christ spoken to the world of the awfulness of sin. Men, looking upon it, see the cost of their disobedience and are brought to repentance.

755 *Misunderstanding God*

A young man said, "Mother died when we children were small, and after awhile father brought home a new wife. We never took the trouble to find out what she was like; we had made up our minds that we hated her. We treated her badly. Once in awhile father found it out, then he punished us, and so severely that we were sorry for what we had done and resolved to behave ourselves. But we never knew what repentance meant till we saw her real, noble self and learned to love her. That was repentance that cut to the quick." It is so with repentance toward God. We see his great love and his true attitude towards us, and our sins grow black as night beside them. We are ready to fall at the feet of Jesus and cry, "What must I do to be saved?"

756 The Prodigal Son

On one occasion when preaching on the returning prodigal, a pastor paused, looked at the door, and shouted out, after he had depicted him in his wretchedness, "Here he comes, slipshod! Make way—make way—make way, there." Such was the approach to reality, that a considerable part of the congregation turned to the door, some rising on their feet, under the momentary impression that some one was entering the chapel in the state described. In the same sermon, paraphrasing the father's reply to the son that was angry and would not go in, he said: "Be not offended; surely a *calf* may do for a *prodigal, shoes* for a *prodigal*, a *ring* and a *robe* for a *prodigal,* but **ALL** I have is **YOURS**."

757 Reverie of Repentance

There are thousands of people who are given to what may be called the reverie of repentance. There are thousands of people who feel sad that they are such wicked creatures. Really they feel that it is too bad. They at times fall into a minor key. Perhaps if they are educated to music they sit down to the piano and play touching airs and sing of the wickedness of the heart till tears flow down their cheeks. They pity themselves that they are

so pitiable. But how much repentance is there in all this? Is there any definiteness in it? Does the person say, "I am sin-sick." Does the person say, "I am unscrupulous, I am untrustworthy, I give way to debauchery in this direction and to animal appetites in that"? Does the person follow the example of that surgeon who when called to dress a wound, probes it in all directions and cleanses it thoroughly before he binds it up? Does he sit down and explore his heart with a searching, minute examination? No; he does not want to go particularly into it. He merely wants to have a feeling of regret in view of his general sinfulness.

758 A Boy's Rebuke

"And saying, Repent ye: for the kingdom of heaven is at hand." (Matt. 3:2)

In an area of Scotland, there was once a tower called the "Tower of Repentance." What gave the tower its name we are not told, but it is said that an English baronet, walking near the castle, saw a shepherd boy lying upon the ground, reading attentively. "What are you reading, lad?" "The Bible, sir." "The Bible, indeed!" laughed the gentleman; "then you must be wiser than the parson. Can you tell me the way to heaven?" "Yes, sir, I can," replied the boy, in no way embarrassed by the mocking tone of the other; "you must go by way of yonder tower." The gentleman saw that the boy had learned right well the lesson of his book, and, being rebuked, he walked away in silence. Do you, the reader of this illustration, know anything of repentance? If not, then learn!

Resurrection

759 *Belief in the Resurrection*

"I see no greater difficulty," says Pascal, "in believing the resurrection of the dead or the conception of the Virgin than the creation of the world. Is it less easy to reproduce a human body than it was to produce it at first?"

760 *"The Lord Is Risen"*

Philip Henry used to call the Lord's day the queen of days, the pearl of the week, and observed it accordingly. His common salutation of his family or friends, on the Lord's day in the morning, was that of the primitive Christians—"The Lord is risen, He is risen indeed;" making it his chief business on that day to celebrate the memory of Christ's resurrection; and he would say sometimes, "Every Lord's day is a true Christian's Easter day."

761 *Christ's Resurrection*

The Christian man's faith must be always upon the resurrection of Christ, when he is in trouble; and in that glorious resurrection he shall not only see continual joy and consolation, but also victory and triumph over all persecution, sin, death, hell, the devil, and all other tyrants and persecutors of Christ and of Christ's people; the tears and weeping of the faithful dried up; their wounds healed; their bodies made immortal in joy; their souls forever praising the Lord, in conjunction and society everlasting with the blessed company of God's elect, in perpetual joy. But the words of St. Paul in that place, if they be not marked, shall do little profit to the reader or hearer, and give him no patience at all in this impatient and cruel world.

762 *Nature's Teachings*

On the subject of the resurrection, J. Pearson remarks, "Besides the principles of which we consist, and the actions which flow from us, the consideration of the things without us, and the natural course of variations in the creature, will render the resurrection yet more highly probable. Every space of twenty-four hours teaches this much, in which there is always a revolution amounting to a resurrection. The day dies into a night, and is buried in silence and in darkness: in the next morning it appears again and revives, opening the grave of darkness, rising from the dead of night. This is a diurnal resurrection. As the day dies into night, so does the summer into winter. The sap is said to descend into the root, and there it lies buried in the ground; the earth is covered with snow, or crusted with frost, and becomes a general sepulchre. When the spring appears, all begin to rise; the plants and flowers peep out of their graves, revive, and grow, and flourish. This is the annual resurrection."

763 Symbol of Resurrection

The writer of "Faraday's Life" supplies us with the following: The churchyard at Oberhofen, Switzerland, was beautiful, and the simplicity of the little remembrance-posts set upon the graves very pleasant. One who had been too poor to put up an engraved brass plate, or even a painted board, had written with ink on paper the birth and death of the being whose remains were below, and this had been fastened to a board and mounted on the top of a stick at the head of the grave, the paper being protected by a little edge and roof. Such was the simple remembrance; but Nature had added her pathos, for under the shelter by the writing a caterpillar had fastened itself, and passed into its death-like state of a chrysalis, and having ultimately assumed its final state, it had winged its way from the spot, and had left the corpse-like relic behind. How old and how beautiful is this figure of the resurrection! Surely it can never appear before our eyes without touching the thoughts.

Salvation

764 Being Saved "as by Fire"

There is such a fate as being saved, yet so as by fire (1 Cor. 3:15), going into the brightness with the smell of fire on your garments.

765 Child Believer

The little child who believes in Christ may seem to be insignificant in comparison with the prophet with his God-touched lips, or the righteous man of the old dispensation, with his austere purity; as a humble violet may seem by the side of a rose with its heart of fire, or a white lily, regal and tall.

766 Seek Christ

Alexander Maclaren says: "If you do not seek Christ, as surely as He is parted from our sense you will lose Him; and He will be parted from you wholly; for there is no way by which a person who is not before our eyes may be kept near us except only by the diligent effort on our part to keep thought, and love, and will, in contact with Him; thought meditating, love going out towards Him, will submitting. Unless there be this effort, you will lose your Master as surely as a little child in a crowd will lose his nurse and his guide, if his hand slips from out the protecting hand. The dark shadow of the earth on which you stand will slowly steal over His silvery brightness, as it did last night over the moon's, [Total lunar eclipse—August 4, 1884] and you will not know how you have lost him, but only be sadly aware that your heaven is darkened."

767 Reliance upon God

Archbishop Magee states: "In what consists the entire of Christianity but in this—that feeling an utter incapacity to work out our own salvation, we submit our whole selves, our hearts and our understandings, to the Divine disposal; and that, relying upon God's gracious assistance, ensured to our honest endeavors to obtain it, through the mediation of Jesus Christ, we look up to Him, and to Him alone, for safety? Nay, what is the very notion of religion, but this humble reliance upon God?"

768 The Narrow Way

A party of tourists were scaling a lofty peak. The path along which the guide led them was very narrow, and in some places a wall had been built to keep the hikers from stepping aside. A young woman of the party complained loudly of the narrowness and inconvenience of the trail. "Let us take the path over yonder," she said, pointing to a winding road a little distance away.

"It is broader than this one; plus, it is shady and I can see such beautiful flowers on either side." The guide only shook his head, but when they had reached the summit he called the young woman to him and asked her to look back over the way they had come. Both roads were plainly visible. She saw that the one she had longed to take lay along a dangerous precipice, where a misstep would have resulted in death. The very flowers she had admired covered treacherous places. With tears in her eyes, she turned and thanked the guide for having kept her in the narrow path. So I believe it will be with you, if you let the All-wise Guide mark out your path for you. There may be times when the broad road seems inviting, but eternity will reveal the fact that the narrow way was just narrow enough to keep you from all the things that would have been your ruin.

769 *The Will in Salvation*

In Holman Hunt's famous picture of "Christ the Light of the World" there is no latch of the door *outside.* The Christ stands knocking, waiting to be admitted, but the ivy-adorned door must open from the inside. Our Lord never destroys the will, but sweetly inclines us, makes us willing in the day of His power. It is always "Whosoever will" (Rev. 22:17), or "Ye will not" (John 5:40) that secures or loses us salvation. To Jerusalem, with tears of bitter sorrow, He said, "I would, but ye would not" (see Matt. 23:37).

770 *The Joy of Salvation*

It is said that in Japan all ocean vessels are launched with a very beautiful and poetical ceremony. Instead of breaking a bottle of wine over the bows they take a large wicker cage of singing birds, perhaps fifty or sixty, and as the vessels glide down the shipways they set them free. For a moment they poise in midair, and pipe and carol, filling the place with glad song. So is it when the Spirit of God sets free the soul from the servitude of sin and self. Launched on the waters of God's salvation, songs of rejoicing breathe forth from the soul, for not only peace, but joy, comes by believing. The joy of pardon, purity, friendship with God, find expression in excellent praise.

771 *The Point of Conversion*

The freezing point of water and the melting point of ice touch each other, as it were, at a special temperature. A wonderful point is that 32 degrees of Fahrenheit. A hair's breadth lower and the water becomes ice, a hair's breadth higher, and ice becomes water. So in every truly converted soul there was a point, whether consciously recognized or not, where its whole character and destiny were changed. Before, it was hard, cold, dead; after, it was alive, tender, with the newfound life of God.

772 *Christ Is Seeking Us*

Christ is seeking us by our unrest, by our yearnings after we know not what, by our dim dissatisfaction, which insists upon making itself felt in the midst of joys and delights, and which the world fails to satisfy as much as it fails to interpret. There is a cry in every heart little as the bearer of the heart translates it into its truer meaning—a cry after God. And by all your unrests, your disappointments, your hopes unfulfilled and blasted in fulfillment, your desires that perish unfruited—by all the mystic movements of the spirit that yearns for something beyond the material and the visible, Jesus Christ is seeking his sheep. . . .

—Alexander Maclaren

773 *The Cleansing Power of Christ*

When the Standard Oil Company began to refine petroleum there was a black substance that no one knew what to do with. Black, sticky, stinking, it could not be buried, nor burned, nor run into a stream. If it were buried or burned, everyone complained of the all but endurable stench; if it were run into a stream, it killed all the fish. So the company offered a reward to any one able to solve the problem. A great many chemists, attracted by the promised reward, occupied themselves with the problem. Finally one walked into the office of Mr. Rockefeller with a white shining substance, free from every offensive quality, and extremely useful. It was what we know today as paraffine, used for candles and hundreds of other good, useful purposes.

Sin makes it impossible for us to have a relationship with God the Father. And sin is not necessarily considered offensive or degrading in the sight of men. Sin is just our natural condition, in which we do not care for the Kingdom of Heaven. When that condition has deepened into what even men call wrong, such as wicked practices, there is special reason for haste. Only Christ can help. And He helps in such a glorious way that He not only delivers us from the galling yoke of sin, and from its curse; but makes us sweet and clean, so that we may become both acceptable and useful to the Master.

774 *The Accepted Time*

To be convinced that one should come to the Lord Jesus Christ and confess Him before men where alone He is confessed—in the Church—and then to delay, is a serious thing.

The steamer *Central America,* on a voyage from New York to San Francisco, sprung a leak in mid-ocean. A vessel seeing her signal of distress bore down toward her, and the captain of the rescue ship cried, "Let me take your passengers aboard now." But it was night and the commander of the *Central America* feared to send his passengers away in the darkness; and, thinking they could keep afloat a while longer, replied, "Lie by till morning." About an hour and a half later the lights were missed. All on board perished, because they thought they could be saved better at another time.

"Now is the accepted time" (2 Cor. 6:2).

775 Both Born and Adopted

A lady who adopted a baby orphan girl lavished upon her the same love and care as upon her own children. When the child was old enough to attend school, she one day heard someone there remark that she was "only an adopted child." She ran home crying bitterly, and sobbed out to the lady: "Is it true that I'm not really your little girl," "Why, of course you're my little girl," was the answer. "Isn't this your own home, and aren't May and Josey and Willie and Tom your sisters and brothers?" The child's head was laid in her mother's lap, and the lady stroked her hair soothingly: "But, mother, did you born me?"

We are not by birth children of God. No, sin stamps us as children of the devil by birth. But, the moment we receive Christ as Savior we are adopted as children of God. And not only that—to make assurance doubly sure, God provides an actual birth, a new birth—the second birth. The Scots have a soft, pleasant word for children. They call them "bairns" (many Americans call them "brats," you know). "Bairns" means born ones. Thank God, those who have broken with sin and have accepted Jesus Christ as Savior are both adopted orphans and "bairns." For Jesus' sake God adopts us as Jesus' brethren; and through the Holy Spirit he regenerates us.

Christians are both adopted and born as God's children.

776 The Mocking Officer Silenced

A Soldier began to grieve at his lost condition. Presently he found salvation in the Lord Jesus Christ. At once he became the butt of unseemly jests for both officers and soldiers.

One of the officers asked him, "What good does your piety do you?"

"Sir," the soldier replied, "Before my conversion I was drunk every day. Now I am always sober, as you see. Formerly I was slipshod in the performance of my duty. Now, as you know, I am faithful."

The mocking officer was silenced. The Bible is the best textbook of efficiency.

777 The Open Door

A party of friends wanted to enter a quaint old parish church. Going to the sexton to ask for the key, they received it with the promise that he would join them at the earliest opportunity. When he met them he found them still standing before the door, endeavoring to open it with the ponderous key. Taking the key out of their hands he said, "Excuse me; I should have told you that the door was open." Then he lifted the latch, and the crowd entered the sanctuary without further bother.

One who tries to open an unlocked door with a key will have to stay outside. It is that way with an ordinary door. It is also that way with the Lord Jesus Christ. He is the door! He is the door to the kingdom of heaven.

He is the only door! And this door is open. We need only to step inside through faith in him; and all else will follow: holiness, service, happiness.

778 Changed Lives as Proof of Salvation

A missionary was once asked to give a proof that the cross would eventually triumph. This is what he replied: "When I arrived at my mission station, the Fiji Islands, this is what I had to do first of all: bury the hands, arms, feet, and heads of eighty victims whose bodies had been roasted and eaten at a cannibal feast. I lived to see those very cannibals who had taken part in that inhuman feast gathered about the Lord's table." Such a miracle could be performed by no one but Jesus Christ. The products of civilization—schools, factories, saloons, pornography—would have given them disease and death, as they did to most of our Indians. Jesus came, and those that used to eat each other henceforth loved each other. Well, the same cause always has the same effects: always the Gospel changes hearts.

779 The Older Son

A father who had been a faithful witness of the Lord Jesus, lay upon his deathbed. As he lay dying, he occupied himself in his meditations and prayers altogether with his two sons Henry and Charles. "Lord, save my son Henry," he would pray over and over again. A Christian friend that called upon him thought that the father spoke in delirium; for Henry was a model young man, whereas Charles had roamed the country for years as a tramp. Were his mind clear, the friend thought, he would pray much for Charles instead of Henry, and called the attention of the dying man to his apparent error accordingly. But the father replied: "I am not mistaken; my hope that Charles will be saved is much greater than that of Henry's salvation. Henry is a self-righteous boy who does not realize that he, too, must break down at the cross of Christ as a poor sinner."

Personal uprightness, if deemed sufficient for salvation, is a stronger bar to heaven than sin. In Christ's time, sinners came, while the Pharisees stayed away. They do it still.

780 "Not of Works"

The difference between "coming to Christ," and "trying to come," has been frequently discussed. "Have you come to Christ?" said a minister one day to a thoughtful young man. "No; but I'm trying," was the answer. "And how long are you going to try before you come?" "I don't know; but I am doing what I can." "I doubt that; and besides, I suspect you are doing the wrong thing." "What do you mean?" "I mean that you are trying to do a work; and it is not by *trying* or by *working* that you are to be saved." "But does not Christ say, 'Come'?" "Yes, but He does not say, 'Try to come.'" "But am I not to *try?*" "No, you are to *come;* and your speaking so much about *trying* shows that you are bent on *work-*

ing, and that you suppose coming to Christ is a work to be done." "But how am I wrong in *trying?*" "Suppose I said to you, '*Trust* me, and you shall have a gift from me next week,' would you say, 'I'll try'?" "No, certainly." "If you did, what should I suppose you meant?" "That I was not sure of you at all; and that I really distrusted you." "What then do you mean when you say, 'I'll try to trust Christ'?" "I suppose it must mean that I am not sure whether He is trustworthy." "Yes, it does mean that; and it means also that you imagine *trying* and *trusting* to be works which you have to do." "I see it." "I hope you do; but do consider what you really mean by that word *try.*" As they were telling each other good-bye, the minister said, "Will you come and see me soon, and let me know how you are?" "I'll *try* to come some time." "No," said the minister; "you are not to *try,* but to come." He smiled as they parted, at the peculiar illustration which he himself had given of the difference between *trying* and *coming.*

781 The World's Need for Christ

You remember Pharaoh's dream in Genesis 41. Seven kine, which had escaped from the torturing heat into the comparative coolness of the water, came up onto the banks and began feeding on the sedge. Shortly after, seven lean kine came up, and, finding nothing left for them to eat, by one of those strange transformations common to dreams, swallowed up their predecessors. So the seven shriveled ears devoured those which were rank and good. This is a symbol of a fact that is always happening, and is happening now.

Our rulers, like Pharaoh, are having troublesome visions just now. In our land weak things are destroying the strong; hungry creatures are devouring the flourishing and the fat; the sterile is swallowing up the fruitful: and there is no visible improvement. Those who know how much we spend each year for drink and for our army; for extravagance and show—will understand what I mean. Oh, it is grievous to see how much is being squandered to no purpose on all these things, when our toiling masses are sinking deeper and deeper into misery and need! And where is the cure? It seems beyond our reach. Our wisdom, with its parliaments, its learned articles, its congresses, seems at its wits' end and non-plussed. At this very hour, for want of something better, millions of men are under arms to keep the hungry and weak from further devouring the flourishing and fat. For God Himself is bringing Egypt to despair, that it may learn the need of that Jesus who—like Joseph once—is now hidden from its view. Then these Bibles shall be searched for guidance, and places of Christian worship shall be crowded; and the Rejected One shall reign, and His bride shall be given Him. Then shall earth rejoice; for He cometh to rule in equity, and His reign is goodwill to men!

It may be that seven years of famine have been passing over you, devouring all that you had accumulated in happy bygone times, and leaving you bare. Do you not guess the reason? There is a rejected Savior transferred to some obscure dungeon in your heart. There never can be prosperity or peace so long as He is there. Seek Him forthwith. Cause thyself to run to Him. Ask Him to forgive years of shameful neglect. Reinstate Him on the throne. Give the reins of power into His hand. And He shall restore to thee the years that the cankerworm has eaten.

—F. B. Meyer

782 You Can't Save Others

A little girl was helping to nurse a sick gentleman whom she cared for deeply. He said to her, "Ellen, it is time I should take my medicine. Please go and measure a tablespoon of medicine and put it in a small glass for me." She went quickly and soon returned to the elderly man's bedside. When she returned he made no effort to take the medicine from her. He spoke to her finally and said, "Now, will you drink it for me?" "Drink it for you," she replied in a startled manner. "What do you mean? I am certain I would if it would do you any good, but you must take it yourself."

As sinners, people must come to Christ by themselves—no one else can transfer salvation to them. In the same manner as the girl could not take the medicine for the sick gentleman and make him well, we as sinners must claim Christ's forgiveness for ourselves.

783 A Birthday Celebrated With Friends

For the Christian, life begins at the moment he accepts Christ as Savior. That "new birth" is pictured in the First Epistle of John as an inauguration into a family (5:1). Brothers and sisters in Christ are now in fellowship with the new believer. Nicodemus had an extremely difficult time understanding the differences between a "physical" birth and the new "spiritual" birth. But as Christ explained, it is something new that happens to the individual. One sure sign of a believer is his genuine love for others. His life and relationships with others reveal his new birthday.

When children have a birthday celebration, often friends are invited to participate. For the Christian, the instant he believes, God's love is evident in him and his fellow believers and rejoicing follows as they celebrate the new birth.

—Spiros Zodhiates

784 God Is Our Light

The life of Christ as men have observed it has always been the light of men. What does this mean? What is the relationship between "life" and "light"? In order to understand this concept, we must examine the meaning of light. Light as we know it is something that is derived from an outside force. What influences or powers that source is to the common man somewhat unexplainable. Ultimately, as we examine Creation, God is ascribed to be the initial source of light. Light in a spiritual sense can be interpreted in much the same way. As a blind man protests that since he cannot observe light, light may in fact not exist (and does not exist from his point of view) so those who are spiritually blind cannot observe God's light in existence in his life. It does not benefit a blind man to be in a sunlit world in the same way as a sighted person. Nor does it benefit one steeped in unbelief to recognize God's light through the person of Jesus Christ. This is the result of faith.

—Spiros Zodhiates

785 "Jesus Can Save Me"

A famous general would often take his little son into his arms and talk with him about Jesus. The little boy never grew tired of hearing that sweet story for it was always new to him. One day while sitting in his father's lap, he said to his child, "Would my little child like to go to heaven?" The little boy replied, "Yes, papa," "But," said the father, "how can you go to heaven? Your heart is full of sin. How can you expect to go into God's presence and stand before Him?" "But all are sinners, father," the child answered. "That is true," replied the father; "and yet God has said that only the righteous will stand before Him. How then can my little boy expect to go there?" The dear little fellow's face grew very sad. Suddenly he burst into tears and exclaimed to his father, "Papa, Jesus can save me."

John 14:6 says, ". . . I am the way, the truth, and the life: no man cometh unto the father, but my me."

786 The Choice Is Yours

A northeastern United States pastor once changed places with a prison chaplain. One day while preaching a chapel message he spotted a childhood friend who had become an inmate. Upon the conclusion of his message, he approached his long-lost acquaintance and inquired about his demise. In their conversation there was much joy in their childhood memories until the inmate made a startling acknowledgement. He spoke of the crossroads that each of them had come to in their lives. The pastor had chosen to follow Christ while the inmate had followed a life of sin.

The Bible often speaks of choices that must be made in the life of an individual. Matthew 10:34–39 is the summary of Christ's parable about following Christ and forsaking all else: "He that loveth father or mother more than me . . . and he that taketh not his cross and followeth after me, is not worthy of me" (Matt. 10:37, 38).

Satan

787 How Satan Gets Possession

There is a story of a man who rented a piece of ground, with the agreement that he was to have possession of it until his crop should have matured. He utilized the opportunity and made the ground virtually his own by sowing acorns. The lesson is an obvious one. Give the devil one hour in which to scatter his seed in your heart, and he may stay with you the rest of your lifetime to look after the crop.

788 Cunning Evil

Sir Charles Follett, former Chief of Customs of Great Britain, speaking on the clever tricks of smugglers, says: "We have had many extraordinary dodges come under our notice. For instance, innocent-looking loaves of bread, when accidentally examined, were discovered to have had every particle of crumb removed from them, and the inside crammed with compressed tobacco. This is only one example of manifold specimens of cunning to bring in prohibited goods." How cunning is our great enemy to bring into our souls his contraband! Evil thoughts, desires, and deeds, covered with the most innocent and harmless-looking excuses; so that

we need the wisdom from above if we are not to be unmindful of his devices.

789 Satan's Servants

Spurgeon had this to say about Satan's weapons:

"We saw in the museum at Venice an instrument with which one of the old Italian tyrants was accustomed to shoot poisoned needles at the objects of his wanton malignity; we thought of gossips, backbiters, and secret slanderers, and wished that their mischievous devices might come to a speedy end. Their weapons of innuendo, shrug, and whisper appear to be as insignificant as needles, but the venom which they instill is deadly to many a reputation."

790 Fighting the Devil

It has been said that in Martin Luther's home in Wartburg, Germany, there exists a dark spot on one of the walls which was reportedly caused by the breaking of an ink bottle that Luther threw at the devil. Apparently, Luther heard noises in the wall, and thought the noises were from the devil. Many have explained that Luther actually heard rats crawling in the wall, and perhaps rats would be a more logical explanation, but what does it matter—Luther *thought* it was the devil, and so he hurled the ink bottle at the direction of the noise! Charles Goodel adds to this story, "I wish there were more men today who would fling their ink at the devil, whether by the bottleful or in drops from the pen's point."

791 *Resisting the Devil*

D. W. Whittle tells of a man who came to Charles Finney and said: "I don't believe in the existence of a devil." "Don't you?" said the old man. "Well, you resist him for a while, and you will believe in it."

792 *A Bullet-Proof Armor*

A United States marshal had an encounter with "moonshiners," in the mountains of eastern Kentucky, and though struck by eighteen bullets fired at him by the outlaws, he escaped unharmed because he was wearing a bullet-proof vest and other protective clothing that shielded him from enemy fire. The Christian has the best coat of mail ever invented. We need never to go into battle without knowing that the darts of the enemy have no power to harm us. Christians everywhere need to have emphasis put on Paul's earnest appeal: "Put on the whole armour of God, that ye may be able to stand against the wiles of the devil" (Eph. 6:11).

793 *Luther's Argument with Satan*

Luther once said: "Once upon a time the devil said to me, 'Martin Luther, you are a great sinner, and you will be damned!' 'Stop! Stop!' said I; 'one thing at a time. I am a great sinner, it is true, though you have not right to tell me of it. I confess it. What next?' 'Therefore you will be damned.' 'That is not good reasoning. It is true I am a great sinner, but it is written, *Jesus Christ came to save sinners*; therefore *I shall be saved!* Now go your way.' So I cut the devil off with his own sword, and he went away mourning because he could not cast me down by calling me a sinner."

Self

Self Deception

794 *Reality More Wonderful Than Fiction*

Three princes were sent by the king, their father, to bring back wonders from distant countries: the one whose present should be the most extraordinary was to succeed him on the throne. The youngest, whom the tale-teller evidently favors, brought back a walnut, and his brothers smiled disdainfully. The walnut was cracked, and there came out of it a hazel nut, the hazel nut contained a pea, the pea a grain of hempseed, the grain of hempseed a grain of millet; the grain of millet was opened, and a piece of cloth was drawn from it, twenty feet long. When I read greedily so many beautiful stories; when I saw so many genies, enchanters, fairies, beautiful princesses, and loving and brave princes, many times would I desire, at the end of the volume, to sit and carry on the vision in my thoughts; then I awoke, and wept with grief at living in life, instead of living in fairy tales; but I very early discovered that real life contains a hundred times more wonders than these charming fables; and I became reconciled to my fate.

795 *The Enriched Woodman*

For some time past, a circumstance that appeared strange has attracted my attention. I dare say you remember my speaking to you of a house crowned with thatch, of the thatch covered with moss, of the ridge of the roof crowned with iris, which was to be seen from a certain point in my garden. Well, for several days I perceived the house was shut up, and I asked my servant, "Does not the woodman live up yonder now?" "No, sir, he has been gone now nearly two months. He is become rich; he has inherited a property of 600 livres a year; and he is gone to live in town." He is become rich! That is to say, that with his 600 livres a year, he is gone to live in a little apartment in the city, without air and without sun, where he can neither see the heavens, nor the trees, nor the verdure, where he will breathe unwholesome air, where his prospect will be confined to a paper of a dirty yellow, embellished with chocolate arabesques. He is become rich! He is become rich! That is to say, he is not allowed to keep his dog, which he has had so long, because it annoyed the other lodgers of the house. He lodges in a sort of square box; he has people on the right hand and on the left, above him and below him. He has left his beautiful cottage, and his beautiful trees, and his sun, and his grass carpet so green, and the song of the birds, and the odor of the oaks. He is become rich! Poor man!

796 Falsehood and Fraud

There is nothing of so ill consequence to the public as falsehood, or (speech being the current coin of converse) the putting false money upon the world; or so dark a blot as deception, which as Montaigne says prettily, *is only to be brave towards God, and a coward towards man;* for a lie faces God, and shrinks from man.

797 Modesty and Piety

The following advertisement appeared in a Manchester paper:

"To Drapers, Haberdashers, Warehousemen, etc.—Wanted, by an eminently pious young man, of Scotland, who has been regularly bred to the above branches, a situation as assistant clerk, manager, salesman, or traveler. The advertiser is twenty-four years of age, possessed of excellent health, amiable disposition, good ability, extensive knowledge of the great Scriptural doctrines, strictly evangelical, and would be found of immense advantage in assisting to advance the claims and reign of the Messiah's kingdom, amidst the civil and ecclesiastical opposition so prevalent among the nations of the earth in these latter agitating times. Testimonials and references to several eminent evangelical dissenting ministers and members of the Gospel, as well as to his present employers, of the most satisfactory tendency as to character and ability, *with portrait,* may be had on application. A house favorable to evagelical, Presbyterian, or Independent church principles, affording permanent employment, and progressive advancement of salary, preferred."

798 Which Was the Greater Fool?

In a sermon preached by Bishop Hall, upon his eightieth birthday, he relates the following story:

There was a certain lord who kept a *fool* in his house; as many a great man did in those days for their pleasure; to whom this lord gave a staff, and charged him to keep it till he should meet with one who was a *greater* fool than himself; and if he met with such an one, to deliver it over to him. Not many years after, his lord fell deathly ill. His fool came to see him; and was told by his sick lord that he must now shortly leave him. "And where will you go?" said the fool. "Into another world," said the lord. "And will you come again?—within a month?" "No." "Within a year?" "No." "When then?" "Never." "Never! And what provision have you made for your entertainment where you are going?" "None at all." "No!" said the fool, "none at all? Here, take my staff, then. Are you going away forever, and have taken no arrangement, from where you shall never return? Take my staff, for I am not guilty of any such folly as this."

799 *The Dragon of the Abyss*

Important and striking truth is often conveyed to the mind by fable, and enforced on the attention with great power, as in the following eastern story: "A man was traveling in Syria, leading his camel by the bridle. Suddenly, the animal is seized with a panic of fear; he raises himself with impetuosity, foams and bounds in a manner so horrible that his master abandons him in anguish, and tries to save himself. He perceives at a distance from the road a deep stream; and as he still heard the frightful neighings of the camel, he sought a refuge there, and fell over a precipice. But a shrub held him up. He clung to it with both hands, and cast on every side his anxious eyes. Above him is the terrible camel, of which he does not lose sight for a moment. In the abyss below is a dragon who opens his monstrous jaws, and seems waiting to devour him. At the side of him he sees two mice, one white and the other black, who gnaw in turn at the foot of the shrub which serves him support. The unfortunate man remains there frozen with terror, and seeing no retreat, no means of safety. Suddenly, on a little branch of a shrub, he discovers some fruit. At that moment he ceases to observe the rage of the camel, the jaws of the dragon, and the frightful activity of the mice. He reaches out his hand to-

wards the fruit, he gathers it, and in the sweet taste forgets his fears and his dangers. Do you ask who is this madman, who can forget so quickly a mortal peril? That man is thyself. The dragon of the stream is the ever-open abyss of death. The camel represents the sorrows of life. The two mice who are gnawing at the roots of the shrub are day and night. And in this situation the fruit of pleasure attracts you. You forget the anxieties of life, the threatenings of death, the rapid succession of day and night, to seek the plant of voluptuousness on the borders of the tomb."

800 *Be Prepared*

Long ago, there was a greatly disappointed young man at West Point. He came all the way from Wisconsin to enter the Military Academy, and when, on arrival, he found that several documents with large seals were needed to permit him entry, he felt very badly indeed. He was born and reared in a little town in Wisconsin. He had dreamed of being a soldier and determined to come to West Point for a military education. He had a long, hard trip from Wisconsin to the Hudson. He had spent two months walking and riding on freight trains in making the journey. A sentinel stopped him when he tried to enter the barracks, and explained the necessary requirements to get there. The boy was heartbroken, and cried like a child. The Savior says there will be some deceived like that at the last judgment. People who imagined they were going to get into heaven, and yet, having made no preparation for it, will be turned away at last. Heaven is a prepared place for a prepared people.

Selfishness

801 The Parable of the Oil Well

There was a certain man who had a great possession; and, when he would find a profitable place upon which to bestow it, a friend said to him, "Look, there is for sale in a certain city an oil well. Now, this well is fitted out with the finest machinery, and is capable of producing large returns to its owner." So the man sent and bought the well, and, after many days, he journeyed to the place where it was. When he came to the place he found the well even as his friend had said.

"Surely," he said, "this well must be producing much profit for me." One thing he saw, however, that amazed him sorely. Nearly all of the great wheels and belts were idle. In one corner of the well a part of the machinery was in motion.

"Why is it," he said to the overseer, "that my well is yielding me no return?"

"Not so," replied the man, showing a small vial of oil. "The well is producing splendidly, since it turns out every day enough to keep its machinery perfectly oiled."

Then was the owner of the well greatly angry, and said, "Of what advantage is it to me that I have invested my money in this thing? If it is to do no more than to keep itself whole, it might as well be burned to the ground and its place given to another."

So is he who is satisfied with using the grace of God to keep himself pure and has no concern for others.

802 A Double Reward

A gentleman who was working in a factory as a shipping clerk, found that his salary was hardly sufficient to support his family. "My health, too, seemed to be failing," he said, "and I knew that if I were to become ill, my family would surely suffer. I gave up our apartment near the factory and rented a little house near the edge of town. There was plenty of acreage with the house, and I thought that, by spending my free time in cultivating the land, I might raise enough food to provide more for our necessities. The result was that I raised enough produce to supply us all winter. That was not all. The vigorous work involved in gardening made me more physically-fit and healthy."

We ought not go into the business of seeking souls for our own sakes. Indeed, such a thing is impossible, but there is a reward that we reap in ourselves.

803 Give Him the Best

A young man, who had been employed to act as night watchman for a large corporation, made a practice of spending his days going on pleasure trips and coming to his post at night breathless and exhausted. The result was that he soon lost his position, because of the indifferent manner in which he performed his work. No man can come into the early part of the kingdom and serve God well if he has spent the early part of his life and strength in serving self.

804 The Selfish Desire for Comfort

The Decade of the 90's can be described as a decade that is providing unprecedented levels of comfort for most Americans. Most of us live in air-conditioned houses with a television set hooked up to cable and a VCR in almost every room to provide us limitless entertainment. We have microwave ovens to cook our food in a minute or less, hair-dryers, camcorders, and cellular phones we can carry anywhere. We can even shop at home now on our personal computers via the Internet. Our cars often have plush seats, dual-climate controls, cruise-control, even compact disc players to provide us maximum stereo sound as we zip on down the highway. Most of us can not even fathom going back in time only fifty years ago, when almost all of the aforementioned luxuries did not exist! While there is nothing wrong with enjoying the comforts that modern technology offers us, how many of us live for these things only?

Charles Gore says: ". . . it is a selfish thing to want comfort only.

Christ has something more than that to offer. He offers you a share in His work. He offers you co-operation with Himself, the life of a member of His body which is to carry out His work and witness in the world, which is to be detached from material interests, which is to seek first the Kingdom of God."

805 The Danger of Selfishness

Ella Wheeler Wilcox sings with graphic force the oft-taught truth that the only real danger that can come to us is from within, and not from without:

> Not from my foes without, but those within,
> I pray to be protected hour by hour;
> For that aggressive self that leads to sin,
> And lures to pleasure with seductive power,
> Stands ever by the portal of desire,
> And mocks my spirit when it would aspire.

806 The Fate of Selfishness

A party of sportsmen went to an island off the Georgia coast for a week's hunt. After being there several days they started up the coast in an open boat. Just before nightfall there suddenly arose a violent squall, which rendered the boat unmanageable, and carried them twenty-five miles out to sea, damaging the boat to some extent, and disabling her. The seas were running mountain high, and the frail craft tossed about from wave to wave, threatening every moment to capsize and deliver its helpless occupants to a watery grave. One of the men, believing that the boat would soon go down, conceived the idea of taking a beer-keg, which was the only thing they had that would keep one afloat, and trying to save himself by deserting the rest of the party. Watching his chance, he seized the keg and jumped overboard. He was, of course, soon separated from the boat. All through the darkness of that night he drifted, with no knowledge of the direction in which he was going. Buffeted by the waves and chilled by the icy winds, he clung to the keg as his sole hope of life. After spending an awful night, he drifted to the shore the next day, more dead than alive. In the mean time, the remainder of the party stuck to the boat, and, re-rigging the sails, managed to reach shore about nine o'clock in the evening. Selfishness is always bad as a policy as well as bad as a principle. God has so made the world that in self-forgetfulness rather than in self-carefulness there is the truest safety.

807 Naomi's Unselfishness

Louis Banks has this to say about the Book of Ruth: "In studying the beautiful friendship between Ruth and Naomi, which is told with such graphic force in the Book of Ruth, the emphasis is nearly always placed on the fidelity of Ruth. Of course that is perfect, and nothing could detract from it; but to my mind the unselfishness of Naomi when with broken heart she urges Ruth to go away to her own people, and leave her to go on alone, is as beautiful as is Ruth's fidelity. Ruth was a young woman yet, and might have a reasonable hope of some friendships coming to her wherever her tent should be cast; but Naomi had lived most of her life, and if she lost Ruth she lost the last sweet tie of human fellowship; and yet she was willing to do it on Ruth's account. I think her unselfishness proved her to be worthy of Ruth's undying fidelity."

808 What's Yours Is Not Mine

So far as is known, no bird ever tried to build more nests than its neighbor. No fox ever fretted because he had only one hole in the earth in which to live and hide. No squirrel ever died in anxiety lest he should not lay aside enough nuts for two winters instead of one. And no dog ever lost sleep over the fact that he did not have enough bones buried in the ground for his declining years. So many people put the emphasis on the wrong things. The Bible teaches us to lay up treasures in heaven, not here on earth (Matt. 6:19-34). Also, it is important to remember that God will provide for our needs as we seek to please Him only (Ps. 84:11).

809 An Errand Boy

Some years ago, a poor boy came to London in search of a position of errand boy; he made many unsuccessful applications, and was on the eve of returning to his parents, when a gentleman, being captivated by his appearance, gave him a position, and after a few months, made him an apprentice. He so conducted himself during his apprenticeship, as to gain the esteem of every one who knew him; and after he had served his time, his master advanced an investment for him to start his own business. The boy retired to his closet with a heart glowing with gratitude to his Maker for his goodness, and there solemnly vowed to devote a tenth part of his annual income to the service of God. The first year his donation amounted to ten pounds, which he gave cheerfully, and continued to do so till it amounted to £500. He then thought that was a great deal of money to give, and that he need not be so particular as to the exact amount.

That year he lost a ship and cargo to the value of £1500 by a storm! This caused him to repent, and he again resumed his contributions with a resolution never to retract; he was more successful every year, and after a length of time, retired. He then devoted a tenth of his annual income for several years, till he became acquainted with a party of worldly men, who by degrees drew him away from God; he discontinued his giving, took up gambling, and eventually lost every thing he had, and became almost as poor as when he first arrived in London as an errand-boy. "There is," says Solomon, "that scattereth, and yet increaseth; and there is

that withholdeth more than is meet, but it tendeth to poverty" (Prov. 11:24).

810 A Murmuring Father

A man with a large impoverished family received a phone call from a friend who had just won the lottery. The poor man had just been informed earlier of the birth of his twelfth child. He exclaimed peevishly, "God sends wealth to others, children to me." It afterwards happened, that the God he had so disdainfully murmured against, sent him the wealth which he so eagerly and wickedly longed for. But as He sent him the wished-for wealth, he deprived him of the children he had complained of. He saw them one by one go to the grave before him; and in advanced life, and great affluence, when his last beloved daughter was taken from him, he painfully remembered his former rebellious murmurings against God.

811 A Miner

Years ago, J. M., a miner, of the age of 18, was severely burned in a coal mine, by one of those explosions of inflammable air, which often prove fatal. One of his fellow workers suffered so severely from the fire, that he died only three days after the explosion; but J. M. unexpectedly recovered, and in about three months was healthy enough to return to work. Not improved spiritually, however, by his recent narrow escape from death, he immediately relapsed into his former wicked manner of life. One Saturday evening, he agreed with several of his companions to rob a store, and was heard on the occasion using blasphemous words, cursing the same God who had mercifully restored him to health.

This would be the last time he would ever blaspheme God, for while they were in the getaway car, the driver suddenly lost control and drove head-on into a telephone pole. All passengers in the car were killed, including J. M. Thus died J. M. in the very bloom of youth; a young man of vicious habits and of a depraved heart.

Young people often indulge in sin, under an idea that they have plenty of time to prepare for death; but how often does the Almighty speak in the terrors of his judgments, and say to us, "Be ye therefore ready, for in such an hour as ye think not, the Son of man cometh!" (Matt. 24:44).

812 Two Guilty Cossacks

In Russia, the winter of 1827-28 was unusually severe. This made traveling very dangerous and many were frozen to death. Two merchants, from the interior, set out on a journey to Astrachan, for the purpose of purchasing fish; they drove their own horse-driven sled, and carried their money (about 12,000 rubles) with them. In passing through the desolate wasteland of the Cossacks country they lost their way, and were in great danger of freezing to death. They agreed that one of them should set off on horse-

back, and endeavor to find some village, while the other was to lie covered up in the sled. Deciding by the casting of lots of who should remain, the other, after riding for some length of time, came to a Cossacks village. In the first house he entered lived an old man, to whom, after having warmed himself a little, he related his circumstances, and thoughtlessly mentioned the sum of money which was left with his companion in the sled. The old man questioned him strictly as to the particular spot where his companion was left; but, at last, told him he could give him no assistance, as he was an old man, and had no younger person to send along with him.

The merchant, therefore, went to some of the other houses in the village, and after some time, persuaded two or three men to accompany him to the steppe where his companion was left. They were glad to find him still alive, but he had been robbed of the money. The intensity of the frost, and darkness coming ever so quickly, prevented them from attempting to trace out the robbers, and they returned to the village, intending, the next day to find the thieves. In the meantime, suspicion fell on the old man, who, it was well known in the village, had two sons, both of whom lived at home. The next morning, a large party of Cossacks set out with the merchants in search of the robbers, and traced them a considerable way into the steppe, where the two sons of the old man were found, frozen to death, and the money belonging to the merchants in their possession.

Sin

813 Fellowship with Christ Can Display Our Shortcomings

The higher the temperature the more chilling would it be to pass into an icehouse; and the more our lives are brought into fellowship with the perfect Life, the more we shall feel our own shortcomings.

814 Sin's Effect on One's Conscience

The thick skin of a savage will not be disturbed by lying on sharp stones, while a crumpled rose-leaf robs the sensualist of his sleep. So the habit of evil hardens the cuticle of conscience, and the practice of goodness restores tenderness and sensibility; and many a man laden with crime knows less of its tingling than some fair soul that looks almost spotless to all eyes but its own. One little stain of rust will be conspicuous on a brightly-polished blade, but if it be all dirty and dull a dozen more or fewer will make little difference. As men grow better they become like that glycerine barometer recently introduced, on which a fall or a rise, that would have been invisible with mercury to record it, takes up inches, and is glaringly conspicuous.

815 Babylon and Jerusalem

That the Jews learned at least one lesson from their captivity in Babylon can not be disputed. Never again did they cast their eyes longingly after strange gods. For all that, the lesson was dearly bought. In the day when liberty to the captives was proclaimed, comparatively few of the people responded. While many returned to Jerusalem, many more lingered in Babylon. Some of them, no doubt, were wedded to the ways of Babylon and had no desire to leave it. Others, perhaps, were so bound by domestic and business relations that they could not get away.

The same things are true of those who are carried off into the Babylon of sin. A few return to the Jerusalem of peace, having profited by their bitter experience, but many more never come back at all. They love the ways of sin, or they have become so anchored to its institutions that escape has become nearly impossible. Let the young man who counts upon taking his "fling" among the attractions of a sensual life be warned. He may be among those who will never return to the city of peace.

816 The Wages of Sin

In one of our large industrial towns a plant was erected for the manufacture of artificial flowers. The work was enjoyable, and the wages paid to the employees were far better than they had been able to earn elsewhere. The establishment was looked upon as a godsend, and the proprietor as a benefactor to the community.

Very soon, however, the health of one of the brightest and most capable girls began to fail. She went listless and weary to her work, and when it was done was barely able to drag herself home. One day she was not able to leave her bed, and a week later the undertaker's hearse stood at the door. She had been the support of a feeble mother and several small children. Suddenly other employees went home from the factory white and fainting, to go to work no more. Finally an investigation was made, and it was found that the workers had been all the while inhaling the most deadly chemicals, which were used in the coloring of the flowers. While they had been generously paid in money, a part of the real wages was—death. Does this not make plain the words of Paul, "The wages of sin is death" (Rom. 6:23)? Sin may pay you liberally in mirth or money, but that is not all. There is a part of the pay that can be deferred for a time, but it is sure to come. "The soul that sinneth, it shall die!" (Ezek. 18:20).

817 "If Thy Hand Offend Thee"

"I see you have had the misfortune of losing one of your hands," someone said to a fine-looking man. The gentleman smiled, and hesitated a moment before he answered:

"Yes, or the good fortune. While a man can't exactly rejoice that he must go through life with only one hand, he must acknowledge that it is better than not going through life at all. The loss of that hand saved my life. It was this way: Some years ago I bought a large manufacturing plant, and while I knew nothing about machinery, it always was a wild fascination for me. In spite of the warnings of the work crew, I was always poking about into places that I had been told were dangerous. One day (I never knew just how it happened) my hand was caught in the machine, and in an instant I felt myself drawn into the very jaws of the machine that would have crushed my body into pulp. The foreman saw my danger; however, he knew that by the time the machinery could be stopped it would be too late. Without the least hesitation he seized a great cleaver and, with an accurate blow, severed my hand from my arm. It was heroic treatment, and for awhile it looked as though I should die from the effects of it. You see that I did not."

Could there be found a better illustration of the meaning of the words of Christ, when he said: "If thy hand offend thee, cut it off and cast it from thee: for it is profitable for thee that one of thy members should perish, and not that thy whole body should be cast into hell" (Matt. 5:30)? In spite of every warning, men are continually being caught in the whirlwind of sin and folly, to find at last that their only hope lies in cutting off that which is a very part of them. Many such go limping through the world, thankful for their deliverance and yet, what a sorrowful reminder of the awful cost of sin.

818 Deadly Deception of Sin

In the northeast corner of the great Yellowstone National Park, there is a gloomy ravine which is known as Death Gulch. At the foot of the mountain slopes there is a stream impregnated with sulphate of alumina, which is death to all animal life. A recent visitor saw quite a number of dead bears which had been killed by drinking the water. Sin has its Death Gulch, and how many men and women are first fascinated and then killed by its fatal stream! It seems to invite; it means to slay.

819 Sin's Beginnings

A former Chief of Police of the City of Paris, France, once said concerning the thefts that take place at the great shops there: "This is the beginning. From a gallery one sees a woman—rich or well-to-do—who buys a number of articles, and pays for them, but takes slyly some little insignificant thing. No one will say she is stealing, but she is closely observed. A little later she will annex an article of greater value, and after this she will steal for the pleasure of stealing." Beware of the beginnings of evil; watch and pray

at the first temptation; then the "secret faults" will never lead to the "presumptuous sins."

820 Consequences of Depravity

The fall of man, and the depravity that is ours; as its fruit, is "total," in the sense that it extends to the whole of our human nature. Mind, heart, imagination, will; all are injured and marred in their operation. If a finger be poisoned it is not the finger only that is affected. The poison circulates in the blood, and if it be not expelled the life will be threatened. So sin in the soul is moral blood poisoning. It injures every faculty and power; weakens all that is noble, and biases to all that is opposed to God's absolute reign in the heart. Hence, as Savior, he comes to put away sin, as a whole, and in each one who trusts in Him.

821 The Danger of Delay in Dealing with Little Sins

Years ago, a French naturalist brought a handful of gypsy moths to this country for purposes of scientific experiment. Some of the moths escaped. If taken in hand at once, they could easily have been destroyed, but the State authorities took twenty years trying to decide how to address the problem. Because of the delay, the problem ended up costing the State of Massachusetts over a million dollars. The dangerous multiplication of evil thoughts and the growth of sinful habits are like that. If the wicked thought is driven out at once, it can be done easily; but if permitted to nest in the heart it rapidly multiplies in power and influence.

822 Flying into the Face of Danger

A train running from Long Island City to Patchogue at a late hour at night crashed into a herd of deer which were standing on the track. The animals seemed dazed by the headlight of the engine. Two of them were killed outright, while others were injured. One of the maddened animals jumped up past the cab and landed in the middle of the coal-laden tender. The deer is the most timid and gentle of all animals, and yet when confused becomes the most reckless in its desperation. No one knows of what reckless, foolish deeds he may be capable if once the heart is fascinated and confused by the baleful glare of evil. It is better to keep away from the track where the devil runs his engines.

823 Hereditary Crime

A former police chief of New York City once spoke of one of the precincts as the social plague-spot of the city. The number of arrests in that great, teeming nest of vice and crime are always near the top of the national crime lists. In this former chief's opinion, all the industrious and respectable families, whose employment income permits them to move, will, sooner or later, find homes in the suburban part of the metropolis. The gangs, drug push-

ers and prostitution ringleaders, however, will stick to their old environments like barnacles to the native rock, and will never go until they are driven out. In many neighborhoods generations of criminals have succeeded each other. Mothers have delivered sons whom they knew would eventually be incarcerated. What is needed above everything else, for the salvation of these large cities, is to break up that deadly line of hereditary crime. But it can never be done without downtown churches, backed with abundant means, not just to distribute old clothes and cheap soup, but to preach the old-fashioned Gospel which Paul preached in Ephesus in the spirit that turns the world upside down.

824 The Tragedy of Single Sins

A Frankfort, Kentucky woman was the victim of a strange accident. She arose in the night to get a drink of water, and in drinking she also swallowed a small black spider that had dropped off of the faucet of her kitchen sink—into her drinking glass. She felt the spider going down her throat, but did not know what it was. In an hour or two she became nauseated, and ejected the spider, but not until it had bitten her internally. The poison from the bite soon spread through her system, and her condition became life-threatening. The flesh puffed up in rolls and ridges, her ears swelled so tightly that the blood oozed through the skin, while her tongue swelled till she almost suffocated. Emergency Room physicians worked for several hours, administering all the antidotes known to medical science, and finally saved her life. The little spider that had such a venomous bite is not larger than a pea, and can roll itself up into a complete ball and float on the water like a piece of cork. So a single sin may poison the whole lifeblood of the moral nature. A single sinner in a circle of acquaintance may spread his moral pestilence through a score of hearts. Beware of the tragedy of single sins.

825 Convinced of Sin, yet Fascinated by It

Professor Charles Rice, the botanist, once had a most thrilling experience with a rattlesnake. He was on a botanical expedition with a fellow scientist, and was sleeping in an open tent. He was aroused from his sleep, one morning, to find to his horror a large rattlesnake coiled on his chest with its head raised to strike at the least movement. While he realized his awful danger, the eyes of the snake seemed to fascinate him, and left him powerless to think or act in any way to save himself. The strain was so great that he mercifully swooned away, and his companion on awakening discovered the snake and destroyed it.

There are many times when people are conscious of their sins, and yet are so fascinated by their evil habits that they seem powerless to break away from them, or crush them out of existence; but if we will breathe a prayer to Christ we shall never lack His help in delivering us from the deadly danger of our sins.

826 Blood Will Tell

Mr. Perry, who was with Lieutenant Peary, the great discoverer, on his Arctic trip, snared a beautiful blue fox in Greenland, and decided to make a pet out of it. On returning to this country, Mr. Perry took the fox to his home at Phillipston, Massachusetts, and installed it in a roomy cage. The fox ate well, and was keeping in good condition, and her owner was hopeful of ultimately gaining a place in her affections. But one night she broke out of the cage, went to a neighbor's farm and killed a number of valuable chickens, and was shot to death by one of the farmhands. Beautiful as the blue fox was, she had the true fox blood, and it led her to death.

One may be a blue-blooded sinner, or a fashionable sinner, but such sins are just as truly sins as the most common and vulgar witnessed in the street. They are just as dangerous too. Anywhere and everywhere, "the wages of sin is death" (Rom. 6:23).

827 The Awful Waste of Sin

A little boy led a policeman to a house which appeared at first to be deserted, but at last a little girl appeared at the door and said she kept house for her father and her little brothers. "I am all alone today," said the ten-year-old child. "Daddy is drunk and has gone away, and he has sold all the furniture." On examination it was found that the father was only a few years since a well-known Wall Street broker, and a member of the New York Stock Exchange. He married a beautiful woman out of a splendid family, whose parents gave her a present of ten thousand dollars on her wedding day. This money and all her husband's fortune had been spent in the bars and carry-outs. A month ago, the wife died, and the husband had been drunk nearly ever since. Who can compute the waste that has gone on in that home! No wonder the prophet exclaims: "Wherefore do ye spend money for that which is not bread, and your labor for that which satisfieth not?" (Is. 55:2).

828 "Be Sure Your Sin Will Find You Out"

(Num. 32:23)—Once in a certain part of Germany, a box of treasure that was being sent by railway was found to have been opened and emptied of its contents, and filled with stones and rubbish. The question was, who was the robber? Some sand was found sticking to the box, and a clever mineralogist having looked at the grains of sand through his microscope, said that there was only one station on the railway where there was that kind of sand. Then they knew that the box must have been taken out at that station, and so they found out who was the robber. The *dust under his feet,* where he had set down the box to open it was a *witness against him* (Mark 6:11).

829 The Whole World for a Human Soul

"For what shall it profit a man, if he shall gain the whole world, and lose his own soul?" (Mark 8:36).

When Lysimachus was engaged in a war with the Getae, he was so tormented by thirst, that he offered his kingdom to his enemies for permission to quench it. His exclamation, when he had drunk the water with which they furnished him, is striking. "Ah, wretched me, who for such a momentary gratification, have lost so great a kingdom!"

How applicable is this to the case of those who for the momentary pleasures of sin, part with the kingdom of heaven!

830 Talleyrand's Death-Bed

For nearly half a century this veteran diplomat acted a prominent part in the affairs of Europe. As the prime minister or ambassador of the Directory, the Consulate, the Empire, the Restoration, and the Monarchy of Louis Philippe, he negotiated the important treaties which determined the boundaries of empires and fate of kingdoms, and formed plans which made Napoleon an emperor, and the emperor an exile. Such a man's view of an eventful life of eighty years furnishes instructive lessons to men who are wasting the energies of life on political ambition or worldly aggrandizement. Just before his death, a paper was found on his table on which he had written, by the light of the lamp, such lines as these: "Behold eighty-three years passed away! What cares! What agitation! What anxieties! What ill-will! What sad complications! And all without other results, except great fatigue of mind and body, and a profound sentiment of discouragement with regard to the future, and disgust with regard to the past!"

831 A Highwayman

In the autumn of 1817, a complaint was made at Hatton-Garden police office by two ladies, who stated that they had been robbed in the following singular manner: while walking near Battle Bridge, about six o'clock in the evening, a dog, unaccompanied by any person, sprung suddenly from the roadside and seizing hold of the purse which one of the ladies had in her hand, forcibly snatched it from her, and turning off the road, made his escape.

A constable stated that a dog answering the same description had also robbed a poor woman of a bundle containing two shirts, some handkerchiefs, etc., with which he escaped. Several other instances of a similar nature were mentioned, and the general conclusion was that the animal had been trained up to the business, and that his master was in waiting at no great distance to receive the fruits of the canine plunderer.

Oftentimes, we are the dog which, by submitting to our flesh, attack those others by our tongue and actions. But, in a much more callous way, besides serving another, we serve our own interests and do not care for the feelings of others.

As Paul wrote in Philippians 2, the believer should keep others before himself, so that their joy can be full.

832 Taking Hold

A wise old tutor was once taking a stroll through a forest with a curious youth by his side. The tutor suddenly stopped and pointed to four plants close at hand. The first was a tiny sprout, just coming out of the earth. The second had rooted itself quite firmly in the fertile soil. The third was a small shrub. The fourth had grown into a well-developed tree.

The teacher said to his youthful companion, "Pull up this first plant." The youth pulled it up easily with his fingers. "Now pull up the second." The boy obeyed, and with slight effort the plant came up, root and all.

"And now the third." The boy pulled with one hand, then the other, but it would not come. Then he took both hands, and the plant yielded to all his strength. "And now," said the master, "try the fourth." The youth grasped the trunk with all his might, but hardly a leaf shook. "I cannot move it," he exclaimed.

"Just so, my son," said the teacher, "with all our bad habits. When they are young and small, we can cast them out, but when they are full grown, they cannot be uprooted."

833 The Real Enemy

Many years ago the Pogo cartoon character made a statement that revealed the real cause of human problems. He said, "We have found the enemy and he is us!"

We are quick to blame the devil or someone else for all of life's problems. We continue to beat our heads against an imaginary wall fighting an enemy that does not exist while the real enemy is within. We are self-satisfied, self-centered, self-sufficient, and selfish.

Adam blamed Eve for his sin (Gen. 3:12), but his problem was with self. Eve accused the serpent for causing her sin (v. 13) but her enemy was self. Sin originated with self and sin continues today because people refuse to let go of self. The self we so desperately cling to will be lost until we learn to let go of it. We should not be amazed that Jesus once said that in order to find ourselves, we must first lose ourselves (Matt. 10:39). Yet, most people are desperately clinging to self.

This week a little bird reminded me of self-centered people who are destroying themselves while fighting an imagined enemy. You may consider this strange, but the bird is attacking its own reflection that it sees mirrored in our basement window. The bird repeatedly attacks the basement window. I have seen this phenomenon before and have wondered why some birds do such a thing. I recently found out why. A bird who attacks itself in a mirrored reflection is usually a male bird who has certain territory that he claims as his own. If another male bird enters his territory, he attacks it. Occasionally a male bird

claims a piece of territory that has a house in it with glass windows. When the light is right he sees a reflection of himself and thinks it is an enemy intruding on his territory. He will consistently attack his reflection until the reflection is somehow eliminated, until he gets disoriented, or until he kills himself.

They beat their heads against their own reflection, thinking they are fighting an enemy, while all of the time the real enemy is inside. Every human problem is caused by each individual attempting to make self the center of life. You can see how problems would arise with everyone wanting his or her own private self as the center. You have probably heard some say, "I never had any problems until I met him," or "I do not have any problems when I am by myself." What they say is true because a person who is around only himself has no rivals.

There is a sound biblical solution to all of our problems caused by self-centeredness. Paul said that we must die to self and live for Christ (Rom. 6:11). He said of himself: "I no longer live, but Christ lives in me. The life I live in the body, I live by faith in the Son of God, who loved me and gave himself for me" (Gal 2:20 NIV): When we are in Christ and Christ is in us then we become one with Christ and everyone else who is in Christ. Then we are no longer threatened by our own reflection because self is no longer our goal; Christ is. We can all be one in Christ if we are willing to die to self (Gal. 3:26-28). Self is the real enemy and until you give that self up to Christ you will never find life or peace or happiness.

—Riley L. Walker

834 Man and the World

What's wrong with the world? Confusion, violence, intolerance— man's inhumanity to man abounds! The tragedy in Waco, the strange ethnic-cleansing war in the former Yugoslavia, the starvation in Somalia and other places, the Homosexual march on Washington and on and on we could go. What is wrong? The major problem is MAN!

A small boy filled with all kinds of playful ideas anxiously awaited his father's return from work. An extra long day at the office, however, had taken its toll, and his father longed for a few minutes of relaxation. Over and over again the boy tugged at his dad's leg with yet another suggestion of something they might do together. Well, finally in total frustration the father ripped from a magazine a picture of the world and tore it into a hundred pieces. "Here," he said handing the child a roll of scotch tape, "go and put the world back together." Ah, peace at last, or so he thought. But, in just a few minutes, he was interrupted again, there before him stood his son—and in his hands was a crudely fashioned picture of the world. "Son, that's incredible. How did you do it?" "It was easy," said the boy, "you see on the other side of

the picture of the world was the picture of a man, and as soon as I got man straightened out the world came together."

What a profound answer from a child! How true! Get man fixed and the world will be okay. What implications for man! Our mission from God is to help fix the world. But, how? Technology? Education? Politics? Welfare? Economics? These are not working! There is a deeper problem. It is the sin problem in our hearts. James asked, "From what comes wars and fightings among you? don't they come from your lusts that war in your members?" (James 4:1). **Man is the problem!**

God wants to fix man. Jesus was sent to provide the way. The gospel is the good news that a solution is available. Our business is to take this message. We do not force men! We try to get people to think. The gospel appeals to the intellect, the emotions and will. Let us really get serious about our task to help man and the world.

—Clarence DeLoach, Jr.

835 Think About It

Watch your thoughts; they become words.

Watch your words; they become actions.

Watch your actions; they become habits.

Watch your habits; they become character.

Watch your character; it becomes your destiny.

What starts out as a simple thought may ultimately determine our destiny, even our eternal destiny. The writer of the above statement must have heard or read the words of Solomon found in Proverbs 23:7: "As a man thinks in his heart, so is he." Our thoughts reflect the person we really are. If we have thoughts which are hateful, they will manifest themselves as words—actions—habits. If, however, we fill our hearts with positive things, can anything but good actions result?

Paul summed it up rightly when he wrote in Philippians 4:8, (NIV) "Finally, brothers, whatever is true, whatever is noble, whatever is right, whatever is pure, whatever is lovely, whatever is admirable—if anything is excellent or praiseworthy—think about such things." Think about "these things." If we occupy our time on thoughts concerning "these things," it cannot help but result in an eternal destiny with God the Father.

We are what we think.

—Steven Killpatrick

836 Fable of a Lamb and Mud

The story is told of a lamb and its mother. It seems that the lamb passed a pigpen each morning on the way to the pasture with its mother. Watching the pigs wallow in the mud seemed like fun, and on an especially hot day the lamb asked his mother if he could jump the fence and wallow in the cool mud. She replied, "No." Then the lamb asked the usual question,

"Why?" The mother just said, "Sheep do not wallow."

This did not satisfy the lamb. He felt that she had put him down and exercised force when she should not have. As soon as the mother was out of sight, the lamb ran into the pigpen and jumped the fence. He was soon feeling the cool mud on his feet, his legs and soon his stomach. After a few moments he decided he had better go back to his mother, but he could not! He was stuck! Mud and wool do not mix. His pleasure had become his prison. He was hopelessly bound by his own folly. He cried out and was rescued by the kind farmer. When cleaned and returned to the fold, his mother said, "Remember—sheep do not wallow!"

Sin is like that. It looks so nice, so easy to escape whenever we wish, but it is not so! Pleasures become our prison. Christians should not wallow (2 Pet. 2:14-22).

837 Less Is More

When Latimer resigned his diocese, Foxe tells us that as he put off his vestments from his shoulders he gave a skip on the floor for joy, "feeling his shoulders so light at being discharged of such a burden." To be relieved of our wealth or high position is to be unloaded of weighty responsibilities, and should not cause us to fret, but rather to rejoice as those who are lightened of a great load. If we cease from office in the church, or from public honors, or from power of any sort, we may be consoled by the thought that there is just so much the less for us to answer for at the great audit, when we must given an account for our stewardship.

838 The All-Seeing Eye

The great astronomer, Mitchell, was one day making some observations on the sun, and as it descended towards the horizon, just as it was setting, there came into the rays of the great telescope the top of a hill seven miles away. On the hill was an orchard, and in one of the apple trees were two boys stealing apples. One was getting the fruit and the other was keeping watch. But there sat Professor Mitchell, seven miles away, seeing every movement as plainly as if he were on the spot.

So men think and act now as if God's eye could not see them.

Spiritual

839 The Time Is Short

In a certain factory, where each man was required to finish so much work in a given length of time, bells were rung at intervals to remind the men just how much time they had left. "The men work better when they realize that the day is slipping away from them," the manager explained.

The same thing is true of us concerning spiritual things. We need often to be reminded that "the time is short." "The night cometh when no man can work" (John 9:4). We work better when we realize that the day is slipping away from us.

840 Let Jesus Give You Strength

A boy saw a man lifting great, heavy weights. He would lift them and then put them down just where he found them. He didn't seem to be doing anything in particular; so, eventually, the boy asked the man what he was trying to do. He said that lifting weights would make him strong. At once there was a question in the boy's mind as to why, while he was at it, he did not lift something that needed to be lifted. Like lifting weights for exercise strengthens the participant, so does the "lifting up" of other fel-

low-Christians. Christian exercise, however, differs from physical athletics in this: The man gets strength when he is not making an effort in his own behalf at all. As a rule, his own uplifting and strength come to him as a surprise.

841 Manifestation of the Spirit

When Mr. Moody held in Birmingham the series of remarkable evangelistic meetings which so intensely stirred that city, Dr. Dale, who was warmly sympathetic, yet greatly amazed at the marvellous results which it produced, once said to the famous evangelist that "the work must be of God for he could see no real relation between him (Mr. Moody) and the work that was done." That is ever the proof conclusive of the Spirit's presence and active power. Peter disclaimed all honor for the healing of the lame man: Paul forever protested, "yet not I, but the grace of God which was with me" (1 Cor. 15:10). In all truly Divine blessing and success, there is something which cannot be attributed to merely human causes. Paul plants, Apollos waters—but increase is God's sovereign gift.

842 The Spirit of the Bible

Who built St. Paul's Cathedral in London? So many masons, carpenters, iron-workers, carvers, painters; and then there was Wren. Yes, there was Christopher Wren. He was not a mason, nor a carpenter, nor an iron-worker. He never laid a single stone, drove a nail, or forged a railing. What did he do? *He did it all.* He planned the splendid edifice: inspired with his thought and purpose all their toil, and shaped through every worker. They were his "hands," and, even today, people flock in thousands from all over the world to see the legendary architect Christopher Wren's masterpiece. Who wrote the Bible? Moses, David, Isaiah, John, Paul? Yes. But *the Holy Spirit did it all.* "For the prophecy came not in old time by the will of man: but holy men of God spake as they were moved by the Holy Ghost" (2 Pet. 1:21).

Blindness

843 Blind to Christ's Importance

How men may live in the presence of the noblest inspirations and yet be blind to them is pathetically illustrated in the present condition of the *Last Supper,* by Da Vinci, the greatest and noblest triumph in the whole realm of art.

Of the many acts of vandalism which have been perpetrated in the realm of art none stands out so gross as that through which this immortal work has suffered. Painted on the end wall of the Maria delle Grazie, in Milan, the holy monks were able to gaze upon it as they sat at their table. But so much did they value it, or esteem its spiritual power, that, finding the passage into their dining-hall too distant from the kitchen, they actually made a way through the wall upon which the picture was painted, cutting out as they did so the feet of the Savior! Surely that blindness of soul which makes men dead to spiritual realities was never more astoundingly illustrated. For here were men whose duties were spiritual, and who had consecrated their lives to spiritual things, so blind in soul that they carelessly sacrificed the most spiritual work of art ever produced to the cravings of appetite.

844 Hiding the Light

David Rittenhouse of Pennsylvania was a great astronomer. He was skillful in measuring the sizes of planets and determining the position of the stars. But he found that, because of the distance of the stars, a silk thread stretched across the glass of his telescope would entirely cover a star; and thus a silk fiber appeared to be larger in diameter than a star. Our sun is 886,000 miles in diameter, and yet, seen from a distant star, our sun could be covered, hidden behind a thread when that thread was stretched across the telescope. Just so we have seen some who never could behold the heavenly world. They always complained of dullness of vision when they looked in the heavenly direction. You might direct their eyes to the Star of Bethlehem through the telescope of faith and holy confidence; but, there is a secret thread, a silken fiber, which, holding them in subserviency to the world, in some way obscures the light; and Jesus, the Star of Hope, is eclipsed, and their hope darkened. A very small sin, a very little self-gratification, may hide the light. To some Jesus, as Savior, appears very far off. He shall be seen where the heart lets nothing, nothing intervene.

Deadness

845 Spiritual Vagrancy

Nearly every man acknowledges that it would be a blessed thing to be a Christian, if only he could reap the benefits without the costs. The common drifter has pretty much the same idea about the things that pertain to respectable living. He would have no objections to being well fed, and clothed too, for that matter, if only he could have these things without working for them. "I often feel that you Christians are to be envied," a young man remarked, "but it would cost me something to become a Christian." In other words, he would have been glad to have eaten bread in the kingdom of God, but he was not willing to work for it.

846 "No Interruption to Business"

On a busy city street, a sidewalk in front of a large building was obstructed with building materials. A great scaffolding had been built across the front, and from it was suspended a sign bearing the words, "**We are Open—No Interruption to Business.**" The public, however, seemed not to agree with the proprietor of the store, since not only were there no signs of customers about the store, but passersby even shunned that part of the street. The decision of the storekeeper that his business should not be interrupted didn't settle the matter, after all.

A young man who had been zealous for Christ and the church took on business responsibilities which absorbed the time he had been giving to spiritual activities. "I am not going to let it interfere with my Christian life," he told the pastor, and yet it did. He had piled so many obstructions between himself and the spiritual influences that had once had access to his heart that they ceased to touch him.

A preacher allowed himself to be caught up in politics. "I do not intend that it shall hinder my work as a soul-saver," he said, but that was only one side of the case. People ceased to come to him with their burdens. They saw obstructions between them and the man they had once felt free to confide in, so they passed by on the other side. The Christian's first concern ought to be that nothing shall interrupt him in his legitimate business—that of carrying out the commission of the Master.

847 Pressing Forward

The manager of a large marine engineering corporation once stated in a newspaper interview that it was commonplace to promote his apprentices to the positions of engineers for large steamships. These engineers were advanced from one grade to another in the order of merit or seniority, as vacancies occurred; but a very striking thing usually happened. So long as these men were climbing towards the top of the corporate ladder they were sober, steady, earnest, active, trustworthy in their work, but when they became chief-engineers, then came danger. They had reached the zenith of their ambition, they began to relax their watchfulness, became careless, and often lost their positions. Their lies the danger in the spiritual life; so long as we follow after a Divine ideal we are safe; the instant we dream we have already attained to all that is possible, we are in danger of apostasy.

Growth

848 Sir Isaac Newton on Beginnings

Sir Isaac Newton states that he did not consider that he had any advantage over other men, except that whatever he thought of sufficient importance to begin he had sufficient resolution to continue, until he had accomplished his object.

849 Foundations of a Christian Life

After a while, when a man has fairly committed himself to a Christian life, many of those things which have been against him turn around, and are like winds in his sails to help him. The great thing is to begin—to begin honestly, to begin with the help of Christ and God—to *begin*. For this is one of those cases in which to begin is half the journey. And where a man is willing to say to his companion, or to some friend or Christian brother, "The time past suffices in which I have lived a worldly life, and I am going by the grace of God, to begin to lay the foundations of a Christian life," in many and many cases the crisis is past. You may not have joy today, nor for weeks; but you are on the way toward it. It may not be conversion, but it will stand intimately connected with it. And if anyone reading this shall say, "I am willing to begin a new course," that is no small matter. To make a beginning in the right direction is a great thing.

850 Do Not Live on Past Experiences

All things in this world run their course, "they have their day and cease to be." New movements arise possessing initial force, and inspired by some living message. While the force lasts the movement sweeps down opposition, but with the expenditure of that initial energy nothing else can keep it alive. It cannot live on its past. This finds illustration in the history of art. Through the Renaissance period art blazed into marvellous splendor, difficulties seemingly insurmountable were overcome with ease, the most amazing triumphs were attained by men possessing the smallest resources.

Then with almost dramatic suddenness virtue seemed to pass out of art, the fire of attainment died down in the heart, and a generation of artists arose who, having no inspiration of their own, contented themselves in imitating the works of the inspired men who had gone before. The art historian puts his finger upon the year 1530, after the death of Raphael, as the date when the light went out and art passed into twilight and obscurity. Many attempts were made to keep art alive by the Mannerists and Eclectics, but it was of no use. Art cannot be kept alive by galvanizing it from without. Life comes only from within. It is of no use, therefore, trying to live on past experiences. We must ever go to the source for new inspiration and, like the Israelites, get manna for each new day.

851 The Price of Spiritual Success

A tersely expressed truth was the answer of the business man when his friend asked him if he had met with success in business. "Met with it?" he replied; "I should say I have not. All the success I have attained I had to run after."

Quite the same is true in our spiritual lives. Men and women do not meet the ideal casually. Neither do they become saints while they are asleep.

852 Glorify the Father by Bearing Fruit

Two friends were talking of the family of a prominent man who had just died. "His oldest son was the source of great joy to him," one of them said. "He brought great distinction upon the family name."

"And what of the other two?"

"Oh they were well enough. That is, they never did anything to disgrace their father. Still, they never glorified his name. If it depended upon them, the name would perish with them."

There are Christians of whom something like this might be said. They have never done anything to disgrace the name they wear, but they have certainly not added to its influence and power. Jesus said, "Herein is my Father glorified, that ye bear much fruit" (John 15:8).

853 The Bible, a Christian's Compass

The following quotation is by John Watson: "Life for every one of us is a stormy voyage with cross-currents which are apt to sweep us out of our course, and an occasional tempest that might wreck an ill-managed vessel. He is fortunate who has a good compass, but he is also wise who is careful to adjust his compass; and as a vessel goes into a quiet bay to test the compasses before venturing on the ocean voyage, so should a man return frequently to the gospels, and learn at the feet of Christ the way of life everlasting."

854 Why the Christian School?

Former Vice-president Marshall, speaking on the subject of public education in America, remarked, "The trouble with our American education is that it has in it too much of materialistic science, and too little of God Almighty." If this statement was true in Marshall's time, it is all too true today, when you consider that the subject of God and prayer have been completely eradicated from our public school systems—all under the misinterpreted guise of "separation of church and state." Many years ago, a pastor once stated that the young people of his church who went away to state universities generally lost their interest in church and religion, and that he had learned from sad experience to expect little from them after attending such schools. On the other hand, it can be acknowledged that many young people have returned from Christian colleges with quickened faith, deepened enthusiasm, and increased power for serving the Lord Jesus and His Church. Why this difference?

The Christian college has a Christian standard. The State school, of course, has a worldly standard. There is much talk everywhere about unselfishness, service, patriotism, and charity. In reality, nobody can be unselfish; no one can truly serve others and promote their highest welfare without power from on high. Power is given only to the believer in the Lord Jesus Christ through the Holy Spirit. Without Christian faith, education will promote only the interests of the world.

The highest thing in the world is Christian character. That is the blossom of time and the promise of eternity. Character is more than intellect, more than efficiency at desk or machine, on the bench or at the bar. Christian character means a man God-filled and bound for heaven. And the attainment of Christian character is the aim of the Christian school.

855 Grafted in the Lord Jesus

In Europe, where the state government rules the church, a godly pastor was once ordered to preach good morals, and not faith in Christ. He read the letter of the authorities to the congregation and said: "I have been told to show you how to be good but to say nothing of faith. Let me tell you something. In my garden stands a scrub pear tree, full of hard, bitter fruit. What good will it do to tell that tree to bear sweet, large fruit instead of its tasteless pears? Listen! By nature we are just such scrub pear trees. When the preacher says: "You shall be good and do good works," the reply is, "We can't." Quite true. The pear tree needs to be grafted, and so do your hearts. But this grafting is done when a new life is given by the Lord Jesus, faith in whom God has told me to preach. This I will do; the rest must take care of itself." And it did.

Nourishment

856 Spiritual Arithmetic

J. Chalmers once said: "God calls upon His people to study and practice the rule of *addition*, and He promises to act by the rule of *multiplication*. How slow is the first when compared with the second; and such is the difference between God and man. Yet the latter is connected with the former. *Add* to your faith virtue, etc., for so an entrance shall be administered unto you abundantly into the everlasting kingdom.

"If God can *multiply* grace and peace to us, we can bear for affliction to *subtract* a few comforts, or even for death to *divide* our earthly joys, assured that nothing shall take away our peace and separate us from his love."

857 The Conditions of Spiritual Growth

There is a very odd tree in an orchard in one of the Midwestern states. It is an old apple tree that was planted many years ago, with its limbs in the ground and its roots in the air, and which still lives to bear an occasional apple and sprout branches where roots should be—a curiosity to beholders. The farmer was induced to produce the oddity through an old German legend, in which such an inverted tree played a prominent part. But although it still lives, and occasionally bears an apple, it is only a curiosity and bears no fruit of any respectable amount. The people who try to live Christian lives without being planted in the Christian church, and letting their roots run down into the responsibilities of church life, are very much like that inverted tree. The Chris-

tians who really bear fruit are those who are rooted deep and solid in the garden of the Lord.

858 The Risen Christ, the Life of the Bible

That which keeps the Bible always up-to-date, making it the most live book in the world, is the ever-living Christ who lives in it. As we come to love Him, and are risen with Him, the Bible becomes precious to us. A cultivated literary critic, a lady, who reviewed a book of a certain author, was very severe in her criticism, pointing out many flaws. A few months later, she became acquainted with the author of this book, and married him. Then she re-read the book, and said: "What a beautiful book! What a nice book! There are some mistakes here and there, but they ought to be overlooked." And she began to recommend that book to every one. The book was just the same as it was before, but her relation to the author had changed. Before he was a stranger; now he was her husband. When she began to love him, she began to love his book. When we come into fellowship with the risen Christ, the flawless, mistake-free Bible becomes to us the most live and precious of all the books in the world.

859 The Spirit-Filled Christian

F. B. Meyer defines Holy Spirit filled living best with the following anecdote: "Let there be no thought of what you can do for God, but

Sight

860 Spiritual Insight

There seems to be more erroneous teachings on the subject of what constitutes spirituality than on almost any other subject. We are always looking for the spiritual in the strange and unusual, forgetting that the really spiritual man finds the Bread of Life in the common food of everyday experience. It is the reverent spirit with which we handle things, and not the peculiarly consecrated deeds which we perform, that makes a truly spiritual life. Frederick Langbridge sings in lines that uplift the soul:

> The darkening streets about me lie,
> The shame, the fret, the squalid jars;
> But swallows' wings go flashing by,
> And in the puddles there are stars.

861 Fruit From Old Seeds

"Cast thy bread upon the waters: for thou shalt find it after many days" (Eccl. 11:1).

It is said that, in the hand of one of the mummies found in a pyramid, was discovered a bulbous root, which, being placed in the earth, grew and bloomed a beautiful, but unknown flower, after having been buried for many hundreds of years. So may the good seed of the word of God spring up after many years. We mention a case in point. Some years since, a venerable man, upwards of one hundred years old, was the subject of converting grace. The cause of his conversion was, hearing a text of Scripture, which his righteous mother had taught him in England, nearly one hundred years before!

862 The Evidence of the Countenance

Long before the era of DNA testing and forensics, an inheritance case was decided in Kingston, New York, where an estate of $30,000 was involved, on the evidence of the large and peculiarly shaped noses of two of the claimants. It came out in the hearings that all the male members of the family in question had very prominent noses of a peculiar shape, and the judge finally decided, more upon the physical similarity of their noses than anything else, that these two claimants were the nephews of the man who had left the inheritance. Men will know us as Christians because we show forth the traits of Christ in our daily lives. Our spiritual countenances should be so like His that those who know us best will have no doubt that we are His heirs and are living in His spirit.

Stewardship

863 Making the Best Use of What You Have

There is a vast difference between the man who follows his business with a servile feeling, giving just as little attention to it as he can and yet obtains a living from it, and the man who masters his business, and with enthusiasm seeks to improve it and admire it. John Curzon, a Polish mechanic, who was presented with a gold medal for his inventions, performed a most extraordinary thing when he succeeded in manufacturing a complete watch in the space of eight hours, and from materials on which most watchmakers would have looked with contempt. It appears that the Czar of Russia, hearing of the marvelous skill of Curzon, determined to put him to the test, and forwarded him a box containing a few copper nails, some wood chippings, a piece of broken glass, an old cracked china cup, some wire, and a few pieces of peg-board, with the request that he should transform them into a time piece. Undaunted, and perceiving a golden opportunity of winning favor at the court, Curzon set about his task with enthusiasm, and in the almost incredibly short space of eight hours had despatched a wonderfully constructed watch to the Czar, who was so surprised and delighted at the work that he sent for the maker, conferred upon him several distinctions, and granted him a pension. The case of the watch was made of china, while the works were simply composed of the odds and ends accompanying the old cup. Not only did it keep good time, but only required winding once in three or four days.

864 Ways of Giving

Beecher once said: "Some men give so that you are angry every time you ask them to contribute. They give so that their gold and silver shoot you like a bullet. Other persons give with such beauty, that you remember it as long as you live; and you say, 'It is a pleasure to go to such men.' There are some men that give as springs do: whether you go to them or not, they are always full; and your part is merely to put your dish under the ever-flowing stream. Others give just as a pump does where the well is dry, and the pump leaks."

322

Surrender

865 When an Excuse Does Not Excuse

One of the dangerous things about many of the excuses men make for staying out of the kingdom is that, under some circumstances, they might be reasonable enough. In the parable of the great supper, the man who had bought land was only acting the part of the prudent man when he went out to look at it. That is, he would have been there if there had been nothing more important to take the precedence. The importance of all things must be considered relatively. Ordinarily, it is a profitable thing for you to take a brisk morning walk, but you would be looked upon as insane if you should start out upon one when your house was on fire. The Lord never discouraged men from being prudent and energetic about their business affairs, but we have the injunction, "Seek ye first the kingdom of God" (Matt. 6:33). The land the man had bought could wait; the feast could not.

866 Have a Purpose

A good deal is gained by the young Christian when he makes up his mind as to what his business really is in the world. A queer genius in a remote district invented a wonderful machine. It generated a good deal of power, and seemed to be capable of accomplishing something, if only it were put to the task. "What is it for?" someone asked the inventor. "Well," was the reply, "it might be used for a sausage grinder, or it might do to hitch to a sewing machine. Then I had thought some of using it for a printing press." Because he never thoroughly made up his mind on this point, the wonderful machine was allowed to stand idle.

A good many really forceful people are lost to the church in pretty much the same way. They think they might be useful in this capacity, or perhaps in that. Then they have had an idea of devoting themselves to something else. The consequences are that they have done nothing.

We are disposed to be hard on the rich man who had more of this world's goods than he knew what to do with, and sat down to devise some new way of disposing of them. I am afraid that a good many of us who have no surplus of this sort of wealth are equally guilty. The young person who looks for something by which he may "kill time" needs to remember that he has at command that by which he might bless many who need his ministry.

867 The Great Question

"Did you spend much time in discussing how far Cana was from

Sychar?" one teacher said to another as they came from the classroom. "I didn't mention it," was the quick reply; "I was too much taken up with the thought of how far some of my scholars were from Jesus Christ."

868 Unprofitable Servants

Is it not strange that we need to be urged to do the very things we profess to have adopted for our chief business? Suppose a man answers a rancher's advertisement for a farmhand. The farmer says, "I want you to plow that field and put in a crop, and I will pay you so much." The young man accepts the offer and ostensibly goes to work. Yet all summer long the farmer and his family have to keep coaxing the young man to go out and plow. He even employs a man to come once a week and urge the man to plow. Of course, all this is ridiculous; no farmer would tolerate such conduct, and no farmhand would be so unreasonable to think that he would; still, the ways of too many of the Lord's so-called servants are not much more consistent. We all know that our preachers have to use the time and strength that ought to be spent in saving sinners, in stirring up the saints and exhorting them to plow.

869 The Midnight Wrestle

We are all familiar with the story of Jacob's famous wrestling match with God's angel. In light of the events that transpired, one can hear Jacob say:

"I have seen God face to face" (Gen. 32:30). Our moments of vision come at daybreak: but they are ushered in by the agony of dread; the long midnight vigil; the extreme agony of conflict; the shrinking of the sinew. Yet, when they come, they are so glorious that the frame is almost overpowered with the brightness of that light, and the exceeding weight of glory. The price is dear, but the vision is more than worth it all. The sufferings are not worthy to be compared with the glory revealed.

This is life; a long wrestle against the love of God, which longs to make us royal. As the years go on, we begin to cling where once we struggled; and as the morn of heaven breaks, we catch glimpses of the Angel's face of love, and hear His whispered name: and as He blesses us, we awake to find ourselves living, and face to face with God—and that is heaven itself.

—F. B. Meyer

870 Walk with Me

If the commonest of us do not find opportunity for saving souls, it is because we do not follow in the footsteps of Him whose pathway always lay hard by the door of the needy and sinful.

A company of students were in the habit of going with a favorite teacher to the forest in search of botanical specimens. There were those who invariably brought back valuable trophies; a few, however, reported having found nothing worthwhile. One of the latter complained to the teacher of the barrenness of his search. "Walk beside me tomorrow," the teacher answered, "and I assure you that you will not return empty-handed."

Fellow Christians, if your life has been barren of results, take this to yourself. Go touch with your feet His footprints. I need not remind you where they will lead you. If you follow Him, He will *make* you a fisher of men. It is a costly thing to follow the Son of man, who despised all things that he might win souls for the kingdom of heaven.

Temptation

871 "My Grace Is Sufficient for Thee"

The following lines on the subject of temptation were penned by George H. Morrison many decades ago, but the subject matter is just as pertinent today as it was when he wrote them:

". . . there is the hour when we are assaulted by temptation. Like suffering, temptation is universal, and like suffering, it is infinitely varied. Probably in all the human family no two are ever tempted quite alike. It is true that temptations may be broadly classified, clustered, as it were, around common centers. There is one class that assails the flesh, another that makes it onset on the mind: yet every temptation is so adapted to the person tempted that perhaps in all the ages that have gone on one was ever tempted just like me. To me there is no argument so strong as this for the existence of a devil. There is such subtlety in our temptations that it is hard to conceive of it without a brain. We are tempted with incomparable cunning; temptation comes to us with so much subtlety and so sure that nothing can explain it but intelligence. Temptation is never obtrusive, but it is always there. It is beside us in the crowded street; it

has no objection to the lonely moor; it follows us to the office and home; it dogs our footsteps when we go to church; it insists in sharing in our hours of leisure, and kneels beside us when we go to pray. At one and twenty we are sorely tempted, and say, 'By-and-by it will get better; wait till twenty years have passed away, temptation will no longer assail us.' But forty comes and we are tempted still; not now as in the passion of our youth, but with a power that is far more deadly because it is so hardening to the heart. There is not a relationship so sweet and sacred but temptation chooses it for its assault; there is not an act of sacrifice so pure, but temptation meets us in the doing of it. It never despairs of us until we die. So tempted as we are, is there any hope for us at all against that shameless and malevolent intelligence? Yes, we are here to proclaim that there is hope in unremitting watchfulness, there is hope in every breath of prayer. 'Satan trembles when he sees the weakest saint upon his knees'; but above all there is hope in this: when we are tempted and are on the point of falling, we can lift up our hearts to Christ and hear Him say 'My grace is sufficient for thee' (2 Cor. 12:9). Was He not tempted in all points like as we are, and yet was He not victorious? And now you are His and He is yours; that victory which he had won is yours. It is at your disposal every hour. Say to yourself when you are next tempted, "He is able to keep me from falling. He that is with me is mightier than they that are against me." Better still, say nothing, but just listen as He rises up beside His Father's throne and calls to you, His tempted children, 'My grace is sufficient for thee.'"

872 Sin Betrays

Solomon J. Solomon has a remarkably realistic picture now in the Manchester Art Gallery in Manchester, England, entitled "Samson Betrayed." The moment chosen by the artist is that intensely dramatic one in which Samson, awaking out of sleep, and finding himself bound with stout ropes, bends his mighty muscles to set himself free. He struggles furiously, but in vain; he has been caught in the meshes of sin, and the sinner, however mighty his strength, can never conquer in that fight. The surprise mixed with indignation in Samson's face illustrates that intensely suggestive statement in the narrative which, when awakened, Samson said: "I will go out and shake myself. . . . and he wist not that the Lord had departed from him" (Judg. 16:20). A long course of sin had stolen from him his powers of resistance, and yet so subtly—when he was asleep—was all this done that he himself was unconscious that he had become en-

slaved. This is the very snare and subtlety of sin; it goes on slowly sapping the moral defenses, covering over its work, dulling the senses of the sinner, while at the same time it corrupts the moral character. Then comes the cry, "The Philistines be upon thee"; the sinner wakes as at other times, and says, "I will break loose as before," only to find that his strength has gone, that "the Lord hath departed from him."

Another suggestion powerfully worked out is the attitude of the temptress. Having brought this great man down to the dust by her temptations, no pity awakes within her at his betrayal. On the contrary she swings her lithe body about in glee, and points the finger of mockery at her captive, laughing the while. Added to the shame of defeat, Samson realizes the hollowness of the temptation, how hellish is the heart of sin, full of soft enticements while it lures its victim on, then cruel as hell when it has accomplished its purposes. Sin's purpose, it is to be remembered, is to betray; its secrets will not be hidden.

873 Dangerous Companionship

In Doré's pictures of the Old Testament there is a striking representation of the Great Flood. In a vast range of heaving waters there juts out one solitary boulder of rock. All else is submerged. To this rock, for safety, has swum a huge lioness with her cubs, to which a few desperate human beings also cling. Wild animals and men and women stand side by side, the fierce passions of the one and the fear of the other alike forgotten in a common peril.

Henry Drummond tells of an incident which this picture suggests. Once during some floods in India the whole valley was inundated, and the inhabitants who escaped drowning were gathered on the peak of a solitary hill, which alone remained uncovered. As they stood there, waiting anxiously for the waters to subside, they saw a huge Bengal tiger swimming through the flood with a cub in her mouth, making for the jutting peak. Terrified at her approach they huddled together, but the tiger as it reached the place of safety showed no signs of attack; instead it lay peacefully down, a common terror having driven out its natural ferocity. An English officer, however, who was one of the company, taking his revolver from his belt, went up to where it lay and shot it dead. Being censured for his cruelty, he pointed to the waters now beginning to subside. "Fear," he explained "had for the moment arrested its ferocity, but when the occasion for its continuance disappeared, the old passions would return and it would turn and rend them."

This is true of all evil companionship. For a time their evil influence and passions may be held in abeyance, but sooner or later these emerge to tear, and ravage, and destroy. It is so also with evil thoughts. When first admitted they seem to lie down tame, and without intent to

molest, but soon they arouse themselves. The only way of safety is to destroy them.

874 Inviting Temptation

A young man, who had previously kept a good reputation, was arrested on the charge of being implicated in an extensive robbery. The trial developed the fact that he had been a tool in the hands of others, and that his part in the matter had been that of showing the men the places where they were likely to get the largest returns. The judge was at first disposed to believe the young man's statement that he had never before stepped aside from the path of rectitude. However, his suspicions were aroused by the fact that the boy had been singled out from among all his associates and approached with the proposal that he take part in the robbery.

"A young man who received such a proposal had done something to invite it," the judge declared. Subsequent developments proved that he was right. Those who asked his aid would not have dared to do so if they had not believed that he was for sale. While it is true that all men must meet temptation, it is not a favorable omen when evildoers make bold to ask us to join them in their deeds. We may be above that which they would have us do, but we have at least not kept our colors where they ought to be.

875 Made Strong by Trials

In the following anecdote, F. B. Meyer uses the illustration of a beehive to compare the struggle of bees to that of the Christian:

"A beekeeper told me the story of a hive—how, when the little bee is in the first stage, it is put into a hexagonal cell, and honey enough is stored there for its use until it reaches maturity. The honey is sealed with a capsule of wax, and when the tiny bee has fed itself on the honey and exhausted the supply, the time has come for it to emerge into the open. But, oh, the wrestle, the tussle, the straining to get through that wax! It is the strait gate for the bee, so strait that in the agony of exit the bee rubs off the membrane that hid his wings, and on the other side is able to fly! Once a moth got into the hive, and fed on the wax capsules, and the bees got out without any strain or trouble. But they could not fly; and the other bees stung them to death. Are you congratulating yourself on having an easy time? No hardness, no difficulties, no cross? Beware lest, like the bees, you lose your wing power, and perish miserably in the dust."

876 Drunken Bees

It is said that the honey of certain flowers has an intoxicating effect on bees. But honey may also be changed into alcohol. In former days it was the source of the chief intoxicating drink in England, as well as other countries. It is believed that honey is sometimes thus transformed while still in the flower. Germs of fermentation are ever floating about in the air, and may settle down in the honey-cups which form the feeding-ground of the bee. The sweet juice being changed to alcohol, the bee finds there a wayside tavern. Jean Ingelow must have had reference to this when she sang:

Crowds of bees are giddy with clover.

Keats also writes of:

Honeysuckles full of clear bee-wine.

Edgar Allen Poe speaks of the intoxicating influence of the blue flowers of sephalica:

It still remaineth, torturing the bee With madness, and unwonted revelry.

The sweetest honey of our American citizenship is the liberty which we sip from our free institutions, but when it ferments and changes into license it becomes a deadly liquor that endangers all our civilization.

Thankfulness

877 *Living Gratitude*

We may offer fervent expressions of gratitude in the prayer meeting and sing aloud in the praise service, but our real sense of indebtedness must manifest itself in more practical ways. A king had saved the life of one of his subjects, and every day afterwards she came to his gate with protestations of gratitude. "I can never begin to pay the debt I owe him," she bewailed. One day the king, in his chariot, passed her cottage. He saw in her garden a tree bearing some luscious fruit, and was seized with a desire to taste it. When he sent his servant with the request that he be given some of the fruit to take to the king, she replied that she only had enough fruit to meet her own needs. She thus laid bare the fact that her expressions of gratitude had been mere words which lacked the element of truthfulness.

878 *Ungracious Thanksgiving*

At school, one Christmas, the students gave their teacher a Bible. The teacher was an eccentric man, and as he took it, he said, very coldly: "I thank you very much, but—I see it has no concordance in it." Of course, they were all hurt at this show of ingratitude, and his "I thank you" didn't count for much. I am afraid that a good many of us take our blessings from the hand of God in much the same way. We say, "I am thankful," in a perfunctory manner, "but—I could make things better if I had my way."

When we repine because of the unalterable environments of our lives, we render our words of praise of no effect. A Christian grumbler is a monstrosity, and if we go from the praise service to find fault with everything about us, from the weather to the minister's sermon, we are guilty of dissembling with our lips.

879 *The Prayer of Thanksgiving*

Oh, if we could know with what tenderness the eye of the Father in heaven rests upon us to see if we will only cast ourselves upon Him when we are in trouble! Often, long before we call, the help is on the way. August Hermann Francke was a Lutheran Christian in Germany who had learned the art of prevailing prayer. Francke's ministry in life was taking care of orphans. There were times when his trust in God was sorely tested because bills were due and there was no money in sight. One day, his manager had brought a bunch of bills, and Francke had to confess that he had no money to pay them. About to fall on his knees for the purpose of asking God to remember the cause of these needy orphans, he found it necessary first to dictate a message. Then, before he could fall on his knees to ask for the money, a draft for a thousand dollars was delivered. Thus being reminded of the promise, "Before they call I will answer" (Is. 65:24), he made his way to his chamber to fall upon his knees to stammer forth his thanks.

880 Thankful for Leprosy

Once a Christian Leper in India was heard to pray: "I thank God that he laid leprosy on me because of the lepers I have been able to lead to Christ." He saw his leprosy as part of God's saving plan. That the souls of the lepers might be washed white in the tide of the Savior's blood, God had permitted him to become a leper.

881 Gratitude

A blind woman who was enabled by a very skillful operation to see, asked to be at once taken to see her minister; she had longed for years to see his face who had led her to see in the Lord Jesus the altogether lovely.

882 Ingratitude

In the early days of Carthage, if a general was defeated, he was generally cruelly and unjustly treated by his own people, and sometimes condemned to banishment. In one engagement the leader Malchus be-sieged a city and compelled it to surrender, but was content to put to death only ten of his chief opponents. Not long after the very men he spared plotted against him, brought him to trial, and condemned him to death.

883 Appreciation for Praise

When Leech read the complimentary review of his sketches which Thackeray wrote in *The London Times,* he was hugely delighted and exclaimed with enthusiasm "That's like putting 1,000 pounds in my pocket."

884 For the Living

Ruskin said, "Let us not forget that if honor be for the dead, gratitude can only be for the living."

885 Touching Gratitude

Wordsworth was once so warmly thanked by an old man for cutting through at one blow a root at which he had been long haggling in vain, that the tears in the old man's eyes drew from the poet these lines:

I've heard of hearts unkind, kind deeds
With coldness still returning:
Alas! the gratitude of men
Hath oftener left me mourning.

886 The Attitude of Gratitude

The late Cleon Lyles told of an experience that happened many years ago when he was holding a gospel meeting in a south Arkansas community. He drove out in the country to visit an elderly man. He found the man's tin-roofed shack. In the porch he could see through the window that the man was just finishing his meager meal of beans and salt pork. At that point the man bowed his head and prayed, "I thank Thee, Lawd, I have dined sufficient."

A couple of powerful lessons jump out of this story. First, that man was happy. Though I never met the gentleman, I am certain, based on his prayer, that his life was one of joy and peace. Thankfulness produces joy as surely as day follows night. It's been my observation that grateful people are giving people and giving people are happy people. Gratitude is a powerful attitude that beautifully colors all of life.

Secondly, gratitude is not based on the quantity of one's wealth. With a heart of gratitude a meal of beans and salt pork can become a royal feast. Blessings often follow gratitude rather than the reverse order. A person who is not thankful for his or her one hundred dollars most likely would not be thankful for ten million dollars. For the attitude of gratitude is a condition of heart.

—Jim Howard

Tongue

887 *How Do You Speak of Those Who Are Absent?*

Have you ever noticed that there is usually a dearth of good kind words for the absent one when his name is mentioned in conversation? There may be words of criticism and faultfinding, but how few are the words of commendation! The golden rule suggests that we speak of the absent one as we would have others speak of us.

888 *Silence as a Peacemaker*

George Morrison wrote this beautiful passage dealing with the dangers of a thoughtless tongue:

"One of the first things that make for social peace is a watchful and a charitable silence. No man or woman can ever be a peacemaker who has not learned to put a bridle on his lips. Every student of Christ must have observed the tremendous emphasis He puts on words. Of every idle word, He tells us, in the day of judgment we are to give account. And if you want to understand aright the passion and the depth of that, you will remember the beatitude, "Blessed are the peacemakers" (Matt. 5:9). Think of the infinite harm that can be wrought by a malicious or a thoughtless tongue; think of the countless hearts it lacerates; think of the happy friendships which it chills. And sometimes there is not even malice in it—only the foolish desire to be speaking, for evil is wrought by want of thought as well as want of heart. There is no more difficult task in life than to repeat exactly what someone else has said. Alter the playful tone, you alter everything. Subtract the smile, and you subtract the spirit. And yet how often do we all repeat things that are almost incapable of repetition and so give pain that never was intended. You can say good-bye in such a tone that it is a dismissal of contempt. And yet how seldom do we think of tone, of voice, of eye, of smile, of personality when we pass on the word which we have heard. There are times that call for all outspokenness. No man ever denounced like Christ. "Woe unto you, scribes and Pharisees" (Matt. 23:13–15), "Go ye, and tell that fox." (Luke 13:32). All I know, and yet the fact remains that as we move along life's common ways, one of the mightiest things that makes for social peace is a wise and charitable silence. Not to believe everything we hear, not to repeat everything we hear, or else believing it to bury it unless we are called by conscience to proclaim it, that is a thing that makes for social peace, a thing within our power today, and it may be along that silent road lies our 'Blessed are the peacemakers.'"

Treasure

889 Moth Cannot Corrupt

We wonder a little that the child can take such pride in a soap bubble, not because the bubble is not beautiful, but because it is soon destroyed. The artist puts a bubble upon the canvas and we say of his work that it is a great achievement. Yet the canvas will one day fall to pieces. There is just one thing which we may give ourselves that is absolutely imperishable. One wonders why it is that fellowship in soul-saving is so much sweeter than fellowship of any other sort. It is not transient. It is hardly possible that when they meet over beyond the river of death, those who are friends because they were of the same business tastes will have the same things in common. But soul-savers will undoubtedly have something to talk over, since they will find there the treasures for which they toiled.

890 Refusing the Prize

"There's a man that once offered me ten thousand dollars and I didn't take it," a young man said of a gentleman who passed down the street.

"Why didn't you?"

"Because I did not know it was ten thousand dollars," he answered.

The fact was the gentleman had come to him and given him a bit of advice, to which no heed was given. It turned out afterward that if he had taken the advice it would have made him ten thousand dollars. I think you and I have had a good many experiences like that, only the riches we might have won are imperishable. That day when Duty said, "Go," and you said, "Oh, I can't go," you missed a prize that would have been yours through all eternity.

891 Interest from Heaven

Every schoolboy and schoolgirl knows what is meant by interest; for they often have to do sums that deal with that subject. Now this teacher wants to know whether his readers are drawing interest from heaven? Interest from heaven? Well, a story will have to suffice as a mode of explanation.

A banker had a clerk of whom he thought a great deal. So, one day, he called him into his office and said: "John, you have been a faithful worker. I have thought of rewarding you according to your faithfulness, and for this reason I have remembered you with ten thousand dollars in my will. However, I am still in good health and have no intention of dying sooner than I can help. Now, that you may not have to wait too long for your money, I will pay you interest on it.

Here is the first year's amount. Therewith he handed him six hundred dollars. That was good news for the clerk. He had ten thousand dollars coming to him; and, in addition, he had the interest on it year by year, which was a pledge of the whole amount.

Our inheritance is in heaven. Oh, how much that means! No pain, no sorrow, no darkness; only joy and light forevermore! But, if we are really on the way to heaven, we do not have to wait for death to enjoy our inheritance. Daily we receive the power to pray, strength under temptation, peace with God, inward joy. These blessings are the interest on our capital in heaven. And like the bank clerk's capital it is a gift—Christ's.

892 Losing the Great to Save the Little

A man lost his life in a New York City fire through his own foolishness. He lived with his wife on the fourth floor of an apartment building. The fire started in the kitchen of the apartment occupied by him. A woman living on the same floor first saw the flames, and her cries of terror awakened the tenants. The fire was then crackling fiercely near an airshaft and filled the halls with smoke. An officer came to the man and his wife, and was astonished to see that the man was determined to go back while the wife was trying to drag him to safety. The officer went to her assistance, and they soon pulled the man out of the house. A little later, some firemen who were hauling a line of hose through the scuttle in the roof found the foolish fellow near his flat with his clothing almost burned from his body. He had gone back into his room for some papers, which he had secured, only to have them burn in his hands. He got the papers, but lost his life. There are many that are holding on to worldly treasures at the expense of everything that can make life precious. They are losing their souls to obtain gain that must soon be loss.

893 Where Are Your Treasures?

A miser in Chicago was so suspicious of everybody that he would not trust his money in the bank, but buried it in his cellar. One night some thieves broke into the cellar and dug up every inch of sand and dirt until they found his box of gold and carried it away. The poor old fellow was nearly crazy over his loss. But the old man has many people following his example in the care of priceless treasures. How many there are who are laying away all their treasures in the sand and dirt of this earthly cellar, when heaven's strong vaults are offered to us for their safe keeping. Jesus says: "Lay not up for yourselves treasures upon earth, where moth and rust doth corrupt, and where thieves break through and steal: but lay up for yourselves treasures in heaven, where neither moth nor rust corrupt, and where thieves do not break through nor steal: for where your treasure is, there will your heart be also" (Matt. 6:19-21).

894 Joy in Heaven over Repenting Sinners

A righteous Armenian calling on Mr. Hamlyn, a missionary at Constantinople, remarked, that he was astonished to see how the people were waking up to the truth; how even the most uncultivated were seeking after it as for hidden treasure. "Yes," said he, "it is going forward; it will triumph; but, I shall not live to see it, for I am born an age too soon." "But," said Mr. Hamlyn, "do you remember what our Savior said, 'There is joy in the presence of the angels of God over one sinner that repenteth' (Luke 15:10)? You may not live to see the truth triumphant in this empire; but should you, by Divine grace, reach the kingdom of heaven, and be with the angels, your joy over your whole nation, repentant and redeemed, will be infinitely greater than it could be on earth." He seemed astonished at this thought; but after examining the various passages to which I referred him, he yielded to the evidence with the most lively expressions of delight. "O fool, and slow of heart," he said, "to read the gospel so many times without perceiving such a glorious truth! If this be so, no matter in what age a Christian is born, nor when he dies."

895 A Peep at an Asylum

"Inasmuch as ye have done it unto one of the least of these My brethren, ye have done it unto Me" (Matt. 25:40).

A gentleman visited an asylum for the mentally ill operated by a society of young people, who devote themselves wholly, without pay, to ministering to these poor creatures. The visitor saw what a dreadful life it was, to be associated continually with so many disturbed people. He exclaimed with amazement, "How can you bear this life without being highly paid for the intolerable misery of it?" One young man who was conducting the tour of the hospital smiled and said, "We shall be paid highly some day by Him to whom we minister."

Trust

896 "Having Not Seen"

Dr. Vincent Tymms, relates in one of his sermons the complaint of many non-believers of not being able to see Christ like His disciples did:

". . . Many complain that a written life of Christ is a cold, remote and insufficient means for the production of faith. They envy those who saw the Lord with the eyes of sense, and are ready to murmur: 'If we could only have seen Jesus, and touched His hand, and heard His voice, it would have been easy to believe. If we had been brought up in Nazareth, there would have been no excuse for doubt; but now all the facts are so far away and shadowy; we hear a voice of testimony, but we see no man; no light gleams into our faces from those wonderous eyes.' 'Sirs,' they exclaim, 'we would see Jesus, and if we could see Him we could believe.' But to all such repinings the record of Christ's private relationships provides a standing answer. Flesh and blood cannot reveal the Son of God. They did not reveal Him to His brothers. The sense perceptions we crave as a help to faith were their greatest hindrance. If we believe not the written story, a story which has the confirmation of a world in course of transformation by His influence, neither should we have believed while as yet He was not risen from the dead, and so declared to be the Son of God."

897 Who Is in Control?

Bulstrode Whitlock, Cromwell's envoy to Sweden, was one night so disturbed in his mind over the state of his nation, that he could not sleep. His servant, observing it said, "Pray Sir, will you allow me to ask a question?" "Certainly," replied Whitlock. "Do you think that God governed the world very well before you came into it?" he suggested. "Undoubtedly"—"And do you not think that He will govern the world quite as well when you are gone from it?"—"Certainly"—"Then, I ask you, do you not think that you may trust Him to govern it as long as you are living?"

Many times as believers, we too wrestle with the problems we face, not realizing that God has been with us all the time. For this to be our hope, we must realize God is in control (Heb. 13:5).

898 All the Powers

A mail carrier once said; "I have the greatest sense of security in delivering the mail. All the resources of the government are pledged to support me in carrying out my work. If I have only one small post card in my bag, no man dares to molest me in its delivery. All the police powers of the United States would be thrown into action, if necessary, to secure the safe delivery of that post card. That led me to think about what Jesus said when He spoke the words of the Great Commission: ". . . All power is given unto me in heaven and in earth. Go ye therefore, and teach all nations, baptizing them in the name of the Father, and the Son, and of the Holy Ghost . . . and, lo, I am with you always . . ." (Matt. 28:18-20)

899 When on the Rock

A storm wrecked a ship. The only survivor was a little boy who was swept by the waves onto a rock. There he sat all night long. In the morning he was seen and rescued. One of his rescuers asked him, "Did not you tremble while you were on the rock during the night?" His answer: "I surely did tremble but the rock did not."

We are human. We cannot help but tremble, but the Rock on which we stand never does.

900 "You Can See a Long Way on a Clear Day"

Willard A Scofield relates:

"Several years ago I made two trips in planes owned by the Mission Aviation Fellowship in Zaire, Africa. During the first flight the clouds were dense and the pilot flew barely 1,000 feet above the ground to maintain some visibility. Even at that low level we plunged into clouds, and when we saw light our plane seemed to nearly scrape the side of a mountain. Quickly the pilot pointed his alarmed passengers skyward and we headed back to our station. As we ate lunch, one of the Zairian passengers thanked the Lord for solid ground.

"Several months later I made the same trip when the sky was cloudless and the sun brightened every inch of the savanna land. What joy it was to fly confidently across God's beautiful country. That day we flew a mile high, and we could see the body of water adjacent to our destination, more than 70 miles away. You can see a long way on a clear day!

"The resurrection of Jesus Christ clears our future. We know who we are and we know where we are going. We **can** see a long way!"

901 Two Figures

"The Lord knoweth how to deliver the godly" (2 Pet. 2:9).

The following authentic story will best illustrate and enforce this text. I give it as it was given to me by a friend who had verified the circumstances during a visit to Blankenburg. A godly Lutheran pastor, Sander, of Elberfeld, had been compelled to rebuke an evildoer for some gross sin, and had thereby attracted to himself his malicious hate. The man vowed to repay him. One night the pastor was called to visit a house that could only be reached by passing over a plank which bridged an impetuous torrent. Nothing seemed easier to his enemy than to conceal himself on the bank till the man of God was returning from the opposite end of the plank, to meet him in the middle, throw him into the deep and turbid stream, leaving it to be surmised that in the darkness he had simply lost his foothold. When, however, from his hiding place he caught sight of the pastor's figure in the dim light, he was surprised to see that he was not alone, but accompanied by another. There were two figures advancing towards him across the narrow plank, and he did not dare attempt his murderous deed. And as they passed his hiding place, the one whom he did not know cast such a glance towards him as convinced him of the sinfulness of the act he had contemplated, and began a work in his heart which led to his conversion.

When converted, he sought out the pastor, to confess to him the murderous intention which had so nearly mastered him, and said: "It would have been your death had you not been accompanied." "What do you mean?" said the other; "I was absolutely alone." "Nay," said he, "there were two." Then the pastor knew that God had sent His angel, as He sent him to bring Lot out of Sodom.

—F. B. Meyer

902 Better to Die Than Deny

There was a case of a strong Chinese Christian bishop who, in undergoing much interrogation, finally thought to himself, "If I just deny Christ in front of these two interrogators and they let me go, then I can live rather than being killed, and could do much productive work for Christ." He did deny Christ and was released.

However, about twenty years later, as he was dying, he cried out and encouraged people to never deny Christ, because he had lived in total spiritual blackness and darkness ever since his release from prison. The Spirit of God in no way allowed him to be used of God. He felt that it would have been better to die than to have agonized for twenty years in this horrible spiritual vacuum.

903 Genuine Faith

Joel C. Gregory states:

"First, I believe that the testing we go through demonstrates the genuineness of our faith. In the phrase 'the testing of your faith' (1 Pet. 1:7), the word 'testing' is an almost untranslatable word. The Williams version explains it as showing what is 'genuine in your faith.' The idea refers to iron ore that has gone through the refining fire and comes out the other side clean and pure and genuine. This is the word Job used when he said, 'When he has tried me in the fire, I will come out like gold' (Job 23:10).

"Actually, there may be something suspect about a faith that has never been tested. An army going through basic training is not ready for battle. Not until soldiers have faced the battle, and been under fire, do they consider themselves proven, hardened, worthy. A ship cannot prove that it has been sturdily built as long as it stays in dry dock. Its hull must get wet; it must face a storm to demonstrate genuine seaworthiness. The same is true of our faith. When we hold fast to belief in Christ in spite of life's storms and crushing criticism, that is when we demonstrate the genuineness of our faith."

904 My Dad Knows God

When my son was a small boy playing with his buddies in the back yard, I overheard them talking one day. One of them remarked, "My Dad knows the mayor of the town!" I overheard another say, "That is nothing—my Dad knows the governor of our state!" When I wondered what was coming next in the "program of bragging" I heard my own little son of four years of age say, "That is nothing—my Dad knows God!" I hurriedly left my place of eavesdropping with tears running down my cheeks, I looked up to God and prayed, "Oh God, I pray that my boy will always be able to say, 'My Dad knows God.'"

905 At The Place of the Sea

Have you come to the Red Sea
  place in your life,
Where, in spite of all you can do,
There is no other way but
  through?
Then wait on the Lord, with
  a trust serene,

Till the night of your fear is gone;
He will send the winds, He will
  heap the floods,

When He says to your soul, "Go
  on!"
And His hand shall lead you
  through, clear through,

Ere the watery walls roll down;
No wave can touch you, no foe
  can smite,
No mightiest sea can drown.
The tossing billows may rear their
  crests,

Their foam at your feet may break,
But over their bed you shall
  walk dry-shod
In the path that your Lord shall
  make.
In the morning watch, 'neath
  the lifted cloud,

You shall see but the Lord alone,
When He leads you forth from
  the place of the sea,
To a land that you have not
  known;
And your fears shall pass as your
  foes have passed,

You shall no more be afraid;
You shall sing His praise in a
  better place,
In a place that His hand hath
  made.

—Annie Johnson Flint

906 Spiritual Rest

Rest is not lying in soft beds of
  ease;
Free from all labor, with no one to
  please.
Rest is not quitting, no burden
  to bear.
Rest is reclining in heart, on His
  care.

Rest can be found in trouble
and pain;
When dark clouds are gathered
and threatening rain.
Rest is relief found in life's
darkest hour;
To know He is with us and held
by His power.

Rest is not found by fulfilling
our dreams.
Dreams often vanish; hopes lost,
so it seems.
Rest is the promise our Lord made
to all,
Who faithfully trust Him, refusing to fall.

There remains a sweet rest for
people of grace;
Who enter that rest while in
'seeking His face.'
This life, so uncertain, can
never destroy,
The rest that is found when His
will we enjoy.

Rest is secured, the hour of
believing.
Today you may enter, His will
now receiving.
His yoke now is easy, the burden is light.
He draws near to comfort and
steady your plight.
Rest comes the moment you
answer His call.
Depend on Him fully, no worry at
all.
Rest settles the mind, anxiety
none;
With love now abiding, the
victory's won.

—Phil Simmons

907 A Pilot's Blind Trust

A pilot was experiencing difficulty
in landing his plane because of fog;
and the airport decided to bring
him in by radar. As he began to receive directions from the ground
he suddenly remembered a tall pole
in the flight path, and appealed in
panic to the control tower about it.
The reply came bluntly, "You obey
instructions; we will take care of
obstructions." How many a Christian
hesitates to obey God's Word because of problems and difficulties!
If we only obey, He is capable of
dealing with the problems and difficulties.

Unbelief

908 "Thou Fool!"

A converted skeptic was asked how he felt in reference to the resurrection and other truths about which he had lampooned. "O, sir," he replied, "two words from God's book conquered me: '**Thou Fool!**'. Do you see this Bible?" taking up a beautiful copy of the Scriptures, fastened with a silver clasp. "Will you read the words upon the clasp that shuts it?" His friend read, engraved on the silver clasp, "Thou Fool!" "There," said the owner, "are the words which conquered me. It was no argument, no reasoning, no satisfying my objections; but God convincing me that I was a fool, and since that day, I have determined that I would have my Bible clasped with those words, 'Thou fool!' and never again come to the consideration of its sacred mysteries but through their medium. I will remember that I am a fool, and only God is wise."

909 The Turmoil Caused by Doubt

The famous philosopher, David Hume, after witnessing in the family of the venerable La Roche those consolations which the Gospel can alone impart, confessed with a sigh that "there were moments when, amidst all the pleasures of philosophical discovery and the pride of literary fame, he wished that he had never doubted."

910 The Sin of Unbelief

"Unbelief among sins," says an old writer, "is, as the plague among diseases, the most dangerous; but, when it rises to despair, then it is as the plague with the tokens appearing that bring the certain message of death with them. Unbelief is despair in the bud; despair is unbelief at its full growth."

911 Teaching of a Straw

It is said of the great Galileo—who had been accused of infidelity because he asserted that the earth orbited around the sun, in apparent contradiction to the Catholic interpretation of Scripture of that time—that, when questioned by the Roman Inquisition as to his belief in the Supreme Being, he pointed to a straw lying on the floor of his dungeon, saying to his accusers that, from the structure of that trifling object, he would infer with certainty the existence of an intelligent Creator. And this is the welcome conclusion to which an attentive examination of the grass of the field inevitably leads.

912 Effects of Unbelief

Unbelief is the occasion of all sin and the very bond of iniquity. It does nothing but darken and destroy. It makes the world a moral desert, where no divine footsteps are heard, where no angels ascend and descend, where no living hand adorns the fields, feeds the fowls of heaven, or regulates events. Thus it makes nature, which is the garden of God, a mere automation, and the history of Providence an accidental succession of events; man, a creature of accidents, and prayer a useless ceremony. It annihilates even the vestiges of heaven that still remain upon the earth, and blocks the way to every higher region.

913 Gospel-Hardened

"Hearing they hear not, neither do they understand." (Matt. 13:13).

A blacksmith's dog used to spend most of its time in the forge, and consequently it got used to the fire. Other dogs came, and the moment the sparks flew they ran away in terror, but the blacksmith's dog would sleep in the midst of all undisturbed. It would scarcely leave the forge, but used to stay in it all night. One night the forge caught on fire, and the dog lost its life in the conflagration.

How many hearers have become too familiar with the warnings of the gospel? Many have taken warning, but many sleep amid the sparks.

Unity

914 Unity by Higher Life and Fellowship

Two men may start to ascend some lofty Alpine peak from points many miles apart down in the valley. They climb the steeps, they scale the narrow ledges that overlook the chasm; at times they are shrouded in the cloud-mist, and you begin to say they will never meet. Ah! but wait a while. Before the night falls they reach the sun-gilt summit, and resting their weary limbs and, refreshing their hungry and thirsty spirits, they find time and taste for pleasant communication before they fall asleep in the little hostel on the mountaintop. So many who seem hopelessly divided in opinion and creed when on the lower plane of life and experience, have only to climb to loftier heights of Divine truth to discover their oneness in the Lord, and their enjoyment of His bounty, and therein their fellowship one with the other. More abundant life, is the Divine philosophy of more abiding unity between Christians.

915 Christian Unity

After the battle of Gettysburg, one of the most disastrous in the American Civil War, a man went into a hospital bearing with him aid and comfort which Massachusetts had sent, and he went around from cot to cot inquiring, "Any Massachusetts soldiers here?" Not a word. Nobody answered. But by-and-by a voice cried, "No! only *United States* Soldiers here." So in the great campaign it is our glory and distinction, not that we are members of this or the other denomination; we are *Christ's Soldiers,* carrying on His holy war against all evil.

Vanity

916 Death-Bed Advice

Monsieur de L'Enclos, a talented man of Paris, educated his daughter, Ninon, with a view of the vain world in which he lived. On his deathbed, when she was about fifteen, he addressed her in this language: "Draw near, Ninon; you see, my dear child, that nothing more remains for me than the sad remembrance of those enjoyments which I am about to quit forever. But, alas, my regrets are useless as vain. You who will survive me must make the best of your precious time."

917 After Fifty Years

After the death of Abderamen, caliph of Cordova, the following paper was found, in his own handwriting: "Fifty years are elapsed since I became caliph. I have possessed riches, honors, pleasures, friends: in short, everything that man can desire in this world. I have reckoned up the days in which I could say I was really happy, and they amount to FOURTEEN!!!"

918 A Nobleman's Pride

A late English Earl felt great pleasure and some pride in leading his visitors over his extensive estate, and pointing out its beauties. One gentleman, fatigued with viewing the arbor, footpaths, orchards, rivulets, waterfalls, etc., sat down in one of the pleasure houses along with the Earl, to whom he said, "Well, my lord, all this and heaven would be grand; but all this and hell would be terrible."

919 The Duke of Luxemburg's Deathbed

This illustrious man, on his deathbed, declared, "That he would then much rather have had it to reflect upon, that he had administered a cup of cold water to a worthy poor creature in distress, than that he had won so many battles as he had triumphed in." All the sentiments of worldly grandeur vanish at that unavoidable moment which decides the eternal state of men.

920 The Vanity of Conquest

When Pyrrhus, king of Epirus, was making great preparations for his intended expedition into Italy, Cineas, the philosopher, took a favorable opportunity of addressing him thus: "The Romans, sir, are reported to be a warlike and victorious people; but, if God permit us to overcome them, what use shall we make of the victory?" "You ask" said Pyrrhus, "a thing that is self-evident. The Romans once conquered, no city will resist us; we shall then be masters of all Italy." Cineas added, "And having

346

subdued Italy, what shall we do next?" Pyrrhus, not yet aware of his intentions, replied, "Sicily next stretches her arms to receive us." "That is very probable," said Cineas, "but will the possession of Sicily put an end to the war?" "God grant us success in that," answered Pyrrhus, "and we shall make these only the forerunners of greater things; for then Libya and Carthage will soon be ours: and these things being completed, none of our enemies can offer any further resistance."

"Very true," added Cineas, "for then we may easily regain Macedon, and make an absolute conquest of Greece; and when all these are in our possession, what shall we do then?" Pyrrhus, smiling, answered, "Why, then, my dear friend, we will live at our ease, drink all day long, and amuse ourselves with cheerful conversation." "Well, sir," said Cineas, "and why may we not do all this now, and without the labor and hazard of enterprise so laborious and uncertain?" Pyrrhus, however, unwilling to take the advice of the philosopher, ardently engaged in these ambitious pursuits, and at last perished in them.

921 A Conceited Young Man

A young man happened to fall into the company of a number of aged Christians, whom he thought to astonish by reciting sublime passages from the poets and orators of history; among other things of that description, he quoted, with great emphasis and energy, the well-known lines of Shakespeare:

The cloud-capt towers, the gorgeous palaces
The solemn temples, the great globe itself;
And, like the baseless fabric of a vision,
Leave not a wreck behind!

Having finished the quotation, he began to pronounce a eulogy upon it, boldly affirming, that there was nothing to be found equal to it in sublimity and grandeur in ancient or modern literature. An elderly Christian, who attentively listened to the whole recitation and comments of the young man, after some time, interrupted the gentleman, and attempted to question his assertion, affirming that he could produce a passage equally sublime. The young man, startled with surprise, challenged the point, on which the old man, in a grave and solemn tone, responded, "And I saw a great white throne, and Him that sat on it, from whose face the earth and the heavens fled away; and there was found no place for them."

"Well," said the young man, overpowered with astonishment, "you have indeed made good your point, that does infinitely surpass it: but please, allow me to ask, where did you find this passage, in which of our classical authors does it occur? For in all my reading, I never recollect discovering such a passage." "Oh," said the old man gravely, "it occurs in a very common everyday book;" and, calling for a Bible, he turned to Revelation, and laying his finger upon Revelation 20:11, he said "There, read for yourself." This complicated the gentleman's confusion; he declared that he had read the Bible over and over again, but that he had never noticed that verse before; and with difficulty could he be brought to believe his own eyes.

Vengeance

922 Malice Produced by Revenge

To be unkind to another man merely because he has been unkind to you serves no good purpose and many evil ones. For it contributes nothing to the reparation of the first injury—it being impossible that the act of any wrong should be rescinded, though the permanent effect may—but, instead of making up the breach of your happiness, it increases the objects of your pity, by bringing a new misery into the world more than was before, and occasions fresh returns of malice, one producing another, like the environment of disturbed water, till the evil becomes fruitful and multiplies into a long succession, a genealogy of mischief.

923 Revenge Is No Reparation

A pure and simple revenge does in no way restore man towards the felicity which the injury did interrupt. For revenge is but doing a simple evil, and does not, in its formality, imply reparation; for the mere repeating of our own right is permitted to them that will do it by charitable instruments. All the ends of human felicity are secured without revenge, for without it we are permitted to restore ourselves;

and therefore it is against natural reason to do an evil that in no way cooperates with the proper and perfective end of human nature. And he is a miserable person whose good is the evil of his neighbor; and he that seeks vengeance in many cases does worse than he that did the injury—or, at least as bad.

924 Vengeful Spirits

Banish all malignant and vengeful thoughts. A spirit of revenge is the very spirit of the devil. Vengeful thoughts make a man more like Satan, and nothing can be more opposite to the temper which Christianity was designed to promote. If your revenge be not satisfied, it will give you torment now; if it be, it will give you greater hereafter. None is a greater self-tormentor than a malicious and vengeful man, who turns the poison of his own temper in upon himself. The Christian precept in this case is, "Let not the sun go down upon your wrath" (Eph. 4:26); and this precept, Plutarch tells us, the Pythagoreans practiced in a literal sense, "who, if at anytime in a passion, they broke out into abusive language, before sunset gave one another their hands, and with them a discharge from all injuries, and so, with a mutual reconciliation parted friends."

925 A Noble Revenge

Thomas Jefferson wrote of some of his political enemies: "Their bitterness increases with their desperation. I shall take no other revenge than by a steady pursuit of economy and peace, and by the pressing forward of my own principles." The best revenge we can take is to continue to proclaim the laws of Christ, and make manifest our intense attachment to Him and His Gospel. This is to overcome evil with good. Go on with your work, is the best way to silence your critics.

Wisdom

926 Why the Bible Is Not Read More

An educated Chinese man was employed by some missionaries to translate the New Testament into Chinese. At first the work of translating had no apparent effect upon the scholar. But, after a time, he became quite agitated and said, "What a wonderful book this is!" "Why so?" said the missionary. "Because," said the Chinese, "it tells me the exact facts about myself. It knows all that is in me. The one who made this book must be the one who made me."

The Bible tells one the fundamental facts about oneself indeed. How superficial, by way of contrast, are human textbooks on psychology, or the human mind! Is this perhaps the reason why many who might be expected to be readers of the Bible neglect daily Bible study? They are not very particular about being the men and women God has intended them to be; and it is surely uncomfortable to hear the Voice they do not care to obey.

927 Knowledge of Christ Not Fully Revealed to Us

The heavens have become grander and more majestic to advancing science and fuller knowledge. Every star was there in the time of the an-cient Chaldean gazers, pursuing its silent march the same as now, but to the human eye what glory has been revealed since! So is it with the glories of the Lamb. All that heaven shall unfold to us has ever dwelt in Him, but, as one suggests, it will be the Sabbath exercise of Eternity to discover how infinitely full those glories were and are.

928 The State of Wisdom in Our World

Joseph Cook says: "There are four stages of culture, and they are universal in every highly civilized quarter of the globe. The first stage is that in which we think we know everything. Then comes the second stage, in which, as our knowledge grows, we are confronted with so many things, we can ask and cannot answer, that we say in despairing mood that we can know nothing. A little beyond that we say we can know something, but only what is just before our senses. Then, lastly, we come to the stage in which we say, not that we can know everything, not that we can know much, but we are sure we can know *enough for practical purposes.* Everything, nothing, something, enough. These are the infantile, adolescent, juvenile, and mature stages of culture." At which point are we?

929 Knowledge and Humility

Writing on Coleridge as an interpreter of Shakespeare, Principal Sharp says, "He taught, and himself first exemplified, that he who would understand Shakespeare must not . . . seat himself on the critical throne, and thence deliver verdict as on an inferior, or at best, a mere equal, but that he has need to come before all things with reverence, as for the poet of all poets, and that, wanting this, he wants one of the senses, the language of which he is to employ."

930 Man's Finite Wisdom

"Know! What do you know? Do you know what the word 'God' means? Do you know what 'holiness' means? Do you know what 'sin' means? Do you know what 'heaven' means? Do you know what 'hell' means? Do you know how to set right what has gone morally wrong in God's world? Nay! We all come within the range of the prayer, 'Father, forgive them, *they* know not what they do'" (Luke 23:34).

931 Our Limited Knowledge

The following excerpt is from Thomas Carlyle:

"To the minnow every cranny and pebble, and quality and accident of its native little creek may have become familiar, but does the minnow understand the ocean tides and periodic currents, the tradewinds and monsoons, and moon's eclipses; by all which the condition of its little creek is regulated, and may from time to time (miraculously enough) be quite overset and reversed?"

932 A Clean Heart

The government artesian well at Lower Brule Indian Agency, South Dakota, is a rarity that has puzzled the geologists of the Northwest. Originally the pressure threw a solid six-inch stream of water to a height of twenty-one feet above the top of the well casing. Soon after the well was completed the pipe began occasionally to become choked and afterward to spout forth blue clay. The blue clay entirely fills the six-inch pipe during the temporary eruptions, and rises slowly above the top of the casing, exactly as sausages emerge from a sausage machine, until the top is so high in the air that it becomes overbalanced; then five or six feet of the length topples over upon the ground. These eruptions invariably begin a short time prior to the advent of windy or stormy weather, and continue until the weather becomes settled. A sinful heart is like that. It spouts forth mire and clay every little while. A man may hide his sinful heart in times of prosperity when everything goes to please him, but when adverse winds come the buried dirt in his heart belches forth. The only way to have a peaceful heart, that will always give forth a pure conversation and life, is to have a clean heart.

933 *Redeeming the Time*

The following illustration is from the pen of F. F. Trench:

"A prophetess came to Tarquinius Superbus, King of Rome, and brought nine volumes of a book, demanding a high price for them. Thinking it too much, he refused, and she immediately burned three, demanding for the six the price of the nine. He still declined to give it, and she burned three more, asking the full sum for the remaining three. He, thinking there must be something extraordinary in the books, and fearing to lose them all, gave for the three the price he had refused for nine.

"So time, as it dwindles, grows more valuable. There are three divisions of man's life—youth, manhood, and old age; and ministers advise men to redeem all this time—youth, manhood, and old age. But in youth men conceive the price they are required to pay in self-denial too great, and they spend it in folly. In manhood they are again advised to redeem the remainder, but they still think the price too great; and then, perhaps, when it comes to the last stage of their lives, they are glad enough to redeem what remains; but here the case is different. The prophetess still demanded but the same price for the remaining three which she had asked for all the nine; but the old, if they are induced to redeem the time at all, which is very unlikely, will have to pay more for the last volumes than they were asked for the whole number at first—the habit of sinning so greatly increases the difficulty of turning to God.

Witness

934 Leaven and Witnessing

The leaven does not leaven the whole mass in a moment, but creeps on from particle to particle.

935 Magnetic Christians

Each tiny particle of a magnet, if it be smitten off the whole mass, is magnetic, and sends out influence from its two little poles. And so the smallest and the feeblest faith is one in character, and one in intrinsic value, with the loftiest and superbest.

936 What Kind of Christians Are We?

What kind of Christians must they be who think of Christ as "a Savior for me," and take no care to set Him forth as "a Savior for you?" What should we think of men in a shipwreck who were content to get into the lifeboat, and let everybody else drown? What should we think of people in a famine feasting sumptuously on their private stores, while women were boiling their children for a meal, and men fighting with dogs for garbage on the dunghills?

937 Being Fed by the Spirit

Let our spirits stretch out all their powers to the better things beyond, as the plants grown in darkness will send out pale shoots that feel blindly towards the light, or the seed sown on the top of a rock will grope down the bare stone for the earth by which it must be fed.

938 The Benefits of Yielding to the Holy Spirit

Loyola demanded from his black-robed militia obedience to the General of the Order so complete that they were to be "just like a corpse," or "a staff in a blind man's hand." Such a regiment made by a man is, of course, the crushing of the will, and the emasculation of the whole nature. But such a demand yielded to from Christ is the vitalizing of the will, and the ennobling of the spirit.

939 Home Evangelism

It may be a hard thing to do, but a person makes a mistake who passes by the humblest member of his own household, and goes outside to invite people to accept Christ. A very worldly woman once said:

"I don't know many Christians, but somehow I can't help regarding them as hypocrites."

"But your sister-in-law, she lives in the same house with you; surely you must acknowledge that she is a devoted Christian."

"That's just it," was the laughing reply. "She has a very lovely disposition, and she just devotes her life to missions and Sunday schools, but she has never said a word to me about becoming a Christian. It's only make-believe with her about souls being in danger. You need not tell *me!* I know that she is fond of me, and if she believed all that, do you think she would not have said something?"

940 There's a Man in There!

In a certain city, a great building was on fire. Along the street were great crowds of men and boys watching the fire. They were retarding the efforts of the firemen, but even the policemen were powerless in their endeavors to keep them back. Suddenly there was a cry: "There's a man in there!" Like a flash the words went from lip to lip, and in an instant the indifferent spectators were eager to do something, even to the risking of their own lives, to save the life that was in jeopardy. Men and women will be ready enough to "throw out the lifeline" when we can get them to realize that someone is actually drowning. Impress the church with the peril of those who are without Christ, and we will have conquered, in great measure, its apathy upon the evangelization of the world.

941 Be Frank

While the soul-winner has need of tact (a name which we give to the wisdom that cometh only from above), anything short of frankness is sure to disgust those upon whom it is tried. Frankness, let us keep in mind, however, does not mean the brutal rudeness that sometimes masquerades under that name. The Christian has always a loving mind toward those he wishes to reach, and is, therefore, kindest in his speech when he is most candid. If you are interested in people, and want them to become Christians, tell them so. Do it delicately and considerately, but do not be a sham about it. A lady visiting in a minister's family was told of some bright, genial people in the neighborhood, who were, however, irreligious, and never even went to church.

"I will go and see them," she said.

"What will you have for an excuse?" said the hostess. "Oh, yes; take this pattern. Mrs. Buchanan asked for it the other day."

"But I do not want an excuse," was the reply. "I want them to know that someone is interested in them."

As a result of that visit, not only the father and mother, but the son, were led to regularly attend church and eventually to become Christians. "It touched me as nothing ever did before," as the mother said afterward, "to know that someone was anxious about me and was praying that I might become a Christian."

942 Only a Block

Many years ago, a city, situated in an arid region, was supplied with water from a beautiful lake far up in the mountains. One day, in the midst of the hot, dry season, the water supply gave out, and the word went from mouth to mouth: "The lake is dry!" Twenty-four hours passed, the people were famishing for water, when one man declared his intention of climbing up to the lake, hoping to find a bucketful of water. Imagine his joy when he found the beautiful lake not dry, but overflowing. All of the water which supplied the city must pass through a great leaden pipe. Into this a block of wood had floated, and had become so closely wedged as to stop the flow of the water.

This is a fair illustration of what a very insignificant block of humanity may do in the way of hindering the progress of God's work in the world. It is a wholesome thought for us to carry home, that there are some souls in the world that will never receive the blessings of the gospel if we do not see to it ourselves.

943 Speaking on Behalf of Christ

"No, I never have anything to say on religious subjects, and do not feel called upon to verbally witness to people that I come in contact with," said a young man. "I believe in testifying by your life instead of your lips."

A little while afterward a friend of the young man was arrested upon the charge of theft. The evidence was circumstantial, and a good deal turned upon the success of the accused in establishing a good reputation. Among those who were

called to testify as to his integrity was the young man in question. He might have said that he preferred to testify for him by his life, but he did nothing of the kind. He went courageously upon the witness stand and spoke in his favor. He was glad of the opportunity to help set his friend right in the eyes of his accusers.

While the service of hands and feet are most valuable, there are times when lip service is not to be despised.

944 A Seed Sown

One day a lady was packing a box of goods for India, when a child brought her a tract, which she just threw into the box. The tract fell ultimately into the hands of a Burmese chief, and led him to Christ. He told the story of his new God and Savior and his new life to his friends. In time many believed and cast away their idols. A church was built, a missionary was sent out, and fifteen hundred souls were won for the Kingdom. The grain of mustard seed can become a mighty force if it be a *living seed.*

945 Recognizing the Value of a Soul

To speak enthusiastically of a Rubens or Rembrandt finely framed and installed in the stately chambers of the National Gallery of Art, is easy enough. It is only to echo the general judgment, to do which we need none of our own. But to know in an instant a masterpiece, when lying in a lumber shop or amid the rubbish of a sales room, when the colors are overlaid with grime, and no signature is to be seen, is to possess the true artistic sense indeed. So our gracious Lord discerned in the men and women of His day, whom others despised, the image of God, though all defaced and marred with sin, and spoke of them as lost sheep, lost pieces of silver, lost souls over whose finding all Heaven would rejoice. He saw worth—soul value—in the apparently unworthy.

946 Poor Illustrators

An article in an illustrated magazine once called attention to the glaring mistakes made by the illustrators of Charles Dickens' books, and particularly to George Cruickshank. Quite a number of very obvious instances were given, at which we feel inclined to wonder how they could possibly have occurred. Yet how many of us are guilty of equal folly as illustrators of the teaching of our Lord Jesus! How few adorn the doctrine, and how often we caricature, rather than expound His will as revealed in His word!

947 The Church's Witness and Safety

Stand on the beach when the storm is raging and search for the lighthouse, and listen to the winds and waves conspiring to quench that light of warning, burning there in order to reveal the cruel rocks around. The sea hurls its foaming billows high into the air, but the light still shines. Fierce gusts of howling wind come down from the clouds and smite upon it, but the light still shines through. So does the Church that has God dwelling within it. Stand on the Rock of His truth, holding forth both His warning and welcoming light. No power can sap its foundations. No wealth can purchase its silence. No cunning can extinguish its light. The gates of hell shall not prevail against it.

948 Rescuing Hidden Treasure

After having been submerged in nearly two hundred feet of water for seven years, the treasure on board the steamer *Skyro,* sunk off Cape Finisterre in 1891, has been recovered by divers. Many efforts had been made without avail, but finally with a more powerful diving apparatus a brave diver descended to the wreck, and blew away the deck with dynamite, and secured $45,000 in precious metal. We ought to be as persistent in seeking after the far more precious treasure hidden under the rough exterior of sinful men and women around us. No treasure ship ever carried freight so valuable as an immortal soul. Well does the Scripture say: "he that winneth souls is wise" (Prov. 11:30).

949 Pulling People Out of Danger

An intelligent dog in the city of Detroit came across a man who was lying insensible on the railroad track, in such a position that he would have been cut in two had a train passed by. As soon as the dog reached the prostrate form, he began to tug at the coat-collar of the unconscious man, vainly trying to drag him out of danger. This persistent tugging seemed to half arouse the poor fellow from the stupor into which he had fallen, and by the time the first man arrived on the scene he was rubbing his eyes and attempting to rise, but was so weak that even after he was placed upon his feet he could not walk without assistance. The dog seemed beside himself with joy when he realized that he had succeeded in interesting someone. He capered and whined, lay down and rolled over, and whirled around in canine ecstasy as he saw the man removed from the track. If a dog has intelligence and love enough to do that, how much more should we, who have received such great blessings of God and have known the pardon of our sins through Jesus Christ, devote ourselves to rescuing the sinful and unfortunate from their danger, and to winning them to Christ who is able to save them.

950 Opportunity

A good rendering of the word opportunity is "opposite a port." Any sailor knows that when you are opposite the port it is best to sail in at once, for if you drift by the harbor's mouth, it may nearly be impossible to beat back against the wind and current. God has put the spirit of missions into all his creation. One thing ministers to another throughout all nature. It is said that even the wasps, when they find honey, go to tell others about it. Surely we ought to be better than the wasps, and joyfully carry the Gospel honey to the ends of the earth.

951 Do Your Duty

A clergyman was once asked by the Duke of Wellington, "How are you getting on with the propagation of the gospel abroad? Is there any chance of the Hindus becoming Christians?" To which the clergyman replied, "Oh no! I do not see anything doing there; I see not reason to suspect any work of the kind being successful." "Well," said the Duke, "what have you to do with that? What are your marching orders? Are they not 'Go ye into all the world, and preach the gospel to every creature'? (Mark 16:15). Do your duty, sir, and never mind results."

952 What a Tract Did

Mr. N. Watts, a Methodist preacher, being appointed to preach, as his custom was, distributed Bible tracts from house to house. At one house a very sullen man was having his tea. When Mr. Watts invited him to the preaching, he said, "I won't come." "Well, now," said Mr. Watts, "come, and we will try to do you good." "I won't come," he replied. "Then perhaps you will read this tract," said Mr. Watts, and without waiting for a reply went to the next door. Some time after, while Mr. Watts was leading a communion service, this man stood up in the gallery, and praised God for what He had done for his soul, stating that it was through reading the tract given to him by Mr. Watts. What encouragement to tract distributers to persevere in their good work.

953 A Strange Messenger

A professional diver said he had in his house what would probably strike a visitor as a very strange chimney ornament—the shells of an oyster holding fast a piece of printed paper. The possessor of this ornament was diving on the coast, when he observed at the bottom of the sea this oyster on a rock, with a piece of paper in its mouth, which he detached, and commenced to read through the goggles of his headgear. It was a gospel tract, and, coming to him thus strangely and unexpectedly, so impressed his unconverted heart, that he said, "I can hold out against God's mercy in Christ no longer, since it pursues me this way." He became, while in the ocean's depth, a repentant, converted and (as he was assured) sin-forgiven man—saved at the bottom of the sea!

954 Irrefutable Argument

"Let your light so shine before men, that they may see your good works, and glorify your Father who is in heaven" (Matt. 5:16).

When Lord Peterborough lodged for a season with Fenelon, archbishop of Cambray, he was so delighted with his piety and virtue, that he exclaimed, at parting, "If I stay here any longer, I shall become a Christian in spite of myself."

A young minister, when about to be ordained, stated that, at one period of his life, he was nearly an infidel. "But," said he, "there was one argument in favor of Christianity, which I could never refute—the consistent conduct of my own father!"

Thus shall we best proclaim abroad
The honors of our Savior God,
When the salvation reigns within,
And grace subdues the power of sin.

955 "The Right to Remain Silent"

Many of us are familiar with the Miranda Act which instructs all peace officers to give the arrested party a review of their rights as a United States citizen. Often we hear these famous lines on television or portrayed over the radio. The one most of us can remember the best is "You have the right to remain silent; anything you say can and will be used against you in a court of law . . ." The first time you hear these words spoken in person, you realize the gravity of the situation.

In a somewhat different way, the believer is asked a different sort of question by the Holy Spirit in our hearts. We are questioned about our faith and trust in God for our eternal salvation on a daily basis by the world, and commanded to witness for the Lord in His Word. As a recent songwriter wrote: "you don't have the right to remain silent if you have been arrested by God's grace." The truth is that we are commanded in the Bible that we do not have the right to remain silent about our faith. Christians are called to tell the world about Christ's death, resurrection, and His saving grace, and to tell of how we have been pardoned for our sins (1 Pet. 3:15). How can we then be silent about the joy of knowing Christ! Share Him with someone today!

Women

956 Rev. William Jay and His Wife

The Rev. William Jay, of England, on the fiftieth anniversary of his ordination, gave his wife the following noble complement. Being presented by the ladies of his congregation with a purse containing 650 pounds, after a few remarks he turned to Mrs. Jay, and said:

"I take this purse and present it to you, madam—to you, madam, who have always kept my purse, and therefore it is that it has been so well kept. Consider it entirely sacred, for your pleasure, your use, your service, your comfort. I feel this to be unexpected by you; but it is perfectly deserved. Mr. Chairman and Christian friends, I am sure that there is not one here but would acquiesce in this, if he knew the value of this female, as a wife, for more than fifty years. I must mention the obligation the public are under to her, if I have been enabled to serve my generation; and how much she has raised her sex in my estimation; how much my church and congregation owe to her watchings over their pastor's health, whom she has cheered under all his trials, and reminded of his duties, while she animated him in their performance; how often she has wiped the evening dews from his forehead, and freed him from interruptions and embarrassments, that he might be free for his work. How much, also, do my family owe to her, and what reason have they to call her blessed! She is, too, the mother of another mother in America, who has reared thirteen children, all of whom are walking with her in the way of the everlasting."

957 The Countess of Huntingdon "Not Ashamed of Me"

As my mother grew better, she frequently took me with her to the Pump Room, and she sometimes told me anecdotes of those she had seen there when a child. On one occasion, when the room was thronged with company—and at that time the visitors of Bath were equally distinguished for rank and fashion—a simple, humble woman, dressed in the severest garb of the Society of Friends, walked in the midst of the assembly, and began an address to them on the vanity and follies of the world, and the insufficiency of dogmatic without spiritual religion. The company seemed taken by surprise, and their attention was arrested for a few moments. As the speaker proceeded, and spoke more and more against the customs of the world, signs of disapprobation appeared. Among those present was one lady with a stern yet high-toned expression of countenance; her air was distinguished; she sat erect, and listened intently to the speaker. The impatience of the hearers became unrestrained; as the Quaker spoke of giving up the world and its pleasures, hisses, groans, beating of sticks, and cries of "Down, down!" burst from every quarter. Then the lady I have described arose with dignity, and slowly passing through the crowd, where a passage was involuntarily opened to her, she went up to the speaker and thanked her, in her own name and in that of all present, for the faithfulness with which she had borne testimony to the truth. The lady added, "I am not of your persuasion, nor has it been my belief that our sex are generally deputed to be public teachers; but God who gives the will can make the exception, and He has indeed put it in the hearts of all His children to honor and venerate fidelity to His commission. Again I gratefully thank you." Side by side with the Quaker she walked to the door of the Pump Room, and then resumed her seat. This lady was the celebrated Countess of Huntingdon.

958 Phillip Henry's Wife

After Mr. Phillip Henry, who came to Worthenbury a stranger, had been in the country for some time, his attachment to Miss Matthews, afterwards his wife, became mani-

fest; and it was mutual. Among the other objections urged by her friends against the connection was this, that although Mr. Henry was a gentleman, and a scholar, and an excellent preacher, he was quite a stranger, and they did not even know where he came from. "True," replied Miss Matthews, "but I know where he is going, and I should like to go with him."

959 The City of Dort, Holland, Preserved by Milkmaids

During the wars in the Low Countries, the Spaniards intended to besiege the city of Dort, in Holland, and accordingly planted some thousands of soldiers in ambush, to be ready for attack when opportunity might offer. On the confines of the city lived a rich farmer, who kept a number of his cows on his grounds, to furnish the city with butter and milk. His milkmaids at this time coming to milk their cows, saw under the hedges the soldiers lying in ambush, but seemed to take no notice of them; and having milked their cows, went away singing merrily. On coming to their master's house, they told him what they had seen, who, astonished at the relation, took one of the maids with him to a magistrate at Dort, who immediately sent a spy to ascertain the truth of the story. Finding the report correct, he began to prepare for safety, and instantly sent to the national government, who ordered soldiers into the city, and commanded the river to be let in by a certain sluice, which would instantly lay that part of the country under water where the besiegers lay in ambush. This was forthwith done, and a great number of the Spaniards were drowned; the rest, being disappointed in their design, escaped, and the town was thus providentially saved. The States, to commemorate the memory of the milkmaids' good service to the country, ordered the farmer a large revenue forever, to recompense him for the loss of his house, land, and cattle; and caused the coin of the city to have a milkmaid milking a cow to be engraven thereon, which is to be seen at this day upon the Dort dollars, stivers, and doights; and similar figures were also to be set up on the water gate of the Dort; and the milkmaids were allowed for their own life, and their heirs a very handsome annuity.

960 Kindness of Women

The following event happened to the late Mungo Park, while in Africa: "I was obliged to sit all day without victuals, in the shade of a tree; and the night threatened to be very uncomfortable, for the wind rose, and there was great appearance of a heavy rain; and the wild beasts are so very numerous in the neighborhood, that I should have been under the necessity of climbing up the tree, and resting among the branches. About sunset, however, as I was preparing to pass the night in this manner, and had turned my horse loose, that he might graze at liberty, a woman, returning from the labors of the field,

stopped to observe me, and perceiving that I was weary and dejected, inquired into my situation, which I briefly explained to her, whereupon, with looks of great compassion, she took up my saddle and bridle, and told me I might remain there for the night. Finding that I was very hungry, she said she would procure me something to eat. She accordingly went out, and returned in a short time with a very fine fish, which she had cooked upon some embers she gave it to me for supper. The rights of hospitality being thus performed towards a stranger in distress, my worthy benefactress, pointing to the mat, and telling me I might sleep there without apprehension, called to the female in fixed astonishment, to resume their task of spinning cotton, in which they continued to employ themselves a great part of the time. They lightened their labors by songs, one of which was composed extempore, for I was myself the subject of it. It was sung by one of the young women, the rest joining in a sort of chorus. The air was sweet and plaintive, and the words, literally translated, were these: "The winds roared and the rains fell. The poor white man, faint and weary, came and sat under our tree. He has not mother to bring him milk, no wife to grind his corn. Chorus, Let us pity the white man, no mother has he," etc. Trifling as this recital may appear to the reader, to a person in my situation the circumstance was affecting in the highest degree. I was oppressed by such unexpected kindness, and sleep fled from my eyes. In the morning, I presented my compassionate landlady with two of the four brass buttons which remained on my waistcoat; the only recompense I could make her.

Works and Service

961 "Is Not This the Carpenter's Son?"

The ultimate results of missionary enterprise may be appropriately illustrated by the following anecdote:

It is related in ecclesiastical history that when the Emperor Julian was setting out upon his Parthian expedition, he threatened to persecute the Christians with the utmost severity, as soon as he returned victorious. Upon this occasion, Libanius, the rhetorician, asked one of them, with an insulting air, what the carpenter's son was doing while such a storm hung over his followers. "The carpenter's son," replied the Christian, "is making a coffin for your emperor." The event proved the answer to be prophetic; for, in an engagement with the enemy, that royal but wretched apostate was mortally wounded, and cried with his expiring breath, *"Vicisti, O Gallilee! I am vanquished, O Gallilean! Thy right hand hath the pre-eminence."*

962 Christ and His Lambs

In a Chinese Christian family at Amoy, a little boy, the youngest of three children, on asking his father to allow him to be baptized, was told that he was too young—that he might fall back if he made a pro-fession when he was only a little boy. To this he made the touching reply, "Jesus has promised to carry the lambs in His arms. I am only a little boy; it will be easier for Jesus to carry me." This logic of the heart was too much for the father. He took him with him, and the dear child was soon baptized.

963 A Hint to Missionaries

Rev. W. H. Medhurst writes: "A Chinese doctor had fixed his station in the center of the market place, with his drugs laid out in order for sale, and bills pasted up, in the Chinese language, inviting people to buy; but as the generality of the people were Malaysians, and as they were likely to be his more numerous customers, he adopted the following method of collecting them together: first he beat a kind of bamboo drum; then he sang a few verses in praise of medicine; and afterwards he commenced in broken Malay to describe his object, and the value of his wares. By this time a great crowd was assembled around him, to whom he described in a lively manner the nature of various diseases, such as blindness, lameness, cholic, etc., pointing out what remedies would be an effectual cure for this and that disorder. In this way he sold a great deal of medicine, and got no small gain by his exertions. Now all that I wish to note is his manner of exciting the attention of the people, and his willingness to be called a fool by his countrymen (as he really was considered), in order to secure his ends, and make a little money. And shall not missionaries, who have nobler ends and better motives, use every means of exciting the attention of the heathen, and become even 'fools for Christ's sake' (1 Cor. 14:10), that they may communicate that knowledge which shall make men 'wise unto salvation' (2 Tim. 3:15)? The practice of the apostles was sometimes to run in among the people, crying, 'Sirs, why do you do these things?' (Acts 14:15) and to 'reason daily in the market with them that met them' " (Acts 17:17).

964 Seed Buried Twenty Years

About the year 1830, an Armenian, residing near the Black Sea, went on a pilgrimage, with thousands of others, to Jerusalem. There he met a man by the name of Yakob Agha, who had been taught by the missionaries, and had embraced the truth as it is in Jesus. From him the Armenian pilgrim gained some knowledge of the better way, and on returning to his home, instead of carrying with him crosses, beads, relics, etc., as was customary, he carried evangelical tracts and portions of the Word of God. These he continued to study, especially the Bible; but he had no one to teach him, or even to sympathize with him in his newly awakened desire for truth. In this course of solitary study and pursuit of truth he persevered more than *twenty years* before he saw the face of a missionary. In this condition he was at last found by Mr. Powers, of the American Board, to whom his history was related. He had once possessed great wealth, but long-continued persecution had spoiled him of his possessions, and left him destitute. He had borne all with meekness, and his case shows with remarkable clearness, not only the immense good which a tract or book may do, but also that the good results may lie hidden from human observation many years, and at least astonish us with their magnitude and value.

965 The Consecrated Cobbler

When William Carey went to India, many a wise man would have said to him, "You may just as well walk up to the Himalaya mountains, and order them to be removed and cast into the sea." I would have said, "That is perfectly true, this Hinduism is as vast and solid as those mountains; but we have faith—not much, yet we have faith as a grain of mustard seed;" and William Carey said, "I will go up to the mountain." Lonely and weak he walked up towards that mountain, which in the eye of man seemed truly one of the summits of human things, far above all power to touch or shake it; and with his own feeble voice he began saying "Be thou removed! Be thou removed!" And the world looked on and laughed. A celebrated clergyman, looking down from his high place in the *Edinburgh Review*, was much amused with the spectacle of that poor man down in Bengal, thinking in his simple heart that he was going to disturb Hinduism; and from his high place he cast down a scalding word, which he meant to fall just as old boiling lead used to fall upon a poor man from the height of a tower. He called him a "consecrated cobbler." All the wise world laughed, and said he was treated as he ought to be treated. However, he went on saying to the mountain, "Be thou removed! Be thou Removed!" and one joined him, and another joined him; the voice grew stronger; it was repeated in more languages than one: "Be thou removed!" I asked the living representatives of the very men who first smiled at this folly, "What say ye now?" "Well," they answer, "you have not got it into the sea yet." That is true; but do you say that the mountain during the last forty years has not moved? No man can say that it is in the same position as it was when William Carey first went up to it. It is moving fast; and I call you to swell that voice, the voice of God's Church, which seems to say, "Be thou removed, be thou removed, and be thou cast into the depths of the sea!" (Matt. 21:21). Cast into these depths it will be; and a day will come when the nations of a regenerated East will write in letters of gold upon the first pages of their Christian history the name of the "consecrated cobbler."

966 Use the Talent God Has Given You

Listen to the eloquent and timely style of George H. Morrison as he defines true Christian Service:

"One of the most familiar scenes in Scripture is the fight of David and Goliath. To me the choicest moment of that scene is when David was getting ready for the fight. I see Saul lending his armor, and it was a very honoring bestowal. I see David, restless and uneasy, handling the great sword as if he feared it. And then I see him laying all aside and crying out, 'I cannot go in these,' and fingering his well-loved sling again. For *Saul* there was but one way of fighting. He had never dreamed of any other way. There was only one tradition in his chivalry, and every fighter must conform to that. But David, fresh from the uplands and the morning and the whispering of God among the hills, must have liberty to fight in his own way. The one was all for immemorial custom. The other was determined to be free. The one said, 'It has been always so,' and the other, 'I cannot go in these.' And remember that it was not Saul who was *in the line of God's election*, but the young stripling from the Bethlehem pasturage who in his service dared to be himself.

"Now in our thought of Christian service, we need to be reminded of that scene. We must guard against narrowing our thought of service into a half a dozen recognized activities. When Christ was on earth, the twelve disciples served Him, and it was a noble and a glorious service. But have you exhausted the catalogue of services when you have named their preaching and their teaching? The woman who washed His feet was also serving, and Martha when she made the supper ready, and the mother who caught up her little child and brought it to Him that it might be blessed. 'I cannot go with these, I have not proved them. I cannot use the helmet and the shield.' Who wants you to? There are hands which can wield no sword but which can carry a cup of water beautifully. There is something thou canst do in thine way—something for which the church is waiting. *Do that,* and do it with thine heart, and perchance thou shalt do more than thou hast dreamed."

967 *What Is Free Will?*

What is free will? George MacDonald says that it "is not the liberty to do whatever one likes, but the power of doing whatever one sees ought to be done."

968 *"Painless" Christianity*

In the sermon *Exercise in Godliness,* H. E. J. Bevan remarks: "It is this great and universal mistake that makes our Christianity so futile at the present day, that we are not prepared to work for it. We feel our want of it but we cannot face

our own personal responsibility for its failure. While blaming everything and everybody else, and setting up something fresh in the way of external organization continually, we are shirking the supreme duty of exercising ourselves daily unto Godliness. . . ."

969 *Will God Rob Man?*

You mean, "Will a man rob God?" You say, "No." We all know that men do rob him. It is not worthwhile to even discuss the question. But the other one? We are not so much in agreement on that subject. The average man who is not a Christian refuses to put himself into the hands of the Almighty because he believes that all God wants is a chance to rob him of everything that goes to make life worth living. Friend, God does not ask you to surrender one of your noble powers; it is only the devil who ever asks that. What the Lord does ask of you is that you let him use them.

In a certain family that traces its lineage back to the days of the pilgrims, there is an heirloom that no amount of money could buy. It is the lantern of the most primitive pattern, and, to the casual observer, would seem to be of little value. This is the secret of its worth. During the Revolutionary War it was borrowed by one of the men who had much to do with the winning of independence. When he returned the lantern it showed signs of hard usage, but it had been made forever glorious by the man who had made use of it. So it is with the powers that we loan to God. They may become worn in His service, but they will be forever after glorious because He used them.

970 The Work We Leave Behind

We are told of Dorcas that, because of her deeds of charity, they mourned for her. They stood by, not merely weeping, but showing the garments that she had made. Have you thought that the work into which many of us put our best time and strength could hardly be exhibited to our credit after we were gone? What if it had been Battenberg doilies, or hand-painted throws for her drawing-room, to which Dorcas had devoted her spare time? However artistic they might have been, they would have seemed tawdry and trifling in such an hour. The homely garments were beautiful because of the beautiful spirit of self-denial which had been wrought into them. We sometimes say that we wish to be remembered by what we have done. The nearest approach to immortality that can be known in this changing world is impressing one's self upon the hearts of our brethren.

971 A New Vision of Man

God has in every location and in every age a special man to do His work. The city of Damascus has never been known to be a hotbed for Christianity, yet when Paul of Tarsus needed advice after his Damascus Road encounter with God, God looked right there for a believer in the person of Ananias, and sent him to minister to Paul. In the explanatory and enabling message to Ananias was contained this statement: "And hath seen in a vision a man" (Acts 9:12). Every day we see men as they appear around us, at work, in the street, in school, on television, but do we see them as they are? It is necessary to see them as they are to determine their real humanity. Half of our global conflicts which now so often make hell out of life (i.e. Bosnia, Chechnya, Liberia, Haiti, etc.) could be avoided if one man could see another through the vision of charity. This vision comes by fervent prayer—for Paul must have been praying when he saw Ananias coming to him.

What the world needs today is a new vision of man. It has seen man as a murderer, brawler, liar, cheater, etc., for in all these personalities he has appeared in this or that distinctiveness. Now it is time for the new man to appear—not a brawler, not a hater, not a hostile character, but the creation of the Christ, the acknowledged Son of God. It is possible that Ananias, when he came into Paul's lodging, did not correspond to the apostle's anticipation of him. Today, the actual men and women we see also fall short of that ideal character sketch that all of us have in mind; but that is no excuse to not continue visualizing the ideal, and striving to transform humanity more and more to the mind of Christ. We should grow weary of this common mentality that says in effect that "human nature never changes," "wars will always exist," or "you cannot expect much progress" and so forth, for it is all mere pessimistic, paganist propaganda. Such talk has no outlook, no moral reason to live and serve God, no real vision for man's future. The saying "All things continue as they are from the foundation of the world" is sound doctrine (2 Pet. 3:4), but it is also used as an excuse for worldliness, crimes against humanity (Hitler, Stalin, Pol Pot), and political corruption on the grandest scale, as we have seen in recent scandals such as Watergate.

It would be a beautiful thing if Christians today, instead of indulging in cynicism, would dream and pray fervently for the next Ananias, or Paul, or John, or Luther, or Spurgeon, or Billy Graham, or any other great Christian leader. We have no right to make excuses for our sins, or to blame our ancestors for our own irresponsibility. Why not become more hopeful of our chances to win as many as we can to Christ, realizing that even in Damascus, God found a righteous man? Why not envision mankind through the eyes of love and hope while we await Christ's return?

972 Unconscious Service

Says the late Andrew Jukes in one of his letters: "Our unconscious service is often the best that we render to anyone. I suppose the rose is not conscious of how it delights others by perfume. The stars know

not how many ships and wanderers they have lighted and guided on their weary journeys. The woman of Samaria little knew how she was refreshing Christ, merely by receiving what He had to give. God is wounded in being rejected. God is gladdened when we receive Him. So each member of the body by its receiving, as much as by its giving, serves the others."

973 Joy over Finished Work

When Robert Moffat was enabled to complete his translation of the entire Bechuana language he was overcome with strange delight and gratitude. He says: "I felt it to be an awful [full of awe] thing to translate the Book of God. When I finished the last verse I could hardly believe I was in the world, so difficult was it for me to realize that the work of so many years was completed. A feeling came over me as if I should die. . . . My heart beat like the strokes of a hammer. . . . My emotions found vent by my falling on my knees and thanking God for His grace and goodness in giving me strength to accomplish my task."

974 Planting for the Future

The late Cecil Rhodes once said: "I remember, in the impetuosity of my youth, I was talking to a man advanced in years, who was planting oak trees. I said to him very gently that the planting of oak trees by a man advanced in years seemed to me rather imaginative. He seized the point at once, and said to me, 'You feel that I shall never enjoy the shade?' I said, 'Yes.' He replied, 'I have the imagination, and I know what the shade will be, and at any rate no one will ever alter those lines. I know that I cannot expect more than to see the saplings; but with me rests the conception, and the shade, and the glory.' Much of our life's activity, perhaps even most of our Christian service is a planting of trees, the shade of which others shall enjoy, rather than ourselves. Yet the confident expectation of this may be a present delight. Even our Lord endured the cross for the joy, not present, but that which was set before Him; the joy of redeeming lost men and women."

975 The Vanishing Cross

A cross is made of two pieces of wood. The shorter piece represents your will, and the longer God's will. Whenever our will opposes God's will, when we do not accept Christ's way, murmur at anything He sends, will not do what He commands, etc., we find we have made a cross. But lay the two pieces side by side, and the cross is gone. So when we quietly accept what He gives, and let our desires lie alongside of His, then we receive the peace of Christ.

976 Consecrated to Good Purpose

When Guttenberg was working in his chamber in St. Abersgot Monastery, he heard a voice warning him that his invention would be the great engine of evil whereby bad men would broadcast the seeds of sin and crime, and so, posterity would curse the man who invented the printing press. He took a hammer, and was actually breaking the type and matrices in pieces when he heard another voice bidding him desist, and declaring that God would use it still more mightily to the spread of His saving truth, and so for the eternal blessing of mankind. So our work is not to destroy the instruments that we use in the service of sin, but make them now the servants of righteousness. Grace can turn a curse into blessing, a fount of bitterness into a fount of life eternal.

977 Freely Ye Have Received; Freely Give

Would to God that this word of the Master might be heeded by all of us as gladly and fully as by that great and good missionary, David Livingstone! To one who extended to him his sympathy for the sacrifices he was compelled to make upon his lonely missionary trips in Africa with their innumerable hardships, he said: "Do not speak to me of sacrifices. There is but One who has made those, namely, He who came from heaven to earth and died for us. I am merely His poor image, having paid only a very little of the debt of gratitude that I owe Him. Therefore say nothing to me of sacrifices. It was a privilege to do what I have done. For it means something to be a missionary."

978 Proud of Labor

In ancient Rome, the bride dressed herself in a long white robe; the pair walked around the altar hand in hand, received the congratulations of their friends, and then the bride, taken with apparent force from the arms of her mother, was conducted to her new home, carrying a broom and a spindle, emblems of the industry that was thought necessary in the household work she was to perform or direct.

979 Meet for the Master's Use

As Christians, Christ intends to use us as vessels (2 Tim. 2:21). But there are conditions of service that we must first meet in order to be used. We must be willing to meet His requirements, wholly, absolutely and without reserve. That means we should be willing to do the seemingly menial duties that He gives to us.

When it comes to serving God, there is no room in the Christian's attitude for the glorification of self. We live in an era where "good self-esteem" is considered one of the most important attributes of one's personality, but Christ wants us to die unto self. We, as vessels, may be plain in appearance in the world's eyes; yet, we are acceptable unto God, if we remain clean vessels as Matthew 5:8 tells us: "Blessed are the pure in heart: for they shall see God."

Sometimes, we as Christian vessels are made fit for Christ's use by being altered by the furnace of affliction and trial. Students of suffering, prosperity, or adversity, become apt scholars in God's school. May we desire to be used of the Master—come what may!

980 Making Disciples

A story is told of the late Dr. R. A. Torrey. Years ago, Dr. Torrey was preaching in a church and noticed a young lawyer in his audience whom he knew. At the close of the meeting, Dr. Torrey went to the man and asked him if he was a Christian. "Yes," the lawyer said, "I consider myself a Christian." "Are you bringing others to Christ?" the minister asked. "No, sir, I am not," he replied; "that is not my business, it is yours. I am called to practice law—you are called to preach." In response to this careless comment, Dr. Torrey then opened his Bible to Acts 8:4, and said, "Will you please read what the word of God says about it?" He read, "They that were scattered abroad went everywhere preaching the word." "Oh, but those were the apostles," he explained. Dr. Torrey then said, "Will you be kind enough to read the first verse." The lawyer then read the verse that says "And they were all scattered abroad . . . **except** the apostles." After reading this, the man had nothing more to say; but, then, what could he say? The command from God is for everyone to go out and make disciples (Mark 16:15). Are you doing this?

981 Aggressive Effort

Spurgeon once delivered this story of a dying man and his Christian friend:

"Brother," said the dying man, "Why have you not been more pressing with me about my soul?"

"Dear James," replied the brother, "I have spoken to you several times." "Yes," was the answer, "you are not to blame; but you were always so quiet over it; I wish you had gone on your knees to me, or had taken me by the neck and shaken me, for I have been careless, and have nearly slept myself into hell."

982 Without a Goal

Several decades ago, the following quotation was printed in *The Toledo Blade:* "There is such a thing as futile speed. Never before in all history were people in such a hurry as now to get nowhere." This quotation is even far more true today, in this era of fast food, drive-thru pharmacies, and rapid transportation. We are so impatient today, but would it not be beneficial to just slow down once in a while and examine our lives to see if our hastiness is really getting us anywhere?

983 Christian Service

The Library of Congress in Washington, D. C. is one of the most fascinating buildings in the world. Each alcove is decorated in themes such as art, music, science, philosophy, history, etc., and each alcove has been given a motto that represents its theme. Mr. A. Lewis tells us that before the motto for the alcove of religion was chosen, a petition was sent out among the leading clergymen in the nation of that time, asking them to participate in a contest to create the best motto. The motto that won the contest comes from Micah 6:8, "And what does the Lord require of thee, but to do justly, and to love mercy, and to walk humbly with thy God."

984 Whose Servant Are You?

The hardships and trials of Paul's life were lifted out of the insignificant and the commonplace because he looked upon them all as so many acts of service for Christ, whom he loved. Love is an easy taskmaster. To have endured hardship and imprisonment for Nero's sake, or as his prisoner, would have galled Paul to the very quick; but when he was in Nero's dungeon for Christ's sake, it was a very different matter. The way to make our lives romantic and splendid is to give ourselves in such complete devotion to Christ that the hard things of life will be endured in the spirit of love for His dear sake.

985 Home Missionary Opportunities

There are some missionary duties that can never be transferred to any one else. God puts us in little circles so that each of us touches some people with more power than anyone else in the world; to them we are peculiarly the missionaries of Christ. The opportunity to do them good is as close to us as our breathing or eating. An employer or teacher or parent can never thrust aside to somebody else the duty of illustrating the spirit of Christ to employees, students, or children. It is not a case where one can send anybody else—one must show forth the mind that is in Christ.

986 *Citizen Soldiers*

On the eve of the Spanish-American War, a Nashville paper says that the mustering in of a military company in that city on the call for volunteers to go to Cuba was marked by an incident worthy of the noblest age of patriotism. At the last moment one man was lacking, and the sergeants were out scouring the camp for some one to take the place, so that the entire regiment could be sworn in. Learning the need, Captain Beyland, who brought down an extra company which had to be distributed among the other companies, retired to his tent without a word to the other officers, who were standing before the men anxiously waiting for one more man to be found. Hope was almost gone, when an erect figure came striding toward the line. When he came in full view, someone said: "It's Captain Beyland." The young man marched up to the line of privates and silently but determinedly took his place in the ranks. He had cut off his shoulder-straps and he took the oath as a private. This noble act thrilled the men, though there was no demonstration of approval from these military men. The colonel of the regiment said: "It is just what we might have looked for in a man like Beyland." We need men like that in every department of duty as citizens—not men only who are willing to wear shoulder-straps, but men with public spirit enough to do ordinary duty in the ranks on common, prosaic days.

Worldliness

987 Triflers

One of the sore trials that sometimes come to the Christian worker is the fact that men so often busy themselves with trifles when weighty matters ought to claim their attention. A preacher, who had been pouring his very soul into an exhortation to men to seek higher and better things, referred, by way of illustration, to the fact that some plants thrive better in the shadow than in the sunlight. At the close of the service a lady came to him and told him that she was so glad that she heard him. The heart of the almost discouraged preacher revived. Imagine his feelings, however, when she went on to say, "I never knew till today what was the matter with my fuchsia. I shall go home and put it in a shady place." In this trial, however, the servant is not above his Lord. Once, when Christ had been speaking to the multitudes upon the high theme of prayer, a man pushed his way to the front and asked Christ to help him get some money that was owed to him.

Sometimes people have so low a conception of the work of the preacher that they would have him leave his work to settle neighborhood quarrels. Men neglect priceless things and devote themselves to trifles, because they have a mistaken idea of values.

988 It Will Trap You

A company of fugitives sought the aid of a guide to pilot them through a dark and lonely cavern, by which alone they could reach a place of safety from their enemies. "You must lay aside your baggage," said the guide. "No man can carry anything with him through the narrow gate." At first they objected. One had this treasure, another that, which it seemed impossible to relinquish. By and by, however, they agreed to comply with the requirements. One fugitive clung secretly to a bag of gold. As it was dark when they set out, he tarried a little behind the rest and hid the treasure in the folds of his robe. When at dawn they reached the place of safety, the man was missing. In trying to creep through a narrow pass, his gold had inescapably wedged him, and he had fallen a prey to his pursuers. So it is with those who would find safety in the kingdom and yet cannot make up their minds to relinquish the world. The treasure sooner or later holds them back and they fall prey to the enemy of souls—Satan.

989 *The Lord's Day or Ours?*

Many people have been inclined to excuse themselves from attending church services on Sunday on the plea that six days of the week are given to work, and they must have some time for themselves. Here is another view of the matter that is worth considering:

"I don't know why you would feel like going to church on Sunday's, now that you have to work so hard all week," someone said to a young woman. "Oh," was the reply, "I feel under more obligation than ever. If I can spend six days, and so much time and strength, working for my own comfort, I would be ashamed not to give a part of one day to the Lord."

Not very many of those who appropriate the Lord's Day for other than its rightful uses, spend it in a way that elevates. Facts demonstrate that a secular Sunday is a thing to be dreaded. In any locality where religion does not prevail it is a day fruitful in riots. A woman whose husband was struggling with the addiction of alcohol, said: "I think we could pull Jim through, if it wasn't for Sunday." We are frequently told that the church is too expensive an institution for the working people, hence they turn elsewhere. It would be interesting to know how much a single Sunday's amusements cost in dollars and cents, to say nothing of the costs that cannot be counted.

One of the simplest, surest ways of settling the question as to how we shall spend the first day of the week—whether in our own pursuits or of our Master's—is to consider the meaning of its name. If I tell you that a certain building is Mr. Smith's, I will scarcely need to add that you are therefore not at liberty to go in and appropriate it to your own private use. So the fact that this day is divinely designated the Lord's ought to stop all discussion as to how we may spend it. We have no right to take possession of it for our worldly pursuits or pleasures.

990 *The Modern Prodigal*

We can only conjecture what the plans of the young man in the parable were when he demanded his portion. He wanted to have a "good time," we are certain of that. He wanted to live a life of sensual pleasure—to throw off everything like restraint. Somehow, though, he could not bring himself to do it under the eye of the father, and in the very shadow of the old home. There was only one way. He must put distance between himself and these things. Many a one has had the same experience.

"There were a good many things I wanted to do." said a repentant profligate, telling his experience, "but because the thought of my mother's teachings would come back to me, I could not quite bring myself to do them. I found that I would have to get away from the memory of her words and prayers before I could really enjoy my freedom." Paul asks "Who shall separate us from the love of Christ?" (Rom. 8:35); then he goes on to enumerate a number of things that cannot do it. There is one agency, however, that can—the man himself. Whoever finds himself a great distance off from his Father's house, may well reflect that it was his own feet that took him there.

991 Thirsting for the World

"The man would never have gone back to his bottle if he had had plenty of nourishing food," said a physician, concerning a recovering alcoholic who had lately returned to drinking. "As long as he was eating and drinking of that which nourished his body, the old appetite did not assert itself."

This thought reminds us of the words of Jesus regarding the living water, "He that drinketh shall never thirst" (John 4:14). It is he that has ceased to drink at this fountain who is in danger. The Christian who is continually drinking in supplies of grace from the Word and from the place of prayer will not thirst after the world. Beware of neglecting the living water. It is the devil's opportunity for suggesting that the wine of the world is pleasant to the taste.

992 Profanity

The wicked practice of swearing, which is so common as to offend the ear in every restaurant and hotel, and which can be heard in almost every motion picture and television show is often mere bravado. Boys think it sounds manly to be profane, and men think it gives force and character to their sayings. Unlike most other vices, it is done openly, and is intended by the swearer for other people's ears. It is a public sin against God, and a public insult to all good men. The boldest blasphemers are often the greatest cowards. A tale is told of a preacher, who told a man with a profane mouth, that he would give him fifty dollars, if he would go into the village cemetery at midnight, and alone with God, repeat the same profanities that he used earlier in the day in public. "Agreed," said the swearer, "an easy way to make fifty bucks." "Well," said the preacher, "come tomorrow, and say you have done it, and you shall have the money." Midnight came. It was a night of great darkness. As he entered the cemetery, not a sound was heard; all was still as death. The gentleman's words came to his mind. "Alone with God!" rang in his ears. He did not dare to utter an oath, but fled from the place, crying, "God be merciful to me a sinner!"

993 The Worldliness of Social and Political Unrest

Rev. Andrew Benvie has a correct representation of this world's state of affairs in his sermon *An Age of Unrest*. This sermon was written in the pre-World War I era, when many nations were preparing for war; however, one does not have to watch the television news or read the newspaper headlines very long to see that things have not changed much since the turn of this soon-to-end century:

"There can be no doubt all the nations of the world are not happy. The nations of the world are not agreed one with another. There are fierce rivalries and much bitterness, and much discontent and many jealousies, and danger everywhere of the great magazine exploding. Christendom is armed to the teeth. Every nation in Christendom is spending millions of dearly earned money on that which is not bread. Millions of able-bodied men are set aside to learn the art of slaughter. Engineers and mechanics of the highest intellectual type are hired at enormous wages to make the most successful deadly instruments of combat. . . ."

The only difference between Benvie's time and the late-twentieth century, is instead of spending "millions" on weaponry, we are spending billions, if not, trillions of dollars on weapons that could potentially kill millions of people with just one push of a button. Matthew 24:6 says that in the last days, "wars and rumours of wars" will exist. How close can we be to Christ's return?

Worship

994 Stained-Glass Windows and Worship

A bit of stained glass may be glowing with angel forms and pictured saints, but it always keeps some of the light out, and it always hinders us from seeing through it. And all external worship and form has such a tendency to usurp more than belongs to it, and to drag us down subtly to its own level.

995 Wonder and Worship

Thomas Carlyle declares that "Wonder is the basis of worship; the reign of wonder is indestructible in man." It is because Jesus the Savior is "The Wonderful"—the full of wonder—whose fullness and sublimity of character can never be fathomed or exhausted, that He will be worshiped forever. In Him dwells all the fullness of the Godhead, and all eternity will be spent in the best employment of knowing Him better, and therefore worshiping and receiving the more.

996 Worship or Natural Emotion

A. K. H. Boyd correctly differentiates worship from natural emotion:

"The enjoyment of noble architecture and music is not worship, and may not be mistaken for it.

The hush which falls on us, walking the aisles of a church of eight hundred years; the thrill of the nerves and heart as the glorious praise begins, whose echoes fail amid fretted vaults and clustered shafts; all that feeling, solemn as it is, has no necessary connection with worshiping God in spirit and in truth. And we may delude ourselves with the belief that we are offering spiritual worship when it is all a mere matter of natural emotion, which the most godless man could share."

997 Useless When Enshrined

Natives of a Third World country were given a sundial. They were thrilled as they learned how to tell time by observing the shadow of the sun on the face of the sundial. As days passed this amazing instrument attracted such interest that the leaders of the tribe decided that it deserved some sort of worship.

To the delight of the leaders, large crowds gathered to worship. However, this created a problem. They now feared for the safety of this remarkable device. It was decided that a beautiful building be erected to house it. This, they thought, would protect it from any would-be thief. The project was completed

333

and a formal celebration was announced. As thousands gathered, the leaders stood before the sundial at which time they made a startling discovery. The sundial, the center of attraction, was now useless. Rather than admit error, the leaders decided to preserve it as a shrine for future generations, thus preserving their dignity.

You may smile as you read this, but isn't this what we have done to the Christian faith? The church started out over nineteen hundred years ago with a strong workable faith, a faith in Christ that would change their lives, a faith that would direct their thinking, a faith that would produce action in the face of opposition. This faith was not "pie in the sky" or wishful thinking. It was reality before anything seen. Today, however, we tend to house our faith in beautiful buildings, hoping to preserve it. Have we enshrined our faith for future generations, hoping that they might guess what faith is all about? Has our faith become useless because of what we have done with it?

—Donald Raub

998 A Man in India

The late Rev. W. Ward, of India, once preached from Ecclesiastes 11:9—"Rejoice, O young man, in thy youth . . ." A notorious drunkard became, under this sermon, very seriously convinced of the importance of salvation; and, with his wife, a short time afterwards made a profession of faith. Previous to this, his employer had used every means he could devise to persuade him to become sober, but in vain. After this change, his employer wished to command him not to attend church, but he replied, "You know, sir, what a drunkard I have been, and how often you have urged me in vain to abandon alcohol; yet by going once to the chapel, I was constrained to do that which none of your reprimands were able to effect: therefore I wish to go again."

999 The Queen and the Bishop

Queen Caroline once pressed Bishop Rundle to tell of her faults. "If it so please your majesty," said he, "I will tell you of one. Persons come from all parts of the kingdom to see your majesty at Whitehall Chapel. It is therefore to be lamented, that you talk to the king so much during the service." "Thank you, my lord bishop," said the queen; "now tell me of another of my faults." "That I will do," said he, "with great readiness at some future time, but first correct what I have just mentioned."

1000 The Freethinker

Collins, the freethinker or deist, met a plain countryman going to church. He asked him where he was going. "To church, sir." "What to do there?" "To worship God." "Tell me, is your God a great or a little God?" "He is both, sir." "How can he be both?" "He is so great, sir, that the heavens cannot contain him; and so little that he can dwell in my heart." Collins declared, that this simple answer from the countryman had more effect upon his mind than all the volumes which learned doctors had written against him.

1001 A Practical Hearer

A poor woman in the country went to hear a sermon, wherein, among other evil practices, the use of dishonest weights and measures was exposed. With this sermon she was much affected. The next day, the minister, according to his custom, went among his hearers, and calling upon the woman, he took occasion to ask her what she recollected from the sermon. The poor woman complained much of her bad memory, and said, she had forgotten almost all that he had delivered: "but one thing" said she, "I remembered; I remembered to burn my bushel." A "doer of the word" cannot be a "forgetful hearer" (James 1:25).

General Index

Scripture Index

Made in the USA
Monee, IL
20 April 2021

65264750R00233